Managing Cities

Managing Cities

THE NEW URBAN CONTEXT

Edited by

**Patsy Healey, Stuart Cameron, Simin Davoudi
Stephen Graham and Ali Madani-Pour**

Centre for Research in European Urban Environments,
Department of Town and Country Planning,
University of Newcastle upon Tyne, UK

JOHN WILEY & SONS
Chichester • New York • Brisbane • Toronto • Singapore

Copyright © 1995 The Editors and Contributors

Published in 1995 by John Wiley & Sons Ltd,
Baffins Lane, Chichester,
West Sussex PO19 1UD, England
Telephone National (01243) 779777
International (+44) 1243 779777

Other Wiley Editorial Offices

John Wiley & Sons, Inc., 605 Third Avenue,
New York, NY 10158-0012, USA

Jacaranda Wiley Ltd, 33 Park Road, Milton,
Queensland 4064, Australia

John Wiley & Sons (Canada) Ltd, 22 Worcester Road,
Rexdale, Ontario M9W 1L1, Canada

John Wiley & Sons (SEA) Pte Ltd, 37 Jalan Pemimpin #05-04,
Block B, Union Industrial Building, Singapore 2057

Library of Congress Cataloging-in-Publication Data
Managing cities: the new urban context / edited by Patsy Healey . . . [et al.].
    p. cm.
Papers from a seminar held in March 1993.
Includes bibliographical references and index.
ISBN 0-471-94922-1. — ISBN 0-471-95533-7 (pbk.)
1. Urban policy — Congresses. 2. City planning — Congresses.
3. Municipal government — Congresses. 4. Cities and towns — Congresses.
I. Healey, Patsy.
HT107.M35 1995
307.76—dc20   94-40240
                                                                                CIP

British Library Cataloguing in Publication Data

A catalogue record for this book is available from the British Library

ISBN 0-471-94922-1 (cl)
ISBN 0-471-95533-7 (pbk)

Typeset in 10/12 Palatino by Mayhew Typesetting, Rhayader, Powys
Printed and bound in Great Britain by Bookcraft (Bath) Ltd

Contents

Contributors

Ash Amin
Centre for Urban and Regional Development Studies, University of Newcastle upon Tyne, UK

Stuart Cameron
Centre for Research in European Urban Environments, Department of Town and Country Planning, University of Newcastle upon Tyne, UK

Graham Cox
School of Social Sciences, University of Bath, UK

Simin Davoudi
Centre for Research in European Urban Environments, Department of Town and Country Planning, University of Newcastle upon Tyne, UK

Michael Dear
Department of Geography, University of Southern California, Los Angeles, USA

Susan Fainstein
Department of Urban Planning and Policy Development, Rutgers University, New Brunswick, New Jersey, USA

Stephen Graham
Centre for Research in European Urban Environments, Department of Town and Country Planning, University of Newcastle upon Tyne, UK

Patsy Healey
Centre for Urban Technology, Department of Town and Country Planning, University of Newcastle upon Tyne, UK

Jean Laterasse
LATTS, Laboratoire d'Ecole Nationale des Ponts et Chaussées, Université de Paris-Marne, Paris, France

John Lovering
Department of Geography, University of Hull, UK

Philip Lowe
Centre for Rural Economy, University of Newcastle upon Tyne, UK

Ali Madani-Pour
Centre for Research in European Urban Environments, Department of
Town and Country Planning, University of Newcastle upon Tyne, UK

Simon Marvin
Centre for Urban Technology, Department of Town and Country Planning,
University of Newcastle upon Tyne, UK

Margit Mayer
Freie Universität Berlin, JF Kennedy Institute, Berlin, Germany

Enzo Mingione
Fundazione Bignascho, Milan, Italy

Jonathan Murdoch
Centre for Rural Economy, University of Newcastle upon Tyne, UK

Hervé Pauchard
LATTS, Laboratoire d'Ecole Nationale des Ponts et Chaussées, Université
de Paris-Marne, Paris, France

Kevin Robins
Centre for Urban and Regional Development Studies, University of
Newcastle upon Tyne, UK

Nigel Thrift
Department of Geography, University of Bristol, UK

Jane Wheelock
Department of Social Policy, University of Newcastle upon Tyne, UK

Preface

This book arose out of informal discussions which began in Newcastle in late 1991 on research priorities in regional economic geography and urban planning. These focused on the relevance of attempting to "manage" change in urban regions at a time when economies, cultures and political institutions were becoming increasingly open to supranational and global influences. This substantive focus was underpinned by evolving conceptual perspectives that are now consolidating into an approach which is being labelled as "institutionalist". In discussion with colleagues elsewhere, an initiative for an ESRC Research Programme was developed. Initially called *Territorial Management in a Borderless World*, this evolved into an ESRC Research Initiative, *The Infrastructure of Territorial Development*. It was put forward for funding to ESRC in Autumn 1992. In the highly competitive climate of social science research in Britain the initiative did not succeed; but as some acknowledgement of the interest of the project, ESRC funds were made available for a seminar around the agenda of the initiative. This book arises from that seminar, held in March 1993 under the heading *Challenges in Urban Management*.

In providing the briefing for the seminar, and in selecting contributors, we focused on the core of our substantive and conceptual interests, which by this time had moved forward. The present editors, with Ash Amin and Kevin Robins from CURDS, and Simon Marvin from CREUE, Town and Country Planning, took responsibility for commissioning the papers and structuring the seminar discussions. The editorial team worked during the seminar and afterwards to record the discussions, in order to develop the overall threads of the book, to organise the various sections and give guidance to the authors. We should like to express our appreciation to all the contributors for their willingness to get involved in the project, to accept our editorial suggestions, and to provide us with suggestions about editorials. As a result, we have found the work of producing this book a stimulating and creative process.

Several of the contributors draw on work which is being published in slightly different forms elsewhere. Amin and Thrift in Chapter 4 draw extensively on a piece written in the European Science Foundation programme on *Regional and Urban Restructuring in Europe* (RURE), published in Amin and Thrift (1994). Wheelock has used the empirical work in Chapter 10 to support a further argument in her chapter in Garrahan and Steward (eds) (forthcoming), *The Paradox of Place: Studies in Urban Continuity and Renewal* (Avebury, Aldershot). Chapter 11 by Mayer is being published in a different form as "Post-Fordism in City Politics" in Amin, A. (ed) (1994), *The Geography of Post-Fordism* published by Blackwell, Oxford. Chapter 12 by Healey has been published in a revised version as "Development Plans: New Approaches to Making Frameworks for Land Use Regulation" in *European Planning Studies* (1994). Part of Chapter 6 by Fainstein is taken from her book *The City Builders* (1994) published by Blackwell, Oxford.

Finally we must make some acknowledgements. Specifically, Wheelock would like to thank the Equal Opportunities Commission and the ESRC for funding her research, and the Wearside families who agreed to be interviewed. Laterasse and Pauchard would like to thank Judith Crew for translating Chapter 7. We would all like to thank ESRC for their, albeit modest, funding of our endeavours. We must also thank the Department of Town and Country Planning at Newcastle University, for providing support and encouragement for our work. We would like to acknowledge the quite exceptional support we have had throughout from CREUE Secretary, Jill Connolly, in helping organise the seminar, and in supporting all our efforts in writing and editing this book; she has been enormously efficient and effective. Finally we would like to thank Anne Lord for her careful proofreading of the text.

The editors
May 1994

Introduction: The City — Crisis, Change and Invention

THE EDITORS

The arguments

City and society

All around us in the western world at the end of the twentieth century, in every arena of life, old orders are crumbling or taking on new clothes. The collapse of the geopolitical global balance of the postwar period has awakened new political instabilities across Europe. Economic relations are being progressively recast in supranational and global terms. The ability to manage these relations to avoid high levels of unemployment and insecure working conditions appears ever more problematic. Demographic change, lifestyle differentiation and the realisation of deep-seated gender, racial and ethnic prejudices in established ways of living undermines assumptions about "normal" behaviour. The struggle of governments to balance public accounts faced with rising demands for spending on social welfare, environmental improvement and economic development has led to strategies which are undermining mid-century welfare state systems. These pervasive uncertainties of contemporary life are acutely symbolised in our concerns about the city and urban life. Cities, once seen as the heart of the innovatory energy and cultural force of western society, now seem to be drifting into becoming decaying and dangerous places.

This book is about the contemporary city and its management. Many commentators describe the city as being in crisis, with urban governments facing rising problems with which they are unable to cope. What is the

Managing Cities: The New Urban Context, edited by P. Healey, S. Cameron, S. Davoudi, S. Graham and A. Madani-Pour. © 1995 The Editors and contributors. Published in 1995 by John Wiley & Sons Ltd.

way forward? There is currently an explosion of discussion arenas in which those interested in city development and city government meet to discuss problems and solutions and exchange experiences. But much of such debate assumes that what the city is and how to govern it are straightforward issues and that the key issues are ones of management technique — how to deliver services; how to foster investment; how to regulate development.

The argument of this book challenges this view. The various contributors share a realisation that what constitutes the city is actively being contested and renegotiated by the dynamics of the economic, social and political relations of contemporary western societies. So also are forms of governance, and consequently of urban governance. Our objective, therefore, is to explore urban relations in contemporary western societies from various points of view and the consequences of these for what it is relevant to "manage" at the urban level, and in what way.

Conceptions of the city

Most people in western societies live and work in urban areas, if by urban areas we mean agglomerations of households, firms and agencies packed together and largely free of farms and forests. Even more of us are included in the *urban regions* which are evolving as activities that were formerly spatially clustered are now dispersed across the landscapes and relationships of farm-based economies. We live in urbanised societies, where our activities, values and expectations are infused by relationships which require the accomplishment of complex activities linking people in their social, economic and public lives. This contrasts with the idealised image of the place-based, largely self-contained rural community, encapsulated in the notion of *gemeinschaft* (Simmel 1971). In European tradition at least, the city has long been equated with *civitas*, with civilisation, and "high" culture (Eagleton 1991), the focal points of regions and nations. Its social diversity and cosmopolitan quality, compared with surrounding rural areas, has often been presented as a creative force, encouraging technical, economic and social innovation. Robins, in Chapter 2, reminds us of Mumford's conception of the city as a crucible. It has also traditionally been associated with governance, the arena where political philosophies are articulated and translated into programmes of action, and where politicians and administrators gather to argue and to organise.

The downsides of urban life have also long been highlighted in the urban literature. A century ago, these were typically associated with the process of industrialisation and its destructive externalities if unregulated. This century, the challenge has been to cope with rapid urban growth caused not merely by industrialisation but also by the general shift from rural to urban societies and the increase in affluence of those in urban areas. The literature on cities over the 100 years from the mid-nineteenth century to the mid-twentieth century is full of accounts of adverse conditions and calls for better management and planning (Hall 1988). Urban planning, along with the development of local environmental services, housing policy and infrastructure development programmes, was promoted as an approach to "tidying up" these adverse externalities. The city thus became a key arena of innovation in local governance. As Dear discusses in Chapter 1, echoing Boyer (1983), urban planning in the twentieth century became a management mechanism to organise and order city growth to reduce the scale of these problems, a modernist planning for modernising societies.

The late twentieth century has seen a resurgence of critical accounts of urban life. The storyline of these accounts tends to emphasise the dangerous and threatening aspects of the city. Los Angeles, once the symbol of a new frontier in innovation in urban form and lifestyle (Hall 1988; Soja 1989), now instead seems to encapsulate these dangers, functioning as a kind of "aversion therapy" in our discussion of the urban.[1] As Dear and Robins emphasise, the city is now often presented as a kind of raw underbelly of the contemporary condition of western societies generally. Within the city, the crises and contradictions of our times seem most concentrated and most visible.

Chapters 1 and 2 explore these troubling perceptions of the urban. Once, it is said, the city, managed by rational principles, was an orderly place. Its spatial order reflected its administrative, social and economic orders. The core of the city was its centre, an administrative, cultural, social and economic node, around which the relations of urban life revolved. It was assumed that these relations were functionally integrated and could be captured in simple socio-spatial models. Such images of the urban were undermined intellectually by economists and sociologists, who saw aspatial relations, revolving around the organs of the nation state or the forces of capital accumulation. More recently, the images have been undermined by urban and regional geographers, who have analysed the ways in which webs of social, economic and political relations link people within and beyond cities. Chapters 4, 5 and 6 show how complex these webs can be, and the breadth of their spatial reach. Such tendencies encourage a view of the urban as fragmenting into relationships operating on a variety of spatial scales. The urban, as a spatial container, to use Mumford's alternative to the crucible metaphor, merely accommodates parts of many such webs, with no necessary connection between them, apart from the sharing of a common space or territory. Chapter 3 discusses how these fragmentation processes create challenges for re-interpreting traditional meanings of "urban" and "rural".

Yet, as recent regional geographers have emphasised, such "cohabitation" of webs of relations in places does matter (Massey 1984). The history and geography of these particular spaces build up cultures, material assets and ways of doing things which make a difference. Chapter 4 stresses the importance of the institutional capacity of places. Fainstein (1994) demonstrates that institutional factors were as critical as property market conditions in the different fortunes of New York's Battery Park project and London's Canary Wharf. Chapter 8 raises the significance of institutional change in the delivery of urban infrastructures on the quality of service provided. Chapter 3 stresses the significance of the distinctive English attitude to landscape and its impact on conceptions of urban regions. The efforts at managing "cohabitation" build up traditions, opportunities and constraints which affect the resources and values of those households, firms and agencies which occupy a territory. This in turn affects the way they engage in their relations with those beyond their territory. Through the dynamics of the negotiation of cohabitation, spaces become places, as Massey argues, and thus an active force in the evolution of relationships. It is this conception of the active force of an urban place which Amin and Thrift seek to capture in their notion of the "institutional thickness" of a place.

Conceptions of change

The shifts in intellectual emphasis — from the city as the hub of a dense, place-based web of relationships to the city as a locus of overlapping webs of relations on diverse spatial scales, from the neighbourhood to the globe — reflects in part a real material change in the way we now live. Companies are no longer oriented primarily to urban region suppliers and markets. As Amin and Thrift argue, this means that deliberate efforts are needed to "pin down" companies to places if places are to capture economic development opportunities. Households are no longer typically nuclear families where the male parent travels to work to the city centre while the female parent uses neighbourhood services and job opportunities, as envisaged by the planners of mid-century (Boyer 1986; Beck 1992). As described in Chapter 9, household forms are more diverse and cultural divisions between the opportunities available to, and expectations of, different groups in society have become more visible. Fewer families can depend on a full-time permanent job in an urban industry or business. Telematics technology has added to the effects of transport technology in liberating households and firms from spatial dependence. Yet, as Graham and Marvin argue, basic urban infrastructures are no longer delivered as a universal standard service. These changes all reinforce the perception of a shift from hierarchical relationships (in households, firms and governance agencies) to more fluid horizontal relationships and networks. In parallel, fragmentation and diversity are accompanied by tendencies to social polarisation and to social and economic exclusion from access to opportunity.

These economic and social changes are reflected in and reinforced by changes in governance. The modernist approach to government provided order, through the universalist welfare state and the machinery for urban planning. These provided a degree of standardisation and predictability in the support services for both social and economic life. Yet they have become ever more difficult to sustain, against both the material realities of the new trans-urban relations described above and the rising agenda of demands for more and more discriminating attention from the interests of all the different relational webs that coexist in an urban area. It is this situation which has given neo-liberal approaches to governance such leverage in the late twentieth century, leading to deliberate attempts to break up the structures of the postwar universalist welfare state as developed in Europe (Batley and Stoker 1991), through strategies of privatisation, and deregulation. One consequence has been the "offloading" to companies, voluntary associations and households of tasks formerly undertaken by the state.

But it also represents a change in the way we think about ourselves. The result has been an increasing fragmentation of agency responsibility within the urban arena. Chapter 5 discusses the diversity of agencies concerned with economic development in English cities. Chapter 11 highlights the multiplicity of community groupings, established for developmental and campaigning purposes, to be found in many European cities. Chapter 12 notes the shift in urban planning systems from comprehensive planning models to a focus on the promotion of individual projects. City governments, once a key locus for the material and ideological integration of urban relationships, have in many places become merely one of many actors in the governance arena, competing for control of agendas and access to resources.

The combined effect of these changes is made spatially manifest in the changing "structure" of urban regions. The multi-nodal urban region has replaced the hierarchy of centres (city centre, district centre and neighbourhoods), which informed the mid-century city planners. Multiple cross-movement within an urban region has replaced the traditional "in–out" radial journey to work. New patterns of socio-spatial clustering are replacing the patterns of gradation from an urban core encapsulated in traditional models of urban ecology (Cheshire and Hay 1989; Piccinato 1993; CEC 1992a). The urban region, as Dematteis (1985) describes it, has become like the relations it accommodates, a space of networks and flows (Castells 1989).

Many of the authors in this book struggle to make sense of the urban in this context. Dear argues that the material conditions of urban regions now require that we move beyond the modernist conceptions of a modernising city which informed urban governance in mid-century, to a postmodern imagery. His argument emphasises the modern as a mental ordering construct rather than a reality. For Dear, the imposition of modernist ordering suppressed the diversity and difference, the disjunctions between relations and the contradictions and dangers inherently present in urban life. These have been revealed once again as, in Dear's words, the modernising impetus has floated away. This suggests that the sense of crisis now associated with the city is the consequence of the collapse of our mental constructs. An urban world, once seen as ordered through functional hierarchies and focused on the organisation of specific objects (houses, factories, households, firms), now appears as a morass of fragmenting and recombining relations, in which the emphasis has shifted to "networking", to making links, to culture and values, and to perceptions and images. This is encapsulated in Amin and Thrift's reference to the city as a thing of fragments, of "bits and pieces".

This conception of a break, between modernist and postmodern conceptions, between Fordist and post-Fordist forms of economic organisation, between industrial and postindustrial society, pervades much of the contemporary literature on western society (e.g. Giddens 1990; Harvey 1989 a, b; Soja 1989; Beck 1992). It represents an interpretive struggle by social scientists to understand the nature of the contemporary conditions unfolding before us, upon which to base predictions and proposals for shaping futures. However, several of the authors in this book challenge the extent of the difference between "then" and "now". Fainstein identifies the continuities in the power of capital to organise our webs of relations and the spatial patterns which result. Lovering reinforces this point, and raises questions about recent policy interest in local economic development strategies. Perhaps, then, the appearance of fragmentation is merely the localised form of a new concentration of economic power. Robins, taking a different argument, emphasises that the tension between order and disorder is not a new phenomenon but a constant theme in discussion of the city. Underlying these debates is both an awareness of the continuity of economic and political power structures and a recognition that the power to maintain and transform structures is carried in images we have of the urban, as well as in control of resources and rules. Such images not only order our analyses, but affect the way people think and act in their various relations, and in the forms, processes and agendas of urban governance.

Innovation and decay

The combination of a material and perceptual "deconstruction" of the "modern" city has all kinds of potential for innovation and development. The disintegration of old orders allows new possibilities to be seen — the creative potential of the diversity of social relations and values, as Dear and Robins emphasise; the flexibility in working practices in developing new products, new markets and more socially-helpful work opportunities;

the opportunities for new political alliances which Mayer notes in Chapter 11 and new ways of developing "self-reliant" social networks discussed by Mingione in Chapter 9.

But it is the destructive side of economic, social and political "restructuring" which feeds our perceptions of crisis in the urban arena. Flexibility in economic and governance structures means the freedom to discard sites and labour forces which no longer have relevance to company or agency strategies. This adds loss of both regular income and social position to households where such job loss is concentrated. Dependency on welfare payments represents a challenge to the dignity of the people in a household, as Wheelock shows in Chapter 10. Meanwhile the level of welfare payments and the quality of service provision is itself falling in many countries, increasing household impoverishment. Changes in social life and culture which open up opportunities for previously exploited and neglected groups — women, people of colour, those from distinctive ethnic communities and those with physical and mental difficulties — awaken divisions and hostilities in the rest of us.

In areas of our cities, where poverty and social diversity are concentrated, the signs of stress are pervasive, in the routinisation of violence, alienation and anger, of crime and stigma. This reinforces exclusionary tendencies, encouraging a defensive sense among the better-off, labelling these stressed neighbourhoods as "outside", not part of the "mainstream", and "other". The spatial expression of such exclusionary differentiation can be found in what in the USA has long been referred to as "white flight", the tendency for the more affluent and more favoured groups to move to neighbourhoods where others like them live, most notably on the urban periphery. Chapter 3 describes how, within rural areas, these groups then become active defenders of an idealised social mix and lifestyle. The result is increasing social–spatial segregation and metropolitan decentralisation (Soja 1989; CEC 1992a). The scale of such outward movement in some cities meanwhile now threatens to extend the problems of the inner city and the peripheral housing estate to large areas of the city.

The perception of crisis is producing an explosion of interest in the city. Much of this is informed by the belief that the quality of a city can become an economic asset in the struggle to capture and retain mobile globalising company investment. It is also fuelled by moral concern for human welfare, and for environmental responsibility. These efforts may be understood as part of a broad attempt to reconstruct new understandings of the contemporary city and its role in our lives, and thereby to provide a basis upon which to work out what we should do about the preoccupying problems. But as this flow of "rethinking the urban" proceeds, people in households, firms and agencies are "inventing" by themselves all kinds of "coping strategies" to deal with the new worlds in which they find themselves.

The range and diversity of these "survival strategies", as Mingione calls them, is a recurring theme in this book. Within the economic arena, researchers are exploring the network-building work of firms, and its contribution to building new institutional cultures and practices in a region, as Amin and Thrift (Chapter 4) and Lovering (Chapter 5) describe. Within the political arena, as Mayer discusses in Chapter 11, new links are being made among diverse social groups and their networks in order to mobilise resistance to some of the more destructive social and environmental consequences of economic change. Chapter 9 argues that forms of economic organisation, long thought to have been displaced by modern capitalism, appear to be growing in significance, from petty commodity production to reciprocal exchange and the unremitting expansion of the criminal economy. Poorer households, in Mingione's account, are turning away from the diminishing opportunities in the formal economy and the welfare state, looking towards reciprocal relationships with friends and kin through which to sustain their survival.

Cities are thus full of local inventions with respect to how to manage survival — for firms and for households. But these inventions only incidentally relate to each other in ways which reinforce mutual benefit and "human flourishing".[2] Many are isolated and precarious. Others are mutually destructive. Thus a restless dialectic appears to characterise contemporary urban life; between innovatory creative processes, which expand their leverage and open up opportunities as they roll along, and destructive forces which inhibit such developments and further break up the relations needed for survival. The various contributors to this book are optimistic or pessimistic depending on how they see the tendencies in this dialectic. Many recognise what is under way as an "invention process", produced through the effort to find new ways of living and doing business in our changed contemporary world. Yet most are also aware of the power of tradition, of capitalist economic relations, and entrenched political elites, to restrict possibilities and capture opportunities.

Urban governance

Where do these changes leave the governance of cities? What roles do formal city governments play in these changes? Are they able to act in the forefront of creative innovation, enabling the "invention process"? Or are they a force of "institutional inertia" as Amin and Thrift suggest? Has city government become a "relict apparatus" of the modernist order, to use Dear's phrase? It is this latter view which reverberates through neo-liberal politics, paralleling neo-marxist and feminist critique of the welfare state (Cockburn 1977). Established city governments, these arguments suggest, both fail effectively to promote flexible market adjustment by the firms in their areas, and are insensitive to the needs of their diverse residents. In addition, it is argued that their organisation — their styles of management and labour relations — are inefficient and inflexible. Neo-liberal strategies have energetically pursued the reform of urban governance, the English case becoming an ideal type for such policies. The goal of restructuring has included deregulation, through contracting out of functions to the private sector, setting up new semi-private agencies to carry out governance tasks, and changing the criteria to which public agencies must work. The result is not only new ways of delivering urban services, but a reorientation of the relations between governance, business and citizens, and all the individual problems and opportunities of workforces caught up in restructuring processes. Chapter 7 shows that in countries where neo-liberal strategies have been less pervasive, as in France, governmental competition can still arise, with conflicts arising from differing technological capacity, as well as different interests.

The "fragmentation" of urban governance, noted in several of the chapters in this book, is itself an innovatory process, with new agencies driven by new criteria and management practices struggling to develop their own "coping strategies". The critical political question which has to be asked of these strategies is whether they facilitate or inhibit the "invention" work within the spheres of the economy and civil society. The political legitimacy of governance in societies which purport to be democratic lies not in the ability to survive, but in the ability to help others to survive and flourish. If the "functional fit" between urban governance and urban economic and social relations, expressed in the idea of modernist urban planning, has been broken up, then we need to ask what new urban governance relations should be invented, if any, to release the opportunities and reduce the tensions of the coexistence in shared spaces of multiple webs of relations. This requires investigation of the relations between governance innovation in the urban arena, and the innovation in other arenas. It is only through such investigation that it is possible to make visible the way evolving urban governance processes are impeding and facilitating the webs of relations which have a locus in a city, and the differential pattern of benefit and harm.

The aims and organisation of the book

Urban researchers and policy makers at the present time have a critical responsibility to contribute to the task of "inventing" appropriate management strategies and institutions for urban regions. It is to this task that this book is addressed. The focus throughout is on urban region change and governance. Each author contributes to an exploration of the relationship from a distinctive point of view. In Part 1, "Reading the City", chapters by Dear and Robins explore changing conceptions of the urban as already noted. This is complemented by an exploration by Lowe, Murdoch and Cox of changes and continuities in the social construction of distinctions between urban and rural in British culture. In Part 2, "The City Economy", chapters by Amin and Thrift, and Lovering, examine debates on the relative importance of the urban dimensions of economic life and the implications for governance activity. Fainstein illustrates these issues through a specific example of urban development in two cases of projects located in the business core of cities at the financial heart of the global economy. In Part 3, "Infrastructure, Technology and Power", chapters by Laterasse and Pauchard and by Graham and Marvin explore the way new technologies and new forms of management are changing the relations of provision for key infrastructures for urban life and economy. In Part 4, "Households Coping with Change", the perspective shifts to the accomplishment of everyday life in the city, challenging many assumptions in mainstream urban analysis about the way individuals deploy their resources. Mingione examines general transformations in the socio-spatial relations of social life. Wheelock draws on research on households at the margins of employment — housings living with male unemployment or with recently established small businesses, to challenge neo-classical behaviour. In Part 5, "Dilemmas of Urban Governance", Mayer looks at the arena of urban politics and its possibilities, and Healey examines alternative approaches to regulating urban development activity. In the concluding chapter, we try to draw the various contributions together to assess the nature and possibilities of urban governance as these are emerging, and, in particular, how these might contribute to improving the quality of life, of economic prosperity and environmental sustainability for twenty-first century cities.

Underpinning the work of the various authors of the book are distinctive conceptions of the city, economy and society and government. Collectively, these represent the theoretical orientation of the book. In the second part of this chapter, therefore, we illustrate these conceptions by examining three "contested" concepts critical to all the contributions. The first elaborates the conception of the "urban". The second clarifies the perspective many of the authors share on social relations. The third notes the meaning of governance in this context, as an introduction to a discussion which is developed further in Chapter 13.

The concepts

The "urban" as an analytical focus

The ambiguity and tensions in discussion of the city are echoed in the analysts' difficulty in defining exactly what an urban area is. Quantitative geographers have sought through measurement to distinguish urban and rural areas. Political scientists have described the city in terms of its administrative units and political organisations. Urban economists have viewed cities as sets of input–output relations (export/import). Sociologists have focused on the distinctive communities and power relations of city life, and on arenas for the organisation of collective consumption. Human geographers and planners have been interested in the dynamics of urban spatial organisation. Students of the humanities have been concerned with the imaginary representation of the city, while political theorists have been attracted to the ancient notion of the democratic "polis".

Whatever view one takes, it is difficult to tie the urban down. It is this definitional difficulty which encourages many analysts to ignore the spatial nature of human relations. Why focus on the spatiality of relations, that is, their location, spatial reach and spatial coexistence? Is it not preferable to focus on people in households, firms and agencies, and their relationships? This analytical option looks increasingly attractive given the weakening of place-based interlocking of webs of relations. As Amin and Thrift argue, localised relational webs very evidently these days are at the mercy of globalising tendencies. Even in terms of spatial patterns, traditional distinctions are evaporating, such as the sharp divisions between urban and rural, town and country, as Lowe, Murdoch and Cox discuss.

This analytical debate has policy implications. Why should policy have a spatial focus, and specifically an urban region focus? As Peterson (1985) has argued, if urban policy at national/federal level is aimed at helping impoverished urban dwellers, why not target benefits at such people directly? Is there any real value in "place-targeting", whether to urban neighbourhoods or urban areas as a whole? Such a conclusion suits all those with interests in the traditional sectoral organisation of the delivery of government services and regulatory regimes. In effect, it leaves spatial coordination to people in households, firms and agencies to negotiate for themselves.

Such challenges to an analytical focus on places have a long history. The argument of this book, outlined above, rejects their conclusions. We argue that relations in places matter. There are three ways in which the challenges to the legitimacy of the urban as a focus of attention can be countered. The first emphasises the significance of spatial proximity. As noted earlier, however many social relations escape from the confines of *gemeinschaft*, the place-based community, households, firms and agencies exist in particular places and share these places with others. How they manage the common concerns which arise from this sharing underpins the notion of local governance as acting for and with local communities. Because coexistence in shared spaces is difficult to negotiate where diverse households, firms and agencies are thrust together at high densities, some form of collective management almost everywhere replaces individual or informal forms of negotiation. This emphasises the core meaning of the urban as an arena for addressing place-based governance dilemmas.

The second challenge emphasises the significance of cultural context, the social worlds in which people live. The contemporary city may be culturally diverse; yet the experience of urban life itself shapes these cultures. As Amin and Thrift describe, through meeting people and exchanging ideas and perceptions, ways of thinking and frameworks for action are moulded. Thus, people's social, economic and political relations are embedded in the particularity of specific places, just as much as they are embedded in their various relational webs. Urban places are, then, particular kinds of places, identified by the density and complexity of the relations within them, and by the distinctive structures and facilities through which daily life is conducted.

This leads to the third challenge to those who argue against the urban as a focus of analytical and policy attention. Whatever problems analysts may have, it is clear that most people know the difference. The urban exists as an image in people's minds, identified with particular landscapes, facilities and opportunities, kinds of experience and ways of doing things. As several of the authors in this book acknowledge, the significance of the urban lies in its imaginary representation. How people in households, firms and agencies react to these images affects where they decide to live or conduct their business. How policy discourse constructs and reacts to images of the urban affects what policies are promoted and where they have effects, as Lowe, Murdoch and Cox illustrate. In this context, the urban is of significance, for analysis and for policy, because of the preoccupying connotations currently carried by the image of the urban.

Thus the case for an analytical and policy focus on the "urban" lies as much in its properties as an image as in its measurable material characteristics. What preoccupies several of the authors of this book, as in much contemporary urban analysis and policy, is an "imagination deficit". Confronted with the experience of urban life, past images no longer carry meaning for us, and the ones we now use encapsulate only fragments of our urban experience.

If so, as Dear and Robins argue, a critical task is to re-imagine the city, in ways which take account not just of its new physical and organisational forms, but of the ways people in households, firms and agencies experience urban life. For some decades, visionaries have been predicting the impact on our societies of mass education, of economic growth, of the information technology revolution, of changes in values about family life, our expectations of health, etc. The challenge for urbanists is now to work out how these changes are affecting the fine grain of social life and economic activity as lived out in particular contexts. What are the new frontiers of innovation — in technology; ways of living; ways of conducting business and forms of governance; where are the backwash effects of destruction; how do these interrelate? How do we conceptualise the place-based embeddedness of the webs of relations in which people now exist?

How we succeed in this endeavour is not just a matter of intellectual interest. Several of the chapters in this book highlight the ways in which the ability of the various relations which bind particular households and firms to their locale may foster innovation and creative forces, or, alternatively, impede them. The organisational capacity of particular places, their "territorial organisation" (Swyngedouw 1992b; Gertler 1992), is now increasingly considered as a factor of production in economic analysis.

The particular history and geography of a place, the legacy of previous relational webs which have organised its economy, its social and political life and its physical structure, may create barriers to adjustment, the "institutional inertia" to which Amin and Thrift refer, just as "institutional history" may create opportunities. So, as they argue, there are economic development reasons for being concerned with the urban arena. In parallel, arguments for the maintenance of an environmental inheritance which is not diminished by exploitation by present generations, the "sustainability" case, direct attention to the quality of urban environments. If Beck's argument is correct, and our contemporary western societies are much more aware of the adverse externality effects, the *risks*, of the way we live and organise our economies, then political attention to risk reduction will grow, particularly to those risks with substantial biospheric consequences. As many now emphasise, the urban arena, with its energy demands, waste production and traffic congestion and pollution, is a significant locus of action for such risk reduction strategies (Nijkamp 1991; Breheny 1992; CEC 1990). Thus, to the extent that social and environmental problems are concentrated in urban areas — problems of poverty and disadvantage; of congestion and pollution — there is moral pressure arising from environmental philosophy to attend to the urban.

So whatever our analytical problems in defining the urban and the urban region, it remains a significant "window" through which to spotlight critical social, economic and environmental problems of our contemporary societies, and the urban agenda remains a worrying dimension of public policy. In conducting analysis on these questions, researchers need not merely to observe the behaviour of households and firms. We need to investigate what use people in households, firms, agencies or other associative forms, make of the urban arena; how they value it, and what meaning they give to it. Similarly, we need to assess how far the governance processes which impact on the urban arena facilitate or inhibit what people are trying to do. On these questions, as the authors of this book often comment, there is a huge deficit of research and imagination.

Urban relations: an institutional approach

Underpinning the above definition, and infusing the chapters in this book, is a significant shift in the way social, economic and political activity is understood. Central to this shift is the perception that individuals do not exist as autonomously choosing actors, making atomistic rational choices in relation to their interests. The ontological assumptions of neo-classical economic theory are thus rejected. Individuality is instead considered as established relationally, through the links we have with other people in various arenas and through the values and cultural norms we acquire as a result. These relations are not, however, seen as freely chosen, completely unconstrained. Individuals in systems of relations may be liberated from many of the constraints of traditional cultures, and from the rules of the Fordist industrial workplace. But they are still in a world structured by power relations deriving from economic, political and cultural organis-ation. These structure the world of opportunities and chances within which individuals inter-subjectively work out their interests and strategies and assert their values and norms. People cannot "step out of the world" as postmodernists such as Derrida (1987) claim, but remain within its evolving history (Habermas 1993).

Nevertheless, within this context, people are not merely at the mercy of structure. Following Giddens (1984), individual agency, in the ongoing flow of relations and actions, re-enacts and reforms power structures through acknowledging them or deliberately seeking to change them. This activity of *structuration*, the interrelation of structure and agency, is actively constructed both through the material flow of resources and through the construction of ideas, images, values and norms. These values and norms then serve to filter how we understand and learn from the flow of experience of our lives. People are thus embedded in their social relations, both shaped by them and actively constituting them through the routines of daily life and through deliberate strategies of relation-building. These relational webs revolve around key nodes where individuals come together — the household, the firm/workplace, the governance agency, the voluntary group. These nodal points are often identified as "organisations".

However, in a relational approach, it is not assumed that organisations are discrete, bounded sets of internal relations. Every manager in a firm lives in a household. Most adult household members work somewhere else, and many engage in a whole range of wider links with kin, friends, and various associations. This gives us a complex mixture of what Mingione refers to as reciprocal and associative relations. The organisation and negotiation of relations within one node is shaped by and affects the negotiation of relations within the other nodes in which a person lives. As Amin and Thrift note, this provides a more developed and richer way of expressing Emery and Trist's concept of the way organisations are located in environments (Emery and Trist 1965). This early management literature presented the environment as "outside" the organisation. The present approach brings the "environment" into an organisation, infusing it with the various values and norms brought in by organisation members. Much of the conflict in firms, in households, in formal agencies and voluntary associations arises from conflicts between these values.

The concept of "embeddedness" is used to capture the way people exist in several relations at once — their household, their workplace, their sports club and their political party — and that each affects the other (Giddens 1990). The concept of "cultural communities" is used to indicate the way stable sets of values may build up among those who routinely share and assert common values and norms, and develop common discourses, or systems of meaning.

This shift in our understanding of social life has strong antecedents, particularly in anthropology (e.g. Geertz 1983; Douglas 1987), and sociology (e.g. Berger and Luckman 1971; and the phenomenologists generally). It has been struggling to find a voice in studies in the fields of management and policy analysis (Crozier 1964; Bryson and Crosby 1992; Handy 1979; Barrett and Fudge 1981; Mazmanian and Sabatier 1989). But its wider significance for the organisation of economic and political life has been highlighted by the scale of change in contemporary societies. This has made us conscious that the values and norms we hold are not universal or natural to the human condition, but are socially constructed, that is, made by active affirmation, through the relations in which we live. As the Fordist vertically integrated company gives way to more flexible company networks operating trans-globally, and as the delivery structures of the universalist, hierarchical welfare state are replaced by new apparently fragmented forms, so people in firms, agencies and households have to renegotiate their relational webs. In doing so, we have all become conscious of cultural difference. The "unity of value and culture", which the powerful used to assume we all shared, has "floated away", along with the apparatus of modernist thought and practice.

This intellectual shift is encapsulated in the adjective "institutionalist". This term derives from a movement within economics, associated in the 1970s with the work of Oliver Williamson (1975). As Amin and Thrift note, Williamson focused on the organisation of transactions and how different arrangements affected profitability. However, it has antecedents in economics which go back much earlier, to the work of Veblen (1919) who understood the economic significance of culture and habits of thought in framing economic judgements, and has been brought vigorously forward in recent years by those interested in evolutionary economics (Hodgson 1988, 1993; Amin and Taylor 1994).

But there has been a parallel and often richer evolution in other fields of inquiry. Policy analysis research began to emphasise the importance of the relations through which policy was articulated and delivered as researchers studied the social relations through which policies were implemented. This work emphasised policy networks and bargaining behaviour (Friend et al. 1974; Rhodes 1981). The work of Anthony Giddens in sociology has provided many working from the tradition of Marxist political economy with a stepping stone to moving away from reductionist models of structural determination to a more sensitive understanding of the way structural driving forces are constructed through the micropolitics of agency interaction, while actively shaping them (Giddens 1984). This tendency has been further reinforced by the work of Michel Foucault on the ethnography of power (Foucault 1979).

Within the fields of economic geography, many of these tendencies have combined to produce more historically sensitive Marxist studies, for example Harvey's work on capital and the built environment (Harvey 1985a, b). Studies of the structural and the contingent in locality change highlight the significance of culture as actively constructed by interaction in places. Much of this work shows the way cultures clash in workplaces and in the household (e.g. Whatmore 1991).

Finally, those interested in the relation between economic and political organisation have moved on from a preoccupation with the "role of the state" and the search for a functional relation between economy and state to empirically based investigation of the fine-grained negotiation of the tensions between economic and political "regulation". In the 1970s the debate focused on the relative autonomy of the state as a power structure, compared with the economy. In the 1980s this debate has been enriched and recast by the contribution of the regulation school. This seeks to identify parallels between modes of accumulation and modes of regulation of the social relations of accumulation (Jessop 1990a, b, 1993). As work has progressed, there has been an effort to move away from economic functionalism to explore how the relations between economic activity and governance processes are actively negotiated in the micropolitics of social relations (Clarke 1992; Peck and Tickell 1992a, b).

This whole body of work represents a major intellectual challenge to economic reductionism (the assumption that our human relations are dominated by economic considerations) and instrumental rationality (the assumption that our behaviour can be primarily explained as derived from rational calculation of our individual interests atomistically conceived). It also challenges structural reductionism (the assumption that human behaviour can be explained by a limited set of general structural forces, such as capital, or the power of elites, or culture). For the "new" institutionalists, agency is multi-faceted, while structure has several dimensions and is actively created by agency as well as shaping microsocial relations.

What then do the "new" institutionalists acknowledge? Firstly, the approach highlights the significance of individual agency. Yet actors are not seen as autonomous individuals, as in neo-classical economics. They are seen as existing in a social milieu, or lifeworld, within which norms, values and ways of doing things are evolved and transmitted, through the meshing of experience and interpretation. The work of interpretation is both a reflective and interactive enterprise, undertaken with others in the social milieu. The collective effort creates *cultural communities* with shared frames of reference.

Cultural distinctiveness is expressed both in what people do, how they go about things, and in how people talk about what they do. Language is the critical medium through which culture is articulated and transmitted, and through which cultural differences are negotiated. It is for this reason that the construction of *discourses* is such an important political and policy task, and the use of discourse so powerful in binding groups together. Individual interests and the strategies of groups are constructed within the context of these cultures, and mesh together rational calculation, moral principle and aesthetic appreciation, Aristotle's *episteme, techne* and *phronesis* (Flyvberg 1993; Habermas 1984). Material interests are thus grasped through cultural frames of reference which give value to certain goods and behaviours and emphasise particular qualities and modes of expression (Geertz 1983).

To understand how cultures are built up and changed, and how they shape the performance of tasks, requires an emphasis on the *dynamics* of social relationships, on the *networks* through which knowledge, experience and forms of representation are developed and exchanged. These may involve direct face-to-face links with other people. But they may also involve acknowledging the worth of non-present and generalised cultural communities, made available through education, the various media, the marketing strategies of firms and agencies, and deliberate proselytising work, as in the strategies of religions, political parties and pressure groups. Cultures encounter each other, in conflicts over meaning and value, as well as over specific interests, anywhere where cultural diversity exists.

Power is exercised within cultures, through the way conformity is negotiated. It is exercised between cultures in the negotiation of access to material opportunity and the discursive terms through which such access takes place. The systematic exercise of power builds up and maintains the *structural driving forces* which are recognised in particular times and places as shaping the evolution of cultures. These driving forces shape and are in turn shaped by the often implicit micropolitics of everyday life, through the way material resources are controlled, social regulation is accomplished and discourses, as forms of representation, evolve. Exactly how individuals, in various groupings, relate to the powerful driving forces which infuse their lives cannot be predicted, since it is an active process of invention. What we do is *contingent* on the particularities of time, place and individual and group capacity. The result is the great diversity of human experience.

While the breakdown of the dominant hegemony of modernist rationalism has exposed the cultural dimensions of our existence, and the differences between us, making us uncertain of ourselves and conscious of our differences with "others" (Geertz 1988), it also makes it much more difficult to locate "cultural communities". These are no longer neatly tied to places, to neighbourhoods, cities, regions and nations. Nor are they to be found necessarily in the key nodes of human interaction — households and kinship networks, firms, formal agencies and informal associations. If individual action is relationally embedded, then so is that of households, firms and agencies. Each of these nodes may be a site of cultural conflict, as Wheelock discusses in Chapter 10, and of the active creation of cultural community. Success in this enterprise in one sphere may generate conflict in the others. The ability to address such conflicts as they arise within the terrain of an urban region is part of what Amin and Thrift describe as the "institutional thickness" of a place. Configurations favourable to the economic development of a place in the contemporary period, they suggest, include relational stability, an "archive of commonly held knowledge", the ability to learn and change, a "high innovation capacity", the extension of "trust and reciprocity", and a widely held sense of a "common project".

The "new" institutionalists thus seek to show why social relations matter to economic and political activity and how this comes about. It does not imply a focus specifically on formal organisations. It emphasises instead how such organisations — a firm, a local government body, a public agency, a pressure group, and the industrial household — are made active by the way people-in-relations realise procedures and activities. In this activating work, an organisation is connected to, and embedded in, the webs of relations which form the social milieux of the various participants.

This new approach is not just a matter of intellectual interest, to provide a richer and more robust explanation of what is going on within the urban arena. It also has considerable implications for the focus and form of policy intervention in urban areas. We examine these implications further in Chapter 13. We now turn briefly to the question of "urban governance".

Managing the urban

It has been argued in this chapter that the urban is best understood as an ensemble of diverse social relations, with different cultural referents and spatial dimensions, which co-exist in the confined arena of urban areas. Further, the particular nature of the ensemble of relations to be found in a place "makes a difference", to the possibilities for economic development, to the environmental qualities of a place, and to the quality of life of the people who live and work there. The institutional relations of a place matter. What are the implications for the management of cities?

As Healey argues in Chapter 12 in relation to land use planning, urban management cannot be understood these days in terms of "top-down" or "command and control" models of governance. Urban governments are not in a position to control the strategies of the various firms and households in their economies. These strategies result from the way people in households and firms respond to the opportunities they see and the pressures on them. Nor are public policies and their implementation a matter of articulating "public interest goals" and then following them through to ensure conformance of behaviour with goals. Public policies are more like experiments, thrown into the relational ensemble, informed by hypotheses about possible effects. At the urban level, city governments may seek to improve the benefits of the coexistence of the relational webs within their areas, or promote the interests of particular actors and their strategies, or just maintain political support. But they are not the sole locus for addressing the concerns people in urban regions may have with respect to managing coexistence in shared spaces. There have always been private arrangements for managing some aspects of the urban region arena. The welfare state tended to diminish the range of activities performed by private arrangements or voluntary collaboration. Its fragmentation and the active promotion of neo-liberal strategies has encouraged new arrangements, both in market forms of provision, through formal strategies of privatisation, and as a result of the "coping strategies" of people in households and firms faced with the withdrawal of the public sector.

Urban management is thus not merely a job of governments. It is the product of the way people in households, firms and agencies seek out ways of making links and establishing common cause with those with similar agendas or some mutuality of interest. Through these processes, as Lovering and Mayer describe, new alliances are formed to influence the terms of coexistence, and influence what local and national governments do. These affect not only the agenda of urban management, what it is seen as necessary to manage; they also affect the styles and processes of management. Thus, as the agencies of formal urban politics — city governments and political parties — struggle to adjust to new circumstances, they are often under active pressure to respond to these new agendas and ways of doing things. At the same time, they too are within relational webs in which typically there are higher tiers of government seeking to shape what they do.

The chapters in this book not only offer suggestions for the new agendas, mechanisms and processes of urban government. They also comment on the struggle of existing city governments to adapt to new conditions. For those concerned with a democratic agenda — that is, forms of urban management which aid the flourishing of the diverse cultural communities which coexist in the urban region arena while enabling the discussion and implementation of ways of identifying and acting on shared problems — a critical issue is how to identify what actions pursued in what way might make a difference. If there is any merit in the conceptual approach outlined here, such actions are likely to focus not just on the provision of goods and services, as city governments did in the past, or the enabling of others to do so, but on the building of links both in social relations and in discourses, between the relational webs in the urban arena. There are many ideas in these chapters on both the opportunities and difficulties of doing this. We try to draw these ideas together in Chapter 13.

Notes

1. This was noted by Patrick Dunleavy during the March Seminar.
2. This Korean concept was brought to our attention by Chang Woo Lee, a research student in the Department of Town and Country Planning, 1988–1993. It draws a traditional analogy with the conditions for plant growth.

Part I

READING THE CITY

ALI MADANI-POUR

On their way back to Marseilles, after three weeks of concentrated discussions at the foot of the Acropolis and on board the steamship *Patris II*, the participants in the Fourth *Congrès Internationaux d'Architecture Moderne* (CIAM) in 1933 formulated their views on town planning as the Charter of Athens. To them the cities were in a state of chaos, suffering from, amongst other things, overcrowding, air pollution, blighted areas and slums, expanding suburbs, lack of open space and of community facilities. These conditions in the cities did not correspond to the "most elementary biological and psychological needs of the great masses of their populations". This was all due to "the uncontrolled and disorderly development of the Machine Age", with its "ceaseless growth of private interests". To save the cities, planned action was required, creating a premeditated order by introducing control into the urban development process, based on the use of "modern technics" and "collaboration of specialists". They asked for large-scale transformation of urban areas into "functional cities", whose four functions — dwelling, work, recreation, and transportation — all stood in a rational relationship to each other and to their city-region (Sert 1944, pp. 246–249).

Sixty years on, from our vantage point, we can see how this modernist manifesto was adopted around the world, was widely put to use,

Managing Cities: The New Urban Context, edited by P. Healey, S. Cameron, S. Davoudi, S. Graham and A. Madani-Pour. © 1995 The Editors and contributors. Published in 1995 by John Wiley & Sons Ltd.

especially in the three decades following the Second World War, and was criticised and discredited afterwards. These ideas, and the practices they evoked, show an overflowing confidence in science and technology, which, when rationally applied, can lead to emancipation by imposing a new order onto the jumble of social and spatial environments. They echoed the optimism and utopianism of the last two centuries based on a linear conception of history as progress and a firm belief in the ability of reason to guide this progress. Yet the modernisation process, as in the past (Berman 1982; Harvey 1985b), proved to be too painful and costly. It dramatically changed the face of many cities but, by its nature, coupled development and displacement, pride and misery. Its functionalist reading of the city was questioned and its solutions were one by one abandoned: rational planning, large-scale redevelopment, strict zoning, high-rise buildings in the parks, demise of the street and so on. The relatively coherent set of prescriptions that this group of avant-gardes brought down from the Acropolis has now been replaced by fragmented collections of ideas and practices. The only apparent string that connects these fragments is their critical reaction to these old certainties. They are hence collectively titled "post"-modernism.

But is postmodernism only a critique of modernism that follows it? Is it a change of style and technique, proposing pragmatic adjustments to the new circumstances, especially when the modernists had proved to be too ambitious and idealistic? Do the modernists and postmodernists share the same concerns for the cities but have different solutions? Or do they see things entirely differently? Is postmodernism an epistemology or an epoch, a theoretical approach or a state of affairs (Hassard 1993)? Is the post-modern "simply a desire, a mood which looks to the future to redeem the present" or a historical period (Docherty 1993)? Is it "a state of mind" (Bauman 1992), "a question of expressions of thought" (Lyotard 1992a)? If it is an epoch, how do we periodise postmodernism? Is it parallel with the global economic and political restructuring known as post-Fordism, where the Fordist mass production and central planning have been replaced with flexibility in production patterns and pluralism in consumption? Is it associated with, as both Baudrillard and Lyotard assume (Featherstone 1988), a move towards a postindustrial age or is it the cultural logic of late capitalism (Jameson 1991) at the stage of globalisation and flexible accumulation of capital (Harvey 1989a)? How do we understand the postmodern space? Is it aestheticised and devoid of any overarching social objectives (Harvey 1989a)? Is it a "multinational space", leaving us unable to grasp it (Jameson 1991)? Facing an increasingly complex and multi-faceted reality, should we continue our attempt to come to an "objective" understanding or should we become content with a relativism that allows us to hold all readings of such reality as valid?

Modernism was essentially based on the possibility and necessity of breaking with tradition and instituting new ways of living and thinking. According to Lyotard (1992a, pp. 64–68), what demarcates postmodernism from its predecessor, besides falling in successive periods, is the decline of the confidence which equated development with progress. For him, the prospect of emancipating all of humanity through planned action, through the efforts of the avant-garde, has all disappeared. What the postmodernists seek now (Lyotard 1992b) is a celebration of difference and waging a war against such grand narratives with their totalising tendencies.

As against this view, Habermas identifies postmodernism with a combination of antimodernism and premodernism in an environment that continues to promote capitalist modernisation processes. He admits that protest and discontent can arise when the modernisation process is guided by standards of economic and administrative rationality. But he argues that we should not abandon the intentions of the Enlightenment, the specialisation of culture to be utilised for the enrichment of everyday life, and should learn from the mistakes of the past, as modernity is still "an incomplete project" (Habermas 1993). The unintended consequences of modernity are due partly to a narrow definition of rationality. Habermas thus sets out to broaden the sphere of reason by incorporating issues of morality, justice and aesthetics alongside the instrumental and scientific rationality (Habermas 1984).

There seems to have been a permanent discourse between order, as an expression of reason, and disorder, representing the diversity and difference caused by the spontaneity of daily life, throughout the history of the western cities. The earliest example of an attempt to impose order on disorders of the urban life was Hippodamus's famous plan of 450 BC for Miletus, which stood in sharp contrast to the disordered geometry of Athens accommodating an unprecedented social diversity (Benevolo 1980; Morris 1979). Roman settlements and the Renaissance ideal cities were other examples of such a drive. But it was in the Enlightenment period, and the long line of utopian schemes, some of which were built as model towns, throughout the nineteenth and the twentieth centuries, that the concepts of order and control were interlinked with the possibility of emancipation of humankind.

Difference and diversity, on the other hand, have always been the essence and reality of urban experience. As the medieval German proverb (*Stadtluft macht frei*) suggested, city air made people free, allowing them to step out from the totalising force of the feudal countryside (Vance 1977). Yet living with difference and diversity could prove a difficult task. The factions of the medieval Mediterranean city, and today's walled neighbourhoods of Los Angeles (Davis 1992), both represent a fear of difference. These spaces represent reorganisation processes searching to create a fragmented and localised, as distinct from a universal, order for a specific group within a spatial limit: to separate "us" from "them", from the Other. In the postmodern era, this tribalism, Bauman (1992) argues, is associated with "privatisation of fear" and the rise of "imagined communities". To the modernist longing for order, the main enemy was the "unlicensed" difference. But we are now bound to live with contingency and difference. To put a brake on tribal hostilities, what is needed is tolerance in the form of solidarity, and "a practical recognition of the *relevance* and *validity* of the other's difference, expressed in a willing engagement in the dialogue" (Bauman 1992, p. xxi).

All chapters in this part contribute to this discourse between order and disorder, between general and particular, between uniformity and difference. The authors offer their readings of the city, which share a critical stance against what they see as the straitjacket of rationalism. They argue that the emerging diversity and plurality of life forms, in their socio-spatial contexts, have not been accounted for in the modernist desire for order. This desire was often accompanied by the homogenising force of the canons that the high culture set, and continues to influence the practices of city management today. They invite us to look at the city with a new "state of mind" and to focus on details of daily practices, where difference is most visible. With this sensibility, they argue, we will be able to see cities in a new light and have a better understanding of the complexities of urban life.

Michael Dear's chapter starts with a general critique of modernist planning and then focuses on Los Angeles as the archetype of postmodern urbanism. He traces the origins of rationalism in American urbanism back to the emergence of a quest for unity, control, and expert skills to be materialised in spatial order. In building the modernist city, however, a separation occurred between capitalist urbanisation processes and planning theory, between material and spiritual, between modernisation and modernism, constituting what Berman (1982) sees as the essence of the twentieth-century dialectic. In Los Angeles, this was best manifest in the subordination of the planning apparatus to the demands of local capital.

Dear is not convinced by the attempts to comprehend the structure of Los Angeles from above. Instead, he asks for a postmodern sensibility, a new way of seeing, which views the city from below. There is no single reality to the city and the key to understand its social life is in focusing on its finely grained microgeography at the street level. The social and spatial fragmentation of the metropolis has given rise to local autonomies and alliances that undermine the formal power structure but are interlinked with the globalised capital and the privatisation processes of the 1980s. This localism, along with the decline of the state responsibility for infrastructure and services, has furthered fragmentation, polarisation, homelessness, crime, and environmental degradation. There is now a sharp contrast between the glossy and prosperous surface of downtown and the city's underbelly, "a hideous culture of malice, mistrust, and mutiny". New ways of creating cities are needed, as there is a non-conformity between this postmodern urbanism, with its absence of a civil will or a collective intentionality, and the obsolete, modernist planning system of the city unable to influence its social heterodoxy.

Kevin Robins starts by reviewing briefly two conservative and radical perspectives that have been influential in the cultural revitalisation and urban regeneration debates during the last decade. He argues that despite some engaging concerns about the subject, especially by the radical approach, they both suffer from a substantial deficit in their rationalistic, idealised images of urban culture. What is missing from these pictures, he suggests, following Mumford, is the question of fear, aggression and anxiety, essential dimensions of urban experience, which must be contained in a civilised environment. In other words, in our understanding of the city, it is not sufficient to resort to reason, as without acknowledging emotions a balance cannot be achieved.

Robins makes the observation that the history of modern city planning has been a futile struggle to impose order and coherence on the seeming confusion and fragmentation of the ever-expanding cities. This has been in part a reaction to fear of the presence of otherness, as represented by the crowd, the woman, and the stranger. The "image of the formless crowd" has caused fears of depersonalisation, fragmentation, and identity loss. Women have been seen, as the feminist writers explain, as a threat to the paternalist order. The stranger is fundamental to the enrichment of the urban experience by bringing new qualities, but his/her mobility and ambivalence are seen as a threat to the established order. The emotions of fear, envy and desire are also aroused by the stranger who lives among us. These emotions can provoke a civilising encounter but also, with the upsurge of violence, can encourage defensive or aggressive behaviour and hence lead to a breakdown of urban culture. The challenge is, therefore, to contain fear creatively and to negotiate common concerns while valuing the difference.

Lowe, Murdoch and Cox outline a strategic process that has been at work to tackle this fear of diversity and disorder: leaving the city altogether and retreating into the countryside, where access to an exclusive environment has ensured a spatial, and therefore social, segregation. They show how, especially since the late nineteenth century, British countryside has come to its prominent cultural status as an alternative to the horrors and dislocations of industrial cities, offering "civilised enjoyment" to dominant social groups. They trace the place of countryside in British culture since the age of Empire, when supply of food from the colonies made the countryside available as a cultural space. This was followed by the interwar call for its protection and distinctiveness, threatened by the encroaching suburbs, and the postwar's state sponsored, agricultural productivism. With dramatic reduction in agriculture's significance, however, the contemporary countryside is where new firms are being relocated in search of pleasant working environments. Lowe, Murdoch and Cox maintain that, throughout these stages, rural space has excluded the city's diversity and has been regarded as an "anchor" for "new traditionalist", "Anglo-centric", class and gender identities. It has become a stable middle-class domain centred on family and on women's traditional role at home. The order and exclusiveness of this space, with its virtues of "peace and quiet", "community" and "neighbourliness", are protected by the planning system, allowing a retreat from the "ex-centric, open-ended and multi-ethnic" urban space.

1

Prolegomena to a Postmodern Urbanism

MICHAEL DEAR

> . . . *The state of theory, now and from now*
> *on, isn't it California? And even*
> *Southern California?*
> (Jacques Derrida, quoted in Carroll, 1990, p. 63)

The practices of everyday life are remarkably constrained. In feudal times, for example, the size and distribution of agricultural settlements was limited by the ability of the farm worker to walk to and from the most-distant fields, and yet still put in a full day's work. Even in today's "global village", most people's lives are restricted by the discipline of the daily journey to work. We can think of an individual's life as being bounded by a "prism" of space and time. Both axes of the prism (time, space) are strictly finite. Human well-being and potential depend upon the resources that a person may readily access within a strictly finite geographical range, as determined by the frictions of time and distance. Thus, in resource-rich environments, individuals may flourish without hindrance; but in resource-deficient settings, access to the means of advancement is inhibited.

Needless to say, the characteristics of individuals as well as places will influence life-chances. For minorities, the poor, the disabled, and women, the time–space prism closes rapidly to become a time–space "prison". It is easy to understand how people come to wear like a scar the "imprint" of

Managing Cities: The New Urban Context, edited by P. Healey, S. Cameron, S. Davoudi, S. Graham and A. Madani-Pour. © 1995 The Editors and contributors. Published in 1995 by John Wiley & Sons Ltd.

an environment, because daily life acts to transmit privilege or poverty. Recall, for instance, how daughters followed mothers into the textile mills; how sons joined fathers down the mine-shaft; and how many Hollywood stars have Hollywood parents.

We can extend our thinking on time and space to encompass the whole of human society. Social life may be conceived as a time–space "fabric", upon which the aggregate biographies of individual lives are engraved. The consequent tapestry is rich and complex, encompassing as it does the fully panoply of social, cultural, political and economic aspirations. One goal of social science is to unravel the structure of this time-space fabric, from the highest level of abstraction to the details of everyday life. Geographers and other urbanists read cities, spaces, places and landscapes in ways analogous to how literary critics read the texts of great writers. Geography's role in this undertaking is to understand how socio-cultural and political-economic change are concretised, or localised, in particular places; and by extension, a principal goal of urban and regional planning is to forge new time–space relationships for the betterment of humankind.

I shall take as my text the city of Los Angeles, which some view as the harbinger of a new, postmodern urbanism, defining a "hyperspace" in which time–space coordinates have been stretched into as yet unknown dimensions (cf. Jameson 1991). For me, postmodernity encompasses a set of perspectives on a most pressing intellectual dilemma: that Rationalism has failed both as an ideal and as a practical guide for thought and social action; and that henceforth, we have to manage without such Enlightenment desiderata as decisive theoretical argument or self-evident truth. In Toulmin's (1990) felicitous phrases, we have moved from a mindset which emphasises the written, the general, the universal and the timeless to one which privileges the oral, local, particular and timely.

Postmodernism's principal target has been the rationality of the modern movement, especially its foundational character, its search for a universal truth (Dear 1988). In Lyotard's (1979) words, postmodernity is openly "incredulous" toward such meta-narratives. The postmodern position is that all meta-narratives are suspect; that the authority claimed by any single explanation is ill-founded, and hence should be resisted. In essence, postmodernists assert that the relative merit of one meta-narrative over another is ultimately undecidable; and by extension, that any such attempts to forge intellectual consensus should be resisted. The deconstruction movement has given further impetus to the demise of modernity (Norris 1982). Deconstruction has emphasised how language limits thought; how our conceptual orderings do not exist in the nature of things but instead reflect our pre-existing philosophical systems. These, in turn, contain conscious and unconscious strategies of exclusion and repression, and are rife with internal contradictions and suppressed paradoxes. Deconstructionists therefore place as much emphasis on what is absent from a text as on what is present therein. According to Derrida and others, we can never completely master language; its effects inevitably go beyond what we can control. Inevitably we fail at the tasks of representation and deciding between various interpretations of the text before us.

For most of its two hundred years of existence, Los Angeles has been viewed as an exception to the mainstream of American urban culture. The city conjures up visions of endless metropolitan sprawl, ubiquitous freeways, inconsequential architecture, idiosyncratic lifestyles, and smog. These images are encouraged and exaggerated by the movies and television programmes that Hollywood has sold to the world. They make it easy to dismiss LA as unreal. But this exceptionalist view is badly misleading. LA is, in many ways, a prototype of twenty-first century North American urbanism. As Garreau (1991, p. 3) pointed out "Every single American city that *is* growing, is growing in the fashion of Los Angeles." Places like Phoenix, Atlanta and Seattle increasingly resemble suburbs of Los Angeles. So do Mexico City and São Paulo. Twenty years ago, the architectural critic Rayner Banham alerted the world to the significance of Los Angeles. But we should not forget that Banham (1973, p. 236) also warned: "Los Angeles threatens . . . because it breaks the rules."

The beautifully named *El Pueblo de Nuestra Reina de Los Angeles de Porciuncula* was founded in 1781. As trumpeted in a 1929 pamphlet issued by the Security Trust and Savings Bank (1929, p. 12): "Thus came into being *a* great American city, destined, as many predict, to be *the* great American city." Boosterism persisted as an integral part of LA's image and purpose throughout its history. In the recent plan for LA 2000, local visionaries imagined the imminent emergence of a "world crossroads city", where just as in times past, citizens would be able to make their "Los Angeles dream come true" (Los Angeles 2000 Committee 1988, p. 87). Of course, there has always been a dark side to the city as well. Bertholt Brecht, fleeing the Third Reich, concluded that "on thinking about Hell, that it must be/Still more like Los Angeles" (quoted in Davis 1990, p. 51). The city's bleak urbanism has provided the source of countless gaudy and grotesque parodies in literature and film. Perhaps best known is Ridley Scott's *Blade Runner*, which evoked a futuristic metropolis of perpetual darkness, a rain-soaked, polyglot inferno of high-tech crime. But Roman Polanski's *Chinatown* captures the reality more accurately: a surficial gloss of striking beauty, glowing light and pastel hues, which together conspire to conceal a hideous culture of malice, mistrust and mutiny.

Casual observers, visitors and residents alike, catch little of the city's underbelly. They are instead persuaded by the glossy, utopian images of the burgeoning World City — a collage of prosperity, fantasy and play: the corporate glitter of LA's downtown citadel; the sunshine, surf and mountains; the city as a giant agglomeration of theme parks. Yet the confusion and chaos that underlie such images are more reminiscent of a Third World nation, a dystopia that is increasingly polarised between haves and have-nots; that is host to the nation's largest population of homeless people; where neighbourhoods increasingly resemble combat zones as warring gangs struggle for turf supremacy. Here, the air, earth and water are perpetually being poisoned. Here, public responsibility for basic human services, including shelter, education and health care, have been progressively abdicated.

I shall not argue here that LA is unique or is a prototype of future urban developments, even though both viewpoints are at some level demonstrably true. I shall instead make a more modest claim: that LA's peculiarities invite us to think differently about aspects of contemporary urbanism.

From modern to postmodern

Barbar the Elephant versus Mickey Mouse

The essence of the problem of postmodern urbanism can be captured, in an entirely serious way, by placing Barbar the Elephant alongside Mickey Mouse. These two cartoon figures provide provocative exemplars of past and future urbanisms.

In her study of the politics of design in French colonial urbanism, architectural historian Gwendolyn Wright (1991) shows how powerful were the myths of colonial order by examining Barbar's 1931 design for the construction of Célesteville, a city of elephants in Africa. Behind a harbour, standardised shuttered huts for native peoples were arranged in neat rows below a hill capped by two monumental buildings: the Palais du Travail and the Palais des Fêtes. The vision of Barbar's creator (de Brunhoff) was one of "social hierarchy, orderly growth, a thriving economy, and effective political authority". All this was to be accomplished (needless to say) without effacing the indigenous African social fabric.

Contrast Barbar's world with that of Mickey Mouse: a vision of the city as a collage of theme parks, best exemplified by the various Disneylands, and in particular by the postmodern archetype, Los Angeles. The emergent reorientations invoked by the postmodern city are nowhere more evident than in Michael Sorkin's edited collection *Variations on a Theme Park*. In his introductory remarks, Sorkin (1992, p. xii) observes that:

> the city has historically mapped social relations with profound clarity, imprinting in its shapes and places vast information about status and power.

However, in Sorkin's "recombinant" city, this earlier modernist legibility has been obscured, and dramatically manipulated: the phone and the modem have rendered the street irrelevant; social hierarchies, once fixed, have become "despatialised"; indeed, space itself is "departicularised" (Sorkin 1992, p. xiii).

Let us, for the moment, grant that this is so. That between the rigidities of modernist planning (in Barbar's colonial guise) and the departicularised places of postmodernity (in Disney theme parks), there is a world of difference. My question is: How and why are modernist legibilities being transformed and the particular spatialities of postmodernity being created?

The origins of rationality in American urbanism

The rationalities of American urban land-use planning may be found somewhere between the end of the nineteenth and the beginning of the twentieth centuries (e.g.; Krueckeberg 1983; Schaffer 1988). The end of the nineteenth century was a period when people searched for "an instinct for improvement" (Boyer 1986, p. 3). The key language of planning at this time referred to such notions as "uplift", "harmony" and "instinct". By the beginning of the twentieth century, less than twenty years later, planning discourse had been realigned to emphasise "unity", "control" and "expert skills". This new disciplinary order had as its goal the use of surplus capital for civilising and socialising purposes. It required state intervention, a revised municipal politics, and the production of a category of experts.

The origins of this emergent social rationality lay in the post-Civil War era, when reconstructionists worried how to discipline and regulate the urban masses, and how to control and arrange the spatial growth of cities (Boyer 1986, p. 9). It did not take long before a host of urban ills were associated with industrialisation and urbanisation, and an intense anti-urbanism was born. This led to a new relationship between the urban populace and social science knowledge, which by the end of the century had called forth a process of city planning. Capitalists joined Reformers to address social and economic needs. First, environmental reform was promoted as a remedy for the social pathologies of urban areas. Secondly, public health legislation was closely followed by the design of model tenements intended to improve the quality of life in urban areas. In an era characterised by "the new totalisation of poverty", settlement houses and charity workers vied for the right to provide relief for groups in need. Thirdly, it became apparent that there was a need for centralised, supervised operations by some form of institutional authority, especially in order to reduce ill-distributed relief. Around this time Charles Mulford Robinson, a journalist who identified himself as a "city improver", remarked upon the strange evil of excessive urban generosity (Boyer 1986, pp. 13–27).

The new totalisation of poverty required an expanded chain of information. A concept of the "curative whole" appeared, reflecting the linkage between pathologies of the individual and pathologies of family, neighbourhood, and city (Boyer 1986, pp. 28–33). As a consequence, attention shifted to new spatial categories and to new environmental causes. The search for a spatial order was principally directed through nature and classical architecture. Robinson was an important figure in the search for municipal art, reflecting the influence of Haussmann (quoted in Boyer, 1986, p. 54) when he wrote:

> . . . it has been found that often there is no better way to redeem a slum district than by cutting into it a great highway that will be filled with through travel of a city's industry. Like a stream of pure water cleansing what it touches, this tide of traffic pulsing with the joyousness of the city's life of toil and purpose, when flowing through an idle or suffering district, wakes it to larger interests and higher purposes.

The birth of a planning mentality meant a new spatial order in American cities, but planning documents quickly zeroed-in on the minute details of the built environment. A concern with physical detail was increasingly abstracted from the motives and conflicts that led to the production of the built environment; civic improvements were recommended without consideration of those vested interests that led to the production of a particular city structure. In short, the process of capitalist urbanisation was overlooked while an idealised/utopian planning theory developed. Planning practice created its own totalisation; for detailed plans to be constructed, an extensive fact file was needed to organise the physical, social, economic and legal/administrative fabric of the city (see Boyer 1986, ch. 4.).

Building the modernist city

The verities of modernist land-use planning and the consequences of the separation of capitalist process from planning theory are convincingly revealed in anthropologist James Holston's (1989) account of the construction of the city of Brasília. Holston noted that the city's modernist plan was founded on the principles of the Athens charter and the philosophy of the Congrès Internationaux d'Architecture Moderne (CIAM) group. The CIAM philosophy concentrated on four functions of the city: housing, work, recreation and traffic; it later added the administrative function to this list. Holston (1989, p. 40) reveals how the modernist city managed to harness mutually antagonistic social and political programmes to a single architectural programme:

Brasília was planned by a left–center liberal, designed by a communist, constructed by a developmentalist regime and consolidated by a bureaucratic authoritarian dictatorship each claiming an elective affinity with the city. Precisely because the CIAM model manages to unite such dissident interest, its brand of modernism has come to dominate development projects worldwide.

The CIAM city was a city of salvation. It was intended to solve the urban and social crises attributed to maladies caused by unfettered private interests. The most important exponent of CIAM principles was the architect Le Corbusier. (His seminal text, entitled *The Radiant City*, includes the following epigraph: "This work is dedicated to authority.") The rationalist metropolis that resulted was a city which dehistoricised the particular — a city distilled into a universal model. The plan was sketched initially by Costa and executed by Neimeyer. Their view was one of "the harmony of the whole" (Holston, 1989, p. 91). Brasil's President Kubiteschek was committed both to modernism and modernisation; he was also a utopianist, who envisaged the architecture of Brasília as a prescription for social change. But how could capitalists and communists both find their visions signified by the same set of symbols? The answer according to Holston (1989, p. 95) lies in the *polysemous* nature of architecture — each group could identify with the break with a colonial past and a leap into the future implied by the plan. Moreover, no priority among the competing political claims represented in the plan could be established.

There is another condition beyond architectural ambiguity that explains how a single plan representation could absorb the multiple significations implied by its communist and totalitarian supporters. The peculiar genius of modernist thought lies in its "empty vessel" quality; anyone can pour identity or signification into that vessel. The abstract ahistoricism and aspatiality of modernist thought has allowed a split to occur between the material side of modernism and the spiritual side of modernism. It is this division that has given modernist thought its remarkable resilience — a chameleon-like ability to satisfy all ideologies at once. At the same time, however, the qualities of ahistoricity and aspatiality also betray modernity's greatest flaw: i.e. its separation of the political economy of modernisation from the culture and spirituality of modernity. Thus, for instance, the rationalities of production and reproduction in capitalist urbanisation have been divorced from the utopian ideals of planning thought as well as from the minutiae of planning practice. This is a (fatal?) recipe for irrelevance. And somewhat predictably, the particular dynamism of Brasilian society destroyed the plan's utopian hopes. Even as the physical design persisted in mutated form, the practices of everyday life pre-empted, even destroyed, the modernist logics that underlie the design (Holston 1989, p. 98).

From modernity to postmodernity

In his examination of the culture of modernity, Marshall Berman (1982) captures the essence of the separation I have just described. Let me use Berman's definitions to clarify some terminology. *Modernity* has been fed by numerous movements including science, industrialisation, demographic change, urban growth, mass communication, nation states, social movements, and the rise of worldwide capitalism. *Modernisation* refers to a state of perpetual becoming. *Modernism* is a discussion about changing visions and values that accompany modernisation (Berman 1982, p. 16). According to Berman, the essence of the twentieth-century dialectic is the relationship between modernisation and modernism. The process of modernisation has engorged virtually the whole world, and the developing global culture of modernism has achieved spectacular triumphs in art and social thought; but as the modern public expanded, it shattered into a multitude of fragments speaking incommensurable private languages. The idea of modernity, conceived in numerous fragmentary ways, thus loses much of its vividness, resonance and depth; its capacity to organise and giving meaning to people's lives is reduced. As a result, we find ourselves today in the midst of a modern age that has lost touch with the roots of its own modernity. As Berman (1982, p. 15) puts it:

> To be modern . . . is to experience personal and social life as a maelstrom, to find one's world and oneself in perpetual disintegration and renewal, trouble and anguish, ambiguity and contradiction: to be part of a universe in which all that is solid melts into air. To be a modernist is to make oneself somehow at home in the maelstrom, to make its rhythms one's own, to move within its currents in search for the forms of reality, of beauty, of freedom, of justice, that its fervid and perilous flow allows.

The consequences for a disoriented, decentred society are profound. According to Berman, first, a dynamic new landscape has been created in which the experience of modernity takes place. Secondly, a radical flattening of perspective has occurred, and been accompanied by a shrinkage of the imaginative range. The twentieth century has in fact lurched towards rigid polarisations and flat totalisations. Open visions have been supplanted by closed visions (for example "both/and" is replaced by "either/or"). Thirdly, the iron cage of a capitalistic, legalistic and bureaucratic framework has closed around us, giving rise to a state of "total administration". Finally, the kind of person constructed by the new modernity is characterised by Marcuse's "one-dimensional man", where people recognise themselves solely through their consumption of commodities (Berman 1982, pp. 18–28).

Using the examples of Charles Baudelaire, Le Corbusier, Robert Moses and Jane Jacobs, Berman reveals that the burgeoning dualism between modernisation and modernism has diminished our understanding of how materialism and spiritualism invade each other. The early Baudelaire portrayed a pastoral vision of modernity, celebrating modern life as a fashion show, a carnival. The later Baudelaire constructed a counter-pastoral vision which poured scorn on the notion of progress and modern life, suggesting that the concept of indefinite progress must be the most cruel and ingenious torture ever invented. It is important to recognise the historical context for Baudelaire's work, viz. the modernisation of Paris by Haussmann on behalf of Napoleon the Third. Through Haussmann, Paris became a unified physical and human space, especially via the construction of the boulevard. Baudelaire's description of life on the boulevard shows how new private and public worlds came into being through the re-creation of the cityscape.

Walter Benjamin pointed out that whereas Marx analysed change as an experience within a world historical context, Baudelaire showed how the same change felt from the inside. Berman (1982, p. 159) quotes Baudelaire's primal modern scene: "I was crossing the boulevard, in a great hurry, in the midst of a moving chaos, with death galloping at me from every side." The archetypal modernist seen here is a pedestrian thrown into the maelstrom of modern city traffic, contending alone against the agglomeration of mass and energy that is heavy, fast and lethal. The street and traffic know no spatial or temporal bounds; they spill into every urban place and impose their tempo on everybody's time, transforming the entire environment into a moving chaos. The boulevard becomes a perfect symbol of capitalism's inner contradictions: rationality exists in each individual capitalist unit, leading to anarchic irrationality in the social system that brings all these units together.

Berman argues that the creation of modernist urban space required that collisions and confrontations do not occur. He uses the example of Le Corbusier's discovery of traffic. After fighting his way through the congestion, Le Corbusier makes a sudden daring leap, identifying totally with the forces that have been bearing down on him:

> On that first of October 1924, I was assisting in a titanic rebirth of a new phenomenon: traffic. Cars, cars, fast, fast! One is seized, filled with enthusiasm, with joy . . . the joy of power. The simple and naive pleasure of being in the midst of power, of strength. One participates in it, one takes part in the society that is just dawning. One has confidence in this new society: it will find a magnificent expression of its power. One believes in it. (Quoted in Berman, 1982, p. 166).

At one moment Le Corbusier is the familiar man in the street dodging the snarling traffic; the next moment his viewpoint has radically shifted, so that now he lives and moves from inside the traffic. He has gone from fighting traffic to joining it. This is the perspective of "the new man" in a car — a paradigm for twentieth-century modernist urban planning. It implies the death of the street: the thesis is that streets belong to people; the antithesis is that there are no streets and no people.

In his search for a revitalised modernism, Berman draws a distinction between the work of Robert Moses and Jane Jacobs. The Moses myth was founded on a conflation of progress and people's rights. Moses was able to release millions of federal dollars following the initiation of several important New Deal agencies, in particular the Federal Housing Administration and the Federal Highway Program. Subsequently, he constructed new and imaginative public places, parkways, and bridges within the New York City area. But Berman suggests that just as the construction of Moses' cross-Bronx Expressway was completed, "the real ruin" of the Bronx began; the fundamental results of Moses' intervention were suburbanisation of the metropolitan fringe and abandonment of the inner city. The direct antithesis of Moses was Jane Jacobs, who recognised that everyday street-life nourished modern experiences and values. She brought the opinions and perceptions of women into the discourse of modernist urbanism, recognised that streets are places of twenty-four hour detail, and drew attention to the ecology and phenomenology of the sidewalk. Jacobs argued that for the sake of the modern, we must preserve the old and resist the new, and her writings were instrumental in provoking a wave of community activism to protect neighbourhoods from further destruction by expressways, etc.

The differences between Moses and Jacobs raise the question of a modernist morality. Returning to the Bronx to recover what was good about the old, Berman discovered a contradiction in the moral imperative of the Bronx. One resident claimed that the Bronx imperative was to *get out* of the neighbourhood in order to achieve success. Berman (1982, p. 328) generalises this sentiment, recognising that the American way to overcome contradictions has been simply to drive away from them. The important change that occurred in the 1970s was that economic depression meant that modern societies lost much of their ability to blow away their past; they were forced to remain and confront their modernism by remembering instead of forgetting:

> At a moment when modern society seemed to lose the capacity to create a brave new future, modernism was under intense pressure to discover new sources of life through imaginative encounters with the past. (Berman 1982, p. 332)

Those who are awaiting the end of modernity can be assured of steady work, according to Berman (1982, p. 346), but:

> . . . if modernism ever managed to throw off its scraps and tatters and the uneasy joints that bind it to the past, it would lose all its weight and depth,

and the maelstrom of modern life would carry it helplessly away. It is only by keeping alive the bonds that tie it to the modernities of the past — bonds at once intimate and antagonistic — that it can help the moderns of the present and the future to be free.

But, I would add, this loosening of the fetters feared by Berman has already occurred; modernism has already floated away, loose, weightless and depthless. This is what has happened; this is what postmodernity is.

The meanings of Los Angeles

[T]he essence of Los Angeles was revealed more clearly in its deviations from [rather] than its similarities to the great American metropolis of the late nineteenth and early twentieth centuries. (Fogelson 1967, p. 134)

Reading the city

Most world cities have an instantly identifiable signature: think of the boulevards of Paris; the skyscrapers of New York; or the churches of Rome. But Los Angeles appears to be a city without a common narrative — except perhaps an iconography of the bizarre! Twenty years ago, Rayner Banham (1973) provided an enduring key to the Los Angeles landscape. To this day, it remains powerful, evocative, and instantly recognisable. He identified four basic "ecologies": surfurbia (the beach cities); the foothills (the privileged enclaves of Beverly Hills, Bel Air etc., where the financial and topographical contours correspond almost exactly); the plains of Id (the endless central flatlands); and autopia (the freeways, a "complete way of life" to Banham).

For Douglas Suisman (1989), it is not the freeways but the Los Angeles boulevards that establish the city's overall physical structure. A boulevard is a surface street that:

- makes arterial connections on a metropolitan scale;
- provides a framework for civic and commercial destination; and
- acts as a filter to adjacent residential neighbourhoods.

Suisman (1989, p. 7) argues that the boulevards do more than establish an organisational pattern; they constitute "the irreducible armature of the city's *public space*", and are charged with social and political significance that cannot be ignored. Their development was a result of a laborious stitching together of the original pueblo, the ranches, and common lands — LA's triple Spanish legacy. Sunset, the city's first boulevard, sprang to life not from city planners with a grand vision, but from private landowners looking for high profit at low risk. As we struggle to understand the late-twentieth century metropolis, Suisman reminds us that a glimpse of this new city had already been imagined along the umbilical cord of Sunset Boulevard in 1892. These vertebral connectors today form an integral link among the region's municipalities. As John Gregory Dunne observed in a television travelogue: "Understand Sunset Boulevard and you've come a long way to understanding Los Angeles."

For Ed Soja (1989), Los Angeles is a decentred, decentralised metropolis powered by the insistent fragmentation of post-Fordism — an increasingly flexible, disorganised regime of capitalist accumulation. Accompanying this shift is a postmodern consciousness, a cultural and ideological reconfiguration altering how we experience social being. The centre holds, however, because of its function as the urban panopticon; the strategic surveillance point for the state's exercise of social control. Out from the centre extend a melange of "wedges" and "citadels", interspersed between corridors formed by the boulevards. The consequent urban structure is at once complex and fragmentary, yet bound to an underlying economic rationality:

> With exquisite irony, contemporary Los Angeles has come to resemble more than ever before a gigantic agglomeration of theme parks, a lifespace composed of Disneyworlds. It is a realm divided into showcases of global villages and mimetic American landscapes, all-embracing shopping malls and crafty Main Streets, corporation-sponsored magic kingdoms, high-technology based experimental prototype communities of tomorrow, attractively packaged places for rest and recreation all cleverly hiding the buzzing workstations and labour processes which help keep it together. (Soja 1989, p. 246)

These three cartoons provide differing insights into the LA landscape. Banham looks at the torso, and recognises three components (surfurbia, plains and foothills), as well as the connecting arteries (freeways). Suisman focuses our gaze less on arteries, and more on the veins that organise everyday life (LA's boulevards). Soja considers the body-in-context, articulating the links between a post-Fordist political economy and postmodern culture to account for the fragmentation and differentiation that comprise Los Angeles. Notice that all three writers maintain a studied detachment from the city, as though a voyeuristic, top-down gaze is needed to discover the objective rationality inherent in the landscape. Yet a postmodern sensibility should be willing, even eager, to relinquish the modernism inherent in these detached representations of the LA landscape. By now, it is commonplace that postmodern sensitivities require new ways of seeing. If we assume that "order is not obvious" (as Robert Venturi observed about Las Vegas), what would a postmodernism from below permit?

Los Angeles as text

Postmodernism is about complication. This is reflected in the LA landscape as an intense localisation and fragmentation of social process. LA's microgeography is extremely finely-grained and variegated. In the manner of Michel de Certeau (1984), the key to understanding its social life lies at the street level, where human beings can be observed in their myriad daily practices. The LA metropolis thus becomes an accretion of the local. There is never any single reality to this city although there have been many singular myths in the minds of its observers.

The social heterogeneity and spatial extensiveness of the metropolis encourage intense and effective local autonomies. These appear in all walks of life, including politics, work, family, culture and environment. One important consequence of metropolitan sprawl is the difficulty of formal urban governance. Los Angeles may yet prove to be the harbinger of a new style of decentred politics. The region is split into many separate fiefdoms, whose leaders constantly battle one another. The problems of political representation include ongoing disputes between county and city governments, the resurgence of the slow-growth/no-growth movements, and the difficulties associated with political participation by ethnic and racial minorities. As the region continues to expand geographically, local government is likely to become increasingly remote and less able to respond to grassroots concerns. As a consequence, formal and informal, legal and illegal alliances rise to press their claims, including those of gays, gangs, feminists, racial and ethnic groups. Their micropowers tend to be exercised within the interstices of the formal power structures, which then become increasingly redundant in the everyday lives of alliance members. And localism becomes critically important in the social construction of individual and social identity. Left to their own devices, and encouraged by the rules of electoral politics, elected officials exercise power within their fiefdoms in an increasingly autocratic and often corrupt manner. And so the bifurcation of formal and informal politics is intensified. Far from being subjected to an intense central surveillance (Soja's conceptualisation), LA sometimes seems to operate on the edge of anarchy. It is not for nothing that the LA City Council has been referred to as a "herd of cats".

In an apparent paradox, the rising pre-eminence of the local in the postmodern city has been facilitated by the appearance of a global capitalism. The emergence of post-Fordism has resulted in an accelerated flow of global capital, and an endless search for cheap labour supplies on an international scale. In the USA, the consequences have been a rapid deindustrialisation (especially in the snowbelt), and (re)industrialisation (in the sunbelt). Los Angeles, in perhaps a typically postmodern way, is experiencing both de- and re-industrialisation simultaneously. Within its limits, the region has, for instance, the vestiges of a major automobile manufacturing industry as well as the glittering towers of a (largely defence-related) high-tech industry. It also has a proliferation of minimum-wage, part-time service industries (e.g. fast food outlets). It is an "informational city" which, at the same time, has a massive informal sector (street vendors on freeway off-ramps; can recycling efforts from the backs of trucks; and so on). The globalisation of capitalism has connected the local ever more effectively to the worldwide developments of post-Fordism; hence, what happens in downtown LA tomorrow may result from yesterday's fluctuations in local labour markets in some Asian or Latin American city.

In social terms, Los Angeles can now fairly be characterised as a First World city flourishing atop a Third World city. This latter term refers to that increasing portion of the population either engaged in the "informal" economy or paid poverty-level wages, and only marginally housed by conventional standards. The postmodern metropolis is increasingly polarised along class, income, racial and ethnic lines. The disadvantaged classes are overwhelmingly people of colour. Their family lives are increasingly disrupted by the demands of a flexible, disorganised capital-ism (for example, the pressure on both parents to work, and the need for several families to crowd together to be able to afford housing). These trends have been aggravated by the strong dose of privatism, as well as the practical effects of privatisation that emerged during the Reagan/Bush era and show little sign of abating in the 1990s.

This acute openness to world trends would probably have been cushioned if it were not for the erosion of linkages, both horizontal and (most especially) vertical, between branches of the state apparatus. The nation-state may be declining in significance, after a century of overarching importance. For instance, the nation-states of Europe are being realigned (albeit fractiously) into a single massive confederation; at the same time, existing federations and many nations are being shattered by resurgent nationalisms (as in the former Soviet Union). In the USA, the rhetorics of "less government" and "more private initiative" have effectively reduced government's overall ability and willingness to address social, economic and political problems. So has the rise of fiscal federalism. Issues of social reproduction, community and the public interest consequently take a back seat; governments and populace collude in the decline of the commonwealth.

This is why the postmodern city is increasingly without a credible infrastructure. Crime is rife. The drug culture is recognised as a rational response by gang-members to the absence of mainstream employment. Health care for the poor is non-existent. The public schools are in a shambles. Homelessness is pandemic in the region. And the welfare system is on the verge of collapse.

The apocalyptic images of the movie *Blade Runner* seem anything but fictitious on many days of the year in Los Angeles. Air quality in the city is the worst in the country, despite increasingly draconian regulations. The physical expansion of the urbanised area has generated further acute, human-induced environmental crises, especially those connected with urban services such as water supply, toxic waste disposal, and sewage. These difficulties, together with LA's especially-hazardous natural environment (earthquakes, floods, landslides, fire — see McPhee 1989), are proving increasingly intractable as southern California continues to act as a magnet for development. Although lip service is paid to environmental issues, the survival of nature in all its forms is a low priority.

The intense localisation, plus the absence of a conventional public transportation network, make decentralisation and diversity possible and even necessary to life in the city. Los Angelenos daily re-invent their city. It is not necessary, for instance, to go downtown to enjoy the principal entertainment and cultural events of the postmodern city. There are major theatre districts also in Pasadena, Hollywood, Long Beach, and Orange County. Art flourishes in Santa Monica, West Hollywood, and other places beyond the downtown. Indeed, downtown LA is not *the* downtown for the vast majority of the region's population. Attempts have been intensified during the past twenty years to create a regional hub at the focal intersection of four major freeways. However, a very large part of the present downtown profile of skyscrapers is, as Davis (1990, p. 138) puts it, "a perverse monument to US losses in the global trade war" which permitted a massive inflow of international capital for downtown speculative real estate investment.

In sum, the analogy that I wish to invoke between postmodern thought and postmodern urbanism is this: that the postmodern city is one in which traditional modes of control are evaporating, and no overarching new rationality has yet appeared as a substitute. In the meantime, emergent forms of economic, social and political relationships rush to fill the vacuum. It is the localisation of these effects that is creating the new geographies of postmodern society — a new time–space fabric.

The transition to postmodernity

The roots and precepts of modern urban planning lie deep in the history of modernity, especially the rationalities characteristic of the Enlightenment and the hegemonies of science. It is a simple task to reach into the past for evidence of appeals to unity, control and expert skills in the history of urbanisation. In the *origins* of Los Angeles, for example, an essentially colonial rationality dominated, inspired by the material and religious imperatives of the Spanish conquerors, and bolstered by a thoroughly systematic code of city planning principles (handed down to the Spanish by the arch-rationalists, the conquering Roman Empire; see Crouch et al. 1982). An equally imposing example of early intentionality was the introduction of a market rationality following the US takeover of Alta California in the mid-nineteenth century. The 1846–1853 land surveys by Ord and Hancock created an urban land and property market where there was as yet no city (Fogelson 1967).

The *maturation* of a distinctly modernist urban planning in Los Angeles can be seen in the emergence of the entrepreneurial and the state-centred growth regimes of the turn of the century (Erie 1992). At this time, an aggressive local boosterism promoted massive public infrastructure investment that pushed LA to the forefront of national urban conscious-ness. It was also the time when a fundamental split occurred between the material and the spiritual in modernist thought — when the modernist/modernisation dialectic was sundered and an idealised utopian planning theory was divorced from the processes of capitalist urbanisation. The most consequential practical manifestation of this fracture was the subordination of the land-use planning apparatus to the exigencies of local capital. In the ensuing instrumentality, planning practice created its own totalisation in the form of detailed information-gathering and regulatory mechanisms. Although city and regional planning had been born from progressive ideas (which persisted, albeit as a muffled chorus), most utopian discourse was henceforward drowned in the sheer scale of the development rush in southern California (Davis 1990, Prologue; Greenstein et al. 1992).

The *apex* of twentieth-century modernist urban planning in Los Angeles is perhaps best represented by the freeway-building era. Transit-rationality was replaced by a freeway-rationality as highways provided an un-stoppable impetus to a decentralisation that existing rail lines had prefigured. The freeways ultimately created the signature landscape of modernist Los Angeles — a flat totalisation, uniting a fragmented mosaic of polarised neighbourhoods segregated by race, ethnicity and class (Bottles 1987; Brodsly 1981).

The *transition to postmodernism* begins in the period of high modernism, when social, political and economic structures begin to remake themselves against the backdrop of obsolescent institutional frameworks. The clash is evident in many ways: when the freeway rationality is confounded by Jane Jacobs' shout from the street; or when the Bronx imperative (still present in the escape to edge cities) is challenged by an uprising by those left behind, who are unable or unwilling to uproot themselves to the new frontier. New social contracts are being written in Los Angeles. Though we remain uncertain about what it looks like, the postmodern hyperspace is with us. In *postmodernity*, we seek ways to understand these new spaces — the texts of an untamed, incongruous urbanism. A postmodern way of seeing abandons, finally, the obsolete canons of modernist thought, replacing them with new conditions of knowing, new prescriptions for understanding and (re)creating cities.

So what is Los Angeles, a postmodern archetype, trying to tell us? In social terms, postmodern LA is a city split between extremes of wealth and poverty, in which a glittering First World city sits atop a polyglot Third World substructure (Davis 1990; George 1992; Martinez 1993; Reid 1992). Economically, it is an emergent world city that is undergoing a simultaneous deindustrialisation and reindustrialisation (Scott 1988; Soja 1989). Politically, it is witnessing a fundamental political realignment as old elites are replaced by place-based coalitions forged from the politics of racial, ethnic and gender tribalisms (Davis 1990, chs. 2–3; Geltmaker 1992; Sonenshein 1993). Postmodern LA is the homeless capital of the USA and the scene of this century's worst urban riots (Davis 1992; Institute for Alternative Journalism 1992; Wolch and Dear 1993). The formal welfare state has collapsed, its place taken by a privatised nonprofit- and voluntary sector-based "shadow state" (Wolch 1990). Planning, too, has become privatised, in a reversal of a century-long trend in which the profession has been progressively absorbed within the apparatus of the state (Dear 1989). The residual modernisms of conventional land-use planning are of course still evident in the postmodern built environment; e.g. the master-planned residential townscapes of Orange County, or downtown LA redevelopment schemes. But such schemes are simply mausoleums of the modernist imagination.

There is now, to my mind, a clear non-conformity between Los Angeles' persistently modernist urban planning and the emergent postmodern urbanism of southern California (cf. Dear 1986, 1989, 1991). The late twentieth-century land-use planning apparatus has floated free from the spirit of the postmodern age. Detached, it becomes a relict apparatus with only the most tangential relationship with the emergent postmodern city. In 1961, John E. Roberts, who joined the LA City Planning Department in 1939 and became its director in 1955, issued this appeal:

> It is our objective to plan for the kind of City that the people of Los Angeles must prefer, for it is the people who make the City; it is the people who are the City. With the continued support of all civic-minded citizens, Los Angeles will steadily enhance its position as a truly Great City. (Los Angeles Department of City Planning 1964, p. 65)

The central irony in this appeal to "the people" who make Los Angeles a "truly Great City" is that it is no longer possible to identify *the* people of Los Angeles. This polycentric, polarised, polyglot metropolis long ago tore up its social contract, and is without even a draft of a replacement. There is no longer a civic will nor a collective intentionality behind LA's urbanism; and the obsolete land-use planning machinery is powerless to influence the city's burgeoning social heterodoxy. *This* is the insistent message of postmodern Los Angeles: that all urban place-making bets are off; we are engaged, knowingly or otherwise, in the search for new ways of creating cities.

2

Collective Emotion and Urban Culture

KEVIN ROBINS

We do not know what to think about the city. We are drawn to the image of the city, but it is also the cause of anxiety and resentment. The city is an ambivalent object: an object of desire and of fear. When Cain built a city, it was "the place where he [could] be himself — his homeland, the one settled spot in his wandering". But the city is also Babel, Babylon; it is the "place of confusion", the place of non-communication, and "when men no longer understand themselves, the city which was the seal of their understanding loses all meaning for them" (Ellul 1970, pp. 5, 19). The city is our own and proper place, but it can come to seem an alien and discomforting environment. We may have a sense of what the "good" city would be, the city where we could be "at home" and where we could be ourselves. But, at the same time, we are haunted by the image of the city as a "bad" object, the city that will refuse us comfort or even overwhelm us.

The culture of cities

Since the early 1980s, an abundant literature on urban regeneration has been raising questions about the culture of cities. The contributors to *A Vision of Europe: Architecture and Urbanism for the European City* (Tagliaventi and O'Connor 1992) reflect the conservative side of the debate, with their call 'to verify, to select, to revive the signs of the urban Golden Age in which it would be possible not only to enjoy the present but also to

Managing Cities: The New Urban Context, edited by P. Healey, S. Cameron, S. Davoudi, S. Graham and A. Madani-Pour. © 1995 The Editors and contributors. Published in 1995 by John Wiley & Sons Ltd.

programme the future" (p. 23). What they see around them now is an urban system in crisis, despoiled and deformed. In his introduction to the volume, Prince Charles characterises contemporary cities as "soulless, degraded and inhuman wastelands". Cities are desolated and depraved places that we can no longer enjoy and in which we can no longer feel at home. The question is whether, in the face of this urban depredation, we can now reclaim "the eternal values of western urban civilisation"; whether we can bring about an urban renaissance in which "our European city might rise again, placing itself on a higher plane and still continue to enjoy the same harmonious and organic growth it has had for millennia" (p. 106). The nature of urban design is closely linked to the nature and quality of life that exists in the city. For the Prince of Wales, "the city should be a collective work of art, its plan and morphology clear and digestible . . . . The artistic dimension of city planning, allied to the political structure and values of a people, should reflect the aspects of human existence it holds dearest". Good urban design has, so it is claimed, the "ability to nurture human life and to give dignity, imbuing people with a sense of belonging and a sense of community".

At the same time, there has also been a more politically radical project working for the "renaissance" of urban culture (e.g. Fisher and Owen 1991; Worpole 1992; Bianchini and Parkinson 1993). Here, too, the agenda has been about recovering a lost object; it is a matter of "re-vitalising" or "re-enchanting" an urbanity that has been damaged and estranged from us. In this case, however, the ideal object (the "good" city, "our" city) has a different imaginary location in the past — it will be Baudelaire's Paris or Sitte's Vienna, rather than Wren's London. Again there is the sense that what has been lost is the cohesion and coherence of the city. What is disturbing is the sense of disintegration, whether it be the fragmentation of urban form, or the privatism and individualism that fractures urban public culture. The "bad" city is a city that is not "whole". To make the city "liveable" again, it is necessary to recover a sense of order and meaning in urban form; urban regeneration must involve a more holistic, comprehensive and integrative attitude to the city. City planners must hold a centre from which the body of the city can be restored to "legibility" and "imageability". They must pit intelligibility against unintelligibility. The "good" city is the one we shall know again in its wholeness, the one whose parts are organised into a pattern of unity. This comprehensible city will again make us feel centred and give us a sense of plenitude. This is the basis on which the city must be "re-imagined".

If this radical perspective shares some of the concerns of the conservative and traditionalist urbanists, it also develops a more robust and engaging vision of what urban culture should be about. As well as recognising the need for security and "sense of place", it puts great emphasis on the vitality and flow of city life. It asks us to imagine a city "which is culturally and socially diverse, a meeting place and a working environment for people of all ages, nationalities and classes; a place where there is something for everyone, a centre of intellectual and political debate, trade, culture and political democracy" (Montgomery 1990 p. 18). There is a concern for the revitalisation of urban public life and the public realm. The increasing privatisation of public space is felt to have restricted the possibilities for casual encounters and spontaneous happenings within the city. This calls for a planning strategy that will re-energise the city centre, making it once again "a potential place for commonality, where some form of common identity could be constructed and where different ages, classes, ethnic groups and lifestyles could meet in unplanned, informal ways" (Bianchini and Schwengel 1991, p. 229). It is a more cosmopolitan image of the city, concerned to rethink the contribution of "minority" cultures in shaping the city's public life. Counterbalancing the concern with civic identity and social cohesion, then, there is a positive commitment to a more complex and challenging urban culture and sensibility.

Both these approaches raise important questions about the culture of cities. They take account of the relation between urban form and the sense of community and stability in urban life. And they consider the stimulation and provocation necessary to make the city an exciting and challenging environment. Yet, in the case of both, there is something missing: there is an imaginative deficit in the claimed "re-imagination" of urban culture. In the end, there is a drawing back from the real issues and difficulties of urban change (Robins 1993). In the following, I want to try to push the discussion of urban culture a little further. Particularly, I shall be concerned with those aspects of urban culture that are absent from the urban regeneration agenda, as it has been elaborated over the past decade or so. It is, no doubt, because of what is lacking that the agenda has sustained a certain charm and appeal. But what is lacking, I shall argue, is so significant that it seriously undermines what has been said about the future of urban life and culture.

Let us pursue the argument by way of Lewis Mumford's classic account of the culture of cities. In *The City in History* (1961), Mumford makes some interesting observations on the origins of urban civilisation. In its earliest days, he argues, the city functioned as a defensive and protective settlement, ensuring the safety and security of its inhabitants. Beyond basic survival, the city served as "a storehouse, a conservator and accumulator" (p. 97), guaranteeing the coherence and continuity of urban culture over time. Mumford refers to "the capacity of the city as a container: it not merely held together a larger body of people and institutions than any other kind of community, but it transmitted a larger portion of their lives than human memories could transmit by word of mouth" (p. 98). This it did because "it is in the nature of good containers not to be changed in composition by the reaction that goes on in them".

The city, in this respect, represents "security, receptivity, enclosure, nurture" (p. 12); it is a supporting and facilitating environment.

But there is, and must be, more than this. Mumford warns of the dangers of a "too-stabilised community", arguing that urban experience is also about "mobilisation and mixture", about "encounters" and "challenges" (pp. 95–96). What made the urban experience vital and exciting was the way in which the city "multiplied the opportunities for psychological shock and stimulus" (p. 96). The city was a challenge to "somnolent provincialism". What was also important was the fact that "it gave the challenge of 'outside' experience to those who lived at home . . . probably from the first, [the city] offered an opening to strangers and outsiders" (p. 96). Mumford suggests that it is precisely this "cultural intermixture" that made the city a civilised place in which to live. "For this reason", he argues, "the stranger, the outsider, the traveller, the trader, the refugee, the slave, yes even the invading enemy, have had a special part in urban development at every stage" (p. 96).

So far, then, we have the city as container and the city as locus of encounter and challenge. These are familiar ideas, and correspond pretty much with those articulated in the urban regeneration literature. But there is a further element in Mumford's thinking. In trying to understand the culture of cities, he takes seriously "the realities of human antagonism and enmity", invoking the city dweller's fear of "the Human Enemy, his other self and counterpart, possessed by another god, congregated in another city, capable of attacking him as Ur was attacked, without provocation" (pp. 50–51). Urban culture is associated with the experience of aggression and violent behaviour. Even when aggression is contained, there is still a fear eating at the soul of the city. Mumford refers to the "deepened collective anxieties" (p. 51) that characterise urban culture, and suggests that urban life may promote a "paranoid psychal structure" (p. 39). Anxiety was provoked, not only by the sense of external threat, but also by the "intensified struggle within: a thousand little wars were fought in the market place, in the law courts, in the ball game or the arena" (p. 52). Urban life was about "struggle, aggression, domination, conquest — and servitude" (p. 52). The city "became from the outset the container of disruptive internal forces, directed towards ceaseless destruction and extermination" (p. 53).

This question of fear and aggression is, I think, fundamental to any understanding of urban culture — and Mumford makes it clear that these "primitive" passions still live in our cities. Fear and anxiety is the other side of the stimulation and challenge associated with cosmopolitanism and the encounter of strangers. It is this fear, and the aggression and paranoia it provokes, that urban culture must hold and contain. It is precisely this dimension of urban life and experience that is missing from the agenda, or agendas, that have been developed around urban regeneration and cultural revitalisation. Here, the culture of cities has been seen in highly rationalistic terms. This is not, of course, to denigrate rational behaviour: it is to argue that rationality is not a given, but rather something that has to be struggled for in the face of the more elemental passions that often threaten to overwhelm it. At its best, urban culture involves some kind of accommodation between provocation and stimulation, on the one hand, and security and stability, on the other. For this to be achieved, it is necessary to acknowledge the significance of passions — both creative and destructive — in urban culture, and then to work towards some accommodation between the dictates of reason and the life of the emotions.

Fear without form

Let us consider the nature of fear in the city. What interests me here is the imagery used to describe the anxieties that are aroused in the urban environment. Donatella Mazzoleni suggests a narrative of dissolution. Once the city was a coherent entity:

> We speak of a city as long as the totality of those who produce and live a collective construction constitute a collective anthropoid body, which maintains in some way an identity as a "subject". The city is therefore a site of an *identification*. The image of the city can be grasped in its totality as a "figure" in a differential relationship with a surrounding . . . . Thus the city has a somatic individuality and a membrane, which may be palpable (in the case, for example, of city walls), or impalpable, and which both surrounds and *limits* its somatic individuality. It guarantees, therefore, the city's concentration of energy, its topological separateness, and, at the same time, the osmotic exchange between internal and external. (Mazzoleni 1993, p. 293)

In this image, the city is the source of our identity: it is where our "we" takes shape; where "we" know our individuality in its difference from what is "out there" and "beyond". When we are centred in this way, we can draw on the city's "concentration of energy" to animate our own happiness and enjoyment. This coherence of the (good) city, Mazzoleni suggests, has now given way to the incoherence of the (bad) metropolis. The metropolis is inhospitable to our needs:

> Metropolises are no longer "places", because their dimensions exceed by far the dimensions of the perceptive apparatus of their inhabitants. The widest sensory aperture, that of sight, is shattered. It was the visual field, in some respect, which defined the city dimensionally: in the metropolis there is no longer pan-orama (the vision of all), because its body overflows beyond the horizon . . . . The mutation does not only concern perceptive behaviour, but also deeply involves the modalities of appropriation and symbolisation of space — since it reaches the horizon, the metropolis is a habitat without a "somewhere else". (pp. 297–298)

This non-place has no centre from which we can impose order and meaning. There is no sense of its totality and its boundedness (its membrane). And there is no outside, no beyond, against which we can experience our separateness and difference. For Mazzoleni, the metropolis can no longer be the site of an identification; in it we cannot hold on to our identity. The city has become "alien", a "beast":

> The metropolitan habitat is now experienced as something which is not only *outside* our body, but also beyond the body, and therefore *other* than the body: it seems to have assumed an alien subjectivity, to have become something with which one has a dialogue, as one would with a stranger. (p. 297)

As one would with a stranger . . . . What a peculiar idea. What does she mean? What happens when the city comes to seem like a stranger? Mazzoleni's gloss seems oblique, elliptical. In the metropolis, she says, "the space around us becomes gigantic, the body shrinks"; we then experience "a return to an 'ancient' state of pre-separation . . . of the loss of the I's borders in a vital mass without surroundings" (p. 298). In this "city as stranger", we no longer know who *we* are. What are undermined are the conditions of order and coherence

The history of the modern city might be seen in terms of the struggle to impose order and coherence in the face of impending disorder and chaos. Totality, integrity, coherence: so much has been invested in them, so much has seemed to depend on them. The desire for order cannot be driven by rational motives. In his chapter, Michael Dear refers to the key role of Le Corbusier in articulating the project of the rationalist metropolis. In *The City of Tomorrow*, Le Corbusier argued that the house, the street, the town,

> . . . should be ordered, otherwise they counteract the fundamental principles round which we revolve; if they are not ordered, they oppose themselves to us, they thwart us, as the nature all around us thwarts us, though we have striven with it, and with it begin each day a new struggle. (Le Corbusier 1947, p. 33)

"Man by reason of his very nature", he says, "practises order . . . . Order is indispensable to him, otherwise his actions would be without coherence and could lead nowhere" (pp. 35, 40). Nature, by contrast, is a "surrounding chaos" and, if we are not vigilant, it threatens to overpower and swamp us. Without the clarity of order — "a geometrical thing" — this chaos will engulf the modern city, Le Corbusier fears. "In the last hundred years", he observes,

> . . . a sudden, chaotic and sweeping invasion, unforeseen and overwhelming, has descended upon the great city . . . . The resultant chaos has brought it about that the Great City, which should be a phenomenon of power and

energy, is today a menacing disaster, since it is no longer governed by the principles of geometry. (p. 43)

"Confusion", Le Corbusier asserts, "is woven into the very texture of our modern cities" (p. 107). For him, Paris has become "a dangerous magma of human beings gathered from every quarter by conquest, growth and immigration; she is the eternal gipsy encampment from all the world's great roads" (p. 43). Le Corbusier is oppressed by feelings of "submersion, cataclysm, invasion" and wants to "bring order once more to a situation which is rapidly getting out of hand" (p. 100). He wants to build a "citadel" against the mob, the rush, the torrent, the chaos of the Great City.

Le Corbusier's defensiveness is manic. The fears that haunt his "plans" are extreme, but their extremity is eloquent and takes us to the heart of what has been defined as the "problem" of the city. Le Corbusier evokes his ideal city in terms of a grid of geometrical cells: "Little by little, and basing each point on cause and effect, I built up an ordered system of the grouping of such cells as would replace with advantage the present chaos to which we are subject" (p. 224). The cell insulates and seals against the menacing flow of the city. The cell is the ultimate boundary for protecting the human against the chaos of the natural order. What is being secured is the clarity and stability of "civilised" identity against the dark and formless flows — the magma, the miasma — that threaten its dissolution. Le Corbusier gives it different names: "savage", "gypsy", "chaos". It is what confounds the ordering process.

Why is Le Corbusier significant? What is our interest in him now? We might answer that it is because he was so exceptional: so extreme in the way he pursued the dream of order; so excessive and manic in his struggle against chaos. There must be some truth in this. But perhaps there is another and better reason why he is still relevant. Perhaps the thing that is significant about Le Corbusier is that he was so *unexceptional*. "Existence is modern", Zygmunt Bauman (1990, p. 165) writes, "inasmuch as it is effected and sustained by social engineering" which has claimed " the right to define order and, by implication set aside chaos, as the leftover that escapes definition". Is it not the case that Le Corbusier's authoritarian rationalism was, and still is, implicit within the principles of modern urbanism generally? Can we not see his heroic utopianism as continuous with more banal planning theory and practice? As Elizabeth Wilson (1991, p. 20) argues, "there is a sense in which all town planning contains both a utopian and a heroic, yet authoritarian, element . . . . The plan is always intended to fix the usage of space; the aim, the state regulation of urban populations." In all planning the management of urban space and culture has been governed by this "colonial imperative". Cities are said to be planned insofar as they are ordered and orderly. In the end, says Richard Sennett (1990, p. 95), "the crowd is a force to be weakened by design". The imperative is to "calm" the flux of urban life and to manage its contingencies and uncertainties. Cities are planned when they are coherent, when they are "legible" and "imageable". Against the threat of disorder and fragmentation, planning has stood for order and wholeness.

But, of course, it is an impossible aspiration. Order is always inconclusive; disorder always threatens to reassert itself. It is not possible to escape the "mingle-mangle" of the city or to tame what Henry Mayhew once called its "wandering tribes" (Stallybrass and White 1986, p. 128). It is the image of the formless crowd that haunts those who want to give form to the urban order. The crowd provokes fears of depersonalisation, fragmentation, loss of identity:

> The crowd is compared to a drunk, delirious, dangerous woman, to an orgy ending in human sacrifices; the crowd, a man-eater or quicksand, swallows up those imprudent enough to fall into her midst; the crowd exerts the attraction and arouses the fear of vertigo; it is a gaping void that fascinates and captures by the thousand those who hurl themselves into it. (Anzieu 1984, p. 140)

The nature of this anxiety and emotional instability "explains the well-known solution to the dangers of a spontaneous crowd: surround it, infiltrate it, organise and discipline it, in other words, establish the supremacy of the paternal over the maternal imego" (p. 140).

Feminist writers on the city have taken up and developed further this question of the gendered nature of anxiety. In *Male Fantasies*, Barbara Ehrenreich (1987, p. xiii) writes, "there is a dread, ultimately, of dissolution — of being swallowed, engulfed, annihilated. Women's bodies are the holes, swamps, pits of muck that can engulf." The male ego is "formed by, and bounded by, hideous dread":

> For that which they loved first — woman and mother — is that which they must learn to despise in others and suppress within themselves. Under these conditions, which are all we know, so far, as the human condition, men will continue to see the world divided into "them" and "us", male and female, hard and soft, solid and liquid — and they will, in every way possible, fight and flee the threat of submersion. They will build dykes against the "streaming" of their own desire. They will level the forests and pave the earth. (p. xvi)

Men's order must suppress women's "nature". Elizabeth Wilson argues that this drama has been at the heart of urban culture. Women's very presence in the city has been a problem. Women are "an irruption in the city, a symptom of disorder, and a problem" (Wilson 1991, p. 9). At the heart of the urban labyrinth, Wilson argues, is the female Sphinx, the "strangling one", the one "who was so called because she strangled all those who could not answer her riddle: female sexuality, womanhood out of control, lost nature, loss of identity" (p. 7). The crowd in the city was feminised; seen and feared "as hysterical, or, in images of feminine instability and sexuality, as a flood or swamp" (p. 7). And "masculine" order and rigidity have always seemed under threat from "feminine" disorder, indeterminacy and fluidity. Women without men in the city "symbolise the menace of disorder in all spheres once rigid patriarchal control is weakened" (p. 157).

What is made clear in recent feminist writings is that urban culture is not created by disembodied, rational beings. Cities contain bodies in motion, and city life is about the experiences of, and shocks to, those bodies. Urban culture is passionate and erotic, but it is also subject to anxieties and tensions. The fundamental issue is then about how we cope with these emotional dimensions to our existence. One way of doing this, as I have been arguing, is by imposing "order" and "form" on what is perceived as threatening. This is the strategy of building dykes. Increasingly, however, such an aspiration must seem an impossible ideal (recall Donatella Mazzoleni's observation that, in the metropolis, "there is no longer pan-orama"). The dream of "wholeness" and "coherence" is an illusion; there is no longer any total vantage point from which the city can be overseen, and "fragmentation" should be considered, not as a pathology, but as part of our condition (Deutsche 1990).

It is a difficult condition. As Elizabeth Wilson (1992 pp. 107–108) argues, "The fragmentary and incomplete nature of urban experience generates its melancholy – we experience a sense of nostalgia, of loss for lives we have never known, of experiences we can only guess at." (One thinks of the "Golden Age" evoked by Prince Charles and his acolytes, and of the idea of public space in the urban regeneration literature.) But what is also made possible, at the same time, is a new basis for experience: one that is based, not on mastery and the imposition of will, but on encounter and engagement with complexity. "The heroism — for both sexes — is in surviving the disorientating space, both labyrinthine and agoraphobic, of the metropolis," Elizabeth Wilson suggests; "It lies in the ability to discern among the massed ranks of anonymity the outline of forms of beauty and individuality appropriate to urban life" (p. 110).

Strange angels

We have considered one set of images around which emotional and unconscious feelings about the city are gathered. I want to turn now to a second familiar image: that of the stranger or foreigner in the city. Cities are made for people from elsewhere. I have already referred to Lewis Mumford's argument that strangers and outsiders, of all kinds, have been fundamental to the life and vitality of cities. The stranger is a resource for urban culture. The existence of strangers makes cities places of encounter, of confrontation and struggle, of tension and conflict. Cities become civilised when they can both contain and harness these energies:

> Only where differences are valued and opposition tolerated can struggle be transmuted into dialectic: so in its internal economy the city is a place — to twist Blake's dictum — that depresses corporeal and promotes mental war . . . . So long as the city performs its essential functions, it keeps struggle and tension within bounds, and heightens their significance. (Mumford 1961, pp. 117, 115)

For Mumford, the stranger adds to the city, which is no city without him and her.

But there are those who have a very powerful sense that strangers take away from the city. As Zygmunt Bauman (1990, p. 150) observes, "strangers bring the outside in, and in so doing they seem to disturb the resonance between physical and psychical distance . . . the fought after coordination between moral and topological closeness, the staying together of friends and the remoteness of enemies". They appear to come as a threat to the known order in which "we" could always orientate ourselves and in which we could feel "at home" with ourselves. Strangers are anomalous, "blurring a boundary line vital to the construction of a particular social order or a particular life-world":

> There is hardly an anomaly more anomalous than the stranger. He stands between friend and enemy, order and chaos, the inside and the outside. He stands for the treacherousness of friends, for the cunning of enemies, for fallibility of order, penetrability of the inside. (pp. 150–151)

The stranger threatens to bring chaos into the social order: "'The other' of order is the miasma of the indeterminate and unpredictable: uncertainty, the source and archetype of all fear" (pp. 164–165). The individual stranger is a discomforting presence. In their numbers, strangers may be feared as an invading mass. Racist and xenophobic panics are driven by "the terror that, without the known boundaries, everything will collapse into undifferentiated, miasmic chaos; that identity will disintegrate; that 'I' will be suffocated or swamped" (Donald 1993, p. 192). Strangers as immigrants and invaders can appear as a "flood", a "tide", as "waves" that will "engulf" us. They can provoke primitive fears of annihilation and dissolution.

The stranger stands for ambivalence, and it is difficult to live with ambivalence. In the face of ambivalence the logic of order and identity is reasserted: "us" against "them". "We" must secure our centrality, and "they" must be pushed out from the centre. "Difference" must become an attribute of "them"; "otherness" must stick to "them". "They" are different, other, alien because they are not "us", because they are not like "us". As William Connolly (1991, pp. 64–66) has argued, "identity converts difference into otherness in order to secure its own self-certainty . . . in order to secure itself as intrinsically good, coherent, complete or rational". But the fear cannot be expunged. "This constellation of constructed others", says Connolly, "now becomes both essential to the truth of the powerful identity and a threat to it. The threat is posed not merely by *actions* the other might take to defeat the true identity but by the very visibility of its mode of *being* as other". Identity is suffused with feelings of anxiety, and these anxieties are projected onto the figure of the threatening stranger. Identity is built around the structure of paranoia, and is defended with paranoid vigilance. It is because the stranger always threatens to expose the imaginary (and manic) nature of the social order, that the social order works so hard to exclude his or her presence from it.

But the stranger cannot be kept out, however much these mechanisms of defence are mobilised. The ambivalence of the stranger makes him or her the focus of conflicting emotions. "Ambivalence expresses fear and desire fused into one" (Wilson 1991, p. 157). If women in the city are feared, they are also desired and needed. And if immigrant strangers provoke feelings of anxiety and resentment, it is also the case that they are envied for their freedom and mobility. Through recognition of this ambivalence, there is the possibility, at least, of coping with the primitive and paranoid mechanisms associated with the xenophobic and racist reactions. There is the potential for working through and modifying anxieties, and even of using the presence of strangers as a resource for enlarging the experience of urban living. It is to the realisation of this potential that Lewis Mumford is appealing when he writes of the transmutation of struggle into dialectic.

There is a creative and uplifting tradition of sociological writing on the city that has been concerned precisely with this question of the civilising potential of "the stranger". Writing at the beginning of the century, Georg Simmel (1971) argued that the stranger brings new and revitalising qualities into urban culture. "Because he is not bound by roots to the particular constituents and partisan dispositions of the group", says Simmel, "he confronts all of these with a distinctly 'objective' attitude, an attitude that does not signify mere detachment and non-participation, but is a distinct structure composed of remoteness and nearness, indifference and involvement" (p. 145). The stranger "contains many dangerous possibilities" because "he examines conditions with less prejudice; he assesses them against standards that are more general and more objective; and his actions are not confined by custom, piety, or precedent" (p. 146). Alfred Schutz (1944, p. 507) refers to the same critical presence of the stranger within the community of the city: "the stranger does not accept the total of its cultural pattern as the natural and appropriate way of life and as the best of all possible solutions of any problem". The stranger possesses "a grievous clear-sightedness" that always challenges the customary and habitual way of life of the community.

Within this sociological tradition, there is the sense that the stranger makes possible "the extension of social relationships" (Wood 1934). Robert Redfield and Milton Singer (1954, p. 69) argued for the necessity for "an enlarged cultural consciousness" in modern cities:

> We refer to the consciousness of cultural differences and the feeling that certain forms of inter-cultural association are of great enough benefit to override the repugnance of dealing with "foreigners". We may call this an enlargement of cultural horizons sufficient to become aware of other cultures and of the possibility that one's own society may in some ways require their presence.

Again noting the freedom of the stranger, Robert Park (1969, p. 137) argues that it is the fact that "he is not bound as others are by the local proprieties and conventions", that makes him more "enlightened" and "cosmo-politan". "As a result of contact and collision with a new invading culture", he suggests, there is a sense of emancipation as "energies that were formally controlled by custom and tradition are released" (p. 136). It has always been the movement and migration of peoples that "has loosened local bonds . . . and substituted for the local loyalties the freedom of the cities" (p. 139). It is this that has constituted the civilised aspect of urban culture.

In the 1990s, in the context of the dramatic transformations affecting European cities, this theme of "the stranger" has been further developed. More psychoanalytically oriented discussions have recognised how much the mechanism of projection conceals conflicts within the self that are mobilised against the stranger. What has been recognised is that the stranger is within; it is the otherness that we cannot surrender to in ourselves. "On a human scale", writes Elie Wiesel (1991), "we are all foreigners: there is a part of us that does not belong to us, something indecipherable and impenetrable. So if foreigners frighten me, it's because they resemble me in some way. They frighten me because, ultimately, I am afraid of myself." I am a person who can arouse fear in the people I meet, and I am frightened by this "strange" part of me. And what of the desire that strangers arouse in me (*despite* my resistance to the loss of control it brings with it)? Does this not actually tell me something about the way I resemble them? I, too, am a person who can be desired by others. And if I desire the other because of his or her "strangeness", then it must be the "strangeness" in me that arouses their desire.

It is a theme that has been most fully developed by Julia Kristeva (1991, 1992). For Kristeva (1991, p. 1), "the foreigner lives within us: he is the hidden face of our identity, the space that wrecks our abode, the time in which understanding and affinity founder". But it is "by recognising him within ourselves, [that] we are spared detesting him in himself". Kristeva poses the choice we have before us: "shall we be, intimately and subjectively, able to live with the others, to live *as others*, without ostracism but also without leveling?" (p. 2). Shall we be able to, both because we have to, and also because estrangement and self-estrangement open up possibilities? "Living with the other, with the foreigner", says Kristeva, "confronts us with the possibility or not of *being an other*. It is not simply — humanistically — a matter of our being able to accept the other, but of *being in his place*, and this means to imagine and make oneself other for oneself" (p. 13). The idea of "a foreigner in his own place" then assumes a wholly different resonance.

This theme of the stranger has remarkable similarities to Richard Sennett's arguments about the value of encounter in urban culture. A man or a woman, says Sennett (1990, p. 148), can become "like a foreigner to him or herself, by doing things or entering into feelings that do not fit the familiar framework of identity, the seemingly social fixities of race, class, age, gender or ethnicity". In order to expose oneself thus, however, "one must do the work of accepting oneself as incomplete", and it is in the city, the metropolis, "in the presence of difference", that people have the greatest possibility to "step outside themselves" (pp. 148, 123). This represents a restatement of what Sennett celebrated, some twenty years ago, as the "uses of disorder" in the city. Here he posed the fundamental question: "why are disorderly, painful events worth encountering?" (Sennett, 1973, p. 109). His answer is that disorder and painful dislocation are central to any civilised, and civilising, social life. There is a regressive tendency in our culture, he argues, to avoid situations of confrontation and exploration; a tendency to build an image or identity that coheres, is unified, and filters out threats in social experience. Against this ordered identity, Sennett argues that "the attempt to deal with 'otherness', to become engaged beyond one's own defined boundaries", is the essence of mature identity and a mature culture (pp. 19, 109). What this calls for is an openness to other cultures, beliefs and ways of life in the city. What it aspires to is an urban culture in which boundaries — territorial, social and psychic — are rendered more permeable, so that individuals and groups can penetrate each other's spaces. Disorder, ultimately, is about a readiness to be out of control, combined with a maturity to handle the consequences.

The very difficult challenge is to make this sensibility the basis of a public and political culture in our cities. Urban politics, as Iris Marion Young (1990b, p. 234) argues, must be conceived "as a relationship of strangers who do not understand one another in a subjective and immediate sense, relating across time and distance". Young points to the danger of communitarianism, where "commitment to an ideal of community tends to value and enforce homogeneity", and emphasises that urban political life must involve "city persons and groups interact[ing] within spaces and institutions they all experience themselves as belonging to, but without those interactions dissolving into unity or commonness" (pp. 234, 237). The opposite danger is to overemphasise difference, failing to recognise the importance of commonality. To simply acknowledge the fact of difference, and to try to live alongside (that is, parallel to) strangers, is not enough. The challenge is to establish a culture that will provide a common ground for negotiating shared concerns at the same time as respecting the value of difference. For Mumford (1961, pp. 116–117), the city is "a place designed to offer the widest facilities for significant conversation". "And if", he argues, "provision for dialogue and drama, in all their ramifications, is one of the essential offices of the city, then one key to urban development should be plain — it lies in the widening of the circle of those capable of participating in it".

Collective emotion and urban culture

"The city manifests humanity's greatest aspiration toward perfect order and harmony", Yi-fu Tuan (1979, p. 145) observes. "An early and essential function of the city was to be a vivid symbol of cosmic order . . . . Corresponding to this desire for physical perfection was the longing for a stable and harmonious society." The modern city may be seen as the most developed expression of this project for order and harmony. The modern city represents the most scientific endeavour to mobilise "the sure paths of reason" (Le Corbusier 1947) to contain the maelstrom and disorder of metropolitan mix. Increasingly, there is a recognition of the limits to such rationalism — this, as Michael Dear argues in this volume, is one of the fundamental issues in the current debate about the postmodern city.

The urban regeneration agendas of the 1980s, which I discussed at the outset of this chapter, were developed in response to this crisis of high-modern urban planning. However, whilst there are important elements in their critique, they make only a partial contribution to understanding the problems of urban culture in the late twentieth century. Their concern has been with the "recovery" of more balanced principles of order and harmony, associated with more humane and civilised expressions of modern urban culture (imagined to have existed at different times in the past). What are left out of account are the forces against which order is asserted. Urban regeneration reflects a more acceptable face of rationalism, and fails to come to terms with the emotional dimensions of urban culture. An idealised, and often utopian, vision of the "good" city is made possible through the disavowal or repression of more threatening and challenging dimensions of contemporary urban life.

Like Michael Dear, I am concerned with the limits to, and failure of, rationalism, though the nature of my concern is somewhat different. Throughout my discussion, I have emphasised the physical, emotional and unconscious aspects of our existence in urban environments. I have sought to explore some of the common themes and images of the urban *imaginaire* — the crowd, the woman, the stranger — because it has been around these that emotional associations and dynamics have collected. Most fundamental is the fear that stalks urban experience, always threatening to overwhelm civility and civilisation. The sense of fear may arouse the need for security and the containment of emotional life. But fear can also be transmuted into the stimulation and provocation of encounter. Most forms of urban discourse that are available to us have been shaped by the rationalist tradition. In consequence, our ability to deal with the collective emotional life of cities is rather limited. Lewis Mumford (1961, p. 46) referred to the "collective personality structure" of cities. I am arguing that this is something that must be taken much more seriously in discussions of the culture of cities; I think we need to extend our understanding of such phenomena if we are to deal with the breakdown of urban culture.

Recent developments in Britain show how urgent this need is, and help to give a particular focus to the broader issue that concerns us. A certain optimism about the possibilities of urban "renaissance" has, in the 1990s, been eclipsed by a mood of depression about our cities. The tragic murder of two-year-old James Bulger, in February 1993, precipitated this mood. Melanie Philips and Martin Kettle (1993) describe the event in terms of "the lost child who wanders off only to be 'rescued' by evil forces". His encounter with these "evil forces" was in a shopping mall, "the place . . . where we are most likely to meet strangers". "James Bulger's death", they suggest, "appals not least because it exposes once again our society's growing indifference and our own increasing isolation. He trusted a stranger and now he is dead." What is evoked is an urban world of random and meaningless violence and violation. "And, of course, the fact that it was all recorded on a security camera makes it even worse . . . . We are therefore doubly affronted, both by being made complicit in this terrible tragedy and by the demonstrable fact that such 'security' devices are clearly anything but."

In his recent book, *The Spirit of the Age* (1993), David Selbourne reflects this same mood of despondency and despair. In his view, our cities are characterised now by "civic dissolution" and "citizen estrangement", and amount to little more than mere conglomerations of people. "Today", he writes, "the metropolis contains millions of citizens who know nothing of its history and traditions . . . . In once-communities, the next man has become a stranger" (p. 317). "When the normal citizen, or ostensible belonger, himself lacks such knowledge", Selbourne observes, "he becomes as strange as a true stranger; at worst, more alien in his own society than the knowledgeable outsider" (p. 326). In this condition of civic disarray, urban society is characterised by increasing and futile acts of violence and aggression. Selbourne provides us with an overwhelming catalogue of murders and mutilations in British cities. With a certain nostalgia for a more coherent sense of community, he concludes that "the giant metropolis, in which violent impulses come increasingly to dictate the responses of half educated strangers towards each other, cannot be the model of civic society" (p. 345). The metropolis is an alien and alienating environment that has dissolved civic bonds and destroyed the sense of obligation and responsibility in urban culture.

The sense of containment is suddenly destroyed, and overwhelmed by a catastrophic sense of fear. In the life of the emotions, it seems, there are no half measures; feelings oscillate between "good" and "bad", with no neutral space. In an urban context, where the shock of encounter and exposure is actually inescapable, exposure to fear is often desired. The point is that, in itself, fear is not necessarily a bad experience, nor is it one that we would always want to refuse. Fear may, in fact, be associated with the emotional stimulus and provocation necessary for us if we are to avoid, both individually and socially, stagnation and stasis. In this sense, ordinary fear may be seen as a functional, and even a creative, element of urban culture. Where it becomes dysfunctional and damaging is when it is implicated in paranoid mechanisms of projection and defence. Paul Hoggett (1992a, p. 346) describes a psychical process through which "a fear which cannot be contained is visited upon the external world where it fuses and blends with the real violence and poison of our social environment". When it does not lead to violence and aggression against the feared other, such a fear may provoke defensive and evasive retreat from the world. If it is engaged with the difficult realities of urban culture, fear may be an essential element of change and development. It is when fear overwhelms the sense of reality that it becomes pathological or defeating.

This matter of collective emotional structures must be a central issue of concern in considering the culture of cities. What is the relation between fear and stimulation? How can fears be creatively contained? How does fear come to destroy the social order? What is needed is a more grounded understanding of both the psychic and the social structures of the emotions. Let me give two examples that seem to me to offer insights into the relation between psychic and social realities. Paul Hoggett (1992b, pp. 23–24) notes the closeness of envy and desire: "Envy occurs when the things you most desire for yourself are the things you most relentlessly attack. They are attacked precisely because they are needed . . . . Envy is both a desperate attempt to deny this sense of lack and an attack upon the thing which prompts it . . . . It is a refusal to recognise that there is a source of anything good beyond one's own (individual or group) subjectivity." Hoggett argues that this complex motion dynamic is central to any understanding of racist and xenophobic behaviour.

In her book, *Goliath* (1993), Beatrix Campbell explores the violence and aggression of the 1991 riots in terms of the psychic and social condition of masculinity. "Men do something dangerous with their *pain* and their *power*", she observes, suggesting that "the crisis of crime [is] a crisis of masculinity" (p. 204). Young men are driven by paranoid and narcissistic forms of behaviour which become a threat even to their own communities. It is the women of the community who seek to manage and contain the violent "masculine tyrannies" (and when they fail, it is these women who are blamed for what the men have done). Campbell's analysis is severe: "Crime and coercion are sustained by men. Solidarity and self-help by women. It is as stark as that" (p. 319). What is of concern, here again, is how the social conditions of urban Britain in the 1990s interact with the emotional condition — the power and the pain — of young men.

In the playing out of these psychic and social dramas, the nature of the urban structure and system is clearly significant, though our understanding of this remains poor. Richard Sennett (1992, p. 3) has described the past fifty years as a "disastrous era" in which cities have become fragmented, "and each fragment is like a homogeneous ghetto — the mall, the housing estate, the industrial park are isolated, self-contained spaces". The consequence of this is that:

> ... class and racial differences, economy and governance are social facts which we experience passively, as spectators of the mass media: we do not live the complexities of society directly and physically, in where we walk, whom we see, or what we touch.

We must consider the implications of these developments — the scale of the metropolis, its fragmentation, the fortification of space, the surveillance cameras, and so on — for the collective emotional life of the city. What happens to its citizens as psychical and physical entities? When we no longer live the complexities of the city directly and physically, how much more difficult does it become to cope with the *reality* of those complexities? To what extent does such insulation and spectatorship encourage paranoid and defensive mechanisms? If we are to make our cities civilised places in which to live, we must come to terms with the "alien subjectivity" that they have assumed.

3

A Civilised Retreat?
Anti-Urbanism, Rurality
and the Making of an
Anglo-Centric Culture

PHILIP LOWE, JONATHAN MURDOCH
and GRAHAM COX

The city is a setting for many forms of life and each may provide the rudiments of a new urban vision. Yet a predominant perception in contemporary society is that civilised living exists beyond the city's boundaries, in the countryside, which is deemed to embody security, neighbourliness, authenticity and the "timeless" values of community life. There is a particular irony in this, for historically cities have usually been portrayed as beacons of civilisation in the wilderness. It was within the city walls, safe from a "savage nature", that humanity could be tamed and society collectively forged. However, with the onset of capitalist development, and the concomitant growth of cities, classes have become separated, both socially and spatially, and from within segregated neighbourhoods each class has built up its own mythologies about the others, fuelling ambivalence to urban life.

For the "pro-urbanists", often political radicals, the city came to stand as a metaphor for social change. Via collective endeavour it presented possibilities for emancipation and from this perspective the radical notion of nationhood, based upon citizenship, emerged. On the other hand, for

Managing Cities: The New Urban Context, edited by P. Healey, S. Cameron, S. Davoudi, S. Graham and A. Madani-Pour. © 1995 The Editors and contributors. Published in 1995 by John Wiley & Sons Ltd.

conservatives and traditionalists the city came to represent a threat to the social and moral order: it promoted a feckless and rootless existence, and gave rise to disease, crime and the worst excesses of the "mob". The true spirit of the nation resided elsewhere and was equated with the country. The growing currency of this latter view has led to an inversion of the Enlightenment vision of urban life. As John Rennie Short (1991) comments, by the late twentieth century, "the city fulfils the same role as the howling wilderness of the sixteenth and seventeenth centuries; a place of base instincts, ugly motives, subterranean fears and unspoken desires, a place which reveals the savage basis of the human condition and frailty of civilised society" (pp. 47–48).

Such an outlook receives singular expression in British society where it is rooted in a specific historical experience. Britain was the first country to experience industrialisation. What by all accounts were the unique horrors and dislocations of that transformation were the more threatening for being encountered for the first time. The result was a striking cultural reaction towards urbanisation, informed by Darwinistic pessimism concerning the prospects for the human condition. Indeed many commentators have argued that, as a nation, Britain has never culturally adapted to urban living. Instead, an alternative vision of an Arcadian Britain has continued to exert a powerful hold. However anachronistic or nostalgic various forms of this vision may have been, it has strongly shaped cultural tastes and opinions as well as the private choices and public decisions of influential and affluent sections of British society, who prefer to see Britain's legacy to modern life as the countryside and its civilised enjoyment, rather than the industrial city and all its works. As the English planner Thomas Sharp put it in 1944: "the English countryside may be claimed to be one of the supreme achievements of civilisation". These ideas have strong resonance. The editor of *Country Life*, a magazine devoted to the maintenance of all that is regarded as valuable in the British countryside, said recently: "From the beginning, *Country Life* has embodied a way of life that many people believe to be the most civilised in the world." That this way of life is rural, not urban, is symptomatic of a profound bias in dominant versions of the national culture, one which has shaped the development of the city and the countryside alike.

Such dominant cultural attitudes in a country which is highly urbanised do not, however, go unchallenged. Hence, Britain's ambivalence to the city is reflected in some of its recent contributions to global culture, most notably the stereotypic styles of punk/alienated urban youth and the "countryman". Although antithetical, both are extensively celebrated in Britain's cultural exports (e.g. films such as *Howards End* and *Brideshead Revisited*; or *Jubilee* and *My Beautiful Launderette*) and are mimicked across the world. In most major western cities one can find examples of both: from the huddle of punks on street corners in downtown areas to the chic little shops selling the "style anglais" in the fashionable shopping districts. As a fashion critic covering the spring shows in Milan recently noted: "Milan is supposed to be the design capital of the world, but the Milanese you see on the street wouldn't be seen dead in Dolce and Gabbana. They spend their money on Barbour, Burberry and Mulberry. Out on the evening passeggio, you could easily kid yourself you were Saturday morning shopping in Cheltenham or Harrogate" (Stafford 1994). These clothes are the sturdy, functional garb of the English country gentleman and emanate from the "civilised enjoyment of the countryside".

In this chapter we wish to examine how the British countryside has come to be accorded such cultural status and how it comes to be so readily embraced by those seeking sanctuary from the city. This, in turn, entails some consideration of how rurality and rural culture have been reconstituted in forms which allow rural areas to be represented as the provenance of dominant social groups and as suitable environments for these groups to retain "traditional" forms of life. In the process of this reconstitution the urban and the rural become differentiated; each "stands for" various forms of life which then become wrapped up in, or excluded from, conceptions of national identity. It is our contention that the countryside lies at the heart of dominant conceptions of British "national" identity, whereas the "urban" sits quite uneasily with such notions of Britishness. The British, or, more specifically, the *English*, countryside has come to be seen as somehow representing all that is "noble" and "timeless" in the nation (Wales and Scotland also have national conceptions of the rural and these differ markedly from those in England, although they are often lost in English definitions of Britain).

To gain an understanding of why the rural presented such an attractive domain to those disenchanted with the city, we must trace certain continuities in the national culture, namely, its anti-urbanism and con-comitant rural bias. As we shall see, the significance of the rural as a cultural "reservoir" is usually in complete contrast to its importance as an economic space (Williams 1975). The economic and cultural functions of the countryside have, in the main, derived from Britain's distinctive global economic position and class structure. The most notable of these, in the age of Empire, was as the "home land" of those members of the upper and middle classes who ventured abroad to administer the colonies. We believe the extension of British rule to all corners of the globe entailed a reconsideration of the "home land". As British dominion began to recede, the rural became more closely associated with "home". This domestic vision has been recast in recent times as the middle class has come to look beyond the city for those values traditionally associated with home ownership, and family-centredness. We argue that one of the consequences of such anti-urban sentiments has been a very British version of "white flight", or, perhaps more accurately, "retreat", from the city.

In order for rural areas to play these roles they must be kept free of other groups and lifestyles; i.e. those that do not "fit" in this mythic national space. In the course of showing how rural areas have been socially made and unmade we shall indicate who has been excluded and why. We will show that in recent times, as the countryside has become of increasing value as a "positional good", tied to the cultural construction of "Anglo-centricity", the need to exclude undesirable, multi-ethnic "others" has become of increasing concern to both rural residents and the central state. The countryside is seen as the repository of a way of life that must be protected: the "urban" must be kept at bay.

The countryside as the home land of the imperial race

Many of the practices and traditions associated with the country lifestyle, although often building on earlier customs, were products of the late nineteenth century, and arose from the particular social and symbolic significance of the British countryside at that time. But, as we noted above, the cultural status of rural Britain had to be reconciled with the country-side's economic character, and we start by outlining the relationship between these two roles.

During the nineteenth century, the UK's approach to international trade was oriented towards the development of its Empire, which in turn rested upon and underpinned its international leadership in industry and commerce. That leadership had initially been built upon the traditional colonial relations that had provided protected markets for trade in luxury goods and cheap manufactures. But it was transformed into a position of dominance through the expansion and ramification of this trade, in association with rapid British industrialisation. The consequence was a marked shift in the UK's international trade towards the import of food and raw materials and the export of equipment, machinery, infrastructure and capital goods. The British Empire was thus crucially organised around the geographical separation of agriculture and manufacturing sectors as poles of imperial exchange (Friedmann and McMichael 1989). A free-trade regime was imposed on colonial markets through a combination of naval power and diplomacy, industrial and commercial might, and a reorganised London discount market with sterling as the international currency. The result was the establishment, for the first time, of a unified, price-regulated world market.

For some of the Continental powers, the maintenance of a large rural population reflected not only the entrenched position of conservative social forces based in rural areas, but also national concerns about food supplies and the need to maintain military reserves based on the peasant stock. In contrast, the economic development of the Empire had proceeded on the assumption that the United Kingdom would supply manufactures, capital and migrants, and the rest of the Empire would supply food and other primary products. Domestic agricultural prosperity and rural people were the casualties. As cheap food flooded into the UK from the 1870s onwards, land went out of arable cultivation, and the rural population declined sharply (between 1881 and 1911 the agricultural population fell from 1 190 000 to 972 000).

The wealth of Empire also contributed to the final, glorious fling of the landed estate as many successful entrepreneurs of the late Victorian and Edwardian periods sought respectability through land purchase and enjoyment through country pursuits, indifferent to collapsing agricultural rents. This process was especially evident in the highlands of Scotland as the new purchasers sustained and reinforced a pattern of ownership that was the most highly concentrated in the UK. By 1912 there were 203 large estates occupying over 3 million acres largely devoted to shooting and stalking (Bryden and Houston 1978; Smith 1992).

As the British countryside became an economic backwater of Empire, it became available as a cultural space, increasingly identified as the "home land" whence the imperial race derived and where, ultimately, it would return. In this way, the development of the Empire provided both the wealth and space to redefine the British countryside as an object and expression of national culture. Although the industries of Newcastle, Manchester and Birmingham were the engine of Empire, its sinews were maintained largely by rural Britain. It was landed families and the older professions who provided much of the finance and the leadership to pacify, administer and exploit Britain's vast colonial territories. From country estates and rural parishes, via the great public schools, sons were sent to the far-flung corners of Empire, not only to recoup family fortunes, but to do what they were born to do — rule — a prerogative increasingly challenged in Britain itself (Cannadine 1990). Rural Britain was thus the nursery of the imperial ruling class. And its aristocratic values of paternalistic authority and chivalry (Girouard 1981), underpinned by an assured sense of racial and social superiority and enlightened self-interest, informed the imperial ideal. Rural Britain was thus presented as a looking glass reflecting what was great, noble and true in the national character. Herein lies the paradox that the nation which staged the industrial revolution increasingly came to see itself in Arcadian terms; at least through its cultural spokesmen, most of whom turned their backs on the Victorian city. The countryside seemed to represent everything the city was not: it offered rustic peace and tranquillity, an escape from the "dirty utilitarian logic of industry and commerce" (Chambers 1990, p. 33).

It is out of this cultural ambivalence that we can trace the rise of preservationism as a social and political movement in late-nineteenth-century Britain. It emerged as part of an intellectual reaction to many of the tenets of economic liberalism and a loss of confidence in the progressive improvement of nature and society. Such a profound shift of opinion arose from a reassessment of the achievements of the nineteenth century and was fuelled by moral and aesthetic reactions to urban squalor and the predicament (and unruliness) of the poor. The Victorians' self-confidence was sapped by the Great Depression of the 1880s and by the intellectual crisis of the post-Darwin years (Burrow 1966). Britain's increasingly disappointing industrial performance in the final decades of the century was matched by a growing equivocation towards industrialism itself which reflected the absorption of the urban bourgeoisie into the upper reaches of British society and its genteel value system — a value system which disdained engineering and trade, and which stressed the civilised enjoyment, rather than the accumulation, of wealth and which preferred social stability to enterprise.

Such observations are presented with considerable emphasis in Martin Wiener's influential book *English Culture and the Decline of the Industrial Spirit* (1981). But whilst Wiener undoubtedly outlines the character of class hegemony after 1850 with great effectiveness, his relentlessly idealist account hardly explains how the counter-revolution embodied in Ruskin's nightmare visions of an industrialised England was so successful. The vision of "Merrie England" which had an impact on the politics of the left as well as the right was parasitic, in fact, on the vitality of other forms of the capitalist spirit. A satisfactory analysis of the ideological aspects of that symbol system needs to explain its relationship to the emerging dominance of the City and the detachment of finance capital from industry and trade. For it was, rather, a renewed manifestation of England's mercantile tradition which furnished the positive momentum for fake archaism, anti-industrial polemics and gentrification (Nairn 1988).

The limitations of Wiener's cultural critique are comprehensively exposed by Rubinstein's (1993) demonstration that, contrary to the popular notion of Britain as "the workshop of the world", manufacturing its way to pre-eminence, it was never fundamentally an industrial economy. Commercial, financial and service-based activities have always been predominant. That predominance, moreover, derived crucially from the role of Empire and the guaranteed profits and markets which it provided. Such security rendered unnecessary the sorts of institutional development and state intervention which were everywhere else associated with the drive to industrialise. Economic liberalism was, therefore, entirely consistent with the central aim of the Empire builders and the British state, which was to sustain and enhance London's place as an international financial and commercial centre. In this way the interests of English gentlemen were furthered. Their need for large yet discreet sources of income to sustain their own image of themselves (Cox 1988) was best served if that income came from land: but monies earned in the City were similarly attractive. Empire, in this view, was the creation of "gentlemen" capitalists seeking to internationalise the earning power of the City so that they might sustain the sorts of income which underpinned the social standing and gentlemanly self-image which they cultivated (Cain and Hopkins 1993). Imperialism has to be seen, therefore, as the ongoing attempt of increasingly unified (Scott 1982) landed and financial classes to extend the basis of their social position in Britain through expansion overseas: a strategy driven by the need to earn income in a particular way. Financial interests have, thereby, enjoyed a sustained primacy in British economic life, and a fundamental separation of interest between the commercial orientation of the City and the requirements of British industry persists (Ingham 1984).

If we seek to identify the components of the gentlemanly ideal which bear on the consumption of the countryside then we confront, time and again, the archaism which is so central to Wiener's thesis. But the prosecution of gentlemanly virtues often demanded, in practice, novel forms of activities which were seen as woven into the very fabric of national life as lived by dominant classes. Thus the "pleasing prospects" afforded by the transformed parkland landscapes of the "big houses" (Williams 1975) had their counterpart in new manifestations of English sporting life: a focus for the aspirations of those whose resources made some sort of participation possible.

Field sports, of course, most obviously exemplify the re-invention of tradition attendant upon fundamental change. Both fox-hunting and shooting had seemed irretrievably threatened by the coming of the railways but proved more than resilient. The former transformed itself from the private, informal recreation of country squires to a highly organised and influential public institution: a social transformation which enabled it increasingly to be presented as both embodying and engendering stability and harmony. The dominant images of the sport provided an enduring mythology, found, in the form of the sporting print, on the walls of countless public houses, hotels and other establishments (Itzkowitz 1977). Shooting was also revolutionised by transport improvements as London businessmen were given ready access to the Highlands and grouse-shooting became a vital feature of the sporting calendar, turning Scotland into a sporting playground (Eden 1979). Whether lowland or upland, the game shooting which was increasingly seen as socially desirable bore only a somewhat attenuated connection to its antecedents. Its scope was changed utterly by the development of the breechloading shotgun (Crudington and Baker 1979). The centre-fire breechloader, firing cartridges, made driven shooting possible and walking up the birds gradually gave way to driving them over lines of permanently constructed butts (Tapper 1992). Notoriously, in the closing years of the century and beyond, competition between estates was often intense. Many of the new owners were not in any way dependent on rental income from their tenant farmers and they worked single-mindedly to adopt the sporting lifestyle they considered appropriate to their properties (Ruffer 1977; Watson 1978).

Thus, many leisured activities, including field sports, were not only transformed during the late nineteenth century but were also subject to the codification and institutionalisation of the previously informal social rules and customs which surrounded them. Even where activities were apparently steeped in tradition — hunting, for instance — they took on new forms, and the contradiction was mediated by accentuating even more wholeheartedly their traditional aspects (Hobsbawn 1983). For the upper middle classes these activities, which had formerly served to set apart an aristocratic ruling class, represented an obvious set of aspirations: "they merely had to be widened and adapted" (Hobsbawn 1983, p. 292). Where it occurred, the accumulation of extensive wealth made possible assimilation to the aristocratic milieu which provided the role model for all aspirants to a gentlemanly lifestyle.

On the other hand, a variety of novel pursuits emerged, such as photography, bird watching, sketching, climbing, cycling and camping, appealing to those — the adventurous, the high minded and the bohemian — who saw in country pastimes the opportunity of escape from stultifying convention (Marsh 1982). Lower social strata, taking advantage of developments in mass transportation and reductions in working hours, also sought to make use of, or to establish, customary rights of access over open country around industrial towns and cities to gain temporary respite from their grim conditions. While this alarmed moralists, landowners and rural traditionalists, social reformers actively encouraged orderly outdoor exercise, out of concern for the physical and mental health of an urbanised population, including its fitness for the needs of imperial defence (Springhill 1977).

Thus the civilised enjoyment of the countryside came to be a widely shared social objective, as did belief that this was a civilising influence. The rural preservation and open-air movements, which championed this objective, campaigned to protect from development stretches of open country close to urban areas, to maintain rural footpaths and rights of way, to promote public rights of access to mountains and common land, to establish national parks and to protect wildlife. The function of rural areas was thereby redefined in part as an urban amenity. The term which came into general currency in the early decades of the twentieth century and signified this new view of rural areas was "the countryside". Significantly, the fiercest struggles in this redefinition of rural space were not with ordinary country people, who remained idealised but neglected, but between the conflicting recreational tastes and means of different urban strata and landed interests, such as the hunting and shooting of the gentry, plutocrats and *nouveaux riches* (G. Cox 1993), the botanising, rambling and golfing of the genteel middle class, and the hiking and coursing of the working class. The battles between these groups over rural space were microcosms of their larger struggles for control over the urban social order.

From home land to home: the British countryside in the interwar and postwar years

After 1919 the plight of rural areas became ever more acute, as they were inexorably tied to the turmoil in international commodity markets. And there was little escape. The whole of the Empire was afflicted by the world depression, and the flow of investment capital from London dried up. Thus employment opportunities for those leaving the land shrank, and the traditional option for the rural unemployed of emigration was also sharply reduced.

Neither was landed capital any longer immune to these forces. Three decades of domestic agricultural recession had taken their toll, and the investment income which had subsidised many estates was sharply attenuated. But it was also in retreat politically, challenged on its own ground by the assertion of tenants' rights, eclipsed nationally by the ascendancy of democratic and urban-based political movements, and decisively defeated in the constitutional crisis of 1911, which had been triggered by Lloyd George's proposals for land taxes. The will of landowning families to assert their traditional interests was then fatally weakened by the loss of innumerable heirs in the First World War. The rapid rise in wages during the war prohibitively raised the cost of maintaining a great estate. Following the removal of wartime agricultural subsidies, many landowners decided, or were forced, to reduce their commitments, often by selling land to their tenants. More than a quarter of all agricultural land changed hands in 1921–22. The very sense that the traditional order of the countryside faced extinction gave added poignancy to the efforts of those who sought to protect its essential features as somehow embodying the true national character.

This was particularly so during the long retreat form Empire. During the interwar years the certainty with which Britain conducted its relations with the colonies waned. In 1926 Balfour recognised the growing tide of nationalism when he declared that the Empire should consist of autonomous communities, all of equal status. Increasing uncertainty began to characterise the administration of the colonies and dominions, reflected in the problems associated with filling foreign civil service posts. In India, for example, during the 1920s and 1930s, more and more native civil servants had to be recruited, until it was evident that the country might become capable of conducting its own affairs. As Pugh (1994, p. 214) notes, "the old confidence in Britain's role steadily crumbled under the pressure of this experience". During this period the number of people emigrating from Britain for the colonies declined, so that by the 1930s more British people were returning than leaving. The symbolic significance of the homeland steadily changed, for increasingly this now became "home", marking a shift to a more inward-looking, introspective, domestic form of rurality (most clearly in evidence in the Home Counties). Retired colonial administrators and merchant adventurers settled across southern England and the rural vision became more and more introspective, with its essential features seen as both "timeless" and "fragile" — an endangered "deep" England (although these retirees were not above refurbishing the countryside with familiar features of Empire, such as the bungalow and rhododendron from northern India). In the words of Stanley Baldwin:

> The sounds of England, the tinkle of the hammer on the anvil in the country smithy, the corncrake on a dewy morning, the sound of the scythe against the whetstone, and the sight of a plough team coming over the brow of the hill, the sight that has been England since England was a land, and may be seen in England long after the Empire has perished and every works in England has ceased to function, for centuries the one eternal sight of England. (Baldwin 1926)

The fragile nature of the traditional rural order was apparent in the weakening of paternalistic landownership and the break-up of some of the great estates which undermined established norms of stewardship and social obligation, and specifically put at risk the maintenance of many fine landscapes and historic buildings. In the words of Patrick Abercrombie, the architect-planner who founded the Council for the Preservation of Rural England: "Even when the estates remained intact the rapport that had existed between local inhabitants and the previous owners had been destroyed. The traditional feeling of being jointly responsible for preserving local amenities had gone" (Abercrombie 1930).

Organised preservation groups did what they could to safeguard important areas and features. The National Trust led the way in acquiring threatened places of special historic interest or natural beauty, which thereby became, in the words of one of its founders, "a bit of England belonging to the English in a very special way" (Hill 1899). Thus great houses and parklands created for the private display of an exclusive inheritance came to be seen as the nation's heritage. Of necessity but also out of conviction, the Trust maintained that its ownership of country houses and estates should be a last resort. Traditional private ownership was the ideal, and the Trust campaigned for tax relief for estate owners, now cast in the role of custodians of the national heritage.

Equally the Trust itself embraced the tradition of paternalistic stewardship in the management of its properties, and in opening to the public the country houses it had acquired, sought to present them as private homes rather than museums or chateaux; i.e. as if lived in by the former owners and furnished with their inherited treasures (in many cases, indeed, owners and their heirs were allowed to continue in residence). The image presented was one of domesticity, however lavish, in an Arcadian setting. What was often obscured was the scale of resources and employment that had been necessary to maintain country estates and hence the extent to which apparently rural and aristocratic lifestyles depended upon wealth earned in the urban industrial and commercial sectors at home and overseas. Detached in this way from connotations of class hegemony, and their rentier underpinnings, stately homes became public shrines to the lives, tastes and pleasures of great families, celebrating values of private ownership and family continuity (Gaze 1988; Wright 1985).

But the greater threat to the countryside was seen to come from without. In its debilitated condition, the countryside seemed unable to resist a rising tide of external pressures. In the context of a growing middle class, the motor car, new trunk roads and commuter railway lines were allowing residential development to break loose from city boundaries. Suburbs mushroomed as cheap mortgages and depressed land values enabled many white-collar workers to buy a villa or a bungalow with a garage for their new Ford 8 or Austin 7. Between the turn of the century and the outbreak of the Second World War, the extent of urban areas nearly doubled to 8% of the total land surface. Greater London grew at an even faster rate and its suburbs threatened to overwhelm much of the south east's countryside.

The rampant and apparently shapeless spread of ribbon development and urban sprawl seemed to imply a creeping disorder, socially and aesthetically, and this stimulated calls for a planned approach to development to maintain the distinctiveness of town and country. As Abercrombie expressed it:

> The essence of the aesthetic of town and country planning consists in the frank recognition of these two elements, town and country, as representing opposite but complementary poles of influence. With these two opposites constantly in view, a great deal of confused thinking and acting is washed away: the town should indeed be frankly artificial, urban; the country natural, rural. (Abercrombie 1933, pp. 18–19)

Now the rural was recast within a domestic framework of middle-class mores in which the older Arcadian virtues came to take on a more modern appeal. That more might be at stake than aesthetics, reaching down to fundamental issues to do with social order and identity, is conveyed in the recurrent use of gender metaphors to characterise the urban/rural divide, in which the countryside is identified as female, with allusions to both the domestic and the natural. As Abercrombie put it: "The English countryside [is] a Ceres, a well-cultivated matron, who duly produces, or should, her annual progeny. If therefore it is true that the town should not invade the country as a town, the regularising hand of man has nevertheless sophisticated the country to serve his needs" (1933, pp. 177–179). The rural planner, Thomas Sharp, wrote in similar vein: "The crying need of the moment is the re-establishment of the ancient anti-thesis. The town is town: the country is country: black and white: male and female. Only in the preservation of these distinctions is there any salvation . . ." (Sharp 1932, p. 11).

The reconstitution of traditional rural boundaries and identities thus became central to the preservationist movement and fed directly into the strategic concerns which were greatly boosted by the outbreak of the Second World War. First, the more Arcadian conceptions of the country-side became of obvious symbolic value in helping sustain morale during a period of intense national sacrifice. But, more importantly, the unique exposure of Britain's reliance on imported food highlighted the strategic significance of domestic agriculture such that the preservation of farm land came to be seen as a matter of national survival. The major focus for these concerns was the official Committee on Land Utilisation in Rural Areas, appointed in October 1941 under the chairmanship of Lord Justice Scott. Formulated at the height of the war, the Scott Report's thinking contributed crucially to the postwar ideology of urban containment and green belts, the establishment of national parks and nature reserves, and state support for farming.

The essential thesis of the Scott Report was that a prosperous farming industry would preserve both the rural landscape and rural communities. Thus the rural community was conceived of as an agricultural community, dependent on the continuance and revival of the traditional mixed character of British farming. The major threat to rural areas, apart from government neglect, was seen to arise from building and industrial pressures which, it was argued, threatened to mar the countryside, take land out of farming and entice labour away from agriculture. The report was optimistic that, if these pressures could be resisted, farm incomes boosted and modern services provided in villages, then traditional rural life would be revived and the countryside preserved. And these assumptions had far-reaching consequences, particularly in shaping the philosophy and objectives of postwar policy for agriculture and land-use planning. The Town and Country Planning Act of 1947 introduced the principle that changes in land use were to be subject to the control of local planning authorities who were to prepare development plans. However, "develop-ment" was defined by the Act in physical terms and specifically excluded agricultural uses and operations. In effect, the legislation accorded farming a pre-emptive claim over all other uses of rural land.

With this prioritisation of agriculture, bolstered by the desire to keep the distinction between the urban and the rural clearly defined, the cultural significance of rural space was maintained. Furthermore, the rural was now coming to be reconstituted through distinctions of class and gender. Most notable was the role of the middle class in defining what counted as rural, and thus what was valuable and in need of protection, noticed in the early 1960s by Ray Pahl in his studies of Hertfordshire villages. Middle-class commuters sought to uphold the sanctity of the village in order to live within a rural community and to be surrounded by a pleasing environment. Having bought their way into such places these commuters then set about trying to mould the social and material shape of the village in a way which was compatible with their preconceptions of rural life (see Pahl 1965, 1966, 1970; for a more recent account of the same phenomenon, see Murdoch and Marsden 1994). The equation they made between the home, the domestic sphere, the family and the rural drew upon and extended well-established cultural conventions. The supposed "time-lessness" of the "rural way of life" was recast within a middle-class view of the stable nuclear family embedded in a community which was itself taking on middle-class attributes. The attraction of the English village to this social stratum is neatly summarised by Val Williams in the following way:

> Being part of a village is like being a member of an extended family and city dwellers, often far from their roots, long for this sense of belonging. Viewed from the city, village life seems so secure, with its bastions of the vicar, the schoolteacher and the local squire. The school is a cosy, well-disciplined place where the old values persist, a log fire burns in the pub and the troubles of the workplace and the home can be forgotten in its flickering ambience. (1993, p. 34)

Again, the rural provided a welcome escape from the urban and allowed a series of new residents to reshape both the material and the cultural forms of rural society. Furthermore, these incomers were also attracted by opportunities to participate in rural recreation, such as rambling, horse-riding, shooting, and so forth (e.g. Curry and Comley 1986; Harrison 1991), activities which came to be seen as part of the "new traditionalist" lifestyle (Urry 1990). As Newby (1980) was to discover, often the active assertion of their ideals, and the pursuit of these leisure activities, on the part of these immigrants alienated the more traditional rural dwellers, particularly those who worked on the land. While agriculture enjoyed a period of state-sponsored prosperity, the farming population could maintain its hold over much of rural life. However, once the industry entered recession in the early 1980s, farmers, and the much depleted ranks of farm workers (full-time agricultural workers declined by 600 000 between 1950 and 1980, a fall of 70%), found the increasing numbers of middle-class incomers usurping much of their traditional influence. Thus the scene was set for another shift in cultural conceptions of rurality.

Consolidating Anglo-centricity

Although depressed conditions returned to British agriculture in the 1980s, the social response has differed markedly from the interwar years. The tremendous increase in farm labour productivity in the intervening period and the growth of the service sector and some manufacturing in rural regions have greatly reduced the countryside's economic dependency on farming. Even in the most rural of areas, agriculture and related industries rarely account for more than 15% of the employed population, and in most rural areas it is a good deal less.

The impact of the contemporary agricultural depression has been profound in catalysing a broader redefinition of the social functions of rural space, away from agricultural production towards a greater emphasis on its consumption role. This is part of a broader restructuring of national economies. The growing internationalisation of capital has also brought a greater degree of locational flexibility, which, for a number of reasons, has partly favoured rural areas:

- Such areas have a relatively low-wage and non-unionised workforce and agricultural labour, shed from small, technologically sophisticated farm businesses, provides a reservoir of transferable, practical skills.
- The small-scale business structure of rural areas and a culture of entrepreneurship may facilitate rapid economic adjustment into flexible systems of production and service provision.
- State support for agriculture, which was to a large extent capitalised in land values, has given rural landowners significant sources of collateral to invest in new businesses.
- Rural areas have become much more accessible as a result of improvements in telecommunications and transportation systems. At the same time, some of the new-wave technologies, particularly biotechnology and information technology, favour rural locations.
- Rural areas are seen to offer more pleasant surroundings in which to work and live than those existing in the modern city and suburbia.

It is, therefore, not surprising that new firm formation rates and employment growth have been higher in small towns and rural areas than in large urban centres (Keeble et al. 1983; Fothergill and Gudgin 1982; Hodge and Monk 1987; Champion and Townsend 1990). Increasingly, in more urbanised regions, service activities have also relocated in rural areas, thereby accentuating an employment pattern already heavily weighted towards the service sector. For the first time since the industrial revolution, rural areas are enjoying a comparative advantage and the consequence is to restore to them some of the diversity they once enjoyed.

In the UK the net effect of these more general trends has been to challenge the dominant role accorded to agricultural productivism. The need to protect agricultural land and promote agricultural productivity at almost any cost was the keystone not only of agricultural policy but also of postwar rural planning. The sectoral crisis in farming has thus also led to an upheaval in the spatial management of the countryside. A wish to wean farmers off their dependence on price supports and the deregulatory instincts of the early Thatcher governments coincided in the 1980s in efforts to free-up the statutory land-use planning system and to open up the countryside to new forms of investment. This, however, stimulated a backlash form the increasingly influential and numerous middle-class groups in rural areas, particularly in the Home Counties, whose Arcadian aspirations would be undermined by new forms of development. In general, therefore, efforts to liberalise rural planning have produced the opposite effect, and the planning system has perversely been strengthened not weakened as a result. This shift is occurring in the absence of the overall strategy for rural areas that was once provided by agricultural productivism. Increasingly, priorities are being set, by default, from below, through the new rural planning system; they have, therefore, a much more localised focus (Lowe et al. 1993).

The shift to a stronger local planning framework, with an enhanced role for forward planning, may well consolidate the hold of the middle-class in rural areas. The role of middle-class political activities in shaping the development trajectories of rural areas is now well documented. For instance, Jo Little argues that "conservative anti-development and *laissez faire* policies not only protect the interests of the middle-classes but actively disadvantage the least affluent. This will result in the continuing (possibly accelerating) social polarisation of rural areas in the future and a reinforcement of middle-class exclusivity in the countryside" (1987, p. 198). Cloke and Little (1990) go on to show how this process may become self-reinforcing, for as more middle-class incomers take up residence they will tend to become involved in local politics and will work to ensure that these planning policies remain in existence. The planning system itself is structured in such a way as to demand a relatively high standard of education from those who choose to participate in it. The existence of the planning system, therefore, provides an arena for middle-class political representation (Lowe 1977). Moreover, within this arena decisions are taken which have real material effects. Planning thus provides not only a focus for middle-class representation but also a means whereby these representations can be translated into spatial forms. Thus the middle-class comes to dominate not just particular forms of housing, labour markets and communities, but also political institutions. As the processes of domination unfold they begin to accumulate; they thus reinforce one another.

As Savage et al. (1992) point out, this privileged position is made up of certain economic, property and cultural assets which become invested in particular (rural) places. Once middle-class members begin to establish themselves in these places they begin actively to mould (politically and culturally) the social and material shape of the locale, often attempting to reproduce certain dominant, or "new traditionalist", conceptions of the rural (Thrift 1989; Urry 1990). The emergent middle-class rural culture reworks already existing dominant cultural discourses associated with the English countryside, characterised as "a bucolic vision of an ordered, comforting, peaceful and, above all, deferential past" (Thrift 1989, p. 26). No matter that this is a mythical rural past, for these elements can be fused into a new idyllic conception of rurality, one which the middle class can now begin to put into effect in reconstituted villages. As agriculture recedes from rural settlements, and barns are converted into "authentic" rural houses for wealthy in-migrants, villages can take on the physical forms of the "new traditionalism", making them hotchpotches of the old and the new where the various elements fuse in a new village, with the "rapid piling of one style upon another" (Ascherson 1993).

The interiors of these houses may also conform to type with Laura Ashley designs becoming "almost a byword for an English middle-class style and fashion which draws upon a mythical Victorian golden age of (rural) living and cultural values" (Pratt 1992, p. 126). Here again the assertion of certain gender identities becomes wrapped up in the "new traditionalism" (see, for instance, Barr and York (1982) on the importance of Laura Ashley to the Sloane Ranger set). As Pratt notes in his review of *Laura Ashley: a Life by Design* (Sebba 1990), Ashley had no sympathy for feminism and believed that women should find fulfilment through the family:

> This is what she seems to have meant by the "moral importance of clothes", believing that women would achieve their ends if they "showed their feminine charms" . . . . Clothes should fit a woman for work (in the home), and should not be made according to a male stereotype of how a woman should look; rather clothes should fit a woman's natural role, in such a state of perfection she would naturally be attractive to men. To Ashley's mind it followed that "the more a woman covered up the more attractive she was to the opposite sex" . . . (Pratt 1992, p. 126)

Such a view has clear affinities with the notion of the village as a stable middle-class domain in which the family is the central unit, where the identity of women is deemed to come from their traditional role in the home and from the concerns of the Women's Institute. Men, on the other hand, commute to work and spend their weekends in the garden, the pub or on the cricket pitch. As Middleton observes in her study of a Yorkshire village:

> Women . . . are seen as "out of place" in most public space in the village. They spend most of their lives in the home, enmeshed in family activities, whilst men of the village fraternise with whomever they find to talk to in public space and predominate in economic, political and cultural activities. The two sexes have distinct lives and inhabit different domains. (1985, p. 132)

Not only is the countryside regarded as an "anchor" for "new traditionalists" class and gender identities, it is also a "white" space. It is now increasingly apparent that ethnic minority groups are confined to the city. There is simply an absence of black faces in the countryside, whether as residents or visitors. Although many black people have long connections to the rural areas in their countries of origin, the English countryside is an alien landscape into which they simply do not "fit". As one black photographer put it, to walk in the Lake District is to "wander lonely as a black face in a sea of white" (quoted in Coster 1991, echoing Paul Gilroy's (1987) book title *There Ain't No Black in the Union Jack*). Thus the experience of black people in Britain is primarily an urban experience. This is borne out by figures quoted in Smith (1989) showing that 43% of Afro-Caribbeans, 23% of Asians but only 6% of all whites live in the inner-city zones of London, Birmingham and Manchester (see also Savage and Warde 1993, pp. 64–68).

The "ghetto-isation" of ethnic minority groups within the city must be understood in the context of the traditional role played by the countryside in English culture, a culture which tends to exclude those who are not white. The ethnic/nationalist significance of the rural can, therefore, be understood in terms of two broad and generalised "national" cultures:

> Here, today, we face the possibility of two perspectives and two versions of "Britishness". One is Anglo-centric, frequently conservative, backward-looking, and increasingly located in a frozen and largely stereotyped idea of the national, that is English culture. The other is ex-centric, open-ended and multi-ethnic. The first is based on a homogeneous "unity" in which history, tradition and individual biographies and roles, including ethnic and sexual ones, are fundamentally fixed and embalmed in the national epic, in the mere fact of being "English". The other perspective suggests an overlapping network of histories and traditions, a heterogeneous complexity in which positions and identities, including that of the "national", cannot be taken for granted, and are not interminably fixed but tend towards flux. (Chambers 1990, p. 27)

The yearning for the rural on the part of the white middle class corresponds in many ways to this portrayal of "Anglo-centricity", as its members draw upon conceptions of the rural which refer back to a time when it represented the "home land" and, more latterly, "home". Within this emerging rural space identities are fixed, making it a white, family-centred, middle-class domain — a domain, moreover, that is imbued with its own mythical history, which selects and deploys particular, nativistic notions of what it is to belong to this Anglo-centric culture. That this is what attracts middle-class in-migrants to the countryside, and what repels them from the urban, is rarely made explicit. Instead the village is extolled for the virtues of "peace and quiet", of "community" and "neighbourliness", virtues which are deemed to be absent from the urban. The latter, on the other hand, is the site for the ex-centric, open-ended and multi-ethnic cultures which are so clearly absent from the rural.

Needless to say the assertion of this "new traditionalist" or Anglo-centric rurality necessitates the exclusion of certain social groups who, as members of other national (urban) cultures, might legitimately make some claim on the countryside. One instance of this is the recent phenomenon of urban youth wishing to escape from the cities into the countryside to participate in "rave" parties. In clamping down on this activity in 1993, by giving the police new powers to break up such parties, the Under-Secretary of State for the Environment said "we are determined to restore peace and quiet to the countryside" (BBC News, 31 March 1993). Another, related, instance is provided by the periodic harassment of New Age travellers who constitute a distressing intrusion into the "bucolic" ambience of rural areas. Yet another is given by the recent commitment on the part of the Home Secretary to make illegal any disruptive activities on the part of hunt saboteurs. Once again disaffected urban youth are making an unwelcome incursion into the countryside, this time to interfere with the pursuit of traditional "country sports". All these perceived threats to the rural way of life are to be dealt with by the Criminal Justice and Public Order Bill which received its first hearing in Parliament in January 1994. The Bill will seek to limit access to private land and property through the criminalisation of aggravated trespass. In such ways does "Anglo-centric" culture attempt to exclude the "ex-centric".

The observation that the English countryside is the preserve of dominant social groups is, of course, by no means new. Neither is the view that the state is often enlisted to uphold this dominance. For instance, in their consideration of the way in which the planning system has moulded both urban and rural areas, Hall et al. (1973) commented:

> An essential feature of the pure system was the creation of communities which were self-contained and balanced. But the new suburban communities of owner-occupied homes in the small towns and villages cater for a narrow spectrum of social classes. Coupled with the concentration of municipal housing in the cities, the result is the development of publicly sanctioned, publicly-subsidised apartheid. (pp. 396–397)

The term "apartheid" was not used to refer to a "colour bar" but simply to a rigid divide imposed between those social groups able to move as they wished and those confined to the (inner) city. However, this seems to have resulted in a very English form of apartheid. Ethnic minorities simply feel they do not belong in the countryside. The countryside, therefore, provides a perfect space within which "Anglo-centricity" may come to be redefined. Rurality is very much at the centre of the struggle to impose Anglo-centric or new traditionalist culture; for rural space, with its mythical history of Englishness, seems much more accommodating than the heterogeneous complexity of the urban. As Mike Phillips, a black writer, says:

> They say, "London isn't the real England, the cities aren't the real England." That always seemed to me nonsense. The notion of the countryside is a last refuge of English nationality, a protection against people who really ought to be foreigners but who somehow seem to have captured part of the island. (quoted in Coster 1991)

Conclusion

The urban/rural distinction is one of the central defining dichotomies of modern society, and we have tried to show here some of the main reasons which have allowed this dichotomy to be maintained. Furthermore, we have argued that the urban and rural have become sites for the "anchoring" of particular identities, from the "gentleman of leisure" to the "housewife" to the white middle class. The context in which dominant conceptions of the rural, and the identities which it partially constitutes, have been defined has changed markedly over the last hundred years. Initially, during the age of Empire, the rural provided a reservoir of both capital and labour to be exported to secure the domination of other lands and was considered as the "home land", by successive waves of settlers, colonial administrators, military men, plantation managers, and missionaries nostalgically looking back. Then, as the Empire began to recede, the rural came to be redefined as "home" for those returning from the colonies and dominions. In the postwar period the rural came to be equated with agriculture but the wholescale restructuring of the industry (a real "agricultural revolution") allowed new middle-class groups, drawn by strong cultural aspirations for the rural life, to re-utilise resources no longer in agricultural use, most notably housing. Moreover, the establishment of the planning system has allowed these new rural residents to pursue the "politics of exclusion" as they attempt to keep development, and thus "others", out. Where earlier generations carved up the globe, the present one must enact its territorial aspirations on a much smaller canvas, through exploring, colonising and ramifying the rural planning system. It is a tribute to the cultural status of rurality that this is still viewed as a "civilising" mission.

The re-creation of the countryside as a "civilised" cultural space entails, therefore, a selective appropriation of the British, or more specifically, English national identity. This mythical past (Porter 1992) informs the actions of those with sufficient resources to bring it into being. Thus rural housing, local environmental features, community life, etc., are woven around traditional features associated with a national past. This is represented as both a "civilised" and a "civilising" past which upholds all that is finest about the nation. After Chambers, we have termed this the assertion of Anglo-centricity and have indicated that the maintenance of this culture depends on the exclusion of others. Such exclusion has been made more pressing by the fact that the Empire has come "home". Britain is now home to many people, from "other" ethnic groups and cultures, who were previously to be ruled from afar. Up to now these "others" have been confined or "contained" within the city. The city has become, therefore, the site for the expression of an "ex-centric" open culture. The rural, on the other hand, is where members of the middle class find a welcome retreat from the "confused" nature of urban life and, in so doing, find a sense of belonging which upholds the long-established, but constantly reworked, forms of identity which are intrinsic to Anglo-centric culture.

Part 2

THE CITY ECONOMY

STEPHEN GRAHAM

Globalism, localism and city economies

The chapters in this part of the book reflect the current dominance of two concerns in debates about city economies. First is the concern to understand the new dynamic interplay between local and global economic forces within which the fortunes of city economies are shaped. Second, there is a concern to analyse the degree to which local institutional intervention can genuinely improve urban economic fortunes given these dynamics. This debate has tended to be polarised between what John Lovering calls the "new localists" (see Chapter 5), and a group of theorists that can be broadly called "globalists" (e.g. Amin and Robins 1991).

Localists argue that new political and economic processes bring a renewed political salience to cities and localities (Cooke 1989; Murray 1991). This arises from the development of new high-tech industrial spaces, a new sense of local political identity, and a shifting down to the local level of many institutional and regulatory structures that previously were the exclusive preserve of the nation state. Parallel movements exist towards a more variegated and locally rooted postmodern urban culture. Together, it is argued, these forces mean that there is an *increased* local potential for policy makers to genuinely improve the economic fortunes of their cities through the development of local economic strategies.

Managing Cities: The New Urban Context, edited by P. Healey, S. Cameron, S. Davoudi, S. Graham and A. Madani-Pour. © 1995 The Editors and contributors. Published in 1995 by John Wiley & Sons Ltd.

Globalists, on the other hand, argue that the previously integrated urban economies of the Fordist era are in fact being *fractured* by the globalisation of capitalism. Whereas previously the firms, institutions and social processes in a Fordist-style city were characterised by a tight integration, today's cities increasingly consist rather of loosely related fragments. Increasingly, the argument goes, these *just so happen* to inhabit the same place; they are oriented more to global economic networks, investors and markets than to specific local needs and resources. This globalisation process therefore works to tightly *confine* the local "manoeuvring space" for genuinely influential policy innovation. This is because the dominant actors shaping the economic fortunes of cities — such as multinational corporations and supranational regulatory organisations — are largely beyond the influence of local policy makers. The result is that such policy makers tend to be reduced to the marketing of their places as centres of investment in increasingly competitive and zero-sum "place marketplaces". Substantially affecting the development fortunes of cities through local policy initiatives becomes very difficult in such a scenario.

So, whilst localists stress the deepening "roots" of local clusters of small firms within specific localities, and their unique entrepreneurial "milieux", globalists argue that capital is in fact tending to "uproot" from its exclusive reliance on particular spaces and places through the globalisation process. This *delocalisation* is reflected through mergers, acquisitions and the centralisation of capital onto ever-larger constellations of firms operating at global scales. These firms construct sophisticated locational strategies on an increasingly global basis.

This localisation/globalisation debate is of fundamental importance in shaping current understanding of the changing development of city economies. It is also crucial to the associated re-examination of the new policy directions being adopted in urban management. Current theories of urban political economy accord economic forces key status as *determinants* influencing the social, geographical and political transformation of cities. Because of this, the importance of city economies goes well beyond the immediate issues of the location, type and quantity of jobs, and the health, or otherwise, of urban economies. The complex global patterning of urban economic growth and decline is seen to help shape the geography of social welfare and political strategies of all spatial scales. This economic debate therefore raises key questions for cities and urban management. These are addressed extremely well by the three chapters in this section.

Economic restructuring and urban entrepreneurialism

Whether one supports the localist or globalist stance, or adopts some blend of the two, it is hard to resist the conclusion that the current round of urban restructuring is interwoven in some way with the greater tying in of urban economies into international urban systems of global capitalist development. This process is associated with a radical restructuring in the current makeup of western urban economies. The traditional specialised industrial districts that first spawned the industrial city are all but a memory in most western cities. Paralleling this often catastrophic collapse of manufacturing has been a growth of some newer sectors. Retailing, media and cultural industries, certain niche manufacturing sectors, producer and financial services, and computer and information services have grown. Most industrial cities have been transformed into postindustrial cities (Savitch 1988). In most western cities, 60% or more of new jobs now derive from information and knowledge-based services.

But this growth has failed to allay the impression that many city economies remain in a condition of deep economic crisis. Serious structural unemployment continues in most cities. Globalisation and the application of new information and communications technologies are leading to the "re-engineering" of many of these "growth" sectors. The results are automation, displacement, job shedding and a spatial shifting round of the jobs that remain. As higher-quality jobs for the corporate classes become scarcer, new lower-order service jobs in leisure and retailing are becoming the basis of job creation in cities. These are often of poor quality and often tend to exacerbate rather than cure poverty (see Chapter 9). The current global recession compounds these problems. Together, the trends have punctured any hope that the 1980s were the start of a long-term urban economic renaissance based on services growth. When combined with national political movements towards neo-liberalism and the cutback of local government finance, this urban economic crisis is increasingly associated with a fiscal and political crisis in urban governance (Pickvance and Preteceille 1991; see also Chapter 11).

This structural economic change has been associated with the ongoing demise of "managerialist" preoccupation of urban government — geared towards the management of public service delivery. In its place, "urban entrepreneurialism" — the proactive encouragement of economic growth through whatever local means are at the disposal of urban governance — is now becoming almost universal (Harvey 1989b; Pickvance and Preteceille 1991). As the economic fortunes of cities move to the top of the local political agenda, urban economic policy making, "public private partnerships", and place marketing are emerging as driving forces in changing approaches to urban management. Central here is the desire to position cities favourably on the global economic networks dominated by the burgeoning multinational corporations.

In the 1980s property boom, the large-scale *physical* redevelopment of parts of cities often took centre stage in this process. Property interests sought to capitalise on the new space demands of the growth sectors whilst reaping the subsidies of urban policy makers (Knox 1993). At this time, urban "regeneration" was all too often equated simply and unproblematically with the physical redevelopment of redundant urban spaces (Healey et al. 1992). These redeveloped spaces helped city managers to try to reposition themselves on global networks by enhancing their postmodern urban imagery — a perceived boost to local economic attractiveness. Susan Fainstein, in Chapter 6, recounts the complex stories behind the grandiose property redevelopment plans in the world cities of New York and London. It was in these global "hot spots" that the processes reached their peaks, symbolised now by the legacy of vast edifices for financial services in Battery Park and Canary Wharf.

Analytical problems in urban economic development

Much ambiguity and uncertainty remains within urban research surrounding the analysis of these processes of urban economic change and the policy shift towards entrepreneurialism. This has been created by the use of a range of often poorly-defined and loosely-applied analytical approaches: "post-Fordism", "postindustrialism", "postmodernism", information economy, being examples. The emphases and interpretations of change vary between these theoretical approaches, even when they are used merely as *working hypotheses* rather than all-encompassing metatheories. It is increasingly clear, however, that the complex web of political, economic, spatial, cultural and technological transformations that together constitute the "urban restructuring" process are not satisfactorily addressed by any one of these approaches (Pickvance and Preteceille 1991).

The rapidity and complexity of change in urban economies, combined with this veritable quagmire of conceptual approaches, has tended to reduce the degree to which empirical work on urban economic restructuring has actually been linked to conceptual debates. The abstract political/economic concepts used often lack a key *intermediate* level whereby their dynamics can be traced in the actions of actors, firms and institutions in specific cities. If it is very difficult to define precisely what a "post-Fordist" economy is in conceptual terms, it will be almost impossible to study real urban development processes using such abstract concepts. This problem is made worse by the growing *invisibility* of many urban economic processes — for example, "hidden" computer networks and private telecommunication networks which link the world's financial centres into one vast electronic financial market, but in an invisible and intangible way. This makes it hard to analyse their tangible effects on the development and management of the cities through which they pass.

The analytical problems have meant that the conceptual debates of localism and globalism, and of postmodernism and post-Fordism, have tended to become detached from a real empirical tradition. The conceptual debate has become dominant. In the 1980s, this resulted in the embedding of certain especially attractive concepts of localism in the minds of analysts and policy makers alike. Bolstering this have been certain interpretations of theoretical debates on regulation theory and flexible specialisation, and the proliferation of local agencies and growth promotion organisations in cities eager to fan the rhetoric of localism (see Chapter 5). As a result, as John Lovering argues, many of the concepts that surround the "new localism" — such as the new industrial district of flexibly specialised small firms — have almost become *mythologised* in the urban policy and studies debates of recent years.

The remarkable persistence of these concepts, once rooted, means that they can continue flourishing without the need for empirical sustenance and despite the build-up of counter-evidence that urban economies are, in fact, *disintegrating* rather than *integrating*. Here the strongest link between urban theory and urban practice occurs at present. According to Lovering, this is open to severe criticism. The almost utopian attachment to single, hegemonic concepts of the "new localism" has led to a failure to document *actual* processes of economic and political restructuring, let alone to suggest improved solutions for policy. To Lovering, this rhetorical localism actually *deflects attention* from the real process at work. These centre on the development of a new global neo-liberal orthodoxy in which the economic and social dislocation of cities becomes intensified in the global context. Thus, localist researchers and policy makers alike are accused by Lovering of "creating discourses rather than jobs".

It is increasingly clear, however, that the binary split between the "localist" and "globalist" arguments is becoming unhelpful. The reality of urban economic change involves a more complex interplay between forces of localisation and globalisation, structure and agency, fragmentation and integration, contingent and general forces, and economic and political factors than has tended to be suggested so far. Urban economic restructuring and policy making is clearly an extremely dynamic and variant process which makes the use of such crude dualities hazardous. Economic change, and political responses to it, are highly variant within and between cities and between different economic sectors.

The neglect of the institutional dimension

The reliance on overly simplified concepts in recent debates on urban economic change has also tended to lead to a neglect of the key importance of the *institutional* dimensions to the processes under way (Logan and Swanstrom, 1990). Implicit in many analyses is an economic and technological determinism or functionalism — urban entrepreneurialism is seen to be made *necessary* in some way because of economic restructuring (Pickvance and Preteceille 1991). Single hegemonic concepts — post-modernism, post-Fordism — are often held up to account for what is in fact a very diverse "untidy reality" of political, economic and spatial change (Walton 1990). Basic assumptions of universal, one-way and hegemonic transformations have meant a key failure to analyse, from a truly comparative empirical perspective, the local, regional and national political *differences* in the institutional development of cities. It is increasingly apparent that cities, in fact, have very different institutional capacities to shape their economies. National political and institutional differences remain very important. These have important consequences for urban economic restructuring and urban policy making (Logan and Swanstrom 1990; Gurr and King 1987).

This political variation and contingency in policy responses to urban economic restructuring is heavily emphasised in this section of the book. Susan Fainstein's comparison of London's and New York's redevelopment policies shows clearly how each was the result as much of the shaping influence of particular national and local policy circumstances as of the pervasive global drive of property capital to invest in grandiose projects in the booming world cities. John Lovering shows that beneath the rhetoric of localism in British cities, there is a particular political project under way at the national level. This involves the imposition of a neo-liberal orthodoxy over urban policy and the intergovernmental system by a centralising, New Right, central government. Finally, much of Ash Amin and Nigel Thrift's analysis stresses the key importance of local institutional capability in securing progressive urban change in the new global era. This capability is very unevenly distributed.

Institutional strategies and urban prospects: towards a normative agenda

As a result of the continuing urban economic crisis and the persistence of those who have argued against the localist thesis, analysis has now moved beyond the often simplistic theoretical suppositions of the 1980s. The "quick fix" of flexible specialisation or a new progressive localism is less often wheeled out as some economic panacea. Much more sophisticated analyses are now developing. These attempt to relate the economic with the political, so bringing them together in sensitive *institutionalist* perspectives of urban restructuring and political economic change.

The three papers in this section are state-of-the-art attempts at this. These approaches are much more amenable to detailed empirical work on *real* city economies and *real* processes of urban governance than are the cruder and more abstract theoretical concepts of early post-Fordist or postmodernist approaches. They are also more able to capture the undoubted political and economic *diversity* and the complexity of political/ economic relations which still characterise western cities.

These approaches also lay the foundations for a movement towards a more sophisticated *normative* agenda, engaging directly with urban policy makers. Again, all three chapters include suggestions for improvements in urban economic policy. These centre on debating the degree to which local "institutional capacity" exists to direct, govern and coordinate local political and economic responses to the structural crisis in cities, through some overall framework of planning and cross-sectoral institution-building. This ties into current debates on the need for urban leadership (Judd and Parkinson 1990b), and the developing power bases of business elites and "growth coalitions" within urban economic policy making (Harding 1991). Amin and Thrift here offer the useful concept of "local institutional thickness" as a way of analysing and improving this local capacity for directing change. As they show, however, building this capacity from scratch is likely to be difficult. It exists in an iterative relationship to the development of city economies: local institutional thickness is influenced by prevailing local economic and political conditions as well as being a factor which goes on to help shape them.

4

Globalisation, Institutional "Thickness" and the Local Economy

ASH AMIN and NIGEL THRIFT

In the age of modernity, the city economy came to symbolise the power-house of capital accumulation. The "Fordist" city, as a locus of mass production, mass consumption, social interaction and institutional representation, became the growth centre of a national economy (Scott 1988). It was a centre of agglomeration — an integrated and self-reproducing economic system. Today, the city economy, as implied in the other chapters of the book, is a thing of fragments, composed of many parallel sectoral logics with few interconnections between them. Thus, the city continues to attract entrepreneurship and investment, but no longer constitutes a cohesive local economic system. In the case of global cities such as London, New York and Los Angeles, it exists as a "central place" in global economic networks and connections (Sassen 1991; Castells 1989). In the case of national cities such as Milan, Paris and Frankfurt it exists as a central node in national administrative, financial, commercial and consumption networks, but not as the industrial power-house which underpins these networks. In the case of the postwar regional centres of mass production such as Turin, Chicago and Birmingham, it exists as a mosaic of deindustrialisation, new inward investment, secondary service activities, regional consumerism and provincial administration. The city economy has thus become increasingly fractured internally, and absorbed into wider networks of capital accumulation. Even in the case of cities in

Managing Cities: The New Urban Context, edited by P. Healey, S. Cameron, S. Davoudi, S. Graham and A. Madani-Pour. © 1995 The Editors and contributors. Published in 1995 by John Wiley & Sons Ltd.

which flexibly specialised industrial districts have been rediscovered (Storper 1989), these localised systems of production and exchange do not contribute, as they did in the past, the engine of growth for the rest of the local economy — they are self-contained islands in a disarticulated city economy.

A major force behind the disarticulation of the local economy is "globalisation". There is still considerable dispute over what the term might mean, let alone what it might portend. Commentators seem willing to agree that a global economy now exists and not just in embryonic form. They seem sure that there is a "dialectic" between the global and the local, and that in some way what counts as the "local" has been transformed by globalisation (Massey 1991b). What remains unclear, however, are the precise ways in which the economies of cities and regions are becoming transformed as a result of their intersection with different aspects of globalisation. This lack of clarity is particularly evident in the analysis of whether globalisation threatens local autonomies and identities to the point of disempowering cities and regions from shaping their own economic future. If there is any truth in the interpretation of globalisation as local threat, how do we account for the persistence of centres of agglomeration in a globalised economy (Amin and Thrift 1992; Storper 1993)? Indeed, what are we to make of suggestions such as that put forward by Margit Mayer in this book, that the post-Fordist economy and polity requires the decentralisation of organisational and governance structures to the level of cities and regions? How does this argument square with the globalisation thesis?

Our aim in this chapter is to try to avoid an analytical polarisation between the local and the global; that is, to go beyond a dualism which considers the world stage as integrated and local economies as fragmented, or vice versa. Via a consideration of the ways in which globalisation and local development are locked together at an institutional level, we want to argue that the question of local economic "integrity" is closely linked to the ability of cities and regions to develop the institutional capability to "capture" global economic flows. Accordingly, the chapter is in four parts. In the first part we look at some of the different processes that are currently subsumed under the heading of globalisation. The second part of the chapter considers how we might understand the "local" in a globalising world. The third part looks at the problem of theorising the institutional base of a city or region. Finally, the conclusion to the chapter raises a number of unresolved issues which this institutionalist perspective throws up regarding the prospect of local "empowerment" in all kinds of locality. Though the chapter does not deal explicitly with the urban economy or particular cities, its relevance lies in offering a broader conceptual framework for discussing urban possibilities in a globalised economy.

The global economy

Most writers seem to agree that the transition from an international to a global economy can be dated from the early 1970s and the breakup of the Bretton Woods system of control of national economies. We can now see some of the fruits of the subsequent reorganisation of the world economy. There are, of course, many of these but seven aspects can perhaps be counted as the most important, in terms of both geography and pervasiveness of influence.

The first of these is the increasing centrality of the financial structure through which credit money is created, allocated and put to use, and the resulting increase in the power of finance over production. Thus Harvey (1989a) writes of the degree to which financial capital has become an independent force in the modern world, while Strange (1991) writes of the increased "structural" power exercised by whoever or whatever determines the financial structure, especially the relations between creditors and debtors, savers and investors. It is particularly the global reach of finance which is striking today, as global money, in a variety of guises, straddles across and to some degree regulates the world's national economies and business transactions.

The second aspect is the increasing importance of the "knowledge structure" (Strange 1988) or "expert systems" (Giddens 1990). Everywhere in economics, sociology, economic sociology, and so on, more attention is being paid to the importance of knowledge as a factor of production. Lash and Urry (1993) even write of a new phase of "reflexive accumulation". The debate can be found in the form of arguments over whether an increase in the educational base of workforces produces higher GNP, in arguments over the importance of learning as a factor in efficient production, the communication of new technologies and the construction of conventions about how to produce, and in arguments over the importance of cognitive and aesthetic reflexivity as cornerstones of modern business conduct (Lash and Urry 1993; Boden 1993). Whatever the form of the debate, it seems clear that the production, and later, distribution and exchange of knowledge is a crucial element of the global and local economic system on a scale that was never the case before. As with the financial structure, owing to the enormous inter-penetration of know-how and scientific culture between nation states and the rise of enabling communications' media and technologies, the "knowledge structure" is becoming less and less tied to particular national or local business cultures, after it has been "released" from its original context of formation.

A third and related aspect is the transnationalisation of technology, coupled with an enormous increase in the rapidity of redundancy of given technologies. In especially the knowledge-based industries such as telecommunications, aerospace, pharmaceuticals and financial services, the development of microelectronics applications has enormously quickened the diffusion of standards and know-how. At the same time, however, the increasing reliance on technological innovation resulting from the combination of new consumption norms, increased competition and the systematisation of the knowledge-base has forced the speed with which technological trajectories are required to change (Dosi et al. 1990; Metcalfe 1988).

Thus at one level, the globalisation of technology represents a levelling of access through the spread of electronic networks and information databases. But, at another level, the greater uncertainty produced by this more complex environment militates against any except those institutions with considerable resources and continuous learning capacity. In other words, the new institutionalised risk environments (Giddens 1991) only reward the adaptable.

The fourth major global force is the rise of global oligopolies. There is a sense in much recent writing that we have now reached a point at which corporations have no choice but to "go global" very early on in their careers, for at least three reasons (Strange 1991):

- because of new methods of production brought about by accelerated technological change
- because of the greater transnational mobility of capital which has made investing abroad easier, quicker and cheaper
- because there have been major changes in the ease of transport and communication.

The result is that national measures of concentration and market share have become less relevant as corporations manoeuvre in global markets, with obvious consequences for the balance of economic power.

Fifth, and a parallel development to the globalisation of production, knowledge and finance, is the rise of transnational economic diplomacy and the globalisation of state power. There is clearly a sense in which we have entered a new era in which governments and firms bargain with themselves and one another on the world stage. In addition, transnational, "plural authority" structures like the UN, G7, the EU and so on have become increasingly powerful (Held 1991). The result appears to be the replacement of the hitherto prevalent system of international stabilisation and rule formation based upon the unchallenged might of nations with the greatest "structural" power (e.g. the United States), by a combination of issue-based agreements between members of "plural authority" structures, and tentative gestures by the most dominant nations to occupy the centre stage in world political economy (Gilpin 1987). For some observers, this is a situation presaging great global institutional and regulatory uncertainty (Lash and Urry 1993; Robertson 1990).

Sixth, and related to the intensification of global communications and international migration, is the rise of global cultural flows and "deterritorialised" signs, meanings and identities. Appadurai (1990) talks of the rise and juxtaposition of global *ethnoscapes* (the continual movement of tourists, immigrants, refugees, exiles and guestworkers across the world); of global *mediascapes* (the instantaneous worldwide distribution, by a diversity of electronic and non-electronic media, of one and the same pastiche of standardised commodities, generalised human values and interests, the cult of consumerism and denationalised ethnic or folk motifs — see Smith, 1990); and of global *ideoscapes* (key concepts and values from the Enlightenment world view, such as "freedom", "democracy", "sovereignty", "rights" and "citizenship", now all evoked by states and counter-movements in different local contexts to legitimate their existence and political aspirations). This is not a process of cultural homogenisation in the hands of readily identifiable national "ethnies" or ideologies, but the fusion of different master narratives (e.g. consumerism, cult of technology, Europeanism) and local vernaculars (e.g. separatism, folklorism, local sacred beliefs, etc.). These are cultural flows which have become "deterritorialised" — separated from their original local and national settings, only to reappear in places as new influences blending in with existing local myths, memories and beliefs (Smith 1990; Hannerz 1992). Global culture, then, is a heterogeneous phenomenon, a juxtaposition of sameness and difference, of the "real" and the "imagined", of intersecting universal and local narratives (King 1991; Bauman 1992).

Finally, the result of the processes described above is the rise of new global geographies. There is an account, increasingly prevalent, in which the processes of globalisation are seen to have produced borderless geographies with quite different breaks and boundaries from what went before. Whether we see the global economy as a "space of flows" (Castells 1989) as almost without a border (Ohmae 1990), as a necklace of localised production districts strung out round the world (Storper 1991), as the centralisation of economic power and control within a very small number of global cities (Sassen 1991), or as something in between these extremes, it is clear that geography is now globally local rather than vice versa.

At work, then, is a multifaceted process of global integration guided by, but not always made in the image of, the most powerful transnational firms, institutions, actors and cultural hegemonies of the capitalist world economy (Chesnaux 1992). The familiar imagery is the simultaneous production and consumption of the same products and images in every corner of the world (Clifford 1988), the restless flow of people, goods, finance, information and ideas across the globe (Hannerz 1992).

The local in the global

Global economy and global society, however, continue to be constructed in and through territorially bound communities. More importantly, these communities continue to represent much more than the situational requirements of global forces. There is now a rich and diverse literature on what "territoriality" or place-boundedness might mean in global times. This is not the place, however, to review the literature. Instead, in what follows, we offer a series of observations on the local–global nexus germane to the later discussion on the scope for local economic "integrity" in a global political economy.

First and foremost, to recognise the global orientation of social and economic processes today is not to play down the significance of place and "territoriality", or to argue the case of homogenisation between places. Globalisation is best seen as a "totality of inter-connected processes and inquiries" (Wolf 1982) flowing through and combining in different ways in different local settings. Indeed, for some observers (e.g. Harvey 1989a; Swyngedouw 1992a), globalisation, seen as the compression and transgression of time and space barriers, ascribes a greater salience to place, since firms, governments and the public come to identify the specificity of localities (their workforces, entrepreneurs, administrations and amenities) as an element for deriving competitive advantage. Place marketing, in this context, is said to constitute a critical element, both for success in the inter-regional competition for investment (Lash and Urry 1993), and for global industry itself to derive competitive advantage and corporate distinctiveness (Ohmae 1989; Porter 1990). On a similar track, Watts has argued that "globalization . . . revalidates and reconstitutes place, locality and difference" (Watts 1991, p. 10), because the cross-cutting of multiple experiences, cultures and images in individual places, yields different hybrids of old and new influences in any given locality.

But, to emphasise the continued significance of local difference is not to suggest that nothing has changed in terms of the way in which places are constituted or relate to the rest of the world. The forces of globalisation described earlier clearly militate against any interpretation of the global as a composition of local settings — separate and relatively self-governing regional social formations held together, as in the past, by place-based norms, identities and rules of social and economic behaviour. Globalisation represents, above all, a greater tying-in and subjugation of cities and regions to the global forces described earlier. However, this is not to play down the significance of place and place-based phenomena, but to see localities as part of, rather than separate from, the global — the product of local, nationwide and transnational influences.

We agree with Kevin Robins that "it is important to see the local as a relational and relative concept, which once significant in relation to the national sphere, now . . . is being recast in the context of globalization . . . as a fluid and relational space, constituted only in and through its relation to the global" (Robins 1991, p. 35). However, we would disagree with the implication that, as a result, the local should be seen only as a "relational" space, because of the territorial indeterminacy and lack of spatial fixity of the economic and cultural influences of today. There is no logical connection between recognising the local as "in and of the global", and abandoning a sense of the local as bounded geographical space, as places with distinctive attributes, as recognisable cities and regions with their own "physicality" and "territoriality". If we accept a definition of territoriality as the basis for living in, assimilating and making sense of the world (Thrift 1983), then there is no reason why globalisation constitutes a threat to "place" identity.

Conversely, there is no reason to cling to a sense of place or place-identification as a haven from complex and unwanted global intrusions (Alger 1990; Harvey 1989a). As Doreen Massey suggests, places are "constructed out of the juxtaposition, the intersection of multiple social relations", and should be seen as "shared spaces", "riven with internal tensions and conflicts" (Massey 1992). The invitation, here, is to see the local as a real territorial arena of social interaction composed of difference and conflict, of related and unrelated connections, of social and economic heterogeneity, of parochial and universal aspirations, and of local and global determinations. But (and this is the point) each setting, with its distinctive sense of place and its "bringing into play of locally sedimented, practice-based knowledge and experience, or the mobilisation of collective memory, always produces a conjuncture of the local and the more global which is in some measure unique" (Pred 1989, p. 221). This account of the local amounts to a recognition of place as both "home" and "the world", an acceptance of cities and regions as increasingly heterogeneous and internally disconnected arenas of social existence (Massey 1992).

Globalisation, thus, redefines localities as territories living with different bits and pieces of the transnational division of labour as well as their own inherited industrial traditions; as territories of contestation between immigrant communities evoking imagined homelands, middle-class dwellers soothed by the distant exotic cultures and working-class communities evoking local traditions; and as territories drawing upon rooted or imagined myths to mobilise a local sense of identity, in order to "capture" the global (e.g. investment) or resist it (e.g. regionalism).

Increasingly, the pressure posed by globalisation is to divide and fragment cities and regions, to turn them into arenas of disconnected economic and social processes and groupings. Nevertheless, places continue to possess specific identities, and mobilisations which seek to transcend the local disconnections. Indeed, it may well be that globalisation has reinforced such tendencies. Place-marketing around carefully selected images of local unity is now a recognised practice by local development agencies to attract international investment. Similarly, the pressure for governance structures at a sub-national scale has grown as a means for securing local interests. Regions have also become an important focus for cultural mobilisation against perceived national or global threats, in defence of place-based identities and communities.

The critical question which follows from the preceding discussion is whether local strategies structured around local common "stories" are sufficient to secure cities and regions a place in the world. Expressed differently, the question is whether place-based politics and policies are appropriate or sufficient for securing acceptable levels of local social and economic well-being. Much of this question, of course, depends on where localities find themselves within the global political economy, in terms of their established strengths and weaknesses. In the next section, we examine the attributes of localities which find themselves as key nodes within global economic circuits, so as to identify the conditions which allow them to exist as "embedded" centres in a global economy.

Embedding the global

The position of cities and regions in the global economy varies of course, as does their window of opportunity onto it. Between old industrial cities, provincial centres of growth and global cities, which all encounter the global in different ways, there exist enormous variations in the characteristics and degree of local economic prosperity. The fact, however, that capital continues to be concentrated in certain geographical agglomerations suggests that globalisation need not always imply a sacrifice of the local. Indeed, the pertinent message to emerge from the growing volume of research on new industrial agglomerations such as Silicon Valley and industrial districts in Italy or in older centres of growth such as the City of London or Hollywood, is that global processes can be "pinned down" in *some* places, to become the basis for self-sustaining growth at the local level.

The question which needs to be answered, then, is why some places continue to remain growth centres in a globalised economy. And here, contemporary research on industrial agglomerations, notably literature on the networks which territorially embed firms, is particularly helpful. In recent times, the concept of agglomeration has come to be treated in new ways as a result of the rise of a new institutional economics and a new institutional sociology. Foremost in the search for explanation has been a re-evaluation of the organisational character of the firm itself, after a period in the 1960s and 1970s when industrial agglomerations were generally believed to exist purely as a means of easing the communication and control problems of large corporations. There are at least five clearly inter-related reasons for this re-evaluation. First, research has shown that the industrial organisation of the firm should be thought of in terms of loosely connected arrays, rather than as organic wholes. The firm is rarely as efficiently organised as the rhetoric of an organisation chart implies. Second, the tasks of coordination and control turn out to be nowhere near as straightforward as previously thought. They involve continual "ad hocery" and improvisation, often on a large scale. Third, firm organisation is often unstable. Certainly, it cannot be assumed that current organisational structures represent, in any sense, an efficient solution. Thus Powell and Di Maggio (1991, p. 33) can declare that:

> We are sceptical of arguments that assume that surviving institutions represent efficient solutions because we recognise that rates of environmental change frequently outpace rates of environmental adaptation. Because sub-optimal organisational practices can persist for a long time, we rarely expect institutions simply to reflect current political and economic forces. The point is not to discern whether institutions are efficient, but to develop robust explanations of the ways in which institutions incorporate historical experiences into their rules and organising logics.

Fourth, the dividing line between firms and their environments is porous and constantly changes. At least since the work of Emery and Trist (1965) , the extent to which a firm can be seen as separate from its environment has been questioned. Just as in the social sciences the death of the subject has been announced, so in work on industrial organisation there has been a corresponding death of the firm: or rather, it is now realised that there are many different firms caught up under one name, just as there are many subjectivities competing for attention in a human subject. Finally, many firms have clearly outgrown agglomerations. They are only ever partly present in such spaces and therefore very often they have both a global and a local identity, or more accurately their identity is a hybrid of the two, in which authority is no longer exercised by easily identified local elites but rather by shifting coalitions of global and local elites.

These are reasons which feed into a theorisation of the firm as a fluid set of organisational interconnections, a network of activities spread across and beyond the individual legal entity. Viewed as such, the perspective on the role of "territory" in industrial agglomerations too has to change in order to incorporate its role as an environment which supports and sustains the industrial "network of activities".

Thus, the literature on industrial agglomerations has generally moved towards a new approach based on a recognition of the importance of an institutional atmosphere in the creation and maintenance of agglomerations. At first, explanations were often couched in terms of the new institutional economics of Williamson (1975, 1985) and others, with the emphasis falling on the role of proximity in lowering the (transactional) costs of a firm. However, it has become clear that the new institutional economics is radically undersocialised as an approach (a deficiency for which it paradoxically overcompensates by producing a radically over-socialised idea of society as a set of bureaucratic hierarchies in opposition to markets) (Granovetter 1985; Granovetter and Swedberg 1992; Swedberg 1991). Thus, more attention is now being paid to explanations couched in terms of a "new institutional sociology" or the "new sociology of economic life", with its emphasis on *networks* of social relations in the economy and particular common forms of understanding that circulate within these networks. Such understandings are seldom explicitly articulated. Instead they exist in a number of forms, as classifications, routines, scripts and other rationalising and rationalised schema.

The result is that attention in the literature on industrial agglomerations has increasingly turned away from "economic" reasons for the growth of new industrial agglomerations, such as product specialisation and the dynamics of local inter-firm divisions of labour. Instead, emphasis is now given to social and institutional factors such as non-market relationships of trust; a strong sense of common industrial purpose; social consensus; local institutional support for business; and agencies and traditions encouraging innovation, skill formation and the circulation of ideas (Hirst and Zeitlin 1991; Sabel 1992; Salais and Storper 1992).

However, the analysis of these characteristics has not been related in any systematic way to globalisation. In a recent paper drawing upon experiences of the City of London and an industrial district in Tuscany (Santa Croce sull'Arno), we have attempted to identify some of the non-economic reasons why localised centres are still needed in the context of global industrial networks (Amin and Thrift 1992). Three reasons for place-centredness appear to be of particular importance in integrated global production filieres, serving to overcome problems of integration and coordination:

- Centres provide face-to-face contact needed to generate and disseminate discourses, collective beliefs, stories about what world production filieres are like. They are also points at which knowledge structures can be tapped into.
- Centres are needed to enable social and cultural interaction; that is, to act as places of sociability, of gathering information, establishing coalitions, monitoring and maintaining trust and developing rules of behaviour.
- Centres are needed to develop, test and track innovations; to provide a critical mass of knowledgeable people and structures, and socio-institutional networks, in order to identify new gaps in the market, new uses for and definitions of technology and rapid responses to changes in demand patterns.

These centres of agglomeration are, thus, centres of representation, interaction and innovation within global production filieres. Seen in this way, what is striking about them is their unique ability to act as a pole of industrial excellence and intelligence, and to offer to the wider entrepreneurial collectivity a well consolidated network of contacts, knowledge structures and institutions. It is this quality which constitutes them as a magnet for further investment and a reason for "territorially embedding" entrepreneurial activity. In other words, these centres are the forcing houses for the construction of worldwide networks of social relations through which discourses circulate and are modulated.

These networks do not all share the same qualities. They differ in the degree to which their members share the same backgrounds (e.g. class or gender or familial ties), institutional ties, and cultural and political outlooks. We might distinguish between at least three types of contact network, each one more tightly drawn than the former and each demanding a greater degree of trust. The first type consists of networks between members of different firms and between firms and major clients. These are often well cultivated by individuals on an enduring basis but they do not necessarily require their members to make major commitments of trust or to share values. A second type consists of networks of specialists who form interest groups, often bound together by particular professional/social institutions. Members of these networks will often have shared specialist knowledge, shared interests, and shared attitudes. Finally, "epistemic communities" (Haas 1992) are tightly drawn interest groups which not only have shared specialist knowledge, shared interests and shared attitudes, but also share a normative commitment to act in particular ways and to follow quite particular policy agendas. Thus, the particular features of centres as "forcing houses" will depend on the nature of the contact networks they represent.

In summary, the new perspective on agglomerations illustrates that success at the local level in securing economic growth cannot be reduced to a set of narrow economic factors. This is not, of course, to claim that economic factors are unimportant — for example, a basic requirement for success seems to be the presence of strategic functions at the top end of a value-added chain. Instead, it is to claim that social and cultural factors also lie at the heart of success and that those factors are best summed up by the phrase "institutional thickness".

Institutional thickness

Institutional thickness is not an easy concept to grasp. It often seems very general, even vague. Yet increasingly it seems that it is these kinds of liminal concepts that hold the key to understanding the workings of the global economy. From the growing literature on institutions and economic development, it certainly seems possible to isolate the following factors.

The first and most obvious of these factors is a strong institutional presence; that is, a plethora of institutions of different kinds (including firms, financial institutions, local chambers of commerce, training agencies, trade associations, local authorities, development agencies, innovation centres, clerical bodies, unions, government agencies providing premises, land and infrastructure, business service organisations, marketing boards, and so on), all or some of which can provide a basis for the growth of particular *local* practices and collective representations in social networks. However, although the number and diversity of institutions constitutes a necessary condition for the establishment of institutional thickness, it is hardly a sufficient one. Three further factors are also important (Powell and Di Maggio 1991).

The second factor is high levels of interaction amongst the network of institutions in a local area. The institutions involved must be actively engaged with and conscious of each other, displaying high levels of contact, cooperation and information interchange which may lead, in time, to a degree of mutual isomorphism. The third factor must be the development, as a result of these high levels of interaction, of sharply defined structures of domination and/or patterns of coalition resulting in both the collective representation of what are normally sectional and individual interests, and the socialisation of costs and the control of rogue behaviour. Finally, there is a fourth factor. This is the development, amongst participants in the set of institutions, of a mutual awareness that they are involved in a common enterprise. This will almost certainly mean that there is a commonly held industrial agenda which the collection of institutions both depends upon and develops. This will usually be no more than a loosely defined script, although more formal agendas are possible. This agenda may be reinforced by other sources of identity, most especially various forms of socio-cultural identification (such as religion, gender and ethnicity).

These, and we suspect, other factors, constitute a local institutional thickness composed of interinstitutional interaction and synergy, collective representation by many bodies, a common industrial purpose and shared cultural norms and values. It is a "thickness" which both establishes legitimacy and nourishes relations of trust. It is a "thickness" which continues to stimulate entrepreneurship and consolidate the local embeddedness of industry. It is, in other words, a simultaneous *collectivisation and corporatisation* of economic life, fostered and facilitated by particular institutional and cultural traditions which appear to have been central to the generation of success within "neo-Marshallian nodes in global networks" (Amin and Thrift 1992). In other words, what is of significance here is not only the presence of a network of institutions *per se*, but rather the *processes* of institutionalisation; that is, the institutionalising processes that both underpin and stimulate a diffused entrepreneurship — a recognised set of codes of conduct, supports and practices which individuals in institutions can dip into with relative ease.

In some nodes (e.g. the City of London) this thickness has persisted over a long period. In others (e.g. Route 128 in Boston) it might be argued that the maintenance of thickness has proved problematic, in particular because of the difficulty of controlling rogue behaviour in an individualistic cultural setting (Saxenian 1991). It should also be remembered that institutional thickness is not always a boon. It can produce resistance to change as well as an innovative outlook. In a perceptive account of restructuring in the Swiss watch industry, Glasmeier (1994) argues that a major obstacle to change has been the inertia of embedded craft-based institutions and cultures in the Swiss Jura to adjust to the norms and parameters of a world watch industry now dominated by whoever can best make advances in quartz technology.

Yet what does seem certain is that local institutional thickness can have a decisive influence on economic development. In situations in which assets for competitiveness are not as it were "locked into" individual firms, place appears to have become of critical importance, as firms gravitate towards localities which offer the best institutional milieu to support their needs. Then ideas, research capability, information, skills, supply structures and services, made widely available through recognisable institutions such as centres of higher education, development agencies, business organisations and other more informal associations, amount to the offer of specific and general infrastructures which can significantly ease the burden of entrepreneurship.

However, official attempts to produce what Sabel (1992) calls "studied trust" in local agglomerations have proved problematic. It has proved relatively easy, through the establishment of various new institutions, to produce heightened levels of interinstitutional interaction, but it has proved much more difficult to force a new collective representation or mutual awareness on these institutions, whether through coercive, mimetic or normative means. Yet what has become clear is that the economic success of localities in a global economy will depend increasingly upon the articulation between institutional thickness and "economic" variables which make it worthwhile for industry to remain in a locality. Finding local economic integrity in a globalised world thus might be possible in principle, but if we take the institutionalising processes identified above seriously, this suggests that the option is probably open best to those localities with proven institutional capability.

Conclusion: institutional thickness and urban regeneration

The argument put forward in this chapter has been that, in an era of globalisation, it is still possible for some localities to develop their economy on a cumulative and circular basis; that is, to "hold down the global" as a basis for endogenous development. It has been suggested that as central nodes of representation, interaction and innovation within global industrial networks, such places are the privileged sites of networks and relationships of exchange articulated on a global scale. In being poles of industrial excellence and expertise, they possess the magnet-like ability to attract new rounds of investment and entrepreneurship, and, thereby, to continue to remain as centres of industrial agglomeration offering a variety of external economies of scope and scale to individual firms.

It has also been suggested in this chapter that the economic success of such centres of agglomeration is strongly dependent on their ability to offer a certain "institutional thickness" to support and embed the economic life of firms and markets. Similar to the line of argument of institutionalists such as Granovetter (1985) and Hodgson (1988, 1993) who have sought to theorise the centrality of social and cultural relations in economic processes, we proposed the need for a broader definition of the term. We suggested that institutional thickness amounts to a combination of features including: the presence of many institutions; interinstitutional interaction; a culture of collective representation; identification with a common industrial purpose; and shared norms and values which serve to constitute the "social atmosphere" of a particular locality. Thus, institutions were broadly conceived to include not only formal organisations, but also more informal conventions, habits and routines which are sustained over time and through space. Similarly, "thickness" is conceived to stress the strong presence of both institutions and institutionalising processes, combining to constitute a framework of collective support for individual agents. Implicit to the argument was also the tacit stress on the inclusive nature of such collective support, reaching out to and involving the majority of individuals and groupings in the local economy.

How does such institutional thickness help a locality to become or remain a "territorialised" economic system? In the most favourable cases, the different determinants of institutional thickness brought together, produce six outcomes. The first is the persistence of local institutions. The second is the construction and deepening of an archive of commonly held knowledge of both the formal and tacit kinds. The third is institutional flexibility; that is, the ability of organisations in a region to both learn and change. The fourth is high innovation capacity, as the common property of a locality. The fifth is the ability to extend trust and reciprocity. Finally, and uniquely, is the sense of a widely held common project, which serves to mobilise the local economic system as a whole with speed and efficiency.

Table 4.1 Institutional dominance

Form of institution	Institutional type		
	Economic	Political	Cultural
Structural–exchange	Centrality in economic transactions	Centrality in elite policy networks / ability to organise policy initiatives	Agglomeration and market centrality in media advertising, art publishing, etc.
Strategic	Headquarters control; role of banks in mobilisation of money capital	Role in national politics, augmented by financial resources and votes	Foundations, cultural projects, etc.
Cognitive aesthetic	Innovation in products, channel investments, management concepts and styles, etc.	Cultural authority of policy centres and foundations, media, press, intellectuals, etc.	Positioning in national and international imagination, ability to generate image

Source: adapted from Di Maggio (1993)

These outcomes are the product of a complex set of institutional conditions, which are not ubiquitously available. This is precisely why only some territories have been able to become centres of economic agglomeration. The development challenge is not only that of creating and consolidating institutional thickness, but of making it work to secure dominance over other competing localities.

Capital cities and core metropolitan regions are clearly one type of locality which can derive competitive advantage from the presence of many institutions of governance in economic, political and cultural life. The recent work of Di Maggio (1993) attempts to position cities within a set of different but overlapping networks of influence that depend upon both institutional type and form of institution (Table 4.1). Di Maggio points to three chief types of institutional dominance that cities can attain: these are economic, political and cultural. In turn, each of the different types of dominance can be related to different forms of institutions. The first of these consists of *structural* networks and results from a single concentration of activities and actors in a place which forces activities and actors in other places to transact/exchange work through them. This is a classical geographical definition of centrality as a network of more or less centralised places which allows external economies and economies of agglomeration to be derived by some places but at the expense of others. Structural networks are usually slow to change because they involve considerable sunk costs, whether these be the weight of corporate headquarters, the main offices of political parties or a conglomeration of museums and art galleries.

A second institutional form is *strategic*; that is, it includes the ability of places to be the core part of influence coalitions. Such networks are less fixed than structural networks, are likely to change more quickly, and result from the ability of coalitions to manipulate much more mobile resources (such as money, capital, jobs or votes). Of course,

> . . . structural dominance still matters, because actors from central places can bring more resources to the table than those in structurally peripheral locations. But the exercise of strategic dominance may operate . . . to set parameters for the routine exchanges out of which structural dominance emerges, laying down the tracks that . . . bear the traffic of short term transactions. (Di Maggio 1993, p. 7)

Finally there is a third institutional form, *cognitive-aesthetic* dominance; that is, the ability of a city to reign over the national or international imagination, such that it is not only a place which is well imaged, but also a place where innovation occurs, tastes are defined and models of management style constructed. Such dominance will rest in part on the willingness of actors in other cities and regions to concede that the ideas/ images formulated in such a city or region are credible. That is, a city or region must have *cultural authority*.

Clearly, different leading cities will have different forms of institutional dominance. Thus Di Maggio points out that New York has high economic and cultural dominance, but very little political dominance because of its inability to control strategic networks. In Britain, London and the South East have high economic, political and cultural dominance. Other cities and regions are not able to achieve the same combination.

Such institutional dominance, of course, is not unique to major cities. One of the interesting revelations of the literature on new Marshallian industrial agglomerations is that institutional thickness and dominance feature also in localities which dominate a particular industry. These might include craft areas in semi-rural settings or inner-city districts, or regional economies clustered around several urban centres and processing a degree of institutional or political autonomy. Though very different in terms of their size and settlement patterns, these agglomerations have in common an institutional thickness centred around a particular industrial cluster. Their institutional capacity in a given industry dwarfs that of other areas competing in the same sector.

Institutional thickness, thus, refers to the capacity of places to develop, consolidate and transmit structures of representation, interaction and innovation. This capacity is independent of the size or "urbanness" of a locality. This is a distinction worth emphasising because, increasingly, the academic and policy literature on urban regeneration appears to be

assuming that cities, as centres of social agglomeration and institutionalisation of socio-economic life, can become centres of economic development
and growth along Marshallian lines.

In many provincial or old industrial cities, for example, emerging policy
action appears, albeit unconsciously, to wish to capture various
institutional powers, through some intuitive belief that local institutional
thickness may be a necessary condition for local economic regeneration.
But less questioned has been whether this is a challenge which such cities
are in a position to meet. One of the distinctive features of less developed
or disadvantaged urban areas is that their historical integration into the
global capitalist project has stripped them of any coherent or cohesive
institutional infrastructure as well as a common agenda which might serve
to develop structures of dominance. More often than not, these cities are
locked into by narrowly bounded alliances between powerful local
politicians, successful local businesses and bodies representing cultures of
"colonisation" (e.g. local branches of transnational corporations, international financial institutions, national business associations, central
government departments, national professional bodies, etc.) (Amin and
Tomaney 1993; Hudson 1992). Thus, while they may well be capable of
developing supply-side initiatives of the sort described above, and going
some way towards interinstitutional collaboration, the key *cultural*
foundations for extended, locally rooted growth (e.g. "studied" trust,
community-wide shared norms, distinctively local traditions, etc.) are likely
to be more difficult to build. Indeed, often the irony is that existing
dominant institutional cultures constitute the main obstacle to changes
which, by definition, represent a threat to local development trajectories
strongly based on sectionalism.

If, therefore, a local institutional thickness which amounts to more than
the sum of many institutions and many initiatives is necessary for
Marshallian local economic regeneration, then the prospects of many
"fragmented" local economies must surely look bleak. However, the case
for the need for *locally based* institutional thickness as a precondition for
urban economic regeneration is not proven. In Britain, and we suspect
elsewhere, part of the insistence upon local "proactivity" appears to be
related to the pursuit of market-led, non-interventionist policy choices at
both the national level, and, to a lesser extent, at the supranational level.
One wonders whether in the context of a different set of national and
supranational institutional choices, the case for local institutional thickness
might somewhat weaken. For instance, the commitment by national
governments and international bodies to a set of industrial and welfare
policies as well as infrastructural programmes (from roads to telecommunications, training and education) in which the objective of promoting
the interests of less favoured cities and regions remains a central priority,
would considerably reduce the pressure for effort only at the local level to

stimulate local economic growth activity. Such a framework would reduce the burden on local areas to develop programmes for which they have limited resources or competence. It would also reduce the onus imposed by Marshallian institutionalism for localities to develop social and cultural attributes beyond their reach.

An *absolute* defence of local institutional thickness, thus, does not necessarily follow from the analysis of the changing nature of the local–global institutional nexus in earlier sections. If anything, our analysis has implied the need to see the local as a part of wider processes, and therefore subject to rules of governance at different spatial scales. The experience of the known industrial agglomerations suggests that what has mattered is having *access* to institutional thickness. If such support can be provided by the national state or other institutions, then the case for local action alone remains unconvincing. This, however, is not to deny that the pursuit of local institutional thickness is not a worthy objective. As the basis for securing local innovation capability, it is clearly indispensable.

In conclusion, there is clearly still some way to go before the ultimate power of the new institutional paradigm can be assessed as an explanation of geographically uneven development. We cannot claim to know much empirically about the strength or range of interactions between institutions in an area, the types of coalition that have resulted, or the construction of mutual awareness and common industrial agendas. Still less can we claim to know about the institutional requirements for economic regeneration in the context of less advantaged cities and regions.

5

Creating Discourses Rather Than Jobs: the Crisis in the Cities and the Transition Fantasies of Intellectuals and Policy Makers

JOHN LOVERING

The news from British cities in recent years has been deeply depressing. The 1990s opened with a panic over "joy-riding" and has seen a more general rise in crime, lawlessness, and fear (Campbell 1993). In 1993 the much-publicised murder of a child by two Liverpool children, the torture to death of a young woman in inner-city Manchester and the murder of a policeman in a drug-gang shooting in London, triggered something of a moral panic over the collapse of the urban social fabric. Wasting no time, the Home Secretary promised to increase the powers of the police and the severity of punishment for offenders, while calling for the restoration of nuclear family values and respect for "authority". If nothing else, this indicated that the classic themes of urban moral panic and social control occupied centre stage in the public debate on the cities (Hall 1988; Rees and Lambert 1985; Savage and Warde 1993). Although there are major national differences, especially concerning the salience of racism and the scale of urban poverty and crime, much the same could be said of the USA and other advanced capitalist countries (Marcuse 1993; Silver 1993; Cross and Keith 1993; Pinch 1993).

Managing Cities: The New Urban Context, edited by P. Healey, S. Cameron, S. Davoudi, S. Graham and A. Madani-Pour. © 1995 The Editors and contributors. Published in 1995 by John Wiley & Sons Ltd.

However, in the academy, and in the corridors of the local and national state, the most influential thinkers of the late 1980s and early 1990s have been preoccupied with a much more comforting story. A distinctive new intellectual and programmatic bias has come to dominate work on urban questions, according to which the chaos that surrounds us now is essentially of the past; the future will be better. This is the implication of a profound historic change in the geography of production which is creating the very real possibility that cities are about to regain economic importance and leverage. This argument is associated with a policy emphasis on the need to construct new social networks linking key local economic and political actors. If these important groups can get their acts together, so the story goes, and if urban management focuses on economic regeneration rather than on the "welfare" issues that have unfortunately preoccupied policy makers in recent decades, a new era of urban economic development may be anticipated. The end of the twentieth century may see something of a return to the urban dynamism of the end of the nineteenth, with a restoration of civic initiative, and a new era of beneficial urban economic change. The vital task now is to get on with reconstructing local governance around the agenda of competition.

This chapter argues that this "New Localist" story is profoundly misconceived and dangerously misleading. It rests on a mistaken analysis of what is actually happening in urban areas, and it is extraordinarily partial and incomplete as a guide to policy. It may help to explain the tone of this chapter to say that it began with my reaction to witnessing far too many sessions where academics have attempted to bamboozle the staffs of local authorities, training agencies, local politicians and members of voluntary organisations into the doctrine I describe here as "New Localist". The New Localist is something of a Straw Person, but certainly an influential one. However, few of the references cited below contain all the sins described herein.

There are indeed many indications of a new "localisation" of economic development, but in reality these are not the consequence of some fundamental autonomous change in the spatial dynamics of capitalist economic development. On the whole, they are the result of political decisions at the level of the national state and international agencies. Correspondingly, the "localistic" character of current economic restructuring has social and spatial implications quite different from, and generally much less benign than, those suggested by the new orthodoxy.

However, this is not meant to suggest that all is doom and gloom. The new political economy of the cities contains new contradictions which raise some new possibilities. The entry of new actors claiming to contribute to local economic policy raises the prospect of new political agendas. The development of new fora for debate and implementation of policy opens up the possibility of broadening the debate about the social meaning and purpose of the city, the nature of the urban polity. At root, the new political economy potentially creates a new politics concerned with the relationship between the local and the global. In order to make the most of it, however, it is first necessary to escape from the intellectual straitjacket imposed by the fashionable "New Localism".

The "New Localism"

Since the mid-1980s, a wave of "localisation" has transformed the organisation of central government, local government, the corporate sector and the voluntary sectors. This is particularly marked in Britain (Townroe and Martin 1992, p. 21; Lawless and Haughton 1992), but is also evident in France (Le Gales 1992) and the USA (Judd and Parkinson 1990a; see also other chapters in this book). This tendency is not only described but also strongly advocated in a flood of glossy policy literature emanating from government departments, local authorities, training agencies, business groups, and innumerable consultants in the UK and elsewhere.

The policy literature draws on academic work, and it is here that the intellectual legitimacy of the New Localism is established. As discussed in the introduction to this volume, in the past decade a number of academic observers have claimed that some sort of historical transition is under way in the organisation of capitalist production. Until recently the most popular narrative concerned the supposed demise of a social form known as "Fordism" and its displacement by post-Fordism. This story now appears to have been absorbed into a wider claim for the social and cultural transition to postmodernity, within which post-Fordism refers to the dimension of production (Cooke 1990b; Cross and Keith 1993; Dear 1991; Harvey 1989a; Soja 1989; Lash and Urry 1993). The story begins with the economy; it is asserted that the regulation of the function of accumulation is shifting down from the national to the local level (Hoggett 1987; Marshall 1989; Stoker 1989). This in turn creates a new local convergence of interests between capital, labour and other local constituencies (Mayer 1992, p. 266). Provided they organise appropriately, cities can now hope to play a more active and rewarding role in the world economy. The corollary is the possibility of a new city-centred form of world economic organisation, of the kind long espoused by Jane Jacobs, formerly dismissed by many as romantic fantasy (Jacobs 1985).

The plot develops through excursions into various empirical case studies which are thought to offer lessons as to how this potential can be realised (Piore and Sabel 1984; Scott and Cooke 1988; Scott 1988; Sabel et al. 1988). The most commonly cited European examples are the so-called "Third

Italy" and Baden-Württemburg, although the list is amended at intervals. The success of such localities is attributed to the existence of networks of private–public relationships through which productive knowledge "embedded" in spatially discrete communities can be mobilised (Granovetter 1985; Harrison 1992; Cooke 1990b). Whatever the intentions of academic authors, these studies tend to be cited as a group by policy analysts who draw relatively simple, transferable lessons concerning the importance of nurturing new networks of producers and bringing about a business environment characterised by trust and cooperation, alongside measures to improve the skills and marketability of local labour (Stoker 1989; Scott 1988). "Networking" is the current policy buzzword, as reflected for example in the recent European Commission White Paper on growth and employment (CEC 1993).

The Right has long argued that the problems of cities are worsened by, if not entirely attributable to, bureaucratic government, and that the solution lies in replacing politicians by managers (*The Economist* 1993). The "New Localist" myth leads to a somewhat similar emphasis; local prospects depend primarily on the construction of a "post-Fordist" apparatus of local governance which can create the conditions for transforming the supply side (Stoker 1990). It is but a small step to argue that the precondition for economic improvement in the cities is "better leadership" (Judd and Parkinson 1990a; Fainstein 1990). The temptation to bring (or rather sell) this good news to practitioners has been enhanced by the growing pressure on academic institutions to generate income. Innumerable consultancy reports and courses advise local policy makers that they are entering a new age and have no choice but to adopt the new policy paradigm, modernising their institutions and habits accordingly (Hoggett 1987; Stoker 1990; Solesbury 1993).

The spurious basis in theory

The academic foundation upon which the New Localism is erected is Regulation Theory (Stoker 1990; Scott and Cooke 1988). The Regulation School emerged through attempts to introduce more sensitivity to civil society and the state into Marxist analyses of capitalist development (Jessop 1992c; Lipietz 1992a). Its best exponents have used it as a heuristic device to explore the way in which these dimensions have been restructured in parallel in specific historic and national contexts (Aglietta 1979; van der Pijl 1989). This is not the way in which it has been used by the theoreticians of the New Localism.

Firstly, they freeze Regulation Theory into a rigid historical transition model, transforming it from an approach to a dogma. Innumerable lists are offered contrasting Fordism to post-Fordism (or modernism to postmodernism). The replacement of a supposedly ubiquitous Fordist economic order by its post-Fordist sequel becomes a grinding historical inevitability. This is a gross distortion of reality — for a sample of critiques, see Thrift (1988), Jessop (1992b), Lovering (1990b), Amin and Malmberg (1992), Brenner and Glick (1991) and Pudup (1992). The enormous diversity of real-world restructuring cannot be reduced to this sort of binary switchover (Gordon 1988; Massey 1993; Amin and Thrift 1994; Lovering 1990a). It is only by forcing reality into the New Localist dualistic formula that the case studies so often cited can appear to confirm the argument. There is in fact nothing new about the emergence of new growth sectors in new places, accompanied by local institutional development. These features have characterised uneven development since the beginnings of industrialisation (Marshall 1987; Harvey 1985a; Storper and Walker 1989). The examples identified as paradigmatic in the New Localist literature may be simply the latest examples.

Secondly, the New Localist appropriation of Regulation Theory reproduces the theoretical problems which tend to subvert the parent theory. These derive from the structuralist separation of the abstract realms of the economic, the political, and civil society. Despite their avowed intentions, Regulation School writers have tended to treat these as empirically separate domains, and to prioritise the first (Jessop 1992b; Brenner and Glick 1991). The New Localism places all the weight on the supposedly autonomous transformation of the regime of accumulation, and as a result treats the mode of social regulation as derivative. (Peck and Tickell (1992b) seem to reproduce this, while Goodwin et al. (1993) and Jessop (1992b) criticise it.) As a result there is no serious analysis of politics and the state, the transformation of "the local" is viewed as an effect of economic forces independent of the state and national and international political influences. In more fashionable sociological language, the constitutive role of reflexivity on the part of policy makers and implementers is ignored (Lash and Urry 1993).

This is to ignore the politically constructed nature of local reality. The legal system defining contracts, the social relationships which are conducive to trust and cooperation amongst employers, the infrastructure of transport links which determine the comparative costs of different localities, etc., have long been national rather than local in origin in western Europe, especially Britain (Reynolds 1992). This has been a critical aspect of state–society relations since the New Deal precipitated the formation of national welfare states (Davis 1987; Savage and Warde 1993).

I would argue that the major influence leading to "localisation" over the past fifteen years has been a series of changes in these political parameters. In Britain the transition from the 1978 Inner Urban Areas Act to the 1987 "Action for Cities", the effective removal of local council control of housing, the requirement for competitive tendering, the obligation on DLOs (Direct Labour Organisations, formerly in-house suppliers of services to local authorities) to make a 5% return, the removal of local authority control of the administration of education and health, the development of urban development corporations, the growing role of the private sector, the development of the TEC (Training and Enterprise Council) network, and the Urban Regeneration Agency, have created a new *de facto* local economic policy apparatus. Yet control of finance and broad policy principles remains highly centralised (especially in Britain). The substance of localisation has also been influenced by other national political/economic strategies, including the deregulation of the labour market and denationalisation of collective bargaining, promotion of the finance sector and property development, and attempts to attract foreign investment (Green 1989; Michie 1992).

Thirdly, the New Localist version of Regulation Theory not only neglects the state, it also neglects non-state dimensions of the social mode of regulation, the complexities of civil society in places and across space. New Localist tracts assert the primordial importance of place, yet a growing literature demonstrates that place is not absolute: its social substance is highly uneven. The extent to which a locality can really be regarded as a coherent crucible of social relations is, to say the least, contentious (Harvey 1993; Massey 1993). Many studies suggest that the geographical contexts within which identity and culture are defined may be changing profoundly, partly because of a "globalisation of culture" (Harvey 1989a; Lash and Urry 1993; Massey 1991a; Featherstone 1993; Robins this volume). Ominously absent from the New Localist story is any serious recognition of the relationship between place and signs of social division such as gender and race (Wilson 1991). The meaning of place and space is highly variable between, and amongst, men and women (Rose 1993; Wheelock this volume). Similarly, the social integrity of "the city" is profoundly limited by the exclusionary effects of institutionalised racism (Keith 1993). The New Localist story begs all the important questions concerning identity, power, and domination. And it does so in an immensely patronising way. Academics and policy makers, who operate within social networks stretched across a wide (often international) geographic space, have decided that the locality that matters for that Other known as "ordinary people" is the city or region they live in.

Localisation in the real world

If the theoretical premises of the New Localism are flimsy, its grip on recent history is no less so. Localisation in practice has been taking place against the background of continued urban economic stagnation. And despite the fanfare, there is little evidence to suggest that this is soon to be reversed.

There has been some highly visible redevelopment in city centres and bursts of activity in "Edge cities"; but there are few signs of overall economic improvement in many, perhaps most, large cities in the advanced capitalist countries. Meanwhile, there is no shortage of evidence that the plight of a large proportion of city dwellers has worsened and will continue to do so (Marcuse 1993). In Britain, urban counties consistently experienced the slowest growth of output in the 1980s, with Merseyside stuck at the bottom of the list (Table 5.1). While Bournemouth, London, Bristol, Leeds and Leicester did relatively well (Champion and Green 1992), it would be absurd to suggest that this means all their citizens benefited significantly. Urban counties monopolise the top of the list of authorities scoring highly on indicators of social deprivation: Knowsley, Manchester, Liverpool, Hackney, Tower Hamlets, Eastington, Southwark, Middlesborough, and Salford (Forrest and Gordon 1993). Those cities which have registered a fall in unemployment appear to have done so mainly because people have moved out.

During the recession of the early to mid 1990s, southern English cities experienced job losses and social crisis on a scale previously reserved for the North. For example, Bristol did relatively well in the 1980s but is suffering classic urban problems in the 1990s. In terms of unemployment rates it has swapped places with Leeds, but while the latter is crowded with gleaming new office buildings, it is also straining under the weight of familiar urban social problems. The British urban "success story" of the 1990s has not seen a reduction in violence, fear and social polarisation.

The focus on place marketing

The proliferation of new economic and labour market actors in cities is sometimes seen as indicating a shift from a "managerial" to a more "entrepreneurial" policy stance (Judd and Parkinson 1990a). This labelling is more than a shade euphemistic. "Entrepreneurship" implies a putting together of various productive activities to bring about a technological innovation, creating something new. Recent developments in many British cities would be more accurately described as "commodification", attempting to package and sell what is already there.

In order to sell a commodity it is necessary to differentiate it from others; the more saturated the market, the more urgent the need for product differentiation. The image industry grew enormously in the postwar decades by presenting itself as an aid to private businesses struggling to sell more-or-less identical products. It soon found additional openings in the political marketplace where politicians were doing much the same. In the 1980s it found profitable new opportunities in the apparatus of the British state. As local government became involved in local economic development it too became a major customer.

Table 5.1 GPD growth rate by UK district 1981–89*

Above UK average		Below UK average	
Clwyd	176.7	Lincoln	104.9
Bucks	175.0	Hants	103.9
Northants	156.8	Gt London	102.7[†]
W. Sussex	154.4	Dyfed	100.7
Cambridge	143.4	W. Midlands	98.2[†]
Surrey	140.2	Lothian	98.0
Oxon	141.8	Gt Manchester	96.4[†]
Berks	142.5	Cleveland	95.7[†]
Dorset	134.8	Nottingham	94.7[†]
Beds	134.6	Mid Glam	94.5[†]
Humberside	133.3	Strathclyde	92.8[†]
Warwick	132.6	Northumberland	92.1
Shropshire	132.2	Highland	90.9
Suffolk	128.7	Tayside	90.4
I-o-W	128.7	Borders	90.1
Wilts	128.4	Dumfries/Galloway	86.1
Hereford/Worcester	127.5	Central Scot	85.1
Gloucester	125.2	W. Glam	82.4[†]
Norfolk	125.0	Durham	81.5
Somerset	124.7	Tyne & Wear	80.0[†]
Gwynedd	121.6	S. Yorks	72.5[†]
Kent	121.0	Fife	66.9
Leicester	120.5	Merseyside	66.6[†]
Cornwall	120.4		
Sth Glam	119.4		
Gwent	118.7		
Staffs	117.0		
Cumbria	116.7		
N. Yorks	115.9		
Grampian	114.0		
Lancs	113.7		
Herts	111.8		
E. Sussex	111.7		
Avon	111.3		
Essex	111.0		
Cheshire	110.6		
Derbys	108.2		
(N. Ireland	105.8)		
Devon	105.7		
W. Yorks	105.5		

* UK average = 105.3
[†] Urban areas

Source: *Regional Trends* 1992, Central Statistical Office, London

From the 1970s, local economic policy consisted largely of efforts to market the locality in order to attract mobile industrial capital (Massey and Meegan 1982; Dicken and Tickell 1992). By the late 1980s the marketing effort was widened to attract property investment (Fainstein and Young 1992; Healey 1992c; Leyshon and Thrift 1990). The growth of the tourist industry has added consumers to the target group for place image-making in the 1990s (Haughton and Lawless 1992). Place marketing is now virtually the core activity in local economic development. It is generally supplemented by some measures to support local enterprise and influence the supply side of the labour market, especially through basic training. But these efforts tend to be modest in the extreme, and in many cases provision has recently contracted as a result of limited public funding. Local economic strategy as a whole now seems to generate more publicity than change. It is certainly not geared to any serious extent towards the supply-side transformation which occupies centre-stage in the New Localist account.

However, if there is not much going on, there are a large number of actors involved in pretending that there is. The growth of Economic Development departments within local authorities, the emergence of professional managers in local government, the sprouting of Urban Development Corporations drawing in private sector developers, the creation of Training and Enterprise Councils (TECs) with a clientele of training providers, and the construction of local business leadership teams, have created a new cohort of local economic-policy actors. Local governance has been part-privatised. Partnership is firmly established as the cornerstone of local authority economic policy, embedded in the requirement in the Local Government and Housing Act 1989 and the creation of TECs, that local economic development policies should focus on objectives relating to the private sector (Peck 1992). In many cities significant industrial interests have coalesced around Business Leadership Teams (Robinson and Shaw 1991). A number of large international and national firms have responded positively, although Britain lacks major private sector urban managers when compared with French industrial interests organised through Chambers of Commerce, German industrialists via the training system, or well-resourced community-minded private companies like Burger King or Hewlett Packard in the USA. Consequently, the TECs spun off from the public sector are usually critical to the new networks. TECs are derived from American Private Industry Councils plus the homeground experience of "Business in the Community". The UK government went further than the USA in insulating the new apparatus from local electorates (Miller 1990, p. 208). Many TECs aspire to move beyond their originally intended training role to take the central role in place marketing, an impulse that appears to have grown as public funding for training has declined (Meager 1991, p. 17).

Business people and development interests have a new prominence in the new local economic-policy apparatus. Robinson and Shaw suggest that as a result "a newly empowered urban elite akin to the philanthropic businessmen of the Victorian era" is emerging (Robinson and Shaw 1991, p. 65; Moore 1991). High-profile examples include John Hall in Newcastle, Don and Roy Richardson in Birmingham, Desmond Pitcher or the Moores family in Liverpool (Blackhurst and Cope 1993). But in many cases the construction of local networks has been hindered by conflicts between commercial and manufacturing sectors (as in Bristol), the lack of a generally acknowledged industrial elite (as in Liverpool) or mutual suspicion between private and public sectors (as in Manchester — Peck 1992). In general, the new band of local entrepreneur-heroes are very far from being latter-day Victorian business-politicians.

Moreover, institution building does not necessarily imply economic transformation (see Chapter 4). Lacking real influence over significant investment decisions, the apparatus of urban economic governance is often under pressure to "spectacularise" policy. This is sometimes literal; fireworks displays in Liverpool and kite festivals in Bristol are both funded by urban development corporations as contributing to a change in the local image. Pleasant though these are, they can hardly be regarded as representing the kind of transformative economic intervention foreseen by the New Localism. Localisation in practice, largely confined to place marketing, is most unlikely to produce a significant net increase in jobs, but it fuels a certain postmodern inventiveness. The Beatles are now everywhere in Liverpool despite the fact that they left town thirty years ago and one of them is dead. They serve as an acceptably uncontroversial place identifier, as indicated by the fact that Paul McCartney was invited to sign the City Challenge bid.

From place marketing to "community"

There is an irresistible tendency for the establishment of a local identity as viewed "from outside" to be accompanied by attempts to establish that identity from the "inside". The result is a number of attempts to "bring the community back in" (Robinson and Shaw 1991).

The term "community" could refer to a territorial organisation, a communality of experience, an aspect of identity, a spatially rooted *gemeinschaft*, or forms of association independent of the state (Young 1990b; Mingione, this volume). While academics mark time pondering the relationship between place-as-community and place-as-commodity in the dim light of the post-Fordism/postmodernism debates (e.g. Soja and Hooper 1993), the apparatus of local governance gets on with the practical business of constructing "community" out of the institutional and personal material to hand.

This has had a major impact on community-oriented organisations, including in many cases those identified with social groups who do not automatically benefit from contemporary economic change. A review of TEC labour market assessments, Local Authority Economic Development statements, or the pronouncements of business leadership teams and urban development corporations would reveal innumerable references "from above" to the need to consider "disadvantaged groups", and lists of organisations or individuals identified with them. From "below", access to grants has become largely conditional upon "playing the training/ employment game" (Ahmed et al. 1993). The admission of selected community-oriented organisations has changed the representation of local interests. Until the mid-1980s the local regional representative of the Trades Union Congress would usually have sufficed to represent employees to local authorities and employers. In the new forums there are likely to be a galaxy of representatives standing for a diversity of ethnic, cultural, gender, or other categories. One organisation, "Common Purpose", has been set up explicitly to create an informed pool of members drawn from diverse local communities who may become future "community leaders".

This reconstruction from above of local economic citizenship is shaped by the patronage of the new regulators, rather than by universalistic norms of the type embodied in traditional democratic processes and at least formally reflected in traditional local government. One effect would seem to be to activate familiar conventional social categories. In Bristol, for example, a measure to target training and employment opportunities on inner-city residents was described by an employer as "focused on the black quarter" (Lovering 1991a). The potential to create a colonial class of "ethnic Godfathers" which Jeffers describes in relation to Labour local authorities in the 1980s remains within the new apparatus of local governance (Jeffers 1993, p. 160; see also Cashmore 1991).

However, the scope for delivering real resources to the new clientele is severely limited. In Britain, initiatives targeted on "disadvantaged groups" are overwhelmingly confined to confidence building, giving information on rights, low- to medium-level training, and job interview guarantees (Lovering 1991a; Peck and Tickell 1992b). These measures are usually implemented by committed people working hard to achieve a modicum of social improvement and a more lasting "demonstration effect". But the impact on the local labour market remains marginal, and is likely to result in the displacement of one low-paid worker by another (Turok 1991). In this context the recruitment of representatives of "disadvantaged groups" to the apparatus of local governance clearly raises the threat of institutional co-optation (Ahmed et al. 1993). The belief that the post-Fordist or postmodern urban economy creates the potential for a significant redistribution of economic benefits and social power, especially to women, minority groups, and environmental interests (Mayer 1992, p. 263), remains a pious hope.

In many US cities, as capital and elite groups moved out, the responsibility for managing what was left was handed over to blacks (Weir 1993, Davis 1993). Localisation in western Europe and especially Britain may be leading to analogous developments, as a new community leadership is recruited to identify with and implement a minimalist strategy based on place marketing. The parallel should not be surprising, since British urban policy in the 1980s has consciously drawn on the US example (Hambleton 1990).

The old behind the new

The argument above is that the reconstruction of local governance in practice has little to do with the emergence of "new regional/local economies", new industrial districts, entrepreneurial cities, etc. anticipated by the New Localism. It has much more to do with the deliberate construction of new local political actors and discourses, from above. Putting this into the language of the Regulation School: real-world localisation is primarily a matter of modifying the mode of social regulation rather than localising the regime of accumulation. Although it has little impact on the trajectory of development of the local economy or the opportunity structures of the local labour market, it has created a new service class, including individuals from business, local government, academia, the community-oriented private sector, voluntary organisations and other interest groups, and perhaps many readers of this book. It also has a significant impact on the *disorganisation* of political interests (Fainstein and Young 1992, p. 233; see also Fainstein, this volume).

Their efforts are unlikely to lead to significant and inclusive economic change. Leading industrialists such as Sir Graham Day are not alone in thinking that the worsening of unemployment and development of an "underclass" will continue (Goodhart 1993), although it is important to beware of the loaded nature of this term (Mingione 1993b; Morris 1993). Against this background, the localisation of institutional structures would seem to represent a change in the form rather than the substance of policy for the cities. The latter continues to consist *de facto* of predominantly *ad hoc* responses to the disruption caused by the continued economic evacuation of urban space. A few global cities contain sectors and groups which are not becoming economically marginal, but these do not include more than a faction of their citizens. London, for example, has a GNP equivalent to that of Saudi Arabia (McWilliams 1993), but it also contains the greatest number of poor people and homeless in Britain. The City of London, the financial centre, employs fewer than half a million people. They have to make their way to work (few of them live nearby) through an environment of increasing squalor, poverty and violence which they strive to ignore and urban managers attempt to obscure (Fainstein et al. 1992).

The New Localist myth diverts attention away from the fact that the *de facto* response to urban economic restructuring is predominantly concerned with social control; the management of social distress and discontent, rather than economic transformation to remove it (Rees and Lambert 1985; Hall 1988). Such policies continue to be mediated by ideologies of the "deserving" versus the "undeserving" poor, cross-cut by ideologies of gender and race (Wheelock this volume; Cross and Keith 1993). The only substantially resourced element of urban policy which can be said to be targeted on young unemployed males, the marginalised children of the Thatcher years, is policing (Campbell 1993). The fable spun by New Localists bears little relation to these realities.

Urban policy as the spatial dimension of national and international policy

The energetic construction of a localised apparatus, and a rhetoric to match, reflect the wider reconfiguration of the national state in the closing years of the twentieth century (Johnston 1993). Two aspects of this are important here. Firstly, the "hollowing out of the state" as it withdraws from welfare and developmental roles (Jessop 1993) has a direct bearing on the cities. Secondly, some of the former functions of the state are being transferred to the international level, creating a new transnational network of policy makers. This has played a major role in establishing a new consensus as to urban management policy paradigms (a consensus of which the New Localism is an offshoot).

The contraction of the welfare state

The creation of a localised economic policy apparatus is closely linked to attempts to reduce central state involvement in welfare and redistributive functions (Le Gales 1992; Marcuse 1993; Davis 1993). Social policy in the 1990s is ubiquitously characterised by a reduction in the "social wage", and weaker efforts to redress inequality in incomes, housing, health and other indicators (Hirst and Thompson 1992, p. 371). It is not often noted that this particularly affects cities. In Britain, the proportion of city dwellers receiving state benefit transfers is significantly higher than the national average. The proportion of households containing only dependent people (children, the sick or retired) in the industrial towns of the North, North West and North East is around three times that of the non-urban South East. The disparity in the percentage unemployed is even greater. The incidence of limiting illness is around twice as high in northern urban areas. The highest concentrations of council housing, and of old people with a car, are in these same urban areas. On all these indicators, Inner London is a massive exception to the rule in the South East (Forrest and Gordon 1993).

While the burden of economic restructuring is disproportionately passed to the cities, city dwellers are disproportionately blamed for the consequences. The vilification of unmarried mothers, and the criminalisation of unemployed young males and ethnic minorities, target social groups which are disproportionately found in the cities. Lone parents account for up to four times as many households in northern cities as in the rural South, and ethnic minorities are largely confined to urban areas. The delegitimisation of the urban poor in the name of the values of the more supposedly "normal" groups who live in the suburbs is an old and dishonourable theme (Hall 1988; Rees and Lambert 1985; Savage and Warde 1993). The political disenfranchisement of the urban poor in the past decade has been more pronounced in the USA than in Britain (Galbraith 1992; Davis 1993), but in this as in other respects, the USA holds up a picture which shows something of the future for European cities, so long as currently fashionable policy orthodoxies prevail (Hambleton 1990).

The "transnationalisation" of the state and the ascendancy of neo-liberalism

Those policy orthodoxies are remarkable international. The role of key policy thinkers in Britain appears to have been to act as channels for ideas developed elsewhere. Perhaps the most important influence on urban outcomes over the 1980s and 1990s has been the denationalisation of policy. There is no space here for a full analysis, and a few suggestions will have to suffice.

A number of observers have drawn attention elsewhere to the "transnationalisation" of the state (Cox 1992; Gill 1992; Leyshon 1992). International organisations such as the IMF, World Bank, GATT, G7, etc., and NGOs (non-governmental organisations) have become important sources of policy and authority alongside national states (Picciotto 1991, p. 53). This fractured and heterogeneous network, described by Cox as a *nébuleuse* rather than a hierarchically ordered apparatus, is not responsible to any formal polity (Cox 1992, p. 30). It does what it does with relative impunity.

One of the truly distinctive features of the world economy in the last decade of this century, especially when compared with mid-century, is that capitalism is now "global but leaderless" (Glyn and Sutcliffe 1992). There is no transnational authority able to develop and administer a framework conducive to the generalisation of national growth strategies (of the kind which characterised the postwar period of growth inadequately described as "Fordism") (van der Pijl 1989). There is no coherent global or regional force able to impose or induce a new set of "regimes of accumulation" oriented towards long-term industrial investment, as happened under US hegemony after the Second World War (Lipietz 1992b; van der Pijl 1989; Ikenberry 1992). The international regulatory space which is sustained by the new "nébuleuse" is oriented to economic priorities other than the growth of output and employment. It is concerned above all with financial goals, especially the reduction of imbalances amongst the leading countries and the restoration of stability (Singh 1992, p. 36).

Process without goals

To various degrees the members of the "nébuleuse" of international and national actors share this neo-liberal agenda of reducing barriers to the flows of capital, especially the constraints imposed by the institutionalisation of labour and non-profit interests within the welfare state. The economic policy discourse at various levels is built predominantly on the metaphor of "enabling" market processes to work effectively, especially via "flexibility". This concern with the process of *adjustment to* market forces is matched by an almost complete lack of interest in the *structuring of* market forces (Dunford 1990). The organisational project on which agreement can be established tends to focus on *process* (adaptation) rather than goals (economic or social objectives). This rather extraordinary implication of neo-liberalism is vividly expressed in the policy prescriptions which regularly issue forth from the IMF and World Bank. The World Bank, for example, recently summarised its thinking on urban policy in the Third World in terms which should be extremely familiar to all students of urban policy in the First: policy should give priority to "improving the level and consumption of investment, reinforcing the institutional capacity for operation and maintenance, seeking opportunities for greater private sector involvement" (IBRD 1991, p. 3). The plight of the urban poor is to be alleviated not by redistribution or political empowerment but by "improving their productive contribution".

The same agenda is put more bluntly in a Brookings Institution study of Russia which insisted that "integration to the world economy should be used to drive domestic economic reforms rather than the other way round" (Hewett 1992, p. 2; see also R.H. Cox 1993). This dogma is reflected in Solesbury's assertion that a "welfare perspective" is no longer appropriate for urban policy in Britain (1993, p. 35). Since places are in competition with one another to attract and retain mobile assets, their proper objective can only be to develop and exploit their unique assets in pursuit of competitive advantage. The urban management "policy frame" must be based on the metaphor of the "player" and the "playing field".

The emergence of this international policy consensus suggests that the key development driving the current form of localisation is the precise opposite of that asserted by the "New Localist" story about post-Fordism. Rather than drifting from the national down to the local level, the regulation of the process of accumulation is becoming the business of an (unaccountable) international apparatus. The continued economic crisis of urban society, and the current urban management agenda, reflect a particular politically constructed relationship between the global and the local (Massey 1991a). Spatial development is a subordinate component of an international and national regulatory order tailored to globalising finance capital (Cox 1992; Corbridge 1992; Lovering 1993). The competition between places both reflects and sustains the absence of a national or international partnership around a developmental and socially inclusive economic project.

This is of course an over-generalisation. There are considerable regional and national differences; the triumph of goalless neo-liberalism is much more obvious in Britain, for example, than in France (see Chapter 7), let alone the industrialising countries of Pacific-Asia. At least at the level of rhetoric, the Clinton administration in the USA appears to promise something of a return to an agenda in which goals matter, and in which economic transformation begins with investment in people, shaping rather than following the market (Reich 1991). The "Delors faction" in the European Union represents a desire to shift Europe in a similar direction (CEC 1993). These may or may not augur important changes in the late 1990s.

Conclusion: alternatives

This chapter has argued that the prospects for the cities within the emergent international regulatory order, and national political agendas tailored to it, bear little relation to the brave new economic adventure portrayed by the New Localism (which is essentially a version of neo-liberalism with a radical gloss). The New Localism not only fails to recognise the importance of state structures and policy orthodoxies, it also fails to recognise itself as an active contributor to the latter. It is part of the problem.

It would be wrong to conclude, however, without suggesting that recent developments contain some positive seeds. The fragmentation of the state means that monolithic "boss government" of the kind that characterised many cities in the past will be less easy to maintain in the future. The various local policy actors, armed with their mission statements, are perhaps more clearly identifiable than in the past. But the lack of a forum for accountability leaves a new "democratic deficit". One way forward is therefore to seek to democratise the new apparatus. The attempt to impose an organising principle based on place when the social and economic meaning of place is becoming ever more problematic requires a great deal of ingenuity and is, thankfully, unlikely to proceed smoothly (see Chapter 2). The building of a new local apparatus draws in new participants and prompts new questions, not least that of what a strategic approach to the local economy might achieve and for whom (Lovering 1988; Haughton and Lawless 1992; Robinson and Shaw 1991). "Locality", as Massey has repeatedly stressed, is not a thing but a terrain of struggle (Massey 1993). The emphasis on place marketing to the detriment of distributional issues has already been questioned in a number of cases (in Birmingham, for example, the emphasis on high-profile property-focused development appeared to have been abandoned in 1993).

A wide range of academic work could inform such rethinking and establish a critique of the currently hegemonic ideology of urban management. The dominant policy frame (whether neo-liberal or new-localist) emphasises working *"downwards"* as if the task is to discipline the local into adaptation to the global (Corbridge 1992). This ignores the fundamental question of how local, national and international processes work *upwards* to affect the way the "global" is constituted. This is not only politically oppressive, as has been implied above, it is also intellectually outrageous. It disregards the entire point of radical (and even not-so-radical) work in economic geography since at least the 1970s (Lovering 1989). It entirely ignores the reflexive nature of social interaction and the socially and politically constructed nature of the economy and economic policy (Lash and Urry 1993). Rather than continue to grind out exercises in the (spurious) "logic of post-Fordism", academic resources could be much more productively employed in very different kinds of "thought experiment". Much may be learned, for example, by exploring the implications of different macrostructural scenarios for forms of restructuring and urban prospects.

In the British case, this especially means paying more attention to the European Union (Amin and Malmberg 1992). A modest real-world example helps to make this point; in 1993 the European Commission introduced a 130 million ECU scheme to compensate areas hit by defence job losses. This was a result of a political response at the local level to a spate of unrecoverable job losses, transmitted via internationally organised links (specifically within the European Socialist group) into the embryonic apparatus of the supranational European state. This example shows how local actions, provided they take a coherent political form, can modify the policy and resource context within which the local exists. The proposal following the Edinburgh summit to establish an urban regeneration fund might become another example (CEC 1992b). There has been little debate over the possibility of moving beyond pleas for cash from Brussels to demands to change what it is that "Brussels" represents (Begg and Moore 1992; Lovering 1993).

The neo-liberal (and New Localist) agenda sets an impossible task for reconstruction of city management. Its inevitable failure would seem likely to open up a more ambitious political debate in the 1990s. If intellectual work is to inform this it must abandon the New Localist spectacles and adopt a more theoretically and empirically broad-minded view of the political economy of the city.

6

Urban Redevelopment and Public Policy in London and New York

SUSAN S. FAINSTEIN

American and British local governments have, since the mid-1970s, responded to the pressures of world economic restructuring and cutbacks in national government support by actively pursing private investment. In London and New York, governmental leaders, confronting the flight of manufacturing and recognising the historical advantage of these cities as global control centres, have identified finance and advanced services as the leading edge of their economy. They have promoted these sectors mainly through providing them with appropriate space. Thus, economic development strategies have typically involved subsidies and regulatory relief to property development firms building speculative office space. Whether government programmes for property development actually do stimulate business is, however, an open issue (Turok 1992). Moreover, numerous studies have documented the highly uneven impacts of commercial revitalisation, which has disproportionately benefited highly skilled professionals and managers and offered very little for workers displaced from manufacturing industries (e.g. Parkinson et al. 1988; Squires 1989).

This chapter briefly examines urban redevelopment programmes in London and New York and the roles of planners in effecting urban redevelopment during the period 1980–92. The redevelopment scenario illustrates how the general processes of global change and current fashions in managing economic development are filtered through the particularities

Managing Cities: The New Urban Context, edited by P. Healey, S. Cameron, S. Davoudi, S. Graham and A. Madani-Pour. © 1995 The Editors and contributors. Published in 1995 by John Wiley & Sons Ltd.

of the local economy and polity in these cities. The chapter's main focus is the presentation of some suggestions for more progressive redevelopment policies. Although I am highly critical of many past practices, my argument assumes that flexibility and entrepreneurship in the municipal public sector are necessary to cope with the hypermobility of capital and the new international division of labour.

Economic development strategies

Within the United States, public–private cooperation has always formed the touchstone for urban redevelopment policy. Nevertheless, a detectable shift took place in the character of local programmes after 1974, as the federal government reduced its financial support and withdrew from its oversight role; the 1980 election of Ronald Reagan marked the virtual termination of major federal involvement in local redevelopment activities. The contraction in federal subsidies forced localities to turn to the private sector for start-up funds for major projects. Local governments became increasingly entrepreneurial in attempting to stimulate private investment, actively promoting their available sites and hawking a range of subsidies, training programmes, and expedited procedures designed to facilitate business operations. The departure from the past lay not in the priority given to private-sector desires, but in the heightened level of local governmental initiative in attracting private-sector involvement. In Britain, fiscal stress on the central government similarly constrained subsidies for urban development through the 1970s. Until then Britain had differed from the USA in allocating a larger and more independent role for the public sector, especially in housing construction. A sharp break in programme character also occurred in 1980, after the election of Margaret Thatcher's Conservative government. Although Thatcher's policy diverged from Reagan's in its centralisation of governmental functions, it had a similar thrust of emphasising private enterprise and pressing local governments into the role of supplicants to the private sector.

For much of this century, urban planning in both the UK and the USA concentrated on controlling and improving the physical environment. Until the 1970s, planning's justification lay in comprehensiveness, an orientation to the long-term, protection of the environment, and preservation of the public interest through orderly development and attention to the interests of all social groups. Numerous critics have contended that these goals were never attained, that planning always primarily benefited business interests, and that economic advantage has perennially constituted the real objective of city planning (e.g. Gans 1968; Harvey 1978). Nevertheless, even if planning has always aimed at producing private economic gain, its institutional setting, the rhetoric surrounding its attainment, and the *modus operandi* of planners changed in the 1980s as the manifest intent of planning switched from physical improvement to economic development. At the same time, the earlier construction of urban problems as defined by poverty and inner-city decline was reconstituted in terms of competitiveness and fiscal solvency (Beauregard 1993).

Revisions in the relationship between public-sector planners and private developers have their roots in the global changes that transformed urban economies and increased inter-urban competition. Within an extraordinarily fluid space economy, land development offered private investors opportunities for enormous profit; facilitating such development gave planners some leverage over the private sector. Governmental agencies had largely abdicated their earlier direct role in urban regeneration, whereby they acquired and serviced land and built public facilities. But government could use its tax and borrowing authority to lower development costs and thereby make projects more appealing to the investors on which the development industry depended, without incurring the high front-end expenditures entailed by the previous approach. Moreover, the large scale of the most profitable projects meant that almost none qualified for governmental approval without the relaxation of regulations, nor could they be developed without governmental contributions of infrastructure. This need for public intervention created the opening for bargaining, in which public officials traded governmental approvals or capital spending for private contributions to housing or public facilities. Nowhere was the new style of planning practised with more vigour than in London and New York.

London and New York

The policy histories of London and New York passed through a similar, although not precisely synchronous, set of stages in the years following the Second World War (Buck and Fainstein 1992). During the 1950s and 1960s, active public intervention resulted in large-scale development of housing and transport. In New York, during the politically turbulent period starting in the late 1960s, the city government under Mayor John V. Lindsay followed a two-pronged strategy. On the one hand it targeted the Manhattan core for regulatory relief and New York State funding of development. On the other, it directed federal funds to the poorest areas of the city for housing and community development programmes. Later in the seventies, when Labour controlled both the central and Greater London governments, it mounted a strategy for London similar to Lindsay's in New York in its emphasis on impoverished areas (Lawless 1989). Until its 1986 abolition, the Greater London Council (GLC) endeavoured to fuse an industry-based economic development strategy with political radicalism (Mackintosh and Wainwright 1987), while Labour-dominated borough councils stressed small-scale development and continued provision of social housing.

After the sharp economic downturn of the mid-1970s, however, funds available for inner-city investment shrunk. By the 1980s governing regimes in both cities devoted themselves to stimulating commercial growth (Fainstein et al. 1992). These regimes relied on real-estate development (in contrast to job training or infrastructure investment) as their primary strategies, addressing the office and housing needs of the upper echelons of the financial and advanced service industries participating in world economic coordination.

Publicly sponsored urban redevelopment proceeded through the swapping of public benefits for commitments of private investment, along with the melding of public and private powers into development corporations. These arrangements took a variety of forms, including, among others, the trading of planning permission in return for the construction of affordable housing; provision of cheap land and infrastructure as the *quid pro quo* for commercial investment; relaxation of building-size regulations in return for public amenities; the use of autonomous public agencies to put together deals for private developers; and the collaboration of public agencies with community organisations in low-income neighbourhoods to form local development corporations. In London, private investors within the Isle of Dogs enterprise zone — but nowhere else — received tax exemptions. New York did not have an enterprise zone and thus could offer no exemptions from federal tax and regulatory burdens; it freely, however, gave local capital and tax subsidies throughout the city to firms threatening to decamp for lower-cost environments.

Urban development corporations and other public–private organisations

The British and New York City governments relied heavily on urban development corporations (UDCs) to implement their redevelopment programmes. UDCs retain many of the governmental powers of their participating public agencies while not being subject to normal public-sector requirements, such as holding open public meetings, filing extensive reports of their activities, providing avenues for community participation, and conforming to civil service rules. Although ultimately responsible to public elected officials, UDCs operate much like private firms, employing the entrepreneurial styles and professional image-building techniques more customary to the corporate than governmental world (Lassar 1990; Squires 1989). British and New York development corporations are similar in many respects; the New York organisations, however, have no connection at all with the national government.

The London Docklands Development Corporation

The London Docklands Development Corporation (LDDC), established by Parliament in 1981 as the planning and development agency for 8.5 square miles of territory in East London, was the most prominent partnership agency in London throughout the 1980s. It received title to much of the vacant land in the redevelopment area and sold it cheaply to private developers. Public contributions consisted of an enormous infrastructure programme, overall planning and management, tax breaks within the Isle of Dogs enterprise zone, and a sales and public relations effort. Except for infrastructure planning, most of the energy of LDDC personnel went into selling the area to potential investors, and it mounted an extremely sophisticated and elaborate public relations and sales effort to do so. During the peak of London's property development boom, the LDDC was extraordinarily successful in bringing in private investment. By 1993, however, many Docklands projects, including the flagship Canary Wharf, were in bankruptcy.

The LDDC has been heavily attacked for emphasising roads at the expense of transit, encouraging development in an inaccessible area, causing a bias in the entire transportation investment programme of the UK towards the Docklands, and neglecting the housing and employment needs of the area's original residents (Association of London Authorities (ALA) and Docklands Consultative Committee (DCC) 1991; DCC 1988). (It should be noted, however, that while the service industries moving into the office complexes offered little employment for displaced dockers, they did provide clerical jobs for local women.) During the late 1980s, the LDDC increased its emphasis on job training and social programmes to benefit long-time occupants, but once the post-1989 property slump set in, it backed away from its social commitments and again began to concentrate single-mindedly on maintaining private investment in the area. Furthermore, the structure of the LDDC, under the control of a board appointed by the central government, excluded residents from the planning process (Lawless 1987; Church 1988). In the words of Bob Colenutt, who was employed by the local authorities to monitor Docklands development: "Power in Docklands lies outside the people we represent. It's with the big developers, the LDDC. The local authorities have very little power, and where they do, they don't use it" (interview with author, 12 July 1992).

New York partnership arrangements

In New York an array of development corporations provided the framework through which the city worked with private firms to foster physical development. The Public Development Corporation (PDC), renamed the Economic Development Corporation (EDC) in 1991, acted as the lead agency in collaborations with the private sector (Fainstein et al. 1989). Established as a quasi-independent local development corporation with a board of prominent business people, PDC differed from the LDDC in not having a limited geographical jurisdiction; rather its boundaries were coextensive with the city's. Its role, which has continued under the EDC format, was to act primarily as a financial intermediary, putting together packages of land improvements, tax abatements, and funding for specific development sites (Lin 1991). On several big projects it acted in tandem with New York State's Urban Development Corporation, a similarly constituted intermediary with greater powers of land taking and financing. The Department of City Planning, which technically has responsibility for land-use planning, largely deferred to the PDC/EDC's definition of the city's development strategy.

Other types of partnerships

Public–private partnerships did not comprise only business-dominated arrangements aimed at developing large office structures. Within London, non-profit housing associations have become the major entity responsible for developing affordable housing. They depend for funding on the Housing Corporation, a central government agency. Housing associations have a long history within London, stretching back to the philanthropic and church-based organisations that sponsored improved housing for slum-dwellers in the nineteenth century. While a subset of these associations are neighbourhood-based cooperatives, the great majority are run by boards drawn from outside the communities in which they operate and function as charities rather than community organisations. Most are simply landlords, but many of them also develop housing.

In 1992 the British national government began a new programme, City Challenge, that aims at involving community elements, including small businesses and non-profit organisations, in neighbourhood regeneration. City Challenge, while much more responsive to local communities than the UDC approach, still represents the new mode of planning whereby decision making rests in an agency outside the regular governmental structure. The City Challenge grant programme was intended to stimulate activity by the kinds of elite corporate entities and community development groups long active in American inner cities, but not yet very visible within the UK.

In New York, non-profit community development corporations (CDCs) have become increasingly significant non-governmental actors outside the Manhattan business district. Once incorporated, CDCs are free to seek financing from public and private lenders and grantors. Sources of funding are quite varied, including state and local governments, religious organisations, private philanthropies, and constituent businesses and housing groups. Two national groups — the Local Initiatives Support Corporation (LISC) and the Enterprise Foundation — raise money from foundations and from private corporations, which gain tax credits from investing in low-income housing. These organisations then act as intermediaries, funnelling resources to CDCs, primarily in support of housing construction and rehabilitation, but also for business development in low-income neighbourhoods. A number of banks have also set up autonomous development corporations which lend money in low-income neighbourhoods. These subsidiaries, which are expected to make a profit, generally participate only in projects in which some part of the costs is subsidised.

The consequences

Despite the promising efforts toward a more inclusive redevelopment effort in some parts of London and New York, the major thrust of policy has been and continues to be directed toward large-scale commercial development. (In New York this was the case even under the one-term administration of Mayor David Dinkins, an African–American.) London and New York, along with Tokyo, were the leading centres for financial transactions and associated services during the 1980s, a fact which was expressed symbolically and materially in their landscapes. The speculative nature of the development process led to the inevitable crash, as too much investment went into expensive real-estate for which there was a limited market. At the same time, not all the strategies were wrong-headed, and not all the projects were ill-conceived. Increases in office employment, new technical requirements for information-based industries, and shrinking manufacturing sectors dictated revision of land uses. Competition among places for expanding industries and the prior specialisations of London and New York in finance and business services meant that a strategy catering to those industries made sense. Nevertheless, expansion of commercial space and a high-end service strategy did not necessitate the wholesale neglect of manufacturing, almost total failure to address the housing needs of low-income people, and government's ceding to the private sector the responsibility for setting developmental priorities.

The lead public institutions, in implementing the development projects of the era, operated in isolation from democratic inputs. By focusing on the construction of first-class office space, luxury housing and tourist attractions, and short-changing the affordable-housing, small-business and community-based industry sectors, they prompted developers to engrave the image of two cities — one for the rich and one for the poor — on the landscape. Redevelopment took the form of islands of shiny new structures in the midst of decayed public facilities and deterioration in living conditions for the poor. The symbolic statements made by the new, competed projects are irritating — not because their internal environments are obnoxious in themselves but because of the contrast between them and the rest of the city.

Government might have put a damper on speculation, attempting to smooth out the extremely cyclical behaviour of property investment. Instead it reinforced the conduct of private financial institutions, which were pouring their money into office and luxury residential construction. Developers, because these sorts of projects had the greatest potential for profit, obviously wanted to build them and sold them to the government and financiers (but unfortunately not to tenants at the end). The deplorable outcome was a huge loss in the asset value of space, serious decline in property tax revenue in New York, heavy unemployment in construction and associated industries, and a general dampening of economic activity as the impact of losses in the property sector rippled through the economy.

Over-reliance on the property industry as the vehicle for stimulating economic growth defeated its own purpose. In the short run, during the peak of the real-estate market, deregulation and assistance to developers did not guarantee that benefits would be translated into increased employment. Moreover, when demand was robust, nothing forced developers to reduce prices to occupants even when development costs had been lowered by governmental action. It appears that when prices were very high during the 1980s, government subsidy and regulatory relief had an inflationary effect, much of it being capitalised into land values rather than bringing down the cost of doing business. In its long-term impact, governmental assistance reinforced the expansion of the supply of space at the upper ends of the commercial and residential markets until supply greatly exceeded demand, at which point the market abruptly plummeted.

In the speculative frenzy of the 1980s, developers projected future returns on a linear extrapolation of escalating rents and were therefore willing to pay extremely high prices for land acquisition. They thereby incurred indebtedness which could only be covered through gargantuan buildings and a wholly unrealistic rental structure that was destined to destroy their market as occupancy costs forced tenants out of business. The tragedy for the city as a whole was the destruction of industries ranging from light manufacturing to theatre production that could not easily be restored once cheap space again became available.

In the sobering aftermath of the boom, it has become clear that long-term profitability and growth were injured by the failure to rein in the speculators. Even though economic development was the justification for the pattern of investment that occurred, no-one was responsible for calculating aggregate growth targets. Public officials frequently assert that such projections are outside their realm of responsibility and that it is up to private business to foresee demand and shape supply accordingly. Since public funds and deregulation underpinned property market activity, however, the refusal of government to limit speculative development represented an irresponsible squandering of public resources. The inability to plan comprehensively meant that too much space for the same kind of use was built on too large a scale, while there was insufficient production of needed housing, public services, and infrastructure. Making financial and business services the centrepiece of each city's development strategy was not in itself a mistake; the error lay in emphasising these sectors virtually to the exclusion of all else and overly depending on real-estate as the method of encouraging them. Highly uneven outcomes were foreordained by an economic development strategy that did not stress job training and placement and did not involve aggressive efforts to identify industries with the potential to generate new employment.

In London, developing the Docklands as an office centre was not in itself wrong. The availability of a huge tract of mainly vacant land in the heart of the London metropolitan area represented an enormous asset, and one that rightfully should have been developed for the benefit of all Londoners, not just the small number of nearby residents. It was the government's unwillingness to bolster the enterprise with major social and educational programmes, to halt competitive commercial development elsewhere, and to construct infrastructure in advance of development, that created the ultimate débâcle. The central government's final unwillingness to subsidise Canary Wharf through putting many of its own offices there, which offered the potential of tiding the development over until it became more accessible, reinforced the shortsightedness of the process. Critics of Docklands development oppose forced moving of civil servants to the Isle of Dogs on the grounds that they should not be made to pay for the government's mistakes, and the Treasury opposes the government's paying anything but the rock-bottom rent. In New York, however, use of the strategy of relocating government offices has shored up real-estate markets and is probably worth the disruption and short-term expenditures it causes.

The entrepreneurship demonstrated by the PDC and its counterparts did facilitate investment in the New York economy. Moreover, the PDC did direct some investment to neighbourhood retail centres and manufacturing locations. Like the LDDC, however, it did not plan for infrastructure needs that were not site-specific, and it saw no need to limit the amount of office buildings coming on the market in New York. Whereas the LDDC ultimately made some efforts in the provision of job training and social services, the PDC had no mandate at all to connect its investment activities with social programmes.

Attacks on the development schemes of the 1980s have not been directed only at their economic failures. Many critics have also contended that they stifled diversity by establishing upper- and middle-class preserves in the midst of the city (e.g. Sorkin 1992; Zukin 1991). The goal of urban diversity, however, does not need to be met by developing each site for mixed-use, mixed-income, multicultural purposes. The provision of buffers between groups with conflicting interests and lifestyles makes some sense. Former Mayor Dinkins liked to refer to the fabric of New York as a "gorgeous mosaic"; in a mosaic there is proximity but also separation. Creating spaces that many people enjoy, even if they do not faithfully reproduce the past, and even if they make some people feel like outcasts, is not in itself so terrible. If we wish to prevent the upper class from invading working-class neighbourhoods or wholly isolating itself in suburban enclaves, then we ought not to forbid the creation of housing and offices for the elite in central places if this can be accomplished without causing displacement. Policymakers, however, can do much more for people who do not benefit directly from office development if they address a more comprehensive set of goals, including that of improving neighbourhood housing and commercial districts for the benefit of local residents.

How to do it better

Public redevelopment programmes and assistance to the private sector *can* form part of a progressive programme for long-term economic growth. They need, however, to be within the context of economic planning that coordinates economic and social policy, emphasises equity, counters the business cycle, and has the metropolitan area as its purview. Economic planning has always been largely anathema in the USA and has no constituency among the Tories who now govern the UK. Nevertheless, it is inconceivable that any private business would make capital expenditures without specifying output targets and calculating in advance the impacts of increasing production. Without unduly interfering with the market, government can identify sectors it will assist and only provide that assistance if businesses within the sector conform to the government's strategy. Such planning would only represent intelligent supervision of governmental expenditure. Whatever errors of forecasting might be made, they could not be worse than offering subsidies and exemptions from planning regulations indiscriminately. The assistance provided to developers in London by the LDDC and the Docklands enterprise zone and in New York by a plethora of incentive programmes already constitute market intervention. What they lack are any controls to ensure that the public sector will gain from its efforts.

Strategies

Evaluation of the London and New York experiences indicates the lineaments of a more strategic approach to redevelopment planning. The strategies set forth here include: (1) setting space targets and developing peripheral centres; (2) creating a diverse economic base; (3) metropolitan planning; and (4) public-dominated partnerships.

New development: targeting size and location

The direct cause of the collapse of the property market in both London and New York was the flooding of the market with more space than could be absorbed. Proper economic planning for a city would set levels of desired space for each market sector and each part of the city, with subsidies and regulatory relief geared to these objectives. Implementation of such a scheme would require forecasting of demand and selection of developers by government. Under such a procedure the public sector virtually guarantees a market for privately developed space; in return the private developer can be required to provide a substantial public benefit in the form of infrastructure provision and low-income housing contributions. A precedent already exists in San Francisco, where legislation limits the amount of office space that can be added each year. A panel selects the best development proposal based on financial and design criteria, and developers must contribute to a housing trust. Although San Francisco has been seriously affected by California's recession, it still has the lowest office vacancy rate of any metropolitan market in the USA.

The old central business districts of London and New York are overcrowded and distant from populations living in outer areas. Increasing uses within them is environmentally and socially destructive. The intensive development of peripheral sites still located within the boundaries of the old central city (i.e. inner London and the five boroughs of New York) would provide businesses with less-expensive more-spacious sites than are available within the original CBDs. The purpose is to compete effectively with suburban locations while maintaining the overall centrality that is the strength of the two cities.

Redevelopment of the Docklands in London and of central Brooklyn in New York for large-scale commercial centres justified government investment. The Brooklyn programme, which received significant capital subsidies as well as major tax subsidies from New York City, succeeded in stimulating economic development in a moribund area. Its deficiencies lie not in its locational target, but in the failure of government to ensure that it was connected with job training and placement programmes and that the public sector received more financial return from its sizable input. Similar claims cannot so far be made for Canary Wharf. Its success would have required much greater governmental commitment to infrastructure investment, associated employment and social programmes, assuring occupancy through use by its own agencies, and restrictions of development elsewhere. In return for pledging this kind of support, the government could have retained rights to the site and obtained ground rent of the sort that the Battery Park City Authority receives in New York and spends on low-income housing. The fault of Docklands development was not the concept of a business centre that would serve the whole metropolitan area, instead of just local residents; rather, it was the execution that foreordained its failure.

A diverse economic base

The governments of London and New York both concentrated their attention on a few economic sectors and allowed important industries to be injured by high rents. Rather than seeking ways to encourage economic diversity within the central areas, they let speculative office buildings and high-volume retail establishments drive out all other uses. Numerous small businesses and non-profit organisations were excluded from the cities' cores. While the New York City government was actively bringing down the occupancy costs of Chase Manhattan Bank and Morgan Stanley, it ignored the situation of drama groups, book stores, artists' workshops, galleries, acting studios, coffee houses, rehearsal halls, and specialised shops, which were going bankrupt or losing their leases. Even though many studies have identified the arts as extremely significant components of the economies of New York and London (Port Authority of New York and New Jersey 1993; Coopers & Lybrand Deloitte 1991), arts groups had to leave centrally located space because they could not afford it. New York City's plan for 42nd Street proposed to transform the area from an entertainment to an office district. In London within the West End and the City, developers were encouraged to redevelop the "marginal" space that housed "marginal" businesses. It was somehow assumed that such businesses did not have an economic future rather than regarding them as essential components of the complex fabric of the city and the possible progenitors of future expansion.

Good economic policy would aim to stabilise those economic and geographic sectors which harbour innovation or give the city a unique competitive advantage. London and New York have traditionally been magnets for talented people, who spawn fledgling enterprises. In addition, they afford markets for highly specialised businesses that cannot survive elsewhere. Although the gross revenues of such enterprises may not allow them to bid for expensive locations, they create a milieu that gives the city its special attraction. Policies to encourage economic diversity would reinforce the functions of creativity and specialised activity. Inexpensive refurbishment of older buildings to serve as incubators for a variety of for-profit and non-profit businesses can assist in fostering originality and maintaining complexity. Very moderate commercial rent control, limiting rent increases to three times the rate of inflation upon renewal of a lease and less thereafter, can keep the short-term greed of landlords from driving potentially long-term tenants out of business through rent rises in multiples of the original amount.

Greater emphasis on assisting the non-profit sector presents another strategy for ensuring stable growth. Within both London and New York, an enormous array of non-profit organisations ranging from charitable trusts to trade groups provides large numbers of jobs and is much more insulated from global economic competition than multinational corporations. Public-sector investment in appropriate space for such groups can contribute more to steady overall economic growth than high public expenditures to attract front-office facilities of corporations subject to mergers. Outside the central areas, greater financial and technical support for local enterprises would diminish the need to seek ways of attracting outside investors. Such support could be tied to provisos that the firm receiving assistance stay within the city.

Although manufacturing will never regain its former foothold in the two cities, greater effort can improve the situation of the still sizeable manufacturing sector that remains. Revolving loan funds, assistance in marketing efforts, better environmental and security services, job placement and training programmes, and provision of parking and loading areas in industrial areas would all contribute to industrial retention. In New York, local economic development corporations offer a framework for such assistance that could become much more significant if President Clinton ever fulfils his campaign promise to establish local development banks. Secure funding for CDCs would release their staffs from devoting the greater part of their time to raising money rather than operating programmes. In London, where local development corporations do not exist, cooperatives offer a similar opportunity.

Metropolitan planning

It is an extremely difficult task to devise an appropriate system for land use and economic development planning that takes metropolitan-area-wide considerations into account, operates efficiently and effectively, involves citizens in reviewing development proposals without succumbing to "NIMBYism", and responds to initiatives emanating from urban neighbourhoods. Because planning must cope with genuine conflicts of interest, trade-offs between long- and short-term considerations, and considerable uncertainty over the results of any project, no process will produce a fully satisfactory result. Nevertheless, the creation of a planning framework like the old Greater London Development Plan would allow inputs at various levels.

The current jurisdictional systems of both London and New York make comprehensive planning impossible. London has no authoritative planning unit; New York has one, but only for part of the metropolitan area. London does have adequately staffed local authorities to run the process at the community level, but New York's community boards have insufficient resources and staff support to be vehicles for extensive planning. A significant planning effort in the two cities would require major institutional innovation at the metropolitan and subsidiary levels.

The past failures of planners, as evidenced in highway programmes, urban renewal, and modernist council estates, make recommendations for more planning suspect. Mine are made on the optimistic assumption that planning can learn from its mistakes, that in fact it was learning at the time the urban renewal programme was terminated in the USA and council housebuilding ended in the UK. The effects of destroying social communities and developing out-of-scale projects had become evident. Citizen participation, housing rehabilitation, and coordination of housing and social services had become incorporated into the programmes. There is, therefore, reason to hope that a revival of planning could produce a more sensitive process. Most important, without such an effort the public will remain hostage to "private" decisions insulated from its scrutiny regardless of their public consequences.

Public-dominated partnerships

There are four conceivable sources of risk capital for economic regeneration:

- the private, for-profit sector
- the state
- employee savings and benefit funds
- the non-profit sector.

Each has advantages and disadvantages. To attract private capital to territories not regarded as inherently profitable by capitalist managers, state officials feel compelled to offer incentives with all the likely negative consequences described earlier. Direct state participation in quasi-governmental corporations can save failing industries — not all of which are "lemons" — and permits greater public control of the outcomes than state subsidy of purely private entities. (AMTRAK, the US passenger railroad corporation which connects a number of old US central cities and whose revival has spun off an important employment and retailing multiplier at its stations, is a good example of revitalisation through the use of this kind of instrument.) Such corporations, though, when they are profitable and capitalised on a large scale, tend to behave little differently from private firms (Rueschemeyer and Evans 1985, pp. 57–59) and will also seek least-cost locations. In contrast, firms run directly by the state will be less profit-oriented and, theoretically at least, susceptible to democratic control. They tend, however, to avoid risks, invest insufficiently, and avoid cost-reduction measures.

Critics of business-dominated arrangements who recognise the necessity of tapping into private capital need to devise innovative versions of the public–private partnership. This means an orientation toward the service sector, including the rapidly growing health-care sector; recognition of the importance of management and entrepreneurship; and a coming-to-terms with the multinational corporation. The reality that giant multinational, service-producing corporations dominate economic transactions means that the Left must find ways of tapping into their economic power rather than dismissing them on moral grounds. Public–private partnerships under these conditions are inevitable; what needs to be done is ensure that the public component is more controlling and shares more in the proceeds. Public sponsorship of consulting, computer, high-tech, restaurant franchise, nursing home, home health care, and similar enterprises, as well as small-scale manufacturing, could generate a stable small-business sector to occupy inner-city sites. If such businesses are to thrive, they will involve internal hierarchies with sufficient returns to managers as to induce competent, experienced individuals to assume these roles. They also will have to allow managers discretion in rewarding worker performance. Under such an approach, social equalisation, if it is to occur, would come through redistribution within the tax and welfare system rather than the firm. In other words, even a progressive policy toward inner-city redevelopment will generate serious inequalities in the rewards to labour if it is to stimulate growth.

Eisinger (1988) especially emphasises the expanding public role in identifying product niches for local industry, promoting product develop-ment, training workers for firms in expanding areas, and marketing local outputs. The typical version of these endeavours allows public assumption of the risk and private appropriation of the profit. A better model would be the hotel and convention bureaux of many municipalities, where a tax on receipts supports the marketing efforts of the bureaux. Eisinger notes that some states participate in royalties from inventions that result from state participation in product innovation. As a general rule, the more that public bodies are assured of a revenue stream keyed to profits that derive from public investment, the better the community can protect itself from the continual undercutting of the public fisc caused by anti-tax pressures.

Private decision making and public oversight

Developers who work within central business districts are generally inclined to think that they are dangerously over-regulated — although

London's property entrepreneurs, having experienced the effect of deregulation, are having second thoughts. To the extent that regulation does exist, it is usually tied to environmental rather than economic effects. Government scrutiny of the financial viability of development enterprises is restricted to evaluating bids for particular sites in response to a government's request for proposals. The high externalities of developmental decisions, however, mean that the consequences of developers' decisions are widely felt. Proposals need to be assessed according to their financial impacts on the market as a whole and their likely impact on job creation.

Social equity demands a balanced redevelopment policy that addresses the distributional effects of economic growth and that provides for consumption as well as investment needs. As most studies of redevelopment show, policy aimed at growth usually has little regard for social impacts. Better policy requires the coordination of economic and social programmes, including the integration of employment and redevelopment programmes; linking of housing and office construction; much higher and more consistent levels of subsidy for affordable housing; opportunities for small business in publicly assisted commercial developments; measures to ensure that any corporation that receives public-sector benefits be prevented from cashing in and then decamping; and a return to the public fisc commensurate with its contribution to the development.

Urban governments will not produce a genuinely transformative redevelopment policy at the behest of policy analysts. Without the strong political backing of a progressive movement demanding a different programme, the advice given in this chapter becomes utopian. Yet, one of the reasons for the contemporary exclusive emphasis on market-led development as the strategy for urban regeneration is the absence of counter-formulations. The suggestions presented here for reorienting redevelopment policy, therefore, are addressed to participants in urban movements rather than to governmental officials, in the hope of contributing to a new agenda which is not simply reactive and which does not indulge in nostalgia for a lost industrial age. The institutionalist perspective that informs this volume of essays implies a recognition of structural forces but also of the role of individual leaders and urban movements in transforming those forces and invigorating urban management. The presupposition of this chapter is that better urban management requires the demystification of institutionalised forms like "the free market" and "public–private partnerships", as well as the devising of improved methods for carrying out necessary governmental functions.

Within the context of a global economy characterised by competition among places and centralisation of economic control in a small number of corporations, urban governments have limited options. This context dictates flexibility and entrepreneurship by urban managers — traditionally (but not immutably) private- rather than public-sector traits. We have, in fact, seen in our look at London and New York that these cities have produced public agencies demonstrating these characteristics. The need now is to change the value framework in which these agencies act, so that their ambitions become an increase in local control over the economy, and greater equity in the outcomes of redevelopment, not simply the attraction of investment.

Part 3

INFRASTRUCTURE, TECHNOLOGY AND POWER

PATSY HEALEY

Infrastructure and the city

One of the key tasks of the urbanising effort of industrial society has been the provision of intensive concentrations of physical infrastructure networks. The provision of such networks — roads, rails, ducts and wires — for the movement of people, goods, energy, water, waste, information and entertainment, has enabled companies and households to get access to more effective ways of production, distribution and consumption. Governments at all levels have invested energetically in infrastructure capacity. Often this has meant "retro-fitting" new infrastructure technologies into the existing urban fabric. The provision of infrastructure networks across urban regions has in turn generated new opportunities for urbanisation, encouraging the spread of cities way beyond city cores.

Driving such investments in the past have been two classically modernist conceptions. The first was the need for "functional fit" between urban activities and infrastructure. This is encapsulated in texts such as Chapin's famous *Urban Land Use Planning* (1965). The second was the

Managing Cities: The New Urban Context, edited by P. Healey, S. Cameron, S. Davoudi, S. Graham and A. Madani-Pour. © 1995 The Editors and contributors. Published in 1995 by John Wiley & Sons Ltd.

objective of "universalist" provision, creating a "level playing field" across urban regions and between social groups. Measures of progress to modernity in currently urbanising countries still include such criteria as levels of connection to energy, water, telephone and television systems.

This method of progressively improving urban infrastructure standards, however, has been undermined by a whole series of shifts in the way infrastructure is produced, managed and used. As Graham and Marvin emphasise, so far these have been very little researched from a social scientific point of view. One dimension of the shift is the introduction of new technologies. Both chapters in this part emphasise the role of telematics, as a management tool for other infrastructure networks, and as networks, transforming the speed, range and variety of information exchange. The annihilation of space by time, which Marx saw in the development of rail transport last century, has been massively enabled by these innovations. This technology underpins new urban metaphors, of the city as "a space of flows" in an "informational city" (Castells 1989).

A second dimension reflects changing priorities and values, and changing perceptions of costs and benefits. In the field of transport planning, the critical measure of achievement was a reduction in travel time and cost. Now this has become very complex to achieve, with new investment in capacity generating new demands in such a way that congestion persistently prevents the realisation of hoped-for travel-cost savings (Newman et al. 1988). There is also growing consciousness of the collective adverse consequences of constantly expanding infrastructure capacity to meet travel demand. These costs include local and global pollution, local environmental quality and energy conservation. In many western cities, the major cause of air pollution and ozone depletion is road transport (Button and Rothengather 1993). These environmental downsides of road transport have parallels in the search for new ways of managing water and waste distribution and energy use. Increasing pressure is being put on utility providers, through regulatory instruments, to improve environmental quality. These in turn create pressures for investment in new forms of provision and distribution, as in the current rediscovery of the value of public transport, at the urban, regional and transnational scales. There are also questions about who bears the costs of such environmental improvements.

A third dimension is particularly evident in older cities, where infrastructure networks date from the early industrial period or before. Renewing outworn pipework and sewers is becoming a major expenditure item for local governments and utility companies, which can only partly be offset by opportunities to introduce the new cables and ducts demanded by the new telephone and television companies.

But perhaps the most significant innovation for cities is in the management of physical infrastructure networks. The provision and maintenance of urban networks in the nineteenth century was typically a task of local government, with different patterns of private and public provision in different places (Marvin 1992). A common trend in Europe in the middle of this century was a shift to public ownership.

Neo-liberal policy strategies have now resulted in the conversion of many such large public companies into private firms, able to pursue expansion and diversification strategies, not merely within their own countries and regions, but transnationally — for example US telecommunications companies, and French water companies. Both chapters in this part emphasise two serious consequences of such privatisation for the city. Firstly, private companies are no longer required to achieve objectives of universal levels of service provision. Instead, access to networks and quality of provision is becoming increasingly differentiated, between places and among companies and households. Secondly, urban government no longer has the capacity to direct what is being provided and how much is produced.

Technological innovation and the capacity for differentiation

Physical infrastructure provision is a world of engineering culture, dominated by the language of science, technique and utility, and by the excitement of technological innovation. It remains a core heartland of industrial modernity. A key characteristic of this culture is its neglect of the institutional relations within which technology is produced and used and within which the benefits and costs of technological innovation are distributed.

When the general objective and technological capacity focused on the extension of basic levels of provision, the consequences of this neglect were neither too obvious nor too serious. Present technology, however, is characterised by the capacity for flexibility and adaptability. It allows fine-grained differentiation between categories of users. Consequently, it allows provider companies to target with increasing spatial and social discrimination those demand groups and locations where profits are expanding or secure. This tendency combines with public policy concerns which promote selectively both general management capabilities (for example local government geographical information systems capacity in France) and particular infrastructure projects (such as the French TGV system and the introduction in Britain of new competition in the telecommunications sphere).

Laterasse and Pauchard emphasise how this results in the development of new nodes of urban value in regional spatial structure. In the French situation, this is linked to the location of stations on new rapid regional rail networks. Graham and Marvin comment on the disparities in distribution and access emerging in Britain in relation to a range of utilities. Along with the new nodes goes the peripheralisation of places within existing urban structure. The mid-century urge towards universal provision is now being replaced by an innovative drive which is destroying the "level playing field".

Both chapters argue that technological innovation in infrastructure capacity, combined with innovation in the management of supply, produces new patterns of uneven development across urban regional space. This interrelation between technology and institutions echoes Fainstein's discussion in Chapter 6 of the difference in approach between New York and London in relation to infrastructure provision for urban redevelopment projects. In New York, the institutional context allowed an early and coordinated emphasis on infrastructure improvement. In Britain, infrastructure improvement was negotiated on a project-by-project basis *after* development interest came forward (Fainstein 1994). Fainstein is in no doubt that the former produced a better result than the latter.

Laterasse and Pauchard note another aspect of the institutional dimension to technological innovation. Infrastructure network innovations are designed using models of network development. These assume characteristics of the behaviour of firms and of people. Laterasse and Pauchard note that the models frequently suffer from technical failure. More fundamentally, their assumptions about behaviour reflect a flawed perception of reality. Modernist infrastructure engineers assume that the modernist city and its characteristic modes of behaviour still exist. When this obviously does not reflect realities, adjustments are made at the margin. But as we describe in this book, patterns of relations within which people move around the city and make use of infrastructure services and facilities reflect a much more complex range and variety of ways of living, producing and doing business. The challenge for the infrastructure engineers, as for the rest of us, is to find ways of understanding these new patterns.

Differentiation, marginalisation and exclusion

A technological answer to the tendencies for new forms of spatially and socially uneven development in infrastructure provision is that the technology itself has the capacity to recreate a level playing field. Telematics in particular appears to open up the possibility for universal access to information. It therefore has the capacity to re-integrate the fragments of our urban societies and to contribute to the project of social cohesion. Neither of the chapters in this part accept that such an outcome will necessarily come about. Laterasse and Pauchard suggest that a much better management capacity would be needed to achieve such an outcome.

Graham and Marvin stress the extent to which utilities privatisation in Britain encourages both the marginalisation of those places and those people who cannot afford to pay for services, and the targeting of the most lucrative opportunities for some of the key technological innovations (e.g. teleports, logistics platforms etc. — see Cornford and Gillespie 1992). This reinforces patterns of urban disadvantage in an economic sense as well as a social one.

The potential of new telematics technology to spread information and service benefits widely is often emphasised. But whether this potential is realised depends not on the technology but on the way it is used. This reinforces the importance of the institutional dimension. If social and economic marginalisation in relation to access to physical infrastructure is increasing in our cities, then we have to look critically at the institutional forms of the production and distribution of infrastructure, and at the regulatory regimes through which societal objectives constrain and encourage tendencies in provision. In this section, both chapters highlight the increasing disjunction between urban governance and the provision of physical infrastructure. The core assumption of modernist urban planning, that planning agencies could control this coordination of development and infrastructure, has thus moved beyond complaints about coordination problems. The assumption itself has evaporated.

Infrastructure provision and urban governance

Graham and Marvin highlight the consequences for urban governance of the privatisation of the utilities in Britain. This represents a second stage in the loss of control of utilities at the urban level. The setting up of national and regional utility companies in the 1940s and the 1970s had already made it difficult for urban authorities to shape the investment programmes of the utilities agencies. Privatisation, by emphasising commercial over social and environmental criteria, has widened the distance to such an extent that local governments and their citizens typically know little about what is happening to their utilities networks (Graham and Marvin 1994b).

Laterasse and Pauchard describe a similar disjunction, yet produced by a different process. Coordination between urban development (land allocation and project approval) was formerly within the control of the French national administration of the Ministère de l'Equipement, also responsible for infrastructure provision. With the 1983 decentralisation of powers to local communes, city mayors are now in a position to promote and control development. But infrastructure remains in the hands of the previous more centralist structure. As a result, there are major institutional tensions between the ambitions and strategies of the infrastructure developers and the strategies of the cities. Despite national government assistance given to communes to build up their information systems, Laterasse and Pauchard argue that it is very difficult for cities to develop sufficient knowledge and power to bargain effectively with the larger units. The consequence, they argue, is two processes of territorial development, one which produces "localised territories", driven by the commune mayors, and the other which creates "functional territories", driven by the infrastructures agencies.

Physical infrastructure: integration or fragmentation

Laterasse and Pauchard develop these issues through a discussion of the role of electronic data systems in city management, with a particular emphasis on traffic flows. They argue that these technologies have the potential to make the management of cities more open and dynamic, as well as more efficient. However, this promise is currently compromised by the competition between the institutional arenas within which such systems are being developed.

Graham and Marvin focus on the uneven social and spatial consequences of technological and institutional change in utilities provision. They seek to redress the neglect of this dimension of urban change in contemporary urban political economy. They argue that the utilities arena reveals clearly the new patterns of governance emerging in relation to the "post-Fordist" city.

Both chapters emphasise the contribution of technological and institutional change in the utilities sector to the fragmentation of the relations of the modernist city. The authors describe the various ways in which functional coordination at the urban level is undermined, and the increasing openness of the forms of provision to priorities arising from transnational and global considerations rather than local ones.

These tendencies towards fragmentation and globalisation of physical infrastructure provision within the urban arena have major consequences for urban life and urban economies. Some urban areas and neighbourhoods are vulnerable to marginalisation, in relation to both the quality of basic provision and access to the new telematics opportunities. The ability of urban governments to control the development of their infrastructure assets is also progressively weakened. Yet in much of the urban economic development literature such infrastructures are considered as key assets in the competition for economic success and survival (Biehl 1986).

These conclusions raise serious questions about the extent to which technological innovation can come to the aid of city economies and quality of life. As currently deployed, the new technologies appear to be reinforcing the concentration of opportunity and power in the hands of the most economically dynamic companies, cities and regions. If benefits are to be spread more widely, much more attention needs to be given to the relation between infrastructure provision and urban governance, as Graham and Marvin argue. More generally, if the democratic promise of the new technologies is to be realised, the creation of institutional structures and processes with the capacity to direct technology to the service of cities, their companies and citizens, needs to be given a central place in the discussion of innovation.

7

Information Systems and Territorial Administration: a New Power Struggle, or Multi-Actor Rational Organisation

JEAN LATERASSE and HERVÉ PAUCHARD

Studies (e.g. Laterasse 1991) have demonstrated the challenges and limitations inherent in the movement towards computerised management of both urban technical systems (roads, transportation and all types of mobility in general, water distribution, sanitation, energy, telecommunications, and so on) and city administration itself. The advantages of electronic data systems, particularly of large urban networks, result from the increased efficiency for handling and controlling flow. Data systems also improve the quality of the services involved with these networks, provided that the entire innovative process has been carefully mastered — particularly organisational and human aspects. This means that the users are not thought of as so many elements capable of perturbing the functioning of urban systems, but rather as active partners in the new regulatory policies being set up.

The limits of such moves towards data systems are due to the fact that the solutions provided by new technologies are only partial (and we have just noted that, in any event, resorting to new technologies of data processing must, if they are to work, be integrated into a global attitude concerning change). They are also temporary. This is the case, for example,

Managing Cities: The New Urban Context, edited by P. Healey, S. Cameron, S. Davoudi, S. Graham and A. Madani-Pour. © 1995 The Editors and contributors. Published in 1995 by John Wiley & Sons Ltd.

in the field of transportation, where any improvement in supply is rapidly absorbed by an increase in mobility, particularly in Europe as regards automobiles.

A question might be put as follows: Is not the principal virtue of an electronic management system that it allows the production and dissemination of information that was previously inaccessible (and thus alters how the city functions as a whole)?

An initial application proposed in Laterasse (1991) concerns making data systems available to both citizens and users. Using this method, the "intelligent city" is first and foremost a more *transparent and intelligible city*. One way to achieve this is to develop a debate about the ultimate use of these systems, and how they might supplement or prolong the use of other urban services. More thought is also required, and at the drawing-board stage, concerning the ways in which they make it possible to utilise the *redundancy* or *complementarity* of these services (Laterasse and Deutsch 1991).

In this chapter we explore another path: namely, the implementation, use and induced effects of information systems intended for French city managers, or more generally those actors intervening at different territorial levels in the government of large urban areas in France. What are these data systems? Will they manage urban systems more efficiently, or are they simply new instruments for gaining power, with no real operational objectives? The last question seems especially important. It must be considered in the light of the combined effects of the decentralisation process begun in France, and the quest for more economy in local government and administration, especially through the management of the means by which urban areas function — getting people, merchandise, energy, water, sanitation from one place to another on a gigantic scale (i.e. not on a single downtown scale, but on the scale of metroplex areas, or all suburbs taken together, or the entire employment pool).

Before attempting to answer these questions, it is helpful to recall the political and institutional context within which we have placed the comments — namely the French context, and more specifically the Ile-de-France region. (Nonetheless, we believe that most of our discussion applies to other developed countries.) Until the end of the 1970s France was heavily marked by several centuries of centralising policy. There was the need for extensive parcelling out of responsibilities to local administrations (there are more than 36 000 communities in France, with populations ranging from a few hundred to over two million in Paris).

Decentralisation served to clarify the various areas of responsibility of local governments on the various territorial levels in many areas (local finances, review of building and zoning permits, managing municipal technical networks, education, social work and public health, and so on). At the outset, the decentralisation bills voted into law in 1983 and 1984 made allowance for transferring resources in accordance with the newly acquired powers of local governments. Local elected officials considered that these reforms were positive. However, a certain number of problems remained: the transfer of resources, in a relatively unfavourable economic context, has not always matched the increase in expenditures of local governments, especially as the prerogatives of local governments remain limited. In addition, some of the national services tended to hang on to their former prerogatives in the name of technical competency. In short, decentralisation, rather than a clear-cut transition, has been a complex *process* in which a new type of equilibrium is difficult to define. Within this context, local governments were quick to show an interest in setting up data services, which they perceived as instruments necessary for carrying out their new duties.

We shall examine in turn the different types of data systems and their modes of functioning, the difficulties associated with the capture and use of data, and the role of these data systems in the restructuring of systems of actors in progress.

Information systems available for managers and officials

We shall begin our discussion with a type of electronic data system used increasingly for the management of large infrastructures and large technical systems. The rationale is flow management. The primary goal is not to provide data or information as such to managers; rather, the aim is to furnish *control-command* of the networks which they are "piloting". Nonetheless they do furnish large amounts of data which are increasingly being used (1) for the shaping and evolution of infrastructures, (2) for a more rational and economic management of networks, and (3) to guide socio-economic policies for the regulation of demand (for example, re-evaluation of fare structures).

A current example is SIRIUS (*Système Intelligent de Régulation et d'Information des Usagers* — Intelligent System for User Information and Control) in use on expressways in the Ile-de-France region. This consists of continuous capturing of traffic data over approximately 500 kilometres of roadway (see Figures 7.1 and 7.2). There is a central control station, and four other control stations located at the four cardinal points of the network, each equipped with mainframe computers. These computers must, on the one hand, display the state of traffic on synoptic screens in the central control station (watched by both the operators of SIRIUS and traffic security police). At the same time, they generate messages for drivers, sent via updated message boards. These messages inform users rapidly about the state of the network, and encourage them to choose an alternative itinerary on the same network when there is a traffic jam on one route.

Existing Motorways
Proposed Motorways
Boundaries of "départements"
Areas of "Villes Nouvelles"

Source : "Ministère de l'Equipement"

Figure 7.1   Motorway system and administrative boundaries

Source: Ministère de l'Equipement

Geographical information systems

The other type of information system to which we shall refer here concerns what is more classically understood by the term "electronic data system" for management use, the widespread development of which has been made possible by advances in computer technology. Such systems include municipal data banks, computer-aided land surveys and plans, geographical data, or information systems, and so on. The principle of these data systems is not new, and the first experiences with them in France date back to the 1970s. Then the cost seemed prohibitive for many local administrations, and the difficulties encountered in operating them were a major handicap. The advances in both hardware and software have now completely changed the problem. The first really modern data systems for urban geography appeared in the USA in 1975. They were inspired by military research and research into natural resource management. The tools have been transferred to a European market, where they have progressively been supplemented by others, coming directly from progress achieved in the computer industry in the realm of computer-aided design.

Motorway managed by D.R.E.I.F.
Motorway managed by "Ville de Paris"
Franchised Motorway

Source : "Ministère de l'Equipement"

Figure 7.2   Authorities for motorway management

Source: Ministère de l'Equipement

Whatever the origin of these Urban Geography Information Systems (hereafter referred to as UGISs), the basic principle remains the same: spatial visualisation of the data necessary for the management of urban territories. In order to achieve this, data are treated and analysed by means of tables which define the graphical and non-graphical elements within a veritable System for the Management of a Relational Data Base, in general by stacking the different territorial levels or scales (see Figure 7.3).

It is indeed this spatial visualisation of data which makes an UGIS so attractive for a local administration. In the decentralisation process referred to above, French cities have taken on — in addition to land survey control, which they had always handled — greater responsibility in terms of housing, town planning and social welfare. In these circumstances the importance of legal reference documents such as the *Plans d'Occupation des Sols* (POS) (land-use plans, or zoning maps) tends to be called into question. These documents now seem to be too rigid in view of the rapidity of evolutions, particularly economic, with which local governments are confronted. The published plans are poorly adapted to the managing of urban projects, particularly when such projects attain a certain size. In addition, the upkeep of roads and all the other large technical

**EXAMPLE OF
GRAPHICAL TRANSFORMATION
AT DIFFERENT SCALES**

**EXAMPLE OF
CORRESPONDING
URBAN DATA BASES**

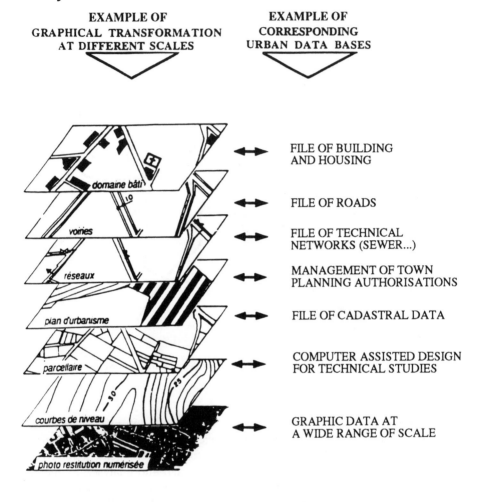

FILE OF BUILDING
AND HOUSING

FILE OF ROADS

FILE OF TECHNICAL
NETWORKS (SEWER...)

MANAGEMENT OF TOWN
PLANNING AUTHORISATIONS

FILE OF CADASTRAL DATA

COMPUTER ASSISTED DESIGN
FOR TECHNICAL STUDIES

GRAPHIC DATA AT
A WIDE RANGE OF SCALE

Original drawing : BCEOM

Figure 7.3 Territorial scales in a relational data base

systems, along with coordination of the various interventions needed, increasingly requires more databases in the form of maps.

Today in France (Dupuy 1991, 1992a), it is estimated that approximately 50% of cities with a population of more than 100 000 have already installed an UGIS, or are in the process of having one installed. These new information systems would appear, to city managers, to be at once more powerful, and more adaptable, than traditional maps and plans, and thus more suited to the present needs of town planning and control.

Examples of applications

Three examples of UGIS creation in the greater Paris metropolitan area, conceived on a supra-urban scale, will be mentioned here (Hayois 1993).

The first is the "zero-pollution" Marne River operation, set up by the river authority. The UGIS covers a territory corresponding to the catchment area, namely 70 kilometres of river and 150 kilometres of tributaries, with about 130 municipalities spread out over three départements in the Ile-de-France region. The goal of the UGIS is to monitor sites where pollution is a risk, and to monitor land development, in order to improve the quality of the catchment and purification systems, and allow tighter control over urban policies (for instance, more control over processes which reduce soil permeability).

The second example concerns the STP, or "Paris Transportation Union", the state-regulated authority organising public transport in the greater Paris area. The area governed by the STP, which has just recently been extended to the entire Ile-de-France region, includes 1281 municipalities and 10.6 million inhabitants (some two million in Paris alone). The stated aims here are to update on a continuing basis the map of public transportation systems, to obtain a global vision of supply, to optimise services to users, to facilitate coordination with all the partner firms of the STP, and to set up a "regional observatory of travel and movement".

The third example concerns the "Schéma Directeur d'Aménagement et d'Urbanisme" (SDAU, "Development Plan for National and Regional Development and Town Planning") in the Ile-de-France region. As part of the decentralisation process, the various municipal authorities, as noted above, have acquired more responsibility over town planning, notably controlling the procedures for obtaining building permits. At the same time, the state has retained the responsibility for working out a development plan, along with the elected assemblies at the level of Region and Département (Regional Council and General Councils) in order to define a long-term land development strategy in the Paris region. The general priority objectives of the SDAU are to master the growth of the region, and control — insofar as it can be controlled — the location of activities, through research on better land allocation, improvements in transportation, and conservation of the environment through better and more rigorous zoning (Rhind 1991).

Methodological considerations

A first and major difficulty in working out an UGIS lies in the acquisition of coherent and homogeneous data, on varying territorial scales. The larger the scale, the more critical the problem (Rhind 1991). The difficulty can be illustrated here numerically. In large French metropolitan areas there are 14 distinct and official statistical categories. The information collected is often combined with data produced for the needs of the individual local administrations concerned. These are all the more diverse since territorial administrations still possess a strong sense of local identity. It is obviously no easy matter to integrate these different types of data, which are sometimes quite detailed, or which contain extremely variable types of aggregation from one territorial unit to another, and which have only rarely been collected specifically for the UGIS.

Problems with databanks and the quality of the models

In certain cases, one might go so far as to question the value of the data. This is especially true when the data rely on measurements in an open milieu, which by their nature are very difficult to make and are not yet subject to methodology and definitions that are universally accepted. Examples are measurement of the parameters of the urban environment such as atmospheric pollution and pollution produced by waste washed into rivers during heavy storms; but also, to a lesser degree, measurements of population movements.

Concerning road traffic in the Ile-de-France region, before SIRIUS went into operation another information system was used. Essentially the system was based on observations by the gendarmerie, either on the ground or from helicopters, and this continued to function for quite some time after the start-up of SIRIUS. Large disparities were noted between the information furnished by the two systems. It is known that the information now produced by SIRIUS, while more reliable than that produced before (which was necessarily more partial), is nonetheless still marred by errors. Further, the commissioning and upkeep of a reliable network on such a large scale takes longer and costs more than was initially thought likely.

In other respects, advances in calculation capacity have meant that, increasingly, UGISs are paired with interactive modelling systems, for example with a view to optimising the working of a system in real-time, or to making forecasts (such as the traffic load on a certain motorway system). These tools are obviously only as good as the data and models being used. Important progress has been made over the past ten years through continuous improvement of databanks and increases in calculation capacities, making possible the comparison of numerous variables. However, there is still the risk of the perverse effects of hasty extrapolations, especially as not all the tools available to city managers have methodological rigour. In general, taking into account the temporal dimension within geographical information systems presents theoretical problems which are difficult to solve, and which require a great deal of accuracy.

The problem of scale

Another illustration of the problems resulting from the spatial visualisation of data can be demonstrated by research currently in progress at the authors' institution. We set out to study the subject of "economic activities" by presupposing that the usual explanations given for the spatial (east versus west) imbalance in Paris between jobs and housing tended to give too much importance to certain territorial rationales (especially fiscal). We also assumed that any study of the localisation of activities (in this instance, measured by the supply of office space) needed more interpretation in terms of the relationship with heavy-duty personal transport systems (trains and motorways). Our objectives were connected to two ideas.

Idea 1: Companies change office locations in relation to public transportation supply

In an unpublished study we showed that office space constructed during the period 19785–89 in the Greater Paris area was largely located close to the railways and major motorways, with preference for the former: 84% of property development offices[1] were located close to[2] both a train access point and at least one motorway access point, while the remaining 16% were located close to only a motorway access point. Our findings of company relocations are shown in Table 7.1

These results confirm that companies prefer to have their offices close to train systems, and suggest in addition a clear "loyalty" to the systems to which they were previously "connected" (only 12% changed). Data on office location and the data showing relocations suggest that when a business moves to another location, the constraints related to access to transportation networks are very much taken into consideration.

Idea 2: How companies plan their relocation also has territorial implications

We also studied the relocations of companies with respect to traditionally defined institutional territories (municipality, département, region). These administer several policy instruments (building permits and professional taxes are applied at the local level, whereas incentives for economic development are applied at the regional level). They are also used for statistical purposes. The results are shown in Table 7.2.

It can be observed that company relocations are fairly evenly divided up, with nonetheless a tendency for moves which go beyond the municipal and departmental levels. This point can easily be explained by the morphology of the Paris départements, especially the zone known as "La petite couronne", composed of the following départements: Hauts-de-Seine,

Table 7.1   Relocations of property development offices according to the nearest transportation access point

Nature of relocation	Number	Percentage
Train ⇒ train	173	66
Motorway ⇒ motorway	59	22
Train ⇒ motorway or motorway ⇒ train	31	12
Total	263	100

Table 7.2   Relocations of property development offices according to territory

Localisation of move	Number	Percentage
Same municipality[3]	67	25
Same département	82	31
Same region	114	43
Total	263	100

Source: Committee on Decentralisation, 1985–89

Seine-Saint-Denis, Val-de-Marne, which forms a *belt* around Paris, while the relocations are essentially *radial* with respect to the train systems involved.[3]

Since the main regulatory divisions in the French administrative hierarchy are the municipalities and départements (and not regions), it thus becomes clear that transportation networks make possible business moves which put these regulations in the wrong, and that business moves present serious regulatory problems in the present politico-administrative territorial system. It is consequently only by means of exhaustive studies, from a holistic point of view (territorial planning), that an understanding of what is variously at stake in linking economic activities/transportation networks can be reached, in terms of the long-term viability of the different options available.

This example, it seems to us, demonstrates how any approach based on data systems, whose spatial extension does not exactly fit the observed processes, runs the risk of producing a partial or imprecise view of the situation. Errors can be induced from a strictly unilateral approach. Here also the classification of spatial data presents both theoretical and practical questions which are difficult to deal with. To put it simply, the data system must be adapted constantly to the phenomenon or process being studied, and the illusion of universality which increasingly more powerful systems are capable of creating is a permanent trap. The managers and decision makers in our cities must be made more aware of these risks.

Data systems, territory, and the roles of the actors

Apart from the foregoing methodological aspects (which are obviously of great importance), what is really at stake from an organisational, institutional, and, in the end, political point of view?

Territorial networks

Several observations need to be considered at this point. The first is that, as Gabriel Dupuy has pertinently pointed out (Dupuy 1991):

> [In France] the computerisation of cities (up to now) has been very introverted. City halls, municipal networks, and inter-municipal networks have been computerised at the municipal level, the district level, the level of the coordinating board of municipalities. Very often, applications have been carried out by and for downtown areas and extended, in a controlled fashion, to suburban municipalities.

This situation can be compared to what we have called the "local sense of identity" (Dupuy uses the term "localised spirit").

Secondly, however, as the example of the offices in Ile-de-France has shown, and as many other examples might demonstrate, networks (especially transportation networks, but also water, energy and others) create new territories, and this reality is being increasingly imposed on municipal management. These new territories might be termed "functional territories", in contrast to the administrative or institutional territories which are constituted by municipalities or départements. These new functional territories often extend over huge geographical areas, far beyond the usual intercommunal regroupings. Their borders, when they can even be called "urban", are very often fuzzy and ill-defined. Functional territories totally ignore the presence of administrative boundaries, just as they are ignored by the flows running through a network and the electronic data systems dealing with them.

The third observation is that, in electronic management systems, the operators intervening in these new territories have found not only tools adapted to their prerogatives, but also a kind of legitimacy. For example, in the case of SIRIUS, and more generally for UGISs connected to devices for the management of large technical systems in real-time, data systems can be constructed within a specific infrastructure, which reinforces the territorial symbolism even further. At the same time it is obvious that this same movement leads operators to look not only to establish their territorial legitimacy, but using this as their starting point, to increase their jurisdiction and authority. And the necessity of producing information upstream of the processes which need to be managed then provides a very convenient excuse. For example, the UGIS constituted by the STP has offered not only to collect data concerning public transportation — which is its primary task — but also to collect an entire mass of other data concerning car use and car parking behaviour, the fleet of all private cars and how often it is renewed, transportation companies including those which function in extremely specific sectors (leisure activities, merchandise, business trips, and so on), as well as general data concerning an entire set of demographic, economic and social elements. At the same time, the management service of SIRIUS is developing, as has already been noted, its own "Movement Observatory". This is being done in the hope of being recognised for assignments going beyond simple traffic management and control, towards the definition of a holistic policy concerning individual travel.[4] The fact that the two operators concerned here depend directly on the central government has no effect on the problem. The same problems come to the fore with, for example, the SDAU, where the policy and authority of the state are confronted with the policies and authority of the local governments.

Reorganisation of territories

The issue which is really at stake here thus appears to belong to the question of a territorial reorganisation of urban management. Not that electronic systems in themselves have created new territories, but computers do provide powerful technical means, unheard of before now, for handling both technical systems and the new territories which they tend to create. At this point, how should the future relationships between the traditional institutional actors and the operators of these new territories be envisaged?

A parallel might be attempted here with work in progress concerning those data systems whose task is to coordinate different urban technical systems. These data systems are *a priori* more modest in their objectives than the UGISs, but they function along the same lines. Moreover, they possess a certain amount of authority, and some conclusions may already be drawn from the vantage point of several years' experience. Just what do they have to say to us? Essentially they say two things.

First, these data systems were developed especially in countries where most technical systems are run by the local government, and their coordination thus naturally falls to these local authorities. In contrast, in places where network managers are numerous, acting in a compartmentalised fashion, and where no one operator predominates (and this is notably the case in France), setting up these data systems presents major problems, and comes up against organisational and cultural problems which are very difficult to surmount.

The second conclusion which can be drawn, reinforcing what we have just said, derives from the fact that, in the realm of technical coordination, a data system is useful only when each partner continuously updates their share of it; and this updating is possible only if each manager of the network *has equal access to* the data bank. To put it plainly, the data systems must be a *common resource,* conceived and managed as such, which presupposes a negotiated approach to the problem, in terms of choice of representation, language, and so on. The French case is interesting. Before decentralisation, the "compartmentalisation" of the actors taking part in the administration and management of technical systems made any cooperation seem hardly possible (Martinand 1986). Today this compartmentalisation is still there; but in areas pertaining to their expertise (for example, the coordination of road works) local governments have obtained significant results. And this is obviously a sensitive area, because the numerous interventions with respect to technical networks (water, drains and sewage, energy, telecommunications) make the digging of trenches necessary.

At this point, one might cite important cases in which this cooperation ended up with the installation of interconnected data systems. Thus, for example, in the Ile-de-France region the operators involved in the networks of gas, electricity and the Syndicate of Water Works together set up a teletechnological server making it possible to systematise the exchange of information on street works so as to make the programmed coordination of interventions easier.

Reorganisation of the actors

The hypothesis we are going to formulate is that this model can be applied to the relationships which will progressively be constructed between institutional actors and new operators. In the French context, at least, it is hardly imaginable that new operators will impose a new division of roles and an uncontrolled enlargement of their range of action in a unilateral manner. Indeed, no signs have as yet been observed of a weakening in the role of local administrations, and of those who manage them. They have on their side both historical and cultural legitimacy, and the continuing distinctive role of the administrative territories in taking care of most of the problems dealing directly with the everyday life of citizens.

In contrast it is quite easy to imagine that, by means of procedures to be negotiated, the authority of the new operators in their specific area of activity (the management of new functional territories) will be recognised by the traditional institutional actors. If the powerful electronic tools being installed can work towards this, it should also be noted that these tools — and, no doubt, on this point Europe can be seen as different from North America — are regarded, except by certain specialists, with a wary and critical eye. Those who use them must first convince others of their utility and reliability. They must also conceive them, following the example of the systems discussed here, as resources held in common. They have to be accessible to the local administration management, and as transparent as possible, with everything that this implies concerning *negotiated procedures*. Under these conditions, data systems will progressively participate in the reorganisation of all the participants involved, which will then be more rational and better adapted to the way in which territories (both functional *and* institutional) overlap, and sometimes even overstep their limits. More generally, they will be adapted to the territorial levels of management of our urban systems.

As an example, consider an elementary version of game theory. If data exchange constitutes a zero-score game, with both winners and losers, it is unlikely that those who stand to lose will encourage these exchanges, and disorder and blockage are foreseeable. If, on the contrary, these exchanges constitute a game with a positive score, in which the possibility exists for each player to win something, then cooperation mechanisms have a better chance of developing. The example of coordination of road works is exemplary here: locally elected officials and the companies handling the technical networks involved all benefit in terms of real financial savings, from such cooperation.

The challenge of standards

In order to evaluate the positive or negative aspects of a game, however, it is not enough simply to take into consideration the economic benefits of the game. Indeed, in the systems of actors at work here, the users themselves are more and more often involved as an active party. The problem of the quality of service which is provided for them, or even taking into account their sensitivity to environmental protection or how areas are developed, becomes more crucial in that these same users are also the voters. At a time when local democracy appears frequently as an important dimension in the solution of ever-more difficult problems confronting local governments, it is also this, without being overly optimistic, which is an important element in favour of the development of *cooperative mechanisms*.

Sharing databanks and information systems which have been conceived on different scales also brings up the question of *standards* (Bensoussan 1991). The stakes here are those previously mentioned: putting into place systems of information which are more or less *open*, more or less *transparent* for all the other actors involved. The UK was the pathfinder here by setting up, as early as 1986, a national transfer form, the NTF. In France in 1989, the Centre National d'Information Géographique (CNIG) assigned the task of solving the problems of geographical information exchange to a working group, which then proposed the EDIGEO form. The need for European standards is recognised by everyone today, and in 1991, a Technical Committee with this job was set up by the Comité Européen de

Normalisation (CEN) (Aigrin and Salge 1992). It is nevertheless quite clear that much work remains to be done, both in defining the appropriate standards, and in applying them to everyone in the same way.

The scientists have a role to play here. Instead of considering that the conception and start-up of these data systems constitute problems for technical development, they ought to consider them as an important topic for research and study, by applying themselves especially to working out rigorous methodologies and by taking an interest in adapting them to concrete problems of territorial management. We believe that the future of geographical information systems should be part of a joint endeavour, as tools to aid in *managing the complexity* of territories, and for potential *renewal of local democracy.*

Notes

1. Offices provided through property development schemes represented approximately 80% of the total supply of offices in the Ile-de-France area during the period of the study.
2. The following figures were agreed upon to represent "proximity": 1500 m using the shortest route to train or subway stations; 3000 m using the shortest route to a motorway exit.
3. In order to take into account the particular status of the city of Paris, which is both a (huge) municipality, as well as a département in itself, we have considered each arrondissement of the city as a separate municipality.
4. A recent issue of the "Cahiers de l'Institut d'Aménagement et d'Urbanisme d'Ile-de-France" (July, 1992) has been published on regional observatories, and the question is insidiously brought up concerning whether it might not be a good idea to set up . . . "an observatory of the observatories"!

8

More than Ducts and Wires: Post-Fordism, Cities and Utility Networks

STEPHEN GRAHAM and SIMON MARVIN

Utility networks — gas, electricity, water and telecommunications — provide the basic infrastructural foundations to the operation of modern economic and social systems. Utilities provide access to energy, water and communications services through extensive physical networks of pipes, ducts, pylons, cables and radio links. Utilities are the conduits or "technological systems" (Hughes 1983) which link firms, organisations and households into wider economic and social structures. As distributed networks, utilities — along with transportation networks — are the very "glue" that holds together modern society. Cities and urban systems, in particular, are today intensely dependent on dense and interwoven lattices of utility networks. Indeed, without them, virtually all aspects of the functioning of the modern "networked" city would be impossible (Tarr and Dupuy 1988; Tarr 1984). For most utility providers, cities play a central role by providing the base for over 80% of all demand for their services.

This pervasive role of utility networks means that they are important both to the economic development of capitalist production and to the reproduction of social relations. Utilities span the production/consumption nexus within cities (Swyngedouw 1989). Utility networks, as large technical and institutional systems, are therefore closely related to the wider society within which they evolve (Gökalp 1992). To adopt

Managing Cities: The New Urban Context, edited by P. Healey, S. Cameron, S. Davoudi, S. Graham and A. Madani-Pour. © 1995 The Editors and contributors. Published in 1995 by John Wiley & Sons Ltd.

regulationist terms, utility networks are key components underpinning both the particular *accumulation system* employed by firms within prevailing productive arrangements, and the associated *mode of social regulation* necessary to stabilise capitalist society into a coherent "mode of accumulation" (Peck and Tickell 1992a, b). It follows that utility infrastructures are important factors in the economic, social and spatial development of cities, regions and space economies. The cost, quality, availability and reliability of these network services, how these vary over space, the technologies they employ, and how their development is regulated are all factors that have important influences upon the development and restructuring of cities and regions. Because of this, the politics of utility regulation are key elements in the wider process of urban management and governance.

The recent renaissance of political–economic analysis of cities has, however, all but ignored the importance of utility infrastructures and their regulation. Extremely influential "regulationist" perspectives, for example, have failed to recognise the crucial relationships between cities and utilities or to analyse the rapid reorientation of utilities which is currently under way (e.g. Moulaert et al. 1988; Peck and Tickell 1992a, b). Dominating this work has been a concern with local economic restructuring within cities in an increasingly global era and its political ramifications (K. Cox 1993; see also Chapters 4 and 5). Urban utility networks tend to be largely ignored or taken for granted in urban political economy. Where urban services are considered, analysis has tended to focus on the collective consumption of welfare services (Pinch 1986), private producer services (Allen 1988) and private consumer services such as retailing (Ducatel 1990). At most, urban utilities are incorporated within brief statements about "urban infrastructure" (Moulaert et al. 1988). By contrast, urban transportation and telecommunications issues have been accorded intensive recent research (Nijkamp 1993; Hepworth and Ducatel 1992; Giannopoulos and Gillespie 1993; Graham 1994). The urban policy literature similarly tends to ignore urban utilities (Marvin 1992).

Recent research on the urban and regional implications of utilities tends to adopt narrow econometric (e.g. Biehl 1986) or simply descriptive approaches of isolated utility developments in specific cities (Tarr 1984). Often these studies focus in isolation on single utility networks rather than adopting a *cross-cutting* and *integrated* perspective over periods of time which attempts to link the development of utilities with wider political and economic trends. As a consequence, understanding of the changing links between utilities and urban development remains extremely under-developed.

The assumption within urban political economy seems to be that urban utilities are a largely unseen, relatively unchanging and *given* infrastructural underpinning for the restructuring and development of cities —

little more than a set of ducts and wires that lie beneath and support the urban fabric. They are not accorded the status of an important element of the economic, social and institutional development of cities worthy of more detailed scrutiny.

This chapter argues that utility networks are too important to be dismissed in this way. The contention here is that it is now more necessary than ever to begin incorporating utilities into our treatment of the changing political economy of cities. Because of their crucial symbiotic role in the economic, social and geographical restructuring of cities and urban systems, and because of their increasingly significant role as actors within the urban political arena, we argue here that the explicit treatment of utility systems within urban political economy is long overdue. Moreover, the profound transformation currently overcoming the regulation, technology and development of utilities makes this all the more important (Marvin and Cornford 1993; Graham and Marvin 1994a, b). Enormous changes in the political economy and technology of utilities are currently under way which change radically the accepted "taken for granted" assumptions about the relationships between urban utility infrastructure and the development and management of cities. These processes are important elements within the wider restructuring of capitalist society. We argue here that they have important but ill-understood implications for the governance and management of cities.

This chapter develops an initial perspective on the dynamic relationships between utilities and the political economy of cities, focusing in particular on the case of the United Kingdom. It analyses briefly the current restructuring of utilities and the implications of this process for cities and urban governance from a historical perspective. We do not pretend to rectify fully the glaring deficit in the treatment of utilities within urban political economy. Rather, we tentatively begin to insert utilities into the debate about cities and restructuring. This is done by attempting to understand, at a broad and general level, the ways in which utilities have been involved in the movement from "Fordism" to a "post-Fordist" era and the ways in which utility regulation and development has been related to urban development during the period from the 1920s to the present day. We also analyse the political, economic and technological trends behind the current reorientation of utilities in the present era and speculate on the significance of these trends for contemporary urban management and governance. We focus in particular on the trend towards the more proactive involvement of utilities in the urban development and policy process as "covert" urban managers. Before developing our perspective, however, it is necessary to explore the fundamental relations between utility networks and the spaces and places within which they operate.

Utility networks, spatiality and urban governance

Utility networks inevitably require the investment over relatively long periods of large amounts of sunk capital within territorially bounded areas. Usually this capital is quite literally *sunk* into the vast hidden lattices of ductwork, pipes, wires and cables that lie beneath modern cities and fill the corridors between them. Because of this, utilities represent classic examples of *locally dependent* capital (Cox and Mair 1988). This makes them intensely dependent on the economic and political fortunes of the localities, cities and regions within which they operate — to an extent which exceeds conventional firms. As Cox and Mair put it: "Public utilities are highly capital intensive, and realizing the values locked up in fixed gas lines, power stations etc. requires the reproduction of a particular spatial pattern of customers who will provide the utility's value inputs" (Cox and Mair 1988, p. 2). The *capital intensity* and *local dependence* of utility networks are centrally important in understanding their relationship with cities and urban governance.

The geographical scale and extent of utility operations is therefore of key significance in understanding the relationships between utilities and urban governance. This stipulates the degree to which utilities can overcome the vulnerabilities created by their dependencies on local economic and political conditions within single localities. A wider geographical scale of operation, or operation within multiple locations, reduces the dependency of utilities on the governance and development of particular localities.

It follows that utilities which are dependent on individual cities or localities are likely to engage more actively in promoting the development of that market area, acting as "growth statesmen" (Logan and Molotch 1987, p. 74) eager to become involved in the growth politics and policies of their host cities or localities. Conversely, nationalised or multilocational utilities will tend to be more insulated from the economic fortunes of single areas. Whilst not a complete solution to local dependence, such multilocationality "reconstitutes local dependence at some broader geographical scale" (Cox and Mair 1988, p. 3). National public ownership reduces such locational dependence even further by centralising the management and financing of utility infrastructure development to the level of the nation state, so effectively divorcing the management and development of utilities from the local political process altogether. Evidence suggests that where utilities are private and local, as is common in the United States, they are much more prone to engage in the promotional growth politics of place — through intimate involvement in local business coalitions and marketing agencies— than they are in nations where utilities operate at the national level or are in public ownership (K. Cox 1993).

Utilities and the "Fordist" city

The first processes of "extensive" industrialisation before the First World War were symbiotically related to the construction of a myriad of small utility systems that co-evolved with the initial industrialisation process. These were often intimately related to the specialised and densely interconnected urban economies of the period. For example, in the North East of England, the North East Electricity Supply Company in the early twentieth century was geared overwhelmingly towards providing modern electricity services and also serviced industrial sites for Tyneside's ship-building, heavy engineering and defence industries (Hughes 1983). During this period, urban utility services were provided by a complex patchwork of municipally and privately owned companies — the electricity and water sectors were dominated by municipal ownership but there was a more significant role for the private sector in gas supply. The extreme local dependence of such utilities on their particular local economies often made these utilities intensely competitive and predatory. They also tended to be intimately involved with the urban and regional politics of their territories. This period can be characterised broadly as one of the *localisation* of urban utilities, and its characteristics are outlined in Figure 8.1.

The movement towards "intensive accumulation" in the interwar period, characterised by the elaboration of mass-production and mass-consumption society (the so-called "Fordist" era), saw an increase in the scale at which utility networks were operated from the local to the regional or national. It also saw a radical improvement in the technological sophistication of utility networks (Hall and Preston 1988). In this period, competitive regulation at the national level tended to give way to monopolistic regulation, as national government intervention grew to dominate national economies. But this process developed unevenly across the utilities sector. The telephone network was taken into public ownership in the early 1900s, while attempts at increasing integration and coordination in the energy sector in the 1920s eventually led to the nationalisation of the fuel industries in the late 1940s. In the water sector there were various attempts to encourage closer cooperation between mainly municipal and some private companies from the 1930s, but the process was not completed until the creation of the Regional Water Authorities in the early 1970s.

The increasing involvement of the nation state in the ownership and coordination of utilities helped create the development of regional, and eventually "national" grids. These distributed increasingly standardised energy, communications and water services. Such networks were necessary to support the integration of cities into national urban systems and markets and helped to underpin the parallel growth of Keynesian regional policies. Widening access to these services also helped to stimulate the modernis-ation of economic and social conditions in a standardised manner (Hughes

	Localisation 1840s–1940s	Nationalisation 1940s–1970s	Global-localisation and privatisation 1980s–?
Utility providers	Private and municipal companies, locally-based	National, public corporations	Local, regional, national and international private companies
Orientation of utility providers	Local monopolies serving premium markets, particularly densely connected industrial economies	National economic development, supply driven, cross-subsidy	Rate of return 'cherry-picking' premium markets, demand-driven
Type of regulation	Mixture of municipal and private firm regulation (through parliamentary acts)	Central government direction and internal management of corporations	Regulated liberalised markets
Objectives of regulators	Protection of local interests	Universal service at standard tariffs, standardised technologies	International competitiveness of national space economy
Production-economic dimensions	Local and regional specialisation and industrialisation, growth promotion	National economic development, regional equalisation and economies of scale	Rebalancing of tariffs, recommodification, local and regional growth promotion, cross-investment
Social-consumption dimensions	Public health, safety and externalities	Universal social access to standard services — mass domestic markets	Social polarisation and fragmentation, 'pay-per revolution' and social dumping
Roles in urban and regional development	Facilitated regional and local industrialisation	Promoted national and regional cohesion	More uneven development, growth coalitions

Figure 8.1 Historical phases of the regulation and development of utilities

1983). We can therefore characterise the Fordist period as one of *nationalisation* in the development of urban utilities (Figure 8.1).

Nationalisation of utilities tended to divorce utility operators in cities from the processes of local politics and government within particular cities in which they had previously been intensely active (Hart 1983). Municipalities and private companies were no longer the operators of a large variety of small utility networks within their areas. Indeed, national political control over the vital "nervous systems" of social and economic life was generally seen to be superior to fragmented municipal and private control. Instead, increasing coordination was able to generate substantial economies of scale, improve the quality of service and standardise tariffs. As nationalisation became more common, and the nation state became the dominant level of utility regulation, municipalities were no longer able to offer cheap utility services as inducements to inward investment from the burgeoning multilocational enterprises through promotion exercises — as they did in the 1920s (Ward 1990). In the electricity sector in the UK, for example, regulatory changes in the 1930s meant that "the important local variations in electrical supply which had underpinned the incentives of the pre-1914 period were being dramatically reduced in the interwar years" (Ward 1990, p. 109).

As private regional companies and local municipal boards gave way to centralised (and often publicly-owned) national utility corporations pushing towards the *equalisation* of infrastructure provision, utilities therefore became less locally-dependent. They also became less of a factor in urban and regional differentiation and local growth politics. This was because the national and regional monopolies were specifically set up to help even out geographical inequalities in infrastructure provision, so overcoming the chaos of fragmented utility development which was increasingly being seen as undermining the drive toward modernisation.

Out of the complex "patchwork" of local utility systems there emerged large, monopolistic and centralised utilities. The huge capital investments necessary to construct these infrastructures required both a protected monopoly status for utility operators and the economies of scale that accrued from the operation at regional and national rather than local levels. As nationally integrated gas, electricity and telecommunications networks were "rolled out" across national space economies, a welfarist emphasis on universal service and tariffing also developed. National public utility corporations were regulated to try to balance the competing needs of industry and production and the growing demands of consumers, in line with the wider elaboration of welfare–Keynesian policies. This occurred through cross-subsidisation between lucrative business markets and consumer/domestic markets. This process supported the emergence of basic utility services as quasi-collective goods available to all on a universal-service/universal-tariff basis (Marvin and Graham 1993).

Increasingly, domestic access to telephone, mains water, gas and electricity services became seen as an accepted norm and social right — a part of the social contract of the time between state, citizen and capital. This drive towards social ubiquity of access was matched by Keynesian regional policies to support spatial cohesion of nation states and the full productive employment of spare regional capacity (Swyngedouw 1989). The advanced provision of subsidised utility infrastructures, as politically induced stimuli to regional development, was a central element in many of the Keynesian regional economic development plans that developed within the period, for example the Regional Economic Planning Councils within the UK. Rather than politically active within such strategies, however, the utilities tended merely to supply the facilitating infrastructure for the wider development programmes.

These processes took away much of the previous variation in the costs and quality of utility services between cities — the source of much previous competition, uneven development and urban political intervention during the localisation era. As the larger networks were gradually elaborated, many of the infrastructural supports that were necessary to support the development of the Fordist city and urban system — near-universal access to electricity, widening access to telephones and gas and cheap, plentiful and efficient water and waste services — were gradually rolled out across national space economies from the cores of the old metropolitan cities (Fishman 1990).

Of course it would be simplistic to interpret this process functionally in an "infrastructure push" manner: the cause and effect relationships between infrastructural development and urban societal change during the Fordist era were complex and symbiotic (Hughes 1983). It is also important to stress that there was a great deal of *diversity* in the histories of specific utilities and how they relate to urban development (e.g. Hughes 1983; Hall and Preston 1988; de Gournay 1988). However, it is possible to argue that — in broad terms — whilst utility networks played a central role underpinning the development of Fordist urban society, they generally tended to become more distanced from urban management and politics during the postwar Fordist era. They were less locally reliant and more centralised than previously, and geared to the national rather than local political agenda. National regulation came to dominate and utilities became incorporated into the Keynesian and welfarist institutions of the nation state (Tarr 1984).

During the postwar period, this process supported the pervasive application of mains electricity, water and gas and connection to the telephone network by both industry and consumers. This in turn underpinned many elements of the spatial and social transformations that came with Fordism. The movement towards the mass production and the consumption of standardised consumer goods (Dunford and Perrons 1983,

p. 326); the integration of disparate cities and localities into functionally integrated national urban systems; the development of multilocational firms; general trends towards time–space convergence and the reduction of spatial variation; and the suburbanisation of cities, were all reliant on the new capabilities offered by nationally integrated utility networks (Capello and Gillespie 1993, p. 26). The Fordist city, as a relatively integrated economic, social and political system spread across a wide urban region, developed an intense reliance on the largely hidden facilitating lattices of utility networks that underpinned it — quite literally. So, whilst many of the urban changes of the period were intimately related to the widening application of large-scale utility networks, the regulation and development of these networks was often increasingly insulated from the local political process within cities as the services were provided and managed by centralised state-owned industries.

"Post-Fordism", cities and the reorientation of utilities

It is increasingly evident that the regulation and development of utilities are now undergoing a second profound transformation. Although it remains unproven, it seems likely that this change is embedded within the wider trends towards a globalising and flexible post-Fordist mode of accumulation within western society. This, however, can only be speculated upon in the absence of more detailed empirical work. What is clear is that the structural crisis of Fordism and the discrediting of monopolistic and Keynesian forms of national policy seem to be pushing utilities in many parts of the western and developing world to be reorientated as privatised and increasingly globalised utility firms. National monopolies are rapidly being replaced by regulated market forces operating at local, regional, national and international scales. This is shifting once again the patterns of locational dependence of utilities and reorienting the relationships between utilities, urban development and urban politics. It is a central argument of this chapter that this process has potentially important implications for urban governance and regulation. We can characterise the emerging era of utility development politically as one of *privatisation* — its dominant characteristic is a movement of utilities from the public or quasi-public domain to the private domain (Figure 8.1). To characterise this phase spatially, we can adopt the phrase of Cooke et al. (1992) and term it an era of *global-localisation*.

The UK provides a good illustrative example of this current reorientation. In the past decade the regulatory regime which governs the development of utilities in the UK has been totally transformed. The 1980s saw the privatisation of all the UK state utility monopolies which had been in place since the interwar or early postwar periods: British

Telecom (1984), British Gas (1986), the water and sewerage industry (1989–90), and the electricity supply industry (1990–91). The Thatcherite neo-liberal proponents of this policy argued that competitive utility marketplaces were needed in the place of "inefficient" and slow-moving public monopolies in order that the UK space economy should have the utility infrastructures necessary to compete globally as a centre of investment. As the social democratic consensus broke down, the institutional infrastructure of nationalised utility monopolies was dismantled, with the income from privatisation being used to support the hard-pressed national public sector budget.

In the place of nationalised public monopolies, new private models for utility development have been brought in, based on the encouragement of new market entrants competing in re-regulated markets. This process of regulatory change is inextricably linked up with the application of new technologies to utility development. These facilitate the competitiveness of individual companies and open up existing networks to competition. Global-localisation also involves a reorientation of utility providers away from the delivery of standardised services on a monopolistic, universal basis, towards the "cherry picking" of lucrative customers in prime competitive and diversified markets.

This process of "re-regulation" has involved profound geographical change. During the nationalisation phase, the national utility monopolies geared themselves towards standardised tariffs and services and geographical *equalisation* between the cities and regions that make up the space-economy. This was based on the notion that they were "natural monopolies" addressing market failures in the interests of national economic development. Emerging now, however, following privatisation, is a much more complex and fragmented range of international, national and, more commonly, *regionalised* utility networks providers. These operate as private firms in search of capital return. The result is a new series of "patchworks" of different utility organisations developing their infra-structures and services with an extremely complex "layering" of spatial dynamics. Intricate patterns of the *relocalisation* of utilities are emerging, with the re-emergence and strengthening of the regional and local-dependency of many utility providers and the emergence of new local infrastructures such as cable TV and combined heat and power. These are combining with *globalisation* — as major utility organisations also try to restructure themselves to compete in increasingly global utility markets to service the burgeoning and highly lucrative utility needs of multinational corporations (McGowan 1993).

This process is underpinning the emergence of global utility networks and a wide range of mergers, acquisitions and cross-investments within the utility sectors, as newly private utility capital attempts to "uproot" from its locational dependence to diversify into global and highly profitable markets. It is increasingly common, for example, for national telecom-munications operators to compete in each others' territories — previously monopolistic — and to set up strategic alliances that allow worldwide coverage of advanced services to be developed (Cooke 1988). This is a key strength in bidding for the custom of multinationals. International financial capital is increasingly the source of utility investments. In addition, an emerging tier of supranational regulatory institutions such as GATT and the European Commission are attempting to support the nascent globalised competitive marketplaces for utilities. This process is backed by the powerful interests of multinationals. The European Commission's current emphasis on the need for improved transeuropean infrastructural networks needs to be seen as a corollary of its policies to establish a single European market for utility services (CEC 1992a). Increasingly, then, the hegemony of the national level in utility politics is being challenged by the supranational and, increasingly, global level. This is eroding further the already tenuous hold of many national and regional utility monopolies and encouraging the ascendancy of the new neo-liberal utility politics across the capitalist world.

Utilities and urban governance in the contemporary city

These changes are extremely rapid, complex and poorly understood. As a consequence, understanding the linkages between utilities and processes of urban development is becoming much more difficult. It remains far too early to define precisely the implications of this type of reorientation of utilities for urban development and governance. Also, despite some evidence that liberalisation and privatisation are generic, global trends in the utility sector, little is known about the generalisability and diversity of these trends, let alone their implications for cities. We know little, as yet, about the varying national tracks being taken by utility liberalisation and privatisation, or how these relate to the initial positions of each country. It is clear, however, that four broad emerging aspects of the reorientation of utilities can be highlighted as being particularly relevant to current debates about the management and development of cities. These are:

- the intensification of social and spatial inequalities in the development of utilities
- the (re)strengthening of the engagement between local and regional utilities with urban politics
- the application of new telematic technologies to utilities
- the increasing convergence between urban utility infrastructures.

This chapter will now explore these four trends, once again from the specific point of view of the UK.

The intensification of spatial and social inequalities in access to utilities

First, the reorientation process has been associated with a renewed intensification of the social and spatial inequalities in access to utilities. Both within and between cities, the reorientation of utilities is a component in the general trend towards the exacerbation of spatial and social inequalities that characterise the current processes of restructuring (Peck and Tickell 1992b). The movement from national utility monopolies geared towards equalisation and public planning to utility marketplaces inevitably supports geographical and social polarisation in the cost and quality of utility infrastructures.

The most profitable "hot spots" or lucrative segments of the utility marketplace — such as the City of London for telecommunications — are the focus of increasingly intense competition between globally oriented utility companies from many nations. Upwards of a dozen telecommunications providers from all over the world now service the financial services firms in the City of London, for example (Graham and Marvin 1994b). The profits to be made within such "hot spots" from high-value-added utility services such as advanced international telecommunications are extremely attractive. But the spatial implications of this reorientation are highly complex and vary between the utilities. For example in the energy sector, gas and electricity utilities are now offering competing packages of services to large industrial and commercial customers. These packages will soon start to reflect the spatial variations in the cost of servicing customers.

At the same time, however, newly privatised utility companies still remain as *de facto* private monopolies in the least lucrative markets — the rural areas, inner cities and the peripheral cities. Here the entrance of competition is deterred by high costs and/or low returns. As newly privatised utility companies become more concerned with the profitability of their investments, and less-geared to long-term "sunk" investments, their investments are likely to become more mobile and fickle. The danger is that they will disinvest from declining or peripheral localities, so withdrawing or at least damaging the vital infrastructural support systems for development within those places. Importantly, this potentially undermines the ability of these localities to compete within the globalising "place marketplace" for inward investment because they will fail to have in place the most up-to-date, efficient and cost-effective urban utility infrastructures which are increasingly necessary to attract mobile multinational capital. This is potentially very significant when the current trend towards the economic fragmentation of cities and the globalisation of the economy are considered (see Chapter 4). This is because it makes such an infrastructural competitive disadvantage of a declining or peripheral city all the more significant.

The increased variation of utility development therefore both reflects and supports the fragmentation of cities. As cities become transformed from integrated economic systems to fragmented local nodes in a globalised economy, so their utility demands are changed also. At the same time, the utility demands of cities are also being changed by the movement towards service and information-based urban economies and the growth of new out-of-centre urban developments spread way beyond the old metropolitan cores (Garreau 1992). Increasingly, urban telecommunications, energy and water service providers are being forced to reorientate themselves to meet the new roles of cities as locations for the nodal connections to wider networks rather than as integrated and coherent localities.

To meet this challenge, and to reflect the movement toward privatis-ation, the technological systems of locally rooted utility networks are now being reconfigured to interconnect on an international basis (McGowan 1993). Such interconnection involves both the *physical* connection of local networks and the *financial and institutional* cooperation of utility companies. This is the fundamental nature of global-localisation in the utility arena which parallels the increasingly global nature of the dominating economic and institutional power networks of multinational capital (Amin and Thrift 1992; Amin and Robins 1991). Utility networks, particularly telecom-munications, are therefore both reflecting and supporting the growing dominance of global corporate networks, within which city authorities struggle to attain nodal status for their territories through place marketing and local economic development policies (Graham, 1994). And as utilities become increasingly privatised and globalised, they are *themselves* emerging as a key component of multinational capital, roaming the globe in search of return on investment (both within and outside the utility sector). The increasingly global investment portfolios of many telecom-munications, water and energy companies reflect both the search for greater profitability, and the desire to reduce the vulnerabilities to the fortunes of single localities within which utilities are, quite literally, rooted.

Because of their importance in piecing together global corporate networks, multinational companies are now intensely aware of the varying utility capacities of different cities. The particular centrality of the *information* infrastructures of global corporations (Bakis et al. 1993) means that the telecommunications and telematics infrastructures of cities and regions are coming under particularly intense scrutiny as a location factor in investment decision making. The cost and quality of other utilities, however — gas, electricity, water and waste services — are of key importance in the locational decisions of many economic sectors, particularly in manufacturing (such as electronics and pharmaceuticals).

This process also threatens the competitiveness of *indigenous* firms and sectors, as the importance of competing internationally grows through the internationalisation of markets. The competitiveness of indigenous firms within cities and regions that are disadvantaged by the reorientation of utilities will be seriously undermined. Finally, this re-regulation and increasing variegation of utility networks threatens the universality of *social* access to basic utility services. Because the cross-subsidies of the monopoly era are now being eroded, areas and social groups at the margins of profitability threaten to be "socially dumped" from utility networks, as their costs are increased to meet the new demands for profitability by utility suppliers (Graham and Marvin 1994a).

The (re)engagement of utilities and urban politics

The second key feature of the reorientation of utilities for cities is the re-emergence of regionalised and localised utility infrastructures. Where utilities were nationalised, as in the UK, the *localisation* part of the process has considerable implications for the urban politics of economic development because it means that utilities are, once again, re-engaging with local politics to support the economic development of their areas. The newly privatised utilities are now often the largest and most profitable private firms within their areas, at a time when local public finances to develop policy initiatives are under severe pressure. And with business involvement in urban politics growing everywhere, utilities are potentially very significant actors within the formation and funding of the new generation of entrepreneurial urban economic policies, simply because it is good for both their long-term economic interests and their local public image (Marvin and Graham 1993). In the UK there is considerable evidence that utilities are already increasing their activities within the many growth agencies, inward investment promotion bodies, arts and cultural development organisations, and "partnership" initiatives that have sprung up across the country in the wake of the application of neo-liberal principles to urban policy. Alan Bruce, in a recent review of the prospects for local economic development policies in the UK, argued that:

> . . . the potential role of utilities in the promotion of local economic development is important. Following privatisation, there are signs that many electricity, gas and water companies are once again seeing that they have a stake in economic expansion. It is easy to see why utilities should again develop such a role. Most are engaged on development programmes that will show a poor return unless their areas expand. Some have significant PR problems. Most are also involved in job-shedding. For these reasons utilities promise to be at the heart of much local economic development at the local and regional levels. Where they are not, the fact that they are now the largest and most profitable private enterprises, means that public bodies will encourage such an involvement. (Bruce 1993, p. 329)

Examples of this renewed involvement of utility operators in urban economic policies include the involvement of BT in urban telematics initiatives in Edinburgh, London and Manchester; the development of many partnership initiatives between cable companies and local authorities (Cornford and Gillespie 1992); the setting up of a specific inward investment bureau within Northern Electric; and the widespread sponsorship of place marketing and urban development agencies by the regionalised water, electricity and gas companies.

The application of telematics technologies to utilities

The third key element of the reorientation of urban utilities is the application of new "telematics" technologies to utility networks (Dupuy 1992b). Currently a new era of control technologies is being harnessed by infrastructure managers in the shape of microelectronics-based computer networks or "telematics" systems (Miles et al. 1988). The previously separate technologies of telecommunication, computing and broadcasting are now converging into an integrated set of "telematics" technologies and services — based on a core group of "digital technologies". Central to these are communications, information and transactions flows between microcomputers and computerised equipment. The new capabilities of telematics are helping to support the liberalisation and globalisation of utility markets by making possible a revolution in the degree to which global infrastructure networks and their management can be controlled in detail. Telematics help to undermine the "natural monopoly" characteristics of urban infrastructures, so allowing private firms to operate them profitably (Robins and Hepworth 1988). What were previously public goods — because it was difficult to monitor and measure the exact consumption of specialised services — are now made private because of the new control techniques of telematics. So, combined with the political movement towards liberalisation, the movement from public monopoly to private marketplace can be seen to have both a technological and a political dimension.

In the search for higher profits in newly competitive markets, telematics provide essential tools when dealing with the massive and complex nature of infrastructure networks. A technological revolution in urban infrastructures is therefore paralleling the political, economic and spatial revolution outlined above. The new capabilities of converging sets of computer and telecommunications technologies for supporting information processing and communications are being applied pervasively across the urban utilities. All aspects of the management, development and control of urban infrastructure networks are becoming increasingly reliant on parallel systems of computer networks (Madden 1992; Dupuy 1992b). Telematics can be used to help keep energy and water production more in line with demand; they allow much more sophisticated control of plant to occur; they support the automation of meter-reading through telemetry; and they support faster and more responsive customer services — particularly to large, lucrative customers (Miles et al. 1988). As Dupuy argues, because of these capabilities, "virtual" systems of computer networks are now beginning to match very closely the "real" hard networks of information, energy and water flows (Dupuy 1992b, p. 67). The result is a movement toward the "real-time" management and development of urban infrastructure networks: decisions can be made on up-to-the-second information based on the real demands, flows and supply operating on a network.

Figure 8.2 provides examples of the application of telematics across the range of urban infrastructures in the UK. Newly privatised utilities are expecting telematics systems to give them a competitive edge and so maintain profitability in increasingly competitive and uncertain markets (Madden 1992). Telematics are being used to cut costs, improve the speed and responsiveness of large organisations and, above all, improve the degree to which enormous network infrastructures can be controlled and organised in competitive ways. They are also being used to extend the capacity of urban infrastructures by allowing the more efficient use of network space. A good example of this is the application of telematics to road transport in such areas as electronic guidance, real-time road monitoring and electronic road-pricing. Importantly, these technologies bring pressures for further privatisation of transport systems because they make possible the transference of road space, network information and telematics services themselves into private goods to be offered by firms in a marketplace for profit. Through telematics it becomes possible to exclude non-payers from networks much more easily and to monitor exactly the use of services to allow precise payment from individual consumers. And the information gleaned from all of this monitoring and processing itself becomes a valuable commodity in the burgeoning information services markets (Hepworth and Ducatel 1992).

To reflect the centrality of telematics to the reorientation of urban utilities, the budgets devoted by UK utilities to telematics went up by 147% in one year between 1989 and 1990 — five times the average for all economic sectors (Madden 1992). This makes utilities the fastest growing sector for telematics investment in the UK. Madden highlights "the vast scale of IT investments in the newly privatised water and electricity industries — and the pivotal role that investment is playing in creating a competing, and competitive, utilities sector" (Madden 1992). Typically, the fragmented IT "islands" inherited from public utility monopolies are being transformed into sophisticated and integrated computer network infrastructures. These are emerging as the basis for all information, communications and transactions flows within the organisation and for

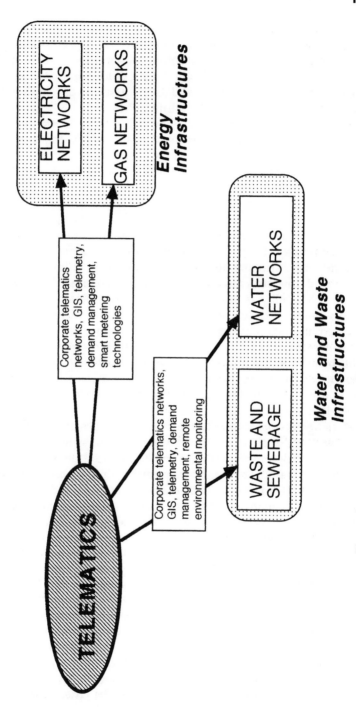

Figure 8.2 The application of telematics to urban utilities in the UK

supporting its relations with customers and suppliers. For example, National Power, the UK's largest electricity generator, is developing one of the largest computing and telecommunication projects ever undertaken by a European company. This will be used to improve customer service, internal flexibility and control and as the basis for developing the "creative service products and complex tariffs" (Madden 1992) now necessary to maintain competitiveness. The view behind the investment was that it "would transform the generator's business by improving efficiency, changing the way it worked with customers and providing revenues in its own right" (R. Wilson 1992).

The convergence of urban utility infrastructures

The final element in the reorientation of urban utilities is the convergence between previously separated infrastructure operators and networks. In the emerging infrastructure and utility marketplaces, cross-investment between utility and infrastructure operators is burgeoning. The new pressure to secure profitability is leading investors to investigate new complementary arrangements between infrastructures that previously were completely divorced in their development within separate public monopolies. This cross-investment is part of a wider trend toward diversification away from core businesses, a process driven by the aim to improve financial performance in utility and infrastructure companies (Brewer 1989). In part, this is a response to the vulnerabilities imposed on utilities by their local dependence.

Once again, telecommunications and telematics are playing a key role in this trend. With all infrastructure operators now developing such strong interests in telecommunications and telematics, many energy, water and transport operators are going a step further. In the post-liberalisation world of British telecommunications, energy, transport and water utilities are amongst the first to invest in new public telecommunications systems to compete for custom with the established operators such as BT and Mercury. The market for advanced telecommunications and telematics services is growing at between 20 and 30% per annum, and a proliferating range of technologies allows niche markets to be entered: cable, personal communication, trunk networks, value-added services and mobile communications.

Existing utility and transport companies are ideally placed to cross-invest into these new utility markets. They possess the necessary large amounts of capital. They already own or control strips of the land, ducts and leeways between the most lucrative business centres that can be used quickly and cheaply to construct new telecommunications networks. In many cases — such as the example of National Power mentioned above — their own sophisticated internal communications networks already have spare capacity that can now be simply resold to outsiders. Finally, they also possess established computer systems to handle billing and customer service as well as expertise in the construction of networks within urban areas.

As we saw above, as liberalisation spreads to be a global phenomenon, this process of cross-investment is taking on a global scale. For example, the current building of urban cable networks in Britain is fuelled overwhelmingly by investment from North American cable and telecommunications investors and French municipal service companies. Increasingly, privatised infrastructure companies face competition at home as well as engaging in competition abroad.

The complex ways in which this dual process of cross-investment and involvement of non-telecoms infrastructures in telecommunications is developing in the UK is summarised in Figure 8.3. This shows graphically how the boundaries between infrastructures are blurring, with the involvement of energy, water and transport companies in telecommunications markets growing particularly quickly. As can be seen from Figure 8.3, this cross-investment and convergence is being paralleled by rapid convergence between computer, telecommunications and broadcasting companies, as the industrial repercussions of technological convergence between these technologies gather pace.

Conclusions

In this chapter we have argued that utility networks need to be incorporated more fully into current debates about urban restructuring, development and politics. Utilities are more than the simple ducts and wires that underpin modern cities. Utilities are the complex and changing technological systems that provide crucial underpinnings to both production and consumption, the development of which relates symbiotically to the wider development and regulation of society. As powerful elements of place-based capital, utilities are key elements within the institutional fabric of urban governance. They are currently undergoing an important reorientation which, we argue, relates to the wider transformation from a Fordist to a post-Fordist society, and which has major implications for the political, economic and technological development of cities.

This reorientation, we argue, involves five interlinked processes: the privatisation of utilities; the development of utility marketplaces; cross-investment between previously separate utilities and geographical areas; the application of telematics technology to utilities; and the emergence of a complex set of spatial dynamics which mixes localisation with globalisation. These processes both support and reflect the wider trends towards the fragmentation of city economies as they become restructured from

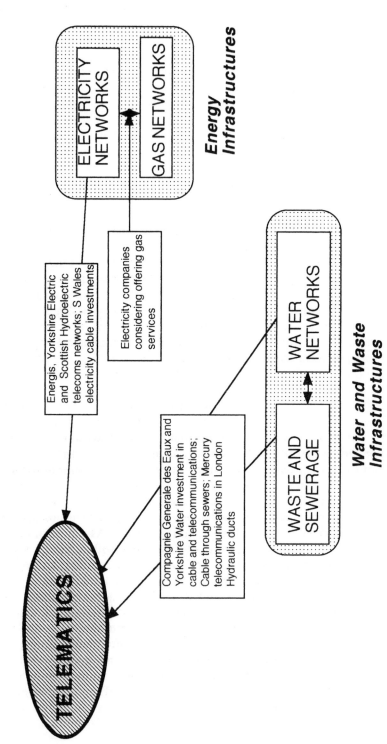

Figure 8.3 The convergence of urban utilities in the UK

Energy Infrastructures

ELECTRICITY NETWORKS

GAS NETWORKS

Energis, Yorkshire Electric and Scottish Hydroelectric telecoms networks; S Wales electricity cable investments

Electricity companies considering offering gas services

Water and Waste Infrastructures

WATER NETWORKS

WASTE AND SEWERAGE

Compagnie Generale des Eaux and Yorkshire Water investment in cable and telecommunications; Cable through sewers; Mercury telecommunications in London Hydraulic ducts

TELEMATICS

coherent and integrated Fordist centres into internally fragmented nodal points situated on global networks. Associated with them is an increasingly complex and variegated "utility patchwork" — a landscape made up of "hot spots" and "cold spots", areas of intense competition coexisting with adjacent areas where even basic social access to utilities seems threatened. Trends towards globalisation and deterritorialisation — as utilities gear themselves up to the profitable global marketplaces — are mixed with trends towards localisation and reterritorialisation — as newly regional and local utilities re-engage with the urban political process to fight for their "patch". Thus utilities are key actors underpinning the social, spatial and economic trends that provide the context for managing cities in the post-Fordist and neo-liberal era.

The scale and speed of these processes mean that their implications for the management and governance of cities remain far from clear. The persistence of wide international and interutility variations in the development and regulation of utilities makes generalisation decidedly hazardous. What is clear, however, is that the sheer local economic weight of privatised utilities is having a greater influence upon urban governance, as utility capital "re-embeds" itself into dependence on particular localities and cities at the same time as developing an increasingly global orientation. This situation in some ways seems to parallel the pre-Fordist case, but this time the global–local dynamics of utilities are more marked. In Britain, certainly, utilities are now proactively beginning to (re)engage in local growth promotion and boosterism, as elements within growth coalitions, to an extent which has not been seen since the interwar period. Certainly, it appears that utilities are of growing importance within the urban political process of alliance and partnerships formation. They have an important role to play in the construction of the local–global dynamics within which the economic and social fortunes of cities are increasingly embedded. The processes of privatisation and global-localisation of utilities raise significant questions about how the relationships between utilities and the social, economic and environmental development of cities should be regulated and by whom. These issues of accountability and power relations in the new era of global-localisation and privatisation have barely begun to be explored (Berrie and Berrie 1993).

The almost complete neglect of utilities within recent theorisations and studies of urban development means that an important "missing link" has been left within current understanding of the city. But it is no longer possible to ignore utilities as actors within the urban arena. A research agenda needs to be constructed so that we can begin to incorporate fully these vital infrastructural, technological and political actors into our theorisation of the management, development and politics of contemporary urban life.

Part 4

HOUSEHOLDS COPING WITH CHANGE

STUART CAMERON

The common theme of a transformation in the nature of contemporary society runs through this book, with the notions of movement from modernism to postmodernism and from Fordism to post-Fordism central to the argument. This section examines some aspects of the experience of this change in the lifestyles of people and households.

The context for the life-chances and economic survival strategies of households is set by the related changes in employment and the economy and in the welfare system and the state implied in the transformation to post-Fordism. This might be characterised by a move from inflexibility/ predictability to flexibility/uncertainty. Talking about the class structure of Fordism, for example, Esping-Andersen (1993) suggests:

> . . . one of its hallmarks was an extremely high degree of career and life-chance predictability . . . . The industrial worker and, for that matter, the routine clerical worker would know that significant upward or outward career mobility was unlikely over the life-course. On the other hand, he or she would face a future of good earnings, job and income stability, a package of fringe benefits and welfare guarantees that allowed, in totem, a satisfactory degree of participation in the prevailing standards of living and consumption in society. (p. 15)

Managing Cities: The New Urban Context, edited by P. Healey, S. Cameron, S. Davoudi, S. Graham and A. Madani-Pour. © 1995 The Editors and contributors. Published in 1995 by John Wiley & Sons Ltd.

It is not accidental that in the opposed characteristics of Fordism and post-Fordism mentioned above — inflexibility/predictability and flexibility/uncertainty — each has what would normally be regarded as a positive and a negative element. With the transformation to post-Fordism the "flexibility", in employment terms, in a regime of flexible accumulation may have a downside in increased insecurity and the often-repeated homily that "no-one now has a job for life". At the same time, the decline of large-scale welfare states — bureaucratic and paternalistic as these might have been — produces fragmentation (discussed in Part 5 in terms of the notion of "governance") and the withdrawal of relatively comprehensive state welfare guarantees.

For the most part, the theoretical contributions to understanding this process of transformation have come from a Marxist tradition. The work of writers such as Offe and O'Connor identified the roots of the breakdown of Fordism in various crises of incompatibility between capitalist accumulation within the market, and the democratic welfare state (e.g. Offe 1984). The Regulation School, in France and the United States, developed out of the structuralist Marxist tradition the concept of the paradigm shift from Fordism to post-Fordism, involving new forms of economic and social regulation. Enzo Mingione discusses the conceptualisation of Fordism and post-Fordism in his chapter and refers to the work of Sayer (1989).

However, these ideas are not incompatible with the ideologies of the New Right, whose analysis would converge in recognising a fundamental instability in the welfare capitalist compromise of Fordism. The divergence between the perspectives deriving from the Marxist tradition and those from the liberal New Right is likely to be normative, and to correspond closely to the "localist–globalist" distinction drawn in relation to economic and industrial change in the introduction to Part 2. A positive view of the outcome of post-Fordism for households — akin to the "localist" position — would emphasise increases in freedom, flexibility and choice. A negative view — akin to that of the globalists — sees rather insecurity, social polarisation and powerlessness in the face of economic forces.

Mingione provides a general review for western societies of the social and employment consequences of these changes. He does not suggest a clear-cut and simple picture, either of the Fordist/post-Fordist transition itself or of its implications for households and societies; but in general his emphasis is on the negative aspects of these changes for many households in the urban system in terms of increasing social polarisation and marginalisation.

Central to the themes of this section, though, is concern with a two-way process. In addition to the question of the impacts — positive and negative — of social and economic transformations, the nature of the household response and adjustment to this new context is examined.

One view of a post-Fordist regime of accumulation — a view perhaps favoured by the liberal New Right — would be to see a reduction in the bureaucracy and inflexibility arising from the decline of the "big battalions" of Fordism as giving freer rein to the emergence of rational economic man, with market relations and economic rationality as the basis for household choices and adjustments. However, quite central to the arguments of both Mingione and Wheelock is a challenge to this view. Both deny that pure economic rationality and relationships dominate the post-Fordist world. Both suggest that personal, non-economic, ascriptive relationships play a crucial role in understanding the behaviour and survival strategies of households within this world. Both writers, in effect, suggest that at the household level no simple, overarching theory is adequate, and particularly not a simple economistic model of behaviour. The economic theories of Polanyi, with their emphasis on reciprocity in economic relations, are acknowledged as an important inspiration both in the chapter by Jane Wheelock, and elsewhere in the work of Mingione (1991).

The roles of different forms of extended family relationships in the economic strategies of households are discussed by Mingione in his chapter. Here he contrasts different family patterns, especially those of northern and southern Europe. The Italian case is, of course, a crucial model in the recent work of Mingione which argues the importance of ascriptive and familial elements in economic relationships (Mingione 1991). This is seen not only in the economy of the "first" Italy in the south, but also in the "third" Italy of the new industrial districts of the north which are widely regarded as at the leading edge of the post-Fordist economy (Mingione 1991, pp. 318–322).

The chapter by Wheelock focuses on a much smaller canvas than that of Mingione, a detailed empirical study of households engaged in small business in the North East of England, and of households with working wives and unemployed husbands. However, the experience of these households "on the margins of employment" in an area of deindustrialis-ation is central to and emblematic of the processes of wider economic and social change.

Again, the central core of the argument put forward by Wheelock is that the households she studied are not dominated by rational economic decision making; that non-economic motivations and familial relationships are at the heart of understanding their behaviour. Indeed, this explains why the *household* is the focus of interest to Wheelock, rather than the individual or the firm. Wheelock describes her methodology as "qualitative" and "holistic". Hers is an approach to the study of economic behaviour and strategies which might be described as more ethnographic than economistic.

This introduction began with the notion of the all-encompassing nature of a transition from Fordism to post-Fordism, and especially the way this model emphasises the link between changes in the structure of economic activity and employment, and changes in welfare provision. The two groups researched by Wheelock include a group — the small business families — which could be seen to be orientated towards the economic system, and a group — families with an unemployed male "head" of household — orientated towards the welfare system. However, Wheelock's chapter tends to emphasise the similarity of the patterns of household response and adjustment between these two groups, perhaps echoing the wider linking of changes in economic and welfare systems.

This is not just a theoretical linkage. Within the European Union, for example, there is a clear concern to complement the fostering of economic change, through the single European market etc., with measures to maintain social cohesion and combat social exclusion. However, there is a strong tendency for European policy makers to look to the informal and voluntary sectors rather than to traditional state welfare provision as the basis for social programmes (e.g. European Foundation 1992). Wheelock provides one picture of the ability of households and communities to adjust to economic marginality, but Mingione's concluding comments perhaps provide a warning against too easy an optimism over the ability of a "bottom-up" response to cope with the challenge of the polarising effects of the changes experienced by a range of types of urban society.

9

Social and Employment Change in the Urban Arena

ENZO MINGIONE

Starting from the late 1960s, it has become increasingly difficult to analyse the directions of social change. This is particularly true for the urban case, which has been strongly conditioned by the typical trends of the previous Fordist decades: that is, suburbanisation and the consolidation of large metropolitan concentrations; increasing employment in large manufacturing and service firms; the tendential prevalence of standardised production and vertical integration; a persistently high rate of economic growth; the crucial importance of nuclear family households with only one (male) breadwinner and of the organisation of mass institutionalised interest groups; increasingly strong nation states with expansive welfare systems. These trends impacted in different ways in different advanced industrial urban contexts but contributed to shape both the realities and the visions of cities conditioned by industrial growth, class division and national boundaries, loyalties and identities.

By contrast, the current patterns of social change largely contradict the earlier Fordist trends. Even if the conceptualisation of "Fordism" and "post–Fordism" can be easily questioned and the discontinuities between the two phases are much less sharp than assumed by many authors,[1] it is generally agreed that the differences in the directions of social change have been substantial and have had a radical impact both on reality and on its interpretation. Interpretations of these new conditions have been problematic: some of the changes have been overemphasised and some underemphasised while others are ignored completely or approached

Managing Cities: The New Urban Context, edited by P. Healey, S. Cameron, S. Davoudi, S. Graham and A. Madani-Pour. © 1995 The Editors and contributors. Published in 1995 by John Wiley & Sons Ltd.

entirely in narrow technical terms. A comprehensive understanding of the characteristics of the post-Fordist transition remains extremely difficult: an in-depth focus on a limited number of aspects results in a distorted sectorial or parochial picture while a sweeping analysis can produce an overly simplistic and abstract vision. These difficulties depend on the weakness of the interpretative paradigms used to understand increasingly complex societies, but also on the distortions that the use of the typical Fordist paradigms is producing. In this respect, the necessity to go beyond the "market" rationale and the economistic and utilitarian paradigm and to recuperate the meanings of household strategies (see Chapter 10) and of different reciprocal and ascriptive aggregations and loyalties becomes increasingly important. As we shall see in the conclusions of this chapter, common — and increasingly global — trends of social change are filtered in different ways by more and more diversified conditions of social life, where age, gender, ethnicity and kinship count as much as personal, professional and market resources and political and associative affiliations.

I shall discuss briefly some important recent transformations in five areas of socio-spatial change. Moreover, I shall criticise some of the distortions and stereotypes that have appeared frequently in the debate during the last two decades, and raise some issues that have not been sufficiently explored. The conclusion will provide some preliminary suggestions for new lines of interpretation, analysis and research.

The question of space and locality

The transformation of space and locality has attracted special attention because of the declining population of large cities, and even metropolitan regions, to the benefit of relatively smaller towns. This phenomenon has generated approaches emphasising counter-urbanisation (Perry et al. 1986) and the hypothesis that the post-Fordist age has produced a radical and permanent change in spatial organisation of the population.[2] The following issues are mentioned as the primary factors in this pattern of change (no order of importance is implied in their listing):

- the decline of the quality of urban life and the increased cost of living in the large cities and metropolitan regions
- the decreasing importance of urban concentration and spatial location in the age of diffused and inexpensive informational and other high-tech systems
- the numerical growth of social groups facing higher costs and decreased benefits of inner-city and suburban residence, such as the elderly, younger, single residents, some professionals and intellectuals in large cities

- the growing environmental consciousness about the worst effects of urban concentration, such as traffic congestion and air and water pollution.

In general, population data tend to confirm these trends but final conclusions about generalised urban decline and counter-urbanisation are extremely premature and problematic. The socio-economic and cultural attraction of large and, particularly, "global" cities (Friedmann 1986; King 1990; Sassen 1991; Mollenkopf and Castells 1991; Fainstein et al. 1992) still seems to be high and growing. The relevance of face-to-face contacts and of highly qualified and powerful, localised social networks is not declining at all, and this is constantly reflected in the intense attention given to these matters by important financial circles in large cities. Moreover, as will be seen below, waves of new immigrants still choose urban centres, and particularly the large metropolitan areas where the expansion of the new service regime of employment is more dynamic (Sassen 1991).

At the same time, the urban space, particularly in global cities, is under increasing pressure due to new and diverse demands. The much expanded role of non-residents (e.g. businessmen, investors, tourists, shoppers, students, cultural visitors and commuters) complicates urban life and produces a new type of socio-economic environment, no longer dependent nearly exclusively on the number of permanent residents (Martinotti 1993). It is on this ground that a fracture between tax-payers' interests (mostly residents and local businesses) and city marketing interests (mostly oriented towards capturing, at whatever the costs, increasing numbers of city users and regular business visitors) is widening fast and in some cases assuming a greater importance than traditional class conflict. At the same time, the built environment's financial cycle, which depends more and more on global interests that are uncontrollable on a local or national scale, is less predictable as a countercycle to national and local industrial trends. The urban and the suburban housing stock are increasingly characterised by schizophrenic tendencies: growing numbers of homeless alongside large numbers of empty apartments in nearby gentrified areas (Marcuse 1993). Although the economic competition for urban space is more complicated, it has not declined in intensity; in fact, the value of urban space has risen dramatically in certain cities.

The second demographic transition

Even more than in the past, the city is at the heart of important demographic and householding transformations. For example, the aging of the population and an increasing proportion of solitary households have attracted the attention of both social scientists and the popular press. But the impact of socio-demographic change has much more profound and diverse consequences. The dramatic restructuring of urban life is readily apparent in the prolonged life after retirement, delayed marriages and child-bearing, more unstable marriages, the patchwork of broken and recomposed households, the decreased number of children per family, and long periods spent outside nuclear arrangements at different ages. Household arrangements typical of the Fordist age, both those characterised by the prevalence of a strictly conjugal nuclear family and the more complex based on various forms of innovative persistence of consanguine solidarity, have been eroded. In addition, these changes, induced by the "second demographic transition" (Lesthaeghe 1991), will probably become increasingly radical in the coming years.

Householding processes, the mixes between conjugal and consanguineous family relations and various other reciprocal/community networks — accompanying radical processes of proletarianisation (in the sense of high dependence on different combinations of monetary wages and welfare service provisions) or, conversely, the adaptation and persistence of small and family businesses — have continued to play a very important role in shaping the different models and variants of welfare capitalism (Esping-Andersen 1990; Mingione, 1991; Wheelock, this volume). In other recent writings (Magatti and Mingione 1994; Mingione 1994a) I have hypothesised that there are important differences between cases, like England, characterised by radical proletarianisation and cases like southern European countries, where small entrepreneurship and self-employment remained persistently diffused and dynamic across different historical phases.

The persistent, but varied, social and economic importance of different household, kinship and communal arrangements applies also to large cities and metropolitan regions where, contrary to simplistic functionalist views on the prevalence of socially isolated standardised nuclear families, varied combinations of family, kinship and community arrangements have contributed substantially to shape the diversified quality of urban life and, in many cases, also the directions of economic development. In this regard, we must now take into consideration the impact of three established trends:

- the increased average length of life, and the consequent higher percentage of the elderly population
- the decline in the birth rate, which is shrinking the extension of kinship networks and, in combination with the previous factor, could strengthen their vertical cohesion[3]
- the increased instability and heterogeneity of family life due to divorce, late marriages and the variety of cohabiting experiences.

Given these new conditions, the capacity of both the conjugal and consanguineous systems to provide support and social integration for an increasing number of marginalised people has been seriously undermined, particularly in the urban areas where the changes have been most rapid and radical.

On the one hand, in those situations where the conjugal system is dominant, as in Anglo-Saxon and Scandinavian low-income and working-class communities, the new trends are immediately apparent: single-parent households, semi-abandoned children, and long-term socially isolated, unmarried or widowed individuals are extremely vulnerable to marginalisation (Buck 1991; Morris 1993; Wacquant 1993). At the same time, a more unstable conjugal system is less able to provide assistance to handicapped, drug-addicted, or mentally or chronically ill members. The number of "dropouts" from the primary social integration system is increasingly sharply and even going out of control in places where the public welfare system is unable and/or unwilling to confront the eroding conditions of family life (this is the basis for the present great differences between the Scandinavian and the English and American cities).

The impact of the transformation of consanguineous systems, which have remained persistently important in most central and southern European societies and in Japan, is equally serious. The effects of a generation made up of large groups of single children born in the 1980s will be felt only when they are in their forties and their parents are in their seventies (Lesthaeghe 1991; Bimbi 1991; Micheli 1992). Moreover, owing to delayed child-bearing, parents in this generation will be markedly older than in the case of previous generations. The future social impact of this demographic change is due to be radical as the horizontal relations between siblings have, up to now, been one of the main factors fostering the adaptation of consanguineous relations in this typology of welfare societies. These relations constitute a base for innovative small entre-preneurship and provide resources with which to look after the elderly and other marginal individuals within a sufficiently large support network (Magatti and Mingione 1994). Recent studies on the Italian case confirm what was argued more than 50 years ago by the American anthropologist Linton (1936). He emphasised the superior capacity for support and adaptability of the consanguineous compared with the conjugal family, as the latter proves too limited and variable in order to face the difficulties to which weak members of the family, in particular children, the elderly, the handicapped or the chronically ill, are exposed for different reasons. The verticalisation of the family will certainly impoverish its capacity in a network of social support and, as a result, increase the demand for provision of economic and welfare assistance from external social institutions, such as the state, private associations, the market, and community organisations. The important role played by a consanguineous family system based increasingly on a strictly vertical intergenerational line, rather than on an extensive number of siblings, may eventually reduce the potential for geographical mobility. Recent surveys of the unemployed (IRES 1992) show that this is already occurring: the young unemployed will not accept a poorly paid job in a location which is outside the area of family and community support, and where the social and economic costs of settling are too high and the loss of support resources is not sufficiently compensated for by the prospect of a long-term monetary income.

It should at least be mentioned that the combination of less favourable labour market conditions (particularly for the younger population, who have difficulty in finding stable full-time jobs) and household support strategies is reducing the geographical mobility and altering the spatial distribution of a large part of the population in industrialised countries. The protection of family and community arrangements is both more important and increasingly problematic as a consequence of reduced opportunities for employment and upward socio-economic mobility. The present conditions in southern European cities, and even in some other cities hard hit by deindustrialisation, will probably extend to a large majority of the urban population of all advanced industrial countries. Migration in general is taking place on a more global scale. However, large sections of the world population which were once highly mobile are now finding it increasingly difficult to migrate.

The current impact of migration in multi-ethnic cities

Major cities are still the destination of migration. The regions of both immigration and emigration have been changing and expanding during the last several decades (Sassen 1988; Mottura 1992). The patterns of migration and integration of migrants have also changed and have become more complex and heterogeneous than in past decades. As we shall see in the next section, the origins of the phenomenon mentioned above are rooted in profound transformations in the employment structure. Here, I shall make some brief observations about the social impact of migration, with regard to emergent types of integration, discrimination and inequalities in large cities.

Most large cities in Europe are coming to resemble North American cities in terms of migration patterns and ethnic diversity and numbers during the peak period of migration. But there is an important difference which complicates the picture. The mix of temporary, seasonal, short-term and medium-term, and long-term and final migration patterns is still very varied in European cities. Immigrant communities face great difficulties not only because they are discriminated against and confined to temporary and informal service jobs, but also because they are increasingly internally divided by different goals and interests. This is illustrated by comparing those individuals who want to save money and make a quick return to their native countries with those who migrate with the intention of staying for a long period. This is especially evident where the resources for ethnic adaptation are increasingly important and purely assimilative strategies have been largely abandoned. It is further complicated by the fact that in some cities there is an ethnic minority with citizenship (like Algerians in Paris or Indonesians in Amsterdam) combining new migrants with the same ethnic origins but different objectives and interests.

Everywhere, however, the situation is overloaded with new tensions arising from the much less stable and more heterogeneous working itineraries of the migrant and ethnic minority populations, and by the failure of assimilative "melting pot" ideals (Petrosino 1991; Balibar and Wallerstein 1990; Ambroso and Mingione 1992). Moreover, the fragmentation of the typologies of insertion of migrants into a greatly diversified range of service jobs and the crisis of trade-unionism reduces the effectiveness of associative organisational resources for migrants and the likelihood of establishing contacts between migrants and local workers.

The fact that the multicultural cities are becoming established realities does not mean that they work well or that discrimination, racism and interethnic tensions have been reduced. On the contrary, we are living through a very uncertain period in this respect (Balibar and Wallerstein 1990; Pugliese 1993b). Neither the spread of the new and old forms of racism, nor the more restrictive migration policies, will stop the present wave of migrations, but they will certainly have a negative effect on urban life in the near future.

Employment transformations

The employment system, while remaining extremely uneven across countries, regions and cities, has changed substantially in the last two decades along two major lines: declining manufacturing employment in medium-sized and large concerns, and increasing diversification of service jobs. The major consequences include a direct loss of jobs, a considerable increase in female employment (particularly among married women), increased instability and heterogeneity of working itineraries, decreased full-time employment for young people and females, and increased numbers of individuals in precarious and low-paid employment. These conditions are unequally distributed across regions, cities and social groups. Moreover, as a whole, they are part of a complex map of social inequalities and forms of integration of the social division of labour (Wright and Martin 1987; Sayer and Walker 1992).

Male wage-earners have been hard hit by job losses, especially in the manufacturing and construction sectors. These conditions are prevalent in some older "industrial" cities and regions, but they are now spreading throughout all Europe. The effects have been severe because of the inadequacy of the new welfare measures adopted (mainly retraining and re-employment schemes aimed at preventing long-term unemployment or occupational downgrading) and of the impact of the expansion of advanced service employment. Moreover, deindustrialisation has had devastating consequences, even in some less-developed regions — like large cities in southern Italy — where it has come on top of more chronic economic problems.

The extremely heterogeneous range of new service jobs has created difficulties everywhere for new entrants into the job market, be they school dropouts or married women. The new jobs have been inadequate in number, but, more importantly, their low quality prevents them from solving the problems of underemployment and unemployment. The time of job-searching has been lengthened considerably, particularly for individuals with poor schooling or inadequate professional qualifications seeking jobs with better pay and more security in order to support their families (Pugliese 1993a). Consequently, these persons are often forced to accept a poorly paid provisional job, which is informal and degrading, and they risk remaining on the margins of official employment for the rest of their lives. When the numbers of poorly paid insecure jobs (unacceptable to the local population) are high, new waves of migrants from less developed countries in the south and, increasingly, from eastern Europe, are attracted. Thus, even the traditionally outmigrating countries of southern Europe now attract waves of new immigrants. This further complicates the complex picture of the conditions of work and of social integration in European cities which, by contrast with North American cities, had retained until recently a less complicated social and ethnic division of labour. What we now have is an unprecedented mix of long-term unemployed individuals, shifting continuously between inadequate forms of employment, and migrants scattered throughout a variety of poorly paid insecure service jobs. This scenario contrasts sharply with that of earlier immigrants to and within Europe, who were employed in the expanding building, mining and manufacturing sectors.

The new service-based regime of employment (Sheets et al. 1987; Sassen 1991) is varied and selective. It lengthens the period of entry, creating difficulties for nearly all individuals. More and more, individuals must make multiple attempts at finding regular employment and seldom enter a stable occupation at the start. During the entry phase, any of life's typical accidents can permanently marginalise vulnerable individuals trapped in run-down areas. What is worse, however, is that this state of affairs leaves an increasing number of workers in forms of employment which are inadequate to support an autonomous life strategy. Furthermore, these conditions are disproportionally concentrated within specific cities or social groups. Neither family, kinship and community arrangements nor state welfare programmes are capable of reintegrating these individuals. Marginalisation is the unavoidable outcome of the above transformations of employment (Buck et al. 1986).

The new forms of work have a particularly negative effect in cities characterised either by deindustrialisation or by a weak, dependent, less-developed industrial history, like southern Europe, Ireland, and the eastern part of Germany. They also have a devastating impact on individuals who cannot find a viable match between work and life strategies in more complex systems of social integration of heterogeneous employment positions. The typical result of exclusion from adequate employment, in combination with poor social integration and support, ranges from the "work-poor" households in England (Pahl 1988; Morris 1990, 1993; Buck 1991) to the impoverished households hard hit by long-term youth unemployment in southern Italy and Spain (IRES 1992; Pugliese 1993a) and the growing numbers in every large city of young adult homeless dropouts (Caton 1990; Marcuse 1989, 1993). The increasingly wide variety of types of marginalisation is a further cause of difficulties, particularly from the point of view of social policies, where it is no longer viable to select just a few important areas for intervention.

Welfare, national crisis and city government

The last consideration leads us immediately on to the difficulties besetting welfare systems. Increasing social complexity and persistent fiscal crises are dominant realities forcing the restructuring of welfare provision in many places. Privatisation, in a variety of styles and forms, has been the most common response. Recourse to "the market" has diminished welfare-state intervention without really solving the new problems posed by the increasing pluralism of demands and scarcity of public resources. Welfare systems, when privatised, are neither more efficient nor less expensive for citizens, but are certainly more patchy and less subject to public control than the more universal ones of twenty years ago. Most responses to the emerging problems encounter difficulties because of much tighter budget restrictions and fierce competition from other, equally urgent and deserving, needs. Under these conditions the risks of marginalisation increase, particularly for those social groups lacking a voice, and even more for individual sliders who are totally neglected by public opinion until they threaten the social order and, consequently, become targets for repression rather than for more constructive kinds of social policy.

The specific interaction between social change and urban welfare and political responses is mediated by diversified historical systems of welfare provision, depending on the complicated balances between state (prevailing in the Scandinavian variants), market (typically predominant in the USA) and family and voluntary support (persistently strong in Germany and even more in southern European countries).[4] Moreover, local responses depend on the systems of decentralisation and devolution from nation state to local authorities, which are also historically diversified along lines which often have little to do with the typology of variants of "welfare capitalism" and which are often changing in different directions. The variety ranges from strong local authorities with independent powers to raise fiscal resources and to implement welfare and local development programmes, to extremely weak local authorities dependent on a highly centralised nation state. Furthermore, relatively more affluent and socially stable cities profit to a greater extent from decentralisation, while poor and problem-ridden communities may be less disfavoured by centralised redistributive programmes, as is well reflected in the north–south divide in Italy. Northern Italian cities are largely favourable to more decentralisation and local autonomy while southern ones generally oppose this move (Mingione 1993a).

There is another reason why urban areas are the front line in the crisis of national democracies and of welfare systems. Large cities and metropolitan regions in particular face great difficulties arising out of efforts to restructure systems of government and to create new forms of socio-economic regulation. The metropolitan cities are too large and heterogeneous to gain from processes of decentralisation and devolution. At the same time they, and even more so the non-metropolitan cities, are too small to raise resources independently for welfare and economic interventions. These areas are already in a precarious position, because a continuing fiscal crisis has sharply reduced their already limited capacity to intervene in crucial welfare areas such as education, health, housing and the environment. Consequently, some of the most important centres of business are also the localities with the worst social problems. Today, cities and even nation states do not have the political resources to ensure that the activities of global business have less unfavourable consequences for local populations and environments.

Conclusions

The urban arena is at the crossroads of social change and is its main testing ground. Obviously, all cities do not have the same problems. Each is diversified and fragmented internally. But, at the same time, urban systems are becoming more complex: both national and continental borders make less and less sense, yet the local socialisation arrangements still continue to condition the identity of individuals to a considerable extent. Paradoxically it is in part true that, in this age of globalisation, local roots may become stronger. Given the complexity of these conditions, any attempt to construct a generalised interpretation or comprehensive theory must remain tentative. In conclusion, I shall try to indicate some of the lines along which local differences matter and provide different responses to the recent trends of social change.

After almost two centuries of urbanisation leading to radical transformations in the quality of social life, the trend of interactions between social life and spatial forms seems to have reached a turning point, at least in the industrialised countries. This has not been, as the founders of sociology at times appeared to believe (Saunders 1981), a process involving the total uprooting of the reference points for community and family identity in favour of an "unbridled" individualisation accompanied by the play of "rational" interests and incorporation into large associative organisations (Mingione 1991). Rather, the process has been a very dynamic and discontinuous one, which has variously reshaped the mixes of sociality in the direction of constantly setting the big city as the privileged and necessary objective of industrial development. Sociological analysis has always highlighted the tensions that have emerged, at various times, between the economic "appeal" of urbanisation and the devastating effect on the quality of social life brought about by the process. In this sense, there is nothing particularly new in the current turning point and we certainly cannot speak of counter-urbanisation. As has been seen throughout this chapter, there is no question of a clear reversal of a trend, but rather a complicated set of changes: from the consolidation of the controversial reality of global cities to the uncheckable decline of the big manufacturing centres; from the renewed dynamism of economically innovative medium-sized cities to the conflictual role of city marketing; from the development of culture, financial operations and information on a planetary scale to the most strongly felt importance of local and particularistic roots and solidarity in the formation of social identities.

Today, huge concentrations of population (the megalopolises that are still on the crest of a wave, the object of special attention and, in many cases, the object of political strategies for development) are an economic necessity, even if they are socially divisive. In Europe, for example, the most structured and widespread urban systems, which developed historically speaking in Germany and Italy, have proved in the last twenty years to be also economically dynamic compared with the megalopolises of London and Paris.[5] Hence we have the increasingly structured and controversial interplay of the different socio-spatial typologies. The different types of cities are inserted in diverse ways into the transformation of occupational systems, which are characterised by a growing lack of decent opportunities for working careers. A sign of this syndrome is city marketing and the anxious attempts to attract supranational institutions and big shows and other events. It is not at all clear whether the competition and processes of transformation will eventually throw up winners or only losers, nor if there are feasible alternatives that are socially more acceptable, less exposed to the damaging effects of global economic competition and less vulnerable to the critical prospects of the transformation of existing welfare systems.

The various welfare systems, having developed historically in diverse contexts, are currently all encountering growing difficulties (Esping-Andersen 1990; Mingione 1991, 1994a). Those that are most exposed to market forces, as in the USA and UK, show a high potential for social polarisation leading to persistent forms of marginalisation and exclusion. And privatisation, the spread of a polarised employment regime in services, and the discriminatory way in which the new waves of migrants are inserted into society and the world of work, are all opening up the prospect of a sharp rise in the number of citizens who are chronically excluded from even minimum citizenship rights.

With regard to the second set of variants of welfare capitalism, those characterised by the persistence of the role of the family, the community and voluntary organisations (and in particular where the family business is not advanced and dynamic as, for instance, in Spain and southern Italy), urban contexts are devastated by the mass unemployment of young people, who are left totally without assistance from public programmes. Such a phenomenon eventually leads to persistent and dangerous forms of generalised impoverishment with a systematic decline in all the norms governing social and working life. Although the life conditions of Afro-Americans in the black ghettoes of the big cities represent the nightmare situation of the underclass, the deterioration of social life in Naples and Palermo can in no way be viewed as a preferable alternative. Furthermore, the demographic transition is radically reshaping the entire social-support capacity of family, kinship and voluntary institutions, which has in any case always been highly uneven within different local, ethnic and social groups. This observation also holds for all the different mixes of welfare provisions, but does of course pose more worrying questions about those where the family and kinship contribution has remained important. An aging population, low birth rate and discontinuity in nuclear family arrangements are upsetting existing householding systems during a historical period of transition in which both a weaker labour market and welfare state are renewing the importance of family solidarity, even in contexts where it had already greatly declined. It is for this very reason that the outcomes of the transformation are difficult to predict in all the various urban contexts of industrialised societies. The new problems of family intervention, in combination with national and international transformations, end by casting a shadow also on those cases, like the third Italy and Baden–Württemburg, which have been viewed as models of post-Fordist socio-economic success driven along by the innovative capacity of small concerns and family businesses (Piore and Sabel 1984).

The third variant of welfare capitalism, namely those combinations based on a traditionally stronger and more direct and universalistic intervention by the welfare state, is now increasingly in difficulty. Dramatic rises in unemployment in Finland and in Sweden herald a more serious situation than might appear at first sight. In those countries, full, costly welfare cover for all unemployed people is the cornerstone of the social system, whatever government coalition is in power. Rising unemployment or, what is even worse, a structural employment deficit can only be dealt with by various combinations of two general policies: a cut in public spending in less crucial areas (the measure preferred by the Right, but which leads to a further fall in employment) or an increase in fiscal pressure and/or public indebtedness (a measure preferred by the Left, but which has the effect of cutting the country off from international markets and damaging economic competitiveness, and may also lead to more unemployment, even if at a slower rate than before). In other words, even the Scandinavian-type welfare systems risk being caught up in vicious circles which undermine the roots of sociality and citizenship.

Social polarisation and the formation of marginalised social groups; mass impoverishment and overall disruption of social life; and persistent and unresolvable forms of collapse of state intervention and of political systems; these represent the three main negative parameters within which the future of advanced capitalist societies is being determined.

Notes

1. For a comprehensive critique of this question in urban studies, see Sayer (1989).
2. For a recent critical discussion of the debate on counter-urbanisation and the new social morphology of large cities, see Martinotti (1993). See also Jones (1990), Sassen (1991), Mollenkopf and Castells (1991), Savitch (1988) and Fainstein et al. (1992).
3. By *vertical* family relations I mean the links involving members of different generations in the strict parental line of descendancy, whereas by *horizontal* family relations I mean those involving siblings within the same generation.
4. This typology is roughly inspired by Esping-Andersen's (1990) "three worlds of welfare capitalism". In recent writings (Mingione 1994a) I have tried to further articulate this explanatory model in order to take into account the number of variants that can be found within each "cluster" and to explain cases, like that of France, which appear difficult to classify and, even more so, to understand applying the Esping-Andersen paradigm.

5.   The case of London can be seen as paradigmatic because financial deregulation has permitted this city to become the most important nodal point of international finance. The number of people working in the City of London is higher than the residential population of the second most important financial centre in Europe, namely Frankfurt. However, the social and economic costs in terms of disruption and polarisation have been extremely high.

10

Household Responses to Urban Change: the Clash Between Incentives and Values

JANE WHEELOCK

Urban areas in large conurbations have suffered considerable deindustrialisation, particularly since the start of the 1980s. The loss of their traditional manufacturing base has meant higher than average rates of unemployment and an increase in low-wage employment, particularly in inner cities. This chapter examines the effects that this economic restructuring has had on households at the margins of employment. The argument is based on qualitative research undertaken (a) with the families of small-business proprietors, and (b) with families with working wives and unemployed husbands, during 1990/91 and 1986/87 respectively. Both studies took place on Wearside, in the North East of England, an urban economy which provides a particularly stark case of the effects on employment of national and international economic restructuring and deindustrialisation (Stone 1993). The empirical analysis was approached holistically, focusing on the integration of lives and livelihoods by examining the household and its paid labour market (formal) and informal (complementary economy) work in each case. This involved what Stanfield (1982) has called "substantive institutional analysis", focusing on the economic character of the household, rather than assuming isolated individuals who maximise economic gain (see also Polanyi 1946).

There were some unexpected findings in both studies. The extent of

Managing Cities: The New Urban Context, edited by P. Healey, S. Cameron, S. Davoudi, S. Graham and A. Madani-Pour. © 1995 The Editors and contributors. Published in 1995 by John Wiley & Sons Ltd.

family involvement in the small-business undertakings interviewed justified positing the existence of a family economic unit, something that had previously been observed only in a rural context in Britain (e.g. Whatmore 1991; Lowe 1988). There was also a marked shift towards more gender congruence in the division of domestic labour in the families with unemployed males. This latter study found that approximately a third of the women were in the labour market, despite the fact that this was not economically rational for the household — due to the combination of low female wages and state benefit rules. Nearly half of the small-business families were no better off than they had been prior to start-up. Again, this seemed to contradict economic rationality; why didn't these families just stay on benefit? Such evidence indicates that the ideology of labour market policy changes during the 1980s, emphasising individual gain as a basis for improving efficiency and discouraging dependency, is at best based on a half understanding.

It is argued that incentives are largely negative in character, with families gaining very little in narrow economic terms. However, family values are often based on non-economic factors, so that those at the margins of employment are prepared to put up with poor economic rewards in an effort to sustain the household. To what extent does this mean that the costs of a market social order are being offloaded onto families in low-paid employment, and can family values of self-reliance and dignity survive the exploitative pressures? Mingione (1991) and others have argued for the importance of family and reciprocally based relations as a basis for understanding the differing processes of economic change and modernisation in the Italian north and south. The conclusions explore the significance of the interrelations between the formal and complementary economies as a basis for understanding the impact of economic change on the household in a British urban environment.

The context of the studies

On Wearside, as with other peripheral local economies, it is very clear that a process of social, or class, and gender recomposition of the labour force has gone on alongside the process of economic restructuring. The two empirical projects undertaken provide typical case studies of such a recomposition. Households with wives continuing to work while their husbands are no longer in the labour market were representative of the Wearside situation at the time of the study, in a double sense. Employment opportunities for male manual workers had declined, and by the mid-1980s unemployment had reached an all-time postwar high, having remained at almost twice the national average since 1971. The prospects for low-paid women workers had, however, remained relatively buoyant. Despite traditionally low levels of female employment, by 1984 women made up 47.5% of the Wearside workforce compared with a regional proportion of 42% and a national one of 43%. Thus, while male employment on Wearside declined by 9.3% between 1981 and 1984, female employment rose by 2.4% (Stone and Stevens 1986).

The number of households relying on a small business or self-employment rose dramatically during the 1980s. At the same time, governments saw indigenous growth based on new small firms as the solution to those problems of economic restructuring and employment decline so typical of Wearside. Unfortunately, academic commentators point out that much of the rise in new firm formation can be put down to the relative decline of large-scale enterprise which has been part and parcel of British deindustrialisation. Indeed, on Wearside, net employment loss from plants with above 500 employees accounted for virtually all the net loss in manufacturing employment between 1973 and 1987, which suffered a 43% fall over the period (Stone 1993).

True, since 1986, as with other regions, the differential between Wearside and national rates of unemployment declined: they were 11.9% compared with 7.4% nationally in 1991. However, evidence of a regional enterprise culture was far from encouraging. Taking the rate of new firm formation as an indicator, Daly (1990, 1991) shows that the Northern region performance is either near to, or at the bottom of, the league table with respect to VAT registrations and self-employment data. And whilst the number of VAT registrations grew substantially in all regions during the 1980s, the North was second lowest at 19.2% rate of growth, and from a low base, with the South East as the highest at 40%. My research set out to find whether extant Wearside small firms — and the families who were involved — had any characteristics which might compensate for this gloomy picture.

Substantive institutional analysis

Substantive institutional analysis is quite different from mainstream economics, which sees itself as the "science of choice". The formal approach to economics emphasises maximising activity, and presumes a world of scarcity. When coupled with rationality, economics thus becomes a science of choice (Stanfield 1982, p. 67). Stanfield follows Polanyi (1946) in his substantivist approach, which, as Waller and Jennings see it, means analysing "the economy as an instituted process of interaction serving the satisfaction of material wants" (Waller and Jennings 1991, p. 488). Economic behaviour is therefore treated as a cultural process where behaviour is learned. The value standard of conventional economics takes a 'more is better' approach, thereby promoting an econocentric culture

(Stanfield 1982, p. 77). Analysing the behaviour of small-business families on Wearside, it was apparent that despite the widespread rhetoric of the enterprise culture disseminated by government throughout the 1980s, the market culture was not the sole determinant of behaviour. The study of households with non-working males also indicates that some families were adopting a work strategy based on a self-respect which actually conflicted with economic rationality. As a result of economic restructuring in the regions there has been a change in the balance of gender power and authority within the household, which has meant a shift in work strategies for men and women within households in a gender congruent direction. As I shall demonstrate, this movement took place not merely in opposition to economic rationality in some cases, but also despite pressures from traditional views of roles and from the state benefit system.

A substantive view of the economic process argues that "the economy is the instituted process or culturally patterned arrangements by which a given human group provisions itself as a going concern" (Stanfield 1982, p. 71). Such an approach makes considerable sense of the value system and culture of survival that lay at the heart of how small-business families in the North East of England behaved. The same can be said of families where men are unemployed and their wives continue to work. A self-respect model of family motivation tends to be associated with a gender congruent lifestyle which involves sharing between husband and wife. Work for such families is not seen as a "disutility", but instead self-respect is being derived from paid and unpaid work. Wives — and to some extent husbands — were deriving self-respect from female participation in paid work, whilst men were also able to gain a rather lesser degree of self-respect from unpaid work. Polanyi (1946) saw market society as one in which the economy is disembedded from society. "The need is to examine the relation of lives to livelihood and subordinate the economy to the lives it properly should serve . . . precisely to re-embed the economy in society" (Stanfield 1982, p. 73). This is what this chapter aims to do in relation to small businesses, whose role in economic regeneration has been so prominent in New Right policies, and to families where wage-earning roles have been reversed.

As Waller and Jennings (1991) point out, there are two further advantages to substantive analysis, though neither of them has necessarily been achieved in practice. One is to address the importance of the links between market and non-market activities, which it is difficult for formalist economic accounts to include. The relations between familial institutions and the market certainly proved crucial to the survival of the small businesses studied. These relations were also significant in structuring work roles for families where the market continued to provide opportunities for female employment, whilst denying a labour market role to men. The second is that gender roles can be unpacked, for "reification of the market in formalist economics constitutes the acceptance of our current prioritization of gender roles as appropriate and natural" (Waller and Jennings 1991, p. 490). This was very apparent from the study of households with male unemployment, though there were also some unexpected findings from the business families. This chapter, then, examines the "economic character" of two types of household, arguing that motivation must be examined in a family, rather than an individual context, and showing that the market culture is not the model for the conduct of life in either household type.

Incentives and values in families with working wives and non-working husbands

The sample of 30 families with children was obtained from a project examining employment potential in Sunderland, which involved a questionnaire interview with a 7% sample of households in selected areas of the city. As an analytical starting point, four categories of organisation of domestic work were distinguished: traditional rigid, traditional flexible, sharing, and exchanged role. In the traditional rigid form of organisation, the husband performs almost no domestic tasks apart from some predominantly male minor tasks such as mowing the lawn. In the traditional flexible household, the wife may still be busy at the weekend or regularly do housework before or after going to work, but her husband will undertake some non-traditionally male minor tasks, as well as, perhaps, washing up, a major gender-neutral task. In the case of sharing households, a range of tasks including some of the five major tasks (vacuuming, washing up, making the main meal, washing and ironing) are shared between husband and wife, or may even be done by the husband. The sharing household often has an ideology of mutual support and company.

In exchanged roles, the husband does a substantial range of tasks, either alone or shared with his wife, whilst she is either the family breadwinner or has more or less full-time employment. The husband may well describe his household routine in some detail, and will have substantial responsibility for the household, at least through the week. Although this form of organisation involves a much looser gender segregation than the others, there will still be residual elements of tradition. An exchanged role organisation implies just that; there has been some exchange of roles between husband and wife, but there is certainly not complete role reversal (for further details see Wheelock 1990a).

When husbands became unemployed, there was some change in organisation of domestic work in nearly half the families (eight from a traditional rigid to a traditional flexible form of organisation, six from traditional flexible to sharing), and there was substantial change in a further six families, including three moving from traditional flexible to exchange roles and two from traditional rigid. In other words, 20 families (nearly 70% of the sample) underwent change towards a less rigid division of labour within the household, while only seven families (less than a quarter) did not. This is a striking indication of the responsiveness of the gender organisation of households to the non-employment of husbands, although it must be kept in mind that even the change to exchanged roles means that there is still a core of household and child-care tasks undertaken by the wife.

It is nevertheless a far cry from the patriarchal image of the North East, made popular by the cartoon character Andy Capp. True, these Wearside families were in circumstances which negated much of the basis for a patriarchal attitude: none of the husbands was in employment, and unemployment makes a nonsense of ideas of a male breadwinner and a family wage. Indeed, wives in full-time employment, particularly, were often regarded as the breadwinner. Negotiations over the gender division of labour within and outside the household were thus subject to a conflict between the traditional (patriarchal) model and the rationality, or maximisation-of-economic-interests model (Yeandle 1984). The state further exacerbates this possibility for conflict within the family. The combination of the unemployment trap with women's low pay undermines the incentive for families to move towards role reversal as a response to male unemployment. It encourages the polarisation of households into those where husbands and wives are both in employment, and households where neither is in employment.

The Wearside sample was surprising in two respects. Firstly, women did work despite the restrictions of the benefit system and their own low earnings. Secondly, the number of hours that some women were prepared to work was unexpectedly high. The popular conception of low-paid female workers is that they are uncommitted to the labour market. This was certainly not the case for the majority of these women: not merely were many prepared to work despite the disincentives of the benefit system and of low pay, but also hours worked and length of time in current job indicated a substantial commitment to the labour market.

The empirical evidence just examined suggests a third model for negotiations over the gender division of household work strategies in addition to the traditional and the economic rationality models: a model of dignity or self-respect. In a substantial proportion of the sample — some 10 families in all — wives continued to work despite the fact that the family was at best only very marginally better off, and in some cases was actually worse off as a result. The concern for self-respect, in some of the sample families at least, was sufficiently strong to overcome both economic rationality and traditional attitudes. The potential for conflict within families where husbands are not working and their wives are in low-paid work is thus high. A case study will illustrate many of these points.

The Bradshaws are an example of a family which has changed from a traditional flexible to an exchanged roles form of organisation. Mr Bradshaw spent 23 years as a butcher until his employer went bankrupt, and he loved his job despite the low pay. When they were first married Mr and Mrs Bradshaw decided that they would share the domestic tasks, at least until they had children. They now have two teenagers, and since their birth Mr Bradshaw has always helped with the housework on a Sunday, something that is most unusual for the men in the sample. When her youngest was about two, Mrs Bradshaw started work again on the twilight shift in a mail-order firm, and as she said of her husband: "He's always helped, taking on nightly duties".

Just over two years before the study interview, Mr Bradshaw was made redundant, and only four or so months later Mrs Bradshaw got full-time work as a warden in sheltered accommodation for the elderly. Possibly because he had always been helpful in the house, both Mr and Mrs Bradshaw had a fairly modest view of the amount of change that took place, but Mr Bradshaw pointed out that he now did housework through the week. Mrs Bradshaw said that she had "much more free time now even though I'm working full-time, because he does most of the household tasks", although she occasionally did some housework in the afternoon when she'd finished work. "He does the housework, while I do the hobbies", she added.

For Mr Bradshaw it was "very belittling really. A man shouldn't do housework. I'll do it, that's it." Of the major tasks he now shared four of them (washing up, vacuuming, shopping and decorating) and he sometimes did the main meal. He did it because "I've nothing else to do and its nice to see a clean tidy house, but there's no financial reward", though there are three tasks he wouldn't do: windows, ironing and washing. Most unusually, the three managerial tasks of planning the meals, making the shopping list and household budgeting were now all shared in the Bradshaw household. Mr Bradshaw also helped his wife with her job, taking out all the rubbish and getting up for difficult male residents in the night. It is worth adding that Mrs Bradshaw earned just enough for her husband to be unable to claim any state benefit at all.

She loved her job — "we should do more for our older people" — and though she knew "it doesn't pay me to work, he worked for me and the kids so why can't I work for him? I wouldn't like to have social workers in". But the job was demanding, "and that's why I need Malcolm around to depend on". Mrs Bradshaw was most appreciative of what her husband did for her, but saw it as very difficult for him to adapt to his new role: "It doesn't matter to me if I work or not. It's more important for men, it's been inbred into them". Mr Bradshaw now bears a substantial domestic burden, but for him it was no substitute for being the breadwinner, and though he was pleased that "we're both independent of the state, at the end of the day we're pounds out of pocket". It was obvious that Mr Bradshaw would dearly love financial recognition for his role in the house, and for the help he gave his wife in her job.

Not merely, then, are households the arena within which the gender conflict between the economic rationality demands of capitalism and the traditional demands of a patriarchal rationality is playing itself out; the household is also the focus for resolving the conflict between market rationality and the urge towards self-reliance and independence from the state. In households where men have become unemployed, it is wives who hold the key to the self-respect which the family can obtain by irrationally working in the labour market in order to avoid dependence on the welfare system, whilst also flouting traditional views of the gender division of labour. Despite Wearside men taking on new roles which by no means correspond to traditional stereotypes, then, adjustment to non-employment is not easy, since the potential for conflict within the family is large.

Incentives and values in small-business families

The second study was undertaken with the families of 24 small businesses set up during the 1980s. There were eight female-headed and eight male-headed businesses in the sample, seven husband-and-wife partnerships and one family partnership. It was posited that small businesses and the self-employed would be likely to make use of the labour of other family members in addition to that of the proprietors themselves, and that this might provide the business with an important element of flexibility. But members of a family do not just have one work role. Any family unit combines work performed to earn income and unpaid work done domestically. In the entrepreneurial family, it is therefore possible that three work roles are being fulfilled: a full-time or part-time job in the formal economy, work in the business, and unpaid work in the complementary economy. Individual families need to combine work for self-consumption with work for income, taking account of the fact that the work they do in the social economy is unpaid.

Given the predominance of labour as a factor of production within small-scale enterprise, flexibility in the use of family labour provides a key to understanding the overall flexibility of such enterprises. In the entrepreneurial family, work for the business unit and work for the family unit are closely interrelated, so that the work strategies adopted justify the use of the term "family economic unit" (Lowe 1988). We can in fact look at the monetarily rewarded aspects of the family's work (business and employment) and at its unpaid work (domestic and caring roles) and develop a model of the internal flexibility of the small firm (for details, see Wheelock 1992b).

The research showed that the family economic unit is able to make use of a wide range of strategies to ensure flexibility in the performance both of direct business tasks and of indirect enabling work. What comes out of the

Wearside study is that family and business needs are integrated with each other in the entrepreneurial family. Like their unemployed counterparts considered in the last section. Wearside entrepreneurial families were adopting a more or less "domesticated" set of values, although in this case it derived from family involvement in the business project of the family, both directly and indirectly. This meant a particularly intense form of domestic value system. It also places the family economic unit at the meeting point of the complementary and the formal economies, and integrates private family roles and public business roles. It is in this integration that the heart of the satisfactions of running a small business are to be found. A case study illustrates many of these features.

> Frank had established his business, initially on a part-time basis whilst he was still undertaking some lecturing, six years prior to interview. He and his wife Fiona were able to devise strategies within the family unit for coping with the illness that Frank developed when the business was four years old. Fiona already had some of the skills necessary for their book-keeping and accountancy business, but Frank had passed on his own skills as he developed them. Fiona was thus in a position to take over the business during the emergency period when Frank was in hospital: "It was a question of actually writing to clients — making sure stuff was collected in, doing quite a lot more administrative work, and taking it in to Frank and working through it."
>
> Frank's illness proved to be a long-term one, possibly stress-related, necessitating permanent adjustments to the business. He strictly limited the number of clients he took on, while Fiona had a rather larger role than she had before, though it remained a part-time commitment which she combined with her own self-employment as a lecturer. Fiona also took on more of the domestic tasks, notably cooking and shopping: "He hasn't got to think about those two and also there's less stress."

For rather more than a third of those interviewed, being part of an entrepreneurial family gave husbands the opportunity to take a role with child-care for which they might otherwise not have had the opportunity. For several of the families interviewed, one of the positive aspects of running a small business was that it provided both spouses with the opportunity of participating in domestic and family life. Frank was explicit on the matter, as was his wife:

> "It also allows us a particular lifestyle which suits us; basically it's very much a mixture of business and home. (Fiona) Almost indistinguishable. (Frank) And allows me to take part in a lot of home activities, child-rearing, housework and so on and it also allows me to cope with the illness we were talking about earlier."

Yet when the costs and benefits for the small business family are examined, the family economic unit is not economically rational, and it is precisely this domestic orientation of the entrepreneurial way of life that constitutes its appeal. Whatever the debate over flexibility as a novel development in the labour process and industrial organisation, it seems widely accepted that the intensity of work has increased since the start of the 1980s in the UK, and the study sample of small businesses on Wearside were no exception. There was an almost universal feeling amongst the sample families that hours are either long, or very long, when you set up in business. Work time can impinge particularly severely on the family when it is located at home, as was the case for well over half the sample when the business was set up. However, there were some non-monetary rewards for the patterns of work involved. For nearly half the sample, running a business meant that husband and wife could spend more time with each other, in some cases because they worked with each other in the business. Indeed, it is the flexibility of business hours that may allow proprietors more time with children or spouses, or to cope with illness for example.

What of monetary rewards? In the Wearside sample, only five families saw themselves as distinctly better off as a result of being in business, with a further six marginally so. Even when looking at this group it is worth realising that some were receiving state benefits beforehand, so that income levels were still not high. Seven families were actually worse off than they had been, with four having about the same income level. Levels of income were such that a number of business families were entitled to draw benefits, including family credit, free school meals or free medical prescriptions, and housing benefit. For a number of businesses, a further enabling income coming into the house was essential.

It is apparent, then, that even modest income rewards were comparatively rare for the entrepreneurial families in the sample. The small-business proprietor (and family members) work long hours to obtain an often meagre financial reward. Why are families prepared to do this? Essentially, the rewards derive from the way of life, which, while demanding, is intrinsically satisfying for most families, despite its problems and pressures in terms of hours of work or uncertain financial rewards. It is a way of life that integrates family and business satisfactions and values. Personal satisfaction is gained from being in control of doing a good job, providing a quality service, with the hope of economic rewards, but with the reality of sheer survival as a baseline. Largely, however, motivations are not individually based, but derive from a focus on the domestic values of the family economic unit.

Internalising the contradictions

I have drawn a picture of two types of household, living on the margins of employment in a restructuring urban economy. Both internalise the contradictions between family values of dignity, self-respect and avoiding the alienation of dependency on the one hand, and being economically rational on the other. It is interesting to make comparisons with some other empirical studies whose outcome also raises questions about the basis for rational choice. Pahl and Wallace's (1985) investigation draws attention to a self-reliant, home-centred way of life amongst a group which is seen as one of the success stories of 'eighties Britain: two-earner, working-class households who own their own home. On the one hand it does not seem economically rational for this type of household to undertake unpaid as well as paid work, for they are in a position to purchase extra consumption goods on the market. On the other hand, such a strategy is conditioned by the availability of employment and by home-ownership, since only then can the materials for home improvements and other self-consumption activities be afforded.

In a study of labour market decisions in low-income households, Jordan et al. (1991) demonstrate the complexity of motivations in the face of unemployment and the casualisation of employment. They characterise their respondents as "frustrated workers" rather than as satisfied beneficiaries of welfare. The men whom they interview give versions of decision making within a normative framework of how men should work (where especially those in temporary work demand dignity) and provide for their families (therefore avoiding certain badly paid jobs). They only respond indirectly to the incentives of wages, taxes and benefits. Jordan et al. are therefore also critical of the rational-choice model of economic behaviour.

Gavin Smith (1994) argues that for the many households involved in the informal economy of the Valencia region of Spain, stresses arise not only from the work itself, but also from the daily existential decisions on how long to stitch shoes, to farm, to cook, to invest time in the friendships necessary to obtain further work, and so on. Smith argues that this represents a kind of transposition of the functions performed by formal institutions, onto the individual person and household. In order to survive, members of households must use and invest in an ideology of shared identity. Smith sees this as amounting to a distinct form of regulation, for which he suggests the term "enterprising love".

In none of these cases does the market mechanism operate in the way that the rational-choice model would suggest. This is because this model fails to take account of non-market motivations based on reciprocity or cooperation. Ben-Porath (1980) argues that such motivations can be incorporated into a narrowly economic model based on price theory, if we take account of the importance of identity as a basis for transactions. Whilst the family plays a major role in the allocation and distribution of resources, the implicit contract by which members conduct their business is very different from any market transaction. Markets involve many buyers and sellers, and are ideally assumed to be replicable, so that value in exchange is independent of the identity of the parties. In the real world, identity is important even in markets, but in the family identity predominates.

A German study of poverty in the Ruhr highlights the costs of maintaining identity-based transactions, showing the poor breaking off their network contacts and isolating themselves in the effort to survive on state benefits (Tobias and Boettner 1992). This appears to be quite a rational strategy, with the expense of travel and the high levels of debt found, for example, in Bradshaw and Holmes' (1989) study of living standards of families on benefits in Tyne & Wear. At the poorest end of the income scale, then, the contradictions may be avoided by abandoning family and friendship networks which entail expenses. But is Ben-Porath's reworking of "rational economic man" the best way forward?

Autonomy and exploitation

It is important to understand the process whereby autonomy and exploitation coexist. The key lies in values that are ignored by politicians obsessed (or overawed) by the individualism of the enterprise culture, or economists who assume the individualism of a "rational economic man". These are the values of reciprocity and cooperation as an irreducible feature of human life. Gudeman and Rivera (1990), following Polanyi (1946), see reciprocity as the obligation to give, receive and return as a mode of integrating the inherent opposition between the Self and the Other. The predominant stream of thought in economics follows Adam Smith in seeing the "propensity to truck, barter and exchange" as a basic economic motivation, with the conflicting interests of self-seeking individuals harmonised through the market mechanism.

Roberts and Holroyd (1992), analysing family firms, suggest that although in boom times formally rational objectives of profit maximisation and accumulation may predominate, other forms of rationality based on family and affective relations and traditional loyalties, or sheer survival are significant in slumps. Certainly, the Wearside economy in the 1980s was scarcely enjoying boom conditions, and it is equally clear that the business families studied were concerned with survival, and sustaining the household, in the context of a domestic, as well as a market value system. Such a value system was also observable in the households with non-working husbands, where again dignity was preserved despite the pressures of economic and patriarchal rationality.

As I have argued elsewhere (Wheelock 1992a), many economists make the error of starting from the individual, rather than from the household and the family. Those who do not, namely the new household economists who follow Gary Becker, persist in positing that household members maximise their individual economic gain, rather than behaving reciprocally (Becker 1965). In the Wearside small business, the family acts as a collective worker by linking family and business lifecycles. In Warwick, Rainbird (1991) saw this in terms of lives having an "interwoven" character. This holistic lifestyle provides the reward of autonomy for the family economic unit. Yet it is also the source of its exploitation through a process in which technical and affective relationships are fused (Roberts and Holroyd 1992). Apparent autonomy for the family means real dependence for the business. A similar conflict is at work in families where husbands are unemployed and their wives continue to work in low-paid employment.

As we approach the end of the century (and the millennium), one of the big questions facing us is how to achieve social integration in a world of insecurity. New Right policy makers and mainstream economists say that there is no dilemma: if the individual pursues his (or more rarely her) self-interest, social harmony ensues. This ignores the fact that people want to contribute to society, as well as to their individual interest; that they want to participate in, and be a part of, their culture. Far from pursuing their own self-interest, significant types of household on Wearside are actually prepared to be exploited in order to play their part in a social enterprise which has two dimensions to it. On the one hand they want to be part of a cooperative family, which, though by no means free of gender-specific roles and conflict, is based on reciprocal values.

The second dimension is the need that people have to undertake purposive work (see Jahoda 1982). A number of the unemployed men said that they would be prepared to work for any wage. In the absence of male employment, changes in the gender division of labour within and outside the household provide for different forms of participation in purposive work, whether paid or unpaid. The success of the small-business form of economic enterprise for the individuals and families involved can be seen as a failure of late twentieth century capitalism. Despite its self-exploitation, self-employment provides for personal dignity and an inherently satisfying way of life for those who stay with this option. The shortcomings of large-scale enterprise can be seen, with Tomer (1987), as a failure of big organisations to invest in the organisational capital needed to ensure effective work from their employees. Bagnasco (1990) perceives it as the outcome of the crisis of Fordism and Keynesianism, where flexible forms of organisation avoid the minute division of labour and state intervention.

The complementary economy and economic restructuring

Mingione has suggested that industrial socio-economic development can only be fully understood by paying attention to "the adaptation and change of reciprocity networks, particularly the house holding process, and to family and kinship strategies" (Mingione 1994b). He argues that it is complex mixes of reciprocal loyalties, adapted and resurgent in innovative ways within modernity, that condition individual economic behaviour and strategies. I have indicated how important these issues are for two key case studies in a restructuring British urban economy. I want to conclude by sketching out the form that the relationships between the formal and the complementary economies take when economic restructuring is going on, arguing that the household is a key institution in this process.

The boundary between the formal economy and the household sector is established in how production decisions within the household are made. How do people make the choice between doing some things themselves (household production) and having others done by someone else (formal economy)? The household in particular, and the economically unmeasured sector in general, are not an alternative society. They enact a set of activities which are complementary to the formal, money economy. Family work strategies provide the interface between the formal and the informal economies. The household, as the unit of reproduction, must apply its working activities to earning and to supplying goods and services directly through self-consumption.

The individuals within a household negotiate or otherwise decide a balance between work for income and for self-consumption. These decisions are made in the light of social and economic changes brought about by economic restructuring, which may alter the gender divisions of labour within the household. Substantive institutional analysis can be used to show that the household is a key institution in the process of evolutionary change. The economic character of the household can be built up from a study of the ways in which judgements about values are made. The work strategies that households adopt are based on diverse and conflicting motivations which incorporate not only economic evaluations, but also traditional patriarchal perceptions of gender roles and a concern for dignity and self-respect. Any re-articulation of work strategies within the household in response to wider economic change is thus subject to four major constraints: economic rationality, pressures from the state benefits system, traditional ideology, and the desire for self-respect.

The cases examined in this chapter, undertaken in an area characterised by extensive deindustrialisation, have shown that families may decide household work strategies on the basis of self-respect, involving a desire to be free both from the constraints of the market and from the state benefits system; a self-respect which may also fly in the face of traditional rationality (see also Wheelock 1990b). Under these circumstances, wives may decide to work in the formal economy, despite wages which may be below benefit levels, whilst their husbands become more involved in the social economy. The result of this is a more gender-congruent division of labour. Similarly, self-employed women and men showed relatively small, but unexpectedly non-traditional, features in the domestic division of labour, running their own business despite the meagre rewards.

A household work strategy based on dignity and self-respect, rather than economic rationality, can be understood in terms of a reconceptualisation of the labour process. The labour process within the household involves the adoption of a personalised way of life. Indeed, one of the hallmarks of the social economy is that it allows the development of a personal way of life, based on home-centred values, which may be at variance with economic rationality. In contrast, the marketed sectors of the economy satisfy private rather than personal needs, needs which are directly circumscribed by market-based values. In other words, when we consider the full range of economic institutions, both formal and informal, and including the household and its members, it becomes imperative to look beyond the stereotyped assumption of "rational economic man" (sic) to gain a proper understanding of people's motivation.

In terms of the implications for the evolution of the total economic system, there is thus an enigmatic interaction between the household and the formal economy. The intimate relationship between the formal and the complementary economies means that the mode of regulation is modified by the personal wishes and aspirations put into effect within the household economy. A substantive institutional analysis of the household thus acknowledges the presence of different family members, and provides the key to understanding the changing ways in which the household and the formal economy interact with each other.

Pahl and Wallace (1985) contrast the way in which self-respect links in with an enlarged domestic economy at the more affluent end of the working-class income scale with unemployed households. They see the former as a "dependent domesticity" in the sense that it relies on the wages of multiple earners in a declining labour market. My own research shows two types of working-class households who are in an intermediate position, with certain of them being able to move towards a household work strategy allowing for self-respect for the family and for the individuals within it. For one group this self-respect is gained through a shift towards gender congruence in the complementary and the formal economies. Self-respect in this case is pursued regardless of market and state welfare pressures. For the small business group, there is also some evidence of non-traditional gender divisions of labour, but the escape from alienation means that the families concerned enjoy very limited financial rewards. Again, the market mechanism and the availability of welfare run counter to these families' bids for self-respect. For the former group particularly, this is a gender-congruent version of Pahl and Wallace's household work strategy; for both groups, it is a form of "independent domesticity". But at what expense to the families and individuals involved? Particularly at a time when rates of family break-up have become so high, should households be forced to internalise the contradictions between the pursuit of dignity and economic self-interest?

Part 5

DILEMMAS OF URBAN GOVERNANCE

SIMIN DAVOUDI

"City" has traditionally been associated with governance, the arena where politicians and administrators manage and organise the city by articulating and translating political philosophies into programmes of action. But, what the appropriate governance forms are for the management of dynamic and sometimes contradictory relations within the urban arena has been the subject of a "restless search" by political communities (Offe 1977). By the end of the century, as Healey in Chapter 12 suggests, the scale of the "restlessness" has increased along with increasing "uncertainty and experimentation about appropriate governance forms for contemporary western late capitalist societies".

Over a hundred years ago, Marx and Engels first emphasised that constant change is inherent in capitalism. "Constant revolutionising of production, uninterrupted disturbance of all social conditions, everlasting uncertainty and agitation distinguish the bourgeois epoch from all earlier ones" (Marx and Engels 1926). Notwithstanding the expectation of continual flux, "we now seem to be witnessing a period of heightened change, where disturbance, uncertainty, and agitation have gathered pace and taken on a new intensity" (Goodwin et al. 1993). "All that is solid"

Managing Cities: The New Urban Context, edited by P. Healey, S. Cameron, S. Davoudi, S. Graham and A. Madani-Pour. © 1995 The Editors and contributors. Published in 1995 by John Wiley & Sons Ltd.

seems to be "melting into air". Observers now speak of "dramatic sea changes" in the nature of capitalism. Discussions are focused around post-Fordist economies, postindustrial societies, and postmodern cultures and lifestyles.

Changes in urban governance

Changes in social, economic and spatial structure of the urban arena are reflected in and reinforced by considerable changes in the way cities are governed and organised.

Within the Fordist mode of regulation, the state played a key role by:

- meeting a variety of needs which the "market" failed to provide for
- becoming involved in widespread planning and regulatory activity (see Chapter 12)
- providing a channel for political conflict (Painter 1991).

It also expressed other aspects of the Fordist mode of regulation such as institutionalisation of collective bargaining (see Chapter 11). Thus, the crisis of the Fordist mode of regulation during the 1970s and 1980s led to the crisis of urban government manifested in the dismantling of the welfare state. Indeed, the recomposition of state activity represents one of the chains marking the passage from a Fordist mode of regulation.

Now, the term "governance" directs attention to the proliferation of service delivery mechanisms and regulatory systems which exist to devise and implement policies. It expresses the shift from provision by formal government structures to the contemporary fragmentation of agencies, and of responsibilities between public, private, voluntary and household spheres. The delivery structure of the universalist hierarchical welfare state is increasingly replaced with new forms and practices of urban governance. The result has been an increasing fragmentation of agency responsibility within the urban arena (Stoker 1988/91). City governments are no longer the key locus for integration of urban relationships but merely one of many actors competing for access to resources and control of agendas.

In an attempt to unwrap the nature of these profound changes, those working from a political-economy perspective have increasingly looked to regulation theory which offers a way of linking and relating changes in the economy to those in society and politics (See Chapter 11). However, changes in the organisation and modes of working of urban governance are being theorised in various ways. Some see them in terms of a shift from managerialism, evident in the universalist policies of the postwar welfare state, to entrepreneurialism, in which losers get progressively neglected (Harvey 1989b), or from welfare to workfare (Jessop 1993). Harvey links this transformation to a paradigmatic shift in capital accumulation from the rigid mass production of Keynesian regulation of Fordism to the flexible accumulation of post-Fordism. Others discuss a struggle between the emergence of new forms of corporatism (e.g. the public policy evaluation culture) and participatory democracy (Fischer 1990). An alternative model is to see these institutional changes as representing a shift from the local government as provider, to enabler (Stoker 1989).

Decay of established processes

However, "we cannot speak of some undifferentiated movement away from one type of regulation and towards another . . . . We are now witnessing a series of diverse and contested changes in the form of local regulation, rather than looking at some nationally (or internationally) determined shift" (Goodwin et al. 1993).

Such conceptions may overgeneralise a more confused and complex process which currently results not only in the fragmentation of local governance activity, but also in the disruption of established channels, networks and alliances through which local governments linked to their citizens and businesses. It results in decay of established forms of political representation. Old networks are disintegrating, new ones forming, focused on new arenas and different forms of representation (Stoker and Young 1993). The instability and fragmentation of relations and networks represent threats to political community and allow powerful groups to impose their criteria and practices discretely and often unchallenged (Mabbott 1993).

Jessop (1992b) argues that, within the broad parameters, the Schumpeterian workfare state can take various forms, such as neo-liberal, neo-corporatist, or neo-statist, within and between countries depending on institutional legacies and the balance of political and economic forces.

In Britain, the impetus for change at the national level is the neo-liberal political philosophy of privatising governance functions, and deregulating areas of economic activity. Competencies, both functionally and spatially, have been removed from local government to different public, semi-public and private agencies. Local governments have been forced to reduce budgets while dependence on central government has increased. The administrative boundaries are once again being reorganised and, following the US model, local governments are under pressure to privatise and contract out a wide range of services. Tasks formerly undertaken by government agencies are being offloaded on to firms and citizens. Within the arena of the urban policy, decision criteria have been shifted increasingly from universalist conceptions of welfare provision in relation to need, to value-for-money and the achievement of measurable outputs.

As Healey suggests, the vocabulary of economic evaluation has penetrated into public policy formulation and implementation. Drawing on the works of Fischer (1990) and Friedmann (1992), Healey argues that "the critical view of the "economisation" of public policy represents it as an attempt to establish a dominant hegemony which crowds out the voices of other systems of meaning, while privileging capital and particularly big capital".

The changes in urban governance relations are not solely and even primarily caused by struggles within the state. These changes mediate wider changes in economic and social life (see Parts 2 and 4). Economic restructuring has in many places removed sections of industry which once had a voice in local politics, through both owners/managers and workers. The new industries, both the large inward investors and the small businesses, are only uncertainly linked to local governance, and in any case, for many such firms, local relationships are relatively unimportant. Meanwhile, patterns of social life are changing dramatically, altering household composition and livelihoods (see Part 4). The recent recomposition of state activity "is based on the emergence of a clear division between subordinate groups who have to depend on reduced public provision, and the more privileged who have access to privatised consumption" (Goodwin et al. 1993). Therefore, it is not surprising to see that informal economic activity in its diversity of forms is increasing, rather than diminishing, in our post-Fordist/postindustrialist times. This diversity is often described in terms of the recognition of gender, race, ethnic, and class cleavages. But, it extends beyond this to a diversification of forms of life (lifestyle) and household economy (livelihood), encouraged but not determined by changes in economic organisation (Mingione 1991). These changes clearly have effects on political life.

Destructive possibilities and innovative opportunities

"The current fragmentation of governance institutions means a fragmentation of arenas for coordination, collaboration and debate" which is likely to lead into "greater inequality of access to urban region resources and further crises of democratic legitimacy for any state action" (Healey in Chapter 12). The crisis of Fordism involved the development of new structural forms, yet the extent to which and the ways in which these new forms constitute a new coherence is questionable. Through what processes could such fragmentation be overcome?

Healey identifies three possibilities: management by criteria and targets; management by partnership; and management by argumentation.

The first approach derives, as already mentioned, from the neo-liberal agenda. It "accepts and deals in fragments", yet represents "a strong and consistent regulatory regime" which has, despite the theory, "strong corporatist tendencies" dominated by politicians, civil servants, and large business interests and shadowed by a few well-organised local pressure groups. Rustin (1989) argues that "no less than in the Keynesian period, state power is being used by the right to construct new class alliances favourable to capital . . . . The Thatcherite strategy is in its own ways as collectivist as Fordism".

The second approach responds to the demand for more spatial coordination through the formation of spatial alliances. The crisis of representation and political involvement is part of the wider contemporary crisis of disjunction between economic and social life and political organisation. Mayer argues that these crises create opportunities for innovation at the local level.

The breakdown of the welfare state has encouraged new arrangements both through formal strategies of privatisation and as a result of the "coping strategies" of firms and households faced with the withdrawal of the public sector. In the arena of economic development, new forms of governance networks linking the private and public sectors, often now referred to as spatial alliances, are developing in many urban regions to overcome the contemporary fragmentation of urban governance (Harding 1992, Lloyd 1992). Such initiatives are often seen as a new way of coordinating the fragments (e.g. the City Challenge initiative in the UK). Yet, they may merely add another fragment.

Healey suggests that "such alliances are typically re-asserting or seeking to establish narrow corporatist frameworks and essentially reflect elite pluralist models of political organisation". In London, for example, since the abolition of the Greater London Council, such a corporate elite has grown up considerably controlling more than £7.5 billion a year of public money through membership of appointed quangos and committees; "a local government without a town hall" (Colenutt and Ellis 1993).

Most of the interpretations of the changes in urban governance in Britain suggest that the trend is towards a form of entrepreneurial technocorporatism in which the local community, except in its business guise, is squeezed out. Yet, empirical research in the field of urban policy evaluation shows evidence of considerable local leverage in a number of programmes which are based on partnership forms of urban governance (Davoudi and Healey, 1994). Mackintosh (1992) stresses the dynamic and variable nature of local governance partnerships, and the way their evolution may change the perceptions, strategies and interests of partners. This serves to reinforce Mayer's point that we know very little empirically about the forms of urban governance which are emerging in different contexts, and the extent to which local innovation, in whatever form, is compromised and structured by wider economic and political relations (Mayer 1992).

Managing spatial coordination

Both Healey and Mayer welcome the emerging new institutional forms but question their sustainability and their innovative capacity. They suggest that the search for coordination mechanisms creates opportunities for a wider range of interests to enter the arena of alliance formation. Yet, they follow different normative discussions in examining ways of including these diverse interests to represent the fragments which, as Healey points out, is the challenge of the democratic management of spatial change in places.

Mayer's discussion focuses on making the most of the emerging "interest bargaining systems" which are available. She argues: "rather than hanging on to the 'old-fashioned' large-scale nationally oriented strategies, rather than demanding specific third-sector or community representation, social movements will need to use their own chip within the structure of the new bargaining system". The task for democratic movements, Mayer argues, is to make the existing forms "accessible and resourceful for marginalised groups threatened by the powerful polarisation processes of post-Fordism".

Healey, however, suggests that the way towards a more democratic management of spatial change is through "participatory forms of management by argumentation". This approach focuses on "the construction of arenas for debates, on the forms of policy discussion and on the mediation of conflicts" — yet, through an "argumentation process" rather than an "arbitration mechanism" which is the key arena of an "interest bargaining" approach (Forester 1992). Management by argumentation, thus, accepts the diversity of interests as well as diversity of systems of meaning. But, drawing on the works of Habermas, Healey concludes: "It is premised on the belief that through forms of interdiscursive reasoning, democratic debate is both possible and desirable in contemporary pluralist societies".

11

Urban Governance in the Post-Fordist City

MARGIT MAYER

This chapter identifies the new practices and forms of urban governance developed, across the western capitalist world, over the last couple of decades and suggests that we interpret them in the light of regulation theory. This means that out of the variety of recent types and styles of urban politics some common trends are filtered out which appear to be, more or less, successful responses to the problems and crises confronting the contemporary city. The regulation approach provides a theoretical framework for contextualising the changes in urban governance within the constraints and possibilities thrown up by the broader restructuring of macroeconomic growth frequently described as "the transition to post-Fordism".[1] This transition is conceived on a rather abstract level, where a post-Fordist growth model delimits some *general forms* within which development will have to take place if the model is to be coherent.[2] On the basis of these general forms it is hardly possible to draw the conclusion that the new model precludes a fairer organisation of social life, nor that it provides a "happier future", for a variety of options and scenarios are possible within this model.[3] Currently observable regional and national differences already underline this openness.[4] But we *can* say that the transition to post-Fordism structurally transforms the terrain of struggle over acceptable living and working conditions. For social movements and local political actors, knowledge of the terrain on which they struggle, of the scope of possibilities and the constraints marking this terrain are of great importance. The soundness of alternative concepts for urban politics

Managing Cities: The New Urban Context, edited by P. Healey, S. Cameron, S. Davoudi, S. Graham and A. Madani-Pour. © 1995 The Editors and contributors. Published in 1995 by John Wiley & Sons Ltd.

and management depends on an adequate understanding of this terrain: its new trenches and new possibilities for alliances and for success.

Thus, this chapter first screens the changes that have occurred in the context of urban governance to see whether they contribute to resolving the dilemmas of urban politics that have become apparent in our recent past, and to what extent they might be consistent with the logic of a new "growth model". In the second part, regulationist analysis is applied to urban politics in order to point to strategic implications that are relevant to the social movements and actors working to develop alternative concepts and practices of urban politics and management.

Changes in urban governance

Many changes have affected local politics over the last two decades, some of which seem to congeal into patterns observable across national and regional distinctiveness. At least three such parallel trends have been identified in recent literatures on urban politics.

First, in all advanced western nations local politics have gained in importance as a focus for proactive development strategies. The background for these developments is the changes in capital mobility and shifts in the technological and social organisation of production, which, among other things, made it increasingly impossible for particular (re)production conditions to be organised/coordinated by the central state. Since the specific conditions of production and reproduction can be orchestrated only by local political systems, their skills in negotiating with supraregional and multinational capital, and the effectiveness with which they tailor the particular set of local conditions of production, have become decisive factors in shaping a city's profile as well as its place in the international urban hierarchy.

Second, there has been an increasing mobilisation of local politics in support of economic development and a concomitant subordination of social policies to economic and labour market policies. This shift in emphasis between different policy fields has often been labelled as a shift towards the "entrepreneurial" city, and it goes hand in hand with a restructuring of the provision of social consumption. Both in the local economic interventionism and in the reorganisation of public services, the local state now involves other, non-governmental actors in key roles.

This constitutes the third novel trend in urban governance, the expansion of the sphere of local political action to involve not merely the local authority but also a range of private and semi-public actors. To coordinate these various policy fields and functional interests, new bargaining systems have emerged, and new forms of public–private collaboration, in which the role of the local authority both in respect to business and real-estate interests, and in respect to the voluntary sector and community groups, is becoming redefined.

The first trend, the development of a "perforated sovereignty" whereby nations become more open to trans-sovereign contacts by sub-national governments, and regional/local forces become more active in advancing their own locational policy strategies directly oriented to the world market, is seen by many observers to contribute to a greater salience of the local state (as well as other local institutions of governance and economic relations). "Greater salience" does not mean greater strength, autonomy or a shift in the balance of central/local relations; in fact, local authorities have extended their strategic and active intervention at a time when they have been under increasing political pressure — in the UK there is even a question mark over their very survival (cf. Page 1993).[5] Despite or because of this, there is a resurgence of local politics, which provides the basis for the other changes in urban governance, on which we will focus here.

Shifts in emphasis between different policy fields

Increased engagement of the local authority in economic development

With central government grants decreasing since the mid-1970s, local authorities have sought to respond to whatever restructuring problems that were manifested in their region. In the declining old industrial areas, anti-unemployment programmes and local labour market policies were put into place (e.g. Maier and Wollmann 1986; Bullman 1991; Getimis 1992); diverse strategies were explored to foster a more favourable business climate; many cities increased spending on culture and leisure facilities, or implemented strategies to upgrade the "image" or the ambiance of a town (cf. Stöhr 1990; Logan and Swanstrom 1990; Mayer 1992). Some local governments seemed to be aware of the increasingly polarised occupational and class structure in their cities and sought to counteract the attendant social disintegration with growth strategies selected according to their social impacts (cf. Heinelt and Mayer 1993). From case studies we can gather that the urban leaders engaged in these diverse activities around local economic development were often far from certain as to how precisely an improvement in the course of urban development might be brought about, except that "industry and employment matters should be important" (Cochrane 1993a, p. 122). Gradually, these activities have consolidated into a more systematic economic development policy oriented explicitly towards nurturing "growth" and, supposedly, employment.

This increased local economic interventionism is expressed not merely in the quantitative growth of local government spending for economic development, but more importantly, in qualitatively different approaches to economic intervention making use of indigenous labour skills and entrepreneurship, emphasising innovation and new technologies, and involving non-state actors in the organisation of conditions for local economic development. While traditionally economic development measures of local authorities would focus on attracting mobile capital (with conventional location inducements such as financial and tax incentives, infrastructure improvement, or assistance with site selection), a shift in the policy approach of economic development offices is now obvious. Subsidies are now targeted to selected industries promising innovation and growth; more public resources are focused on research, consulting and technology transfer, as well as on building alliances embracing universities, polytechnics, chambers of commerce and unions; land is no longer a cheap resource to be offered generously, but a precious one to be developed strategically (Dyson 1988; Parkinson et al. 1988; Cooke and Imrie 1989; Bennett et al. 1990). Instead of seeking to attract capital from elsewhere, strategies focus on new business formation and small business expansion; instead of competing with other jurisdictions for the same investment, efforts are made to strengthen existing and potential indigenous resources (Moore 1983; Eisinger 1988; Robinson 1989). Going beyond traditional booster campaigns (with which development officials have always publicised the virtues of their respective business climate), cities increasingly "market" themselves in the global economy. And finally, the new development strategies frequently include employment strategies involving the so-called "third" and the "alternative sector" (Ashworth and Vogel 1989; Lassar 1990; Mayer 1990).

These diverse efforts to mobilise and coordinate local potential for economic growth together produced the effect of gradually undermining the traditional sharp distinctions between different policy areas. This is particularly true in the cases of labour market and social policy domains, but also educational, environmental and cultural politics have become more integrated with, and are often part and parcel of, economic development measures. A further effect has been institutional changes: new departments and interagency networks have been created within the administration, and new institutions contributing in significant ways to the shaping of local politics have been established and/or supported outside of the local authority, such as Urban Development Corporations, Training and Enterprise Councils, technology centres, growth promotion alliances or local "round tables". The UK and USA, having been first among the OECD countries to experience severe urban economic decline, were also the first to shape national programmes directed specifically towards encouraging economic activities in urban areas, and establish distinct national agencies to administer them (cf. Fox Przeworski 1986). By now, in most countries central state (as well as EU) programmes have been put into place that encourage (in more or less coercive fashion) the emergence at the local/ regional level of such developmental concepts and of the necessary institutional structures, often by tying their subsidies to the condition that the locality reach a consensus about the forms of cooperation among all the relevant actors. Central government in the UK has been particularly domineering in establishing Urban Development Corporations and enterprise agencies, in which it sought to bring together many of the same actors around local economic development yet circumvent left-wing Labour councils (cf. Cochrane 1993b, 29ff).

Restructuring and subordination of social consumption

Besides the mobilisation of local politics for economic development, whereby the local state seeks to organise private capital accumulation by including relevant private actors, the local state has also been significantly restructured in its collective consumption/welfare functions. The pressures exerted by economic restructuring and mass unemployment on the one hand and by shrinking subsidies from central government on the other, and the willingness to accord priority to economic development policies, have pushed one of the formerly central functions of the local state — the provision of collective consumption goods and welfare services — into the background. Not only did local government spending for collective consumption provision decline as a proportion of overall expenditures, but a qualitative restructuring has taken place involving an increase in importance of non-state (private and voluntary sector) organisations or of public agencies directed by market criteria (quasi-governmental agencies) in the provision of public services. In various policy fields where the local state used to be the exclusive service provider, non-governmental agencies have been upgraded or private markets have emerged (e.g. in waste disposal); in urban renewal, environmental and social policies local authorities cooperate more and more frequently with neighbourhood initiatives, self-help or other social movement organisations (cf. Blanke et al. 1987; van Hauff 1989; Evers 1991).

As in the sphere of economic development, in the sphere of social reproduction, too, public sector-led forms of provision and management have been scaled down and complemented or replaced by a variety of private, voluntary, and semi-public agencies and initiatives, and parallel needs for coordinating structures have emerged. What is more, the traditional redistributive policies of the welfare state have been supplemented by employment and labour market policies designed to promote labour force flexibility. For example, in many cities attempts are made to switch from unemployment compensation to job creation and retraining programmes and to generate employment opportunities for specific groups (which directly supplement/replace traditional social policy). A plethora of municipally funded programmes have been established in social, environmental, and urban renewal policy domains, which tend to be hybrid programmes emphasising workfare and job creation while burdening non-profit (third sector) organisations with delivery and implementation of urban repair or social service functions.[6] Though quantitatively rather insignificant, municipal employment and training programmes have served to mobilise and integrate the job-creating potentials from different policy areas. Active labour market policy measures of this kind therefore imply a blurring of the traditional distinction between economic and social policies as they create a real link between the local economy and the local operation of the welfare state: welfare becomes increasingly redefined in terms of the economic success of a local area (which does not imply success of job-creation measures!).

This means that social welfare measures which used to be relatively universal and guaranteed by the national welfare state (while delivered by the local state) have again become an area of struggle and are implemented in a fragmented fashion. This shift away from service provision through unitary and elected authorities towards more fragmented structures with increased involvement of local business, as well as of other private and voluntary sector agencies, has turned local government into merely one part — though maybe the "enabling" part — of broader "growth coalitions".

Further, the new mix of unpaid self-service labour and private and public sector-paid labour contributes to the development of new consumption norms which support the commodification and/or the self-servicing of welfare functions (cf. Jessop 1991b, p. 101).

Thus, the new public–private forms of cooperation in the area of social consumption are also part of structural changes in the municipal action repertoire. Whether local struggles and bargaining processes will result in more egalitarian and accountable models responsive to broad local needs, or in divisive models enforcing polarisation and marginalisation processes, one of the new characteristics of the emerging local "welfare state" that distinguishes it from the past is its role in enabling negotiation with, and initiating activities by, "outside" actors.

Expansion of the sphere of local political action: new bargaining systems and public–private partnerships

The strategies developed to mobilise local potential for economic growth involve actors way beyond those of classical municipal politics. Labour market policy, for example, now involves not only the local authority, but also federal employment offices, individual state programmes (and their local participants), social welfare associations, churches, unions and in many cases individual companies and newly created consultancies. Urban development policy now involves private actors already in planning stages, while the local authority also has a say in implementation processes. Urban social programmes, emphasising self-organised and community-based forms of social service provision and relying on funds from diverse state and other sources, require novel types of cooperation of different municipal actors as well as between municipal and private agencies.

In these novel cooperation processes, spanning different policy fields and bringing together actors from very different backgrounds, bargaining systems have emerged which exhibit round-table structures and are characterised by a cooperative style of policy-making where, instead of giving orders, the local authority is moderating or initiating cooperation. Such non-hierarchical style seems to have been recognised as essential for identifying and for acting on the intersecting areas of interest of the different actors (cf. Hesse 1987, p. 72; Scharpf 1991). The novelty consists in the fact that bargaining and decision-making processes increasingly take place outside of traditional local government structures, and that urban governance becomes based on the explicit representation and coordination of functional interests active at the local level.

The actors participating in the definition and implementation of economic development and technological modernisation programmes tend to be business associations, chambers of commerce, local companies, banks, research institutes, universities and unions. The restructuring of the local welfare state, on the other hand, has expanded the sphere of local political action to include an additional set of actors: welfare associations, churches, unions, and frequently grassroots initiatives and community organisations.[7] Given the new employment structures, the growth of precarious and casualised job relations and structural long-term unemployment, the traditional distinction between these "soft" and "hard" policy spheres has, however, been eroded as municipal programmes are seeking to address "social" problems with economic development and labour market policies.

Besides the new forms of public–private collaboration in economic development and in social service provision, explicit public–private partnerships have also emerged in urban renewal and urban development efforts. Faced with both tight budgets and increasing redevelopment tasks, many city governments have explored new ways of planning and financing urban redevelopment. In order to upgrade their central business districts, to reintegrate old industrial sites, and to develop attractive new projects, they have entered into partnerships with large investors, developers, and consortia of private firms (cf. Healey in Chapter 12).

There is no "typical" public–private partnership, but more and less intensive forms of cooperation and more and less traditional forms of partnership coexist. The concept embraces a range of collaboration types, from mere subsidy relations between the local authority and particular firms, in which local government plays the role of a "junior partner", to joint ventures where state and firms share risks and equity interests on a relatively equal footing. Partnership projects most frequently focus on the physical upgrading of a large area near the central business district (Frieden and Sagalyn 1989; Dekker 1992), but increasingly they also involve development planning and implementation in more neglected neighbour-hoods, in which case the private partners include community development corporations and other neighbourhood-based groups (cf. Simmons et al. 1985, pp. 35ff, 49ff; Costonis 1990; Selle 1991).

In any case, the partnership rests on a "deal" between the public and the private participants: for the local authority's contribution of subsidy, use of governmental powers (planning, assembling of properties, tax forgiveness), and modification of government regulations (zoning, land usage), the private partner is expected to meet certain project goals and to take on later management tasks. The private partner also has to share project returns with the local authority. This may occur through later lease or tax payments, through providing public infrastructure (e.g. subway stations), or through hiring local (minority) workforces in project construction or maintenance (Smith 1989; Molotch 1990).

Private investors gain from such a deal because the local authority's resources offer them attractive ways to expand their activities. In areas with intense development pressures, urban redevelopment provides highly profitably opportunities for private developers, who need access to promising real-estate as well as titles. Large investors such as banks, insurance and construction companies have recognised the potential of this municipal market for some time.

City governments gain from this deal because it allows them to attract more financial resources to urban development and increase their effectiveness in achieving development goals. By combining public powers with entrepreneurial flexibility, organisational capacity, and additional private (venture) capital, complex urban development tasks can be carried out more quickly and efficiently. Further, city governments decrease their dependency on the national government and are able to tailor development more directly to particular local needs. Pressure on limited municipal administrative capacities is relieved and partnerships often work to increase the qualification and flexibilisation of public administrations. Contrary to the total privatisation of public tasks, the city retains, despite limited finances, some control and influence (Kirlin and Kirlin 1983; Heinz 1993). In fact, over the years, public negotiators have become more skilled in obtaining concessions from developers and in holding private partners responsible for meeting performance obligations. Over the years, cities have also moved away from partnerships focusing on large individual development projects (attracting advanced services establishments and other growing sectors along with the reshaping of urban space), as the negative side-effects of their uncoordinated and often private sector-led growth became increasingly obvious (displacement, bipolar job structures, etc.) (cf. Robinson 1989; Squires 1989); instead, more strategic planning efforts have gained in importance. Rather than competing in the construction of new office buildings and festive retail malls, cities seek to identify the particular strengths and indigenous potentials of their locale and to support targets accordingly. This newer approach also incorporates a broader range of interests (including community, housing, and industrial development corporations), and connects the provision of public resources more tightly to the production of certain outcomes by holding firms accountable and setting contractual performance standards (cf. Fainstein and Fainstein 1992, p. 51).

Nevertheless, this "deal" between the public and private sectors contains a high level of ambiguity, as partnership schemes remain sites of continuing political and economic renegotiation: "In effect, what is 'going on' in partnerships is a version of the broader conflict over the future organisation and scope of the public sector" (Mackintosh 1992, p. 221). It is precisely this ambiguous character which allows local government and other "public interest" organisations to play a strategic role.

Both community-oriented partnerships and partnerships focused on redevelopment in growth-promising central areas vary greatly in terms of openness and responsiveness to affected interests, depending on local political traditions and current balances of power. The more horizontal style of the new bargaining systems and project-specific partnerships does not necessarily imply greater openness to democratic influence or accountability to local social or environmental needs. On the contrary, the participants may form an exclusive group representing only selected interests. While there are significant differences in the relative power of business, unions, and community groups, as well as between "established" community groups and more marginalised, unorganised interests, and while new bargaining systems and partnerships vary in their inclusiveness, these new institutional relations and arenas of urban management have altered the political terrain and opportunities for all local political actors. Politics in the sense of arriving at and implementing binding decisions occurs more and more via negotiation and renegotiation among different public and private actors, both of which are affected by the process as each partner tries to "move the objectives and culture of the other towards their own ideas" (Mackintosh 1992, p. 216).

In these partnerships, the distinction between urban (re)development projects and economic development strategies as described above is increasingly blurred, especially in the case of community development projects/corporations which are typically as concerned with industrial and commercial development as with housing and physical renewal. Such partnerships, which usually include some form of community representation, may offer services and technical assistance for local (small) businesses, run job placement services, or help with developing export programmes for the local businesses. They seek to tap whatever local economic development potential exists, thus contributing to the municipal strategy of mobilising indigenous potential for economic growth and regeneration (National Congress for Community Economic Development 1989; Wievel and Weintraub 1990).[8]

On the other hand, the expansion of development corporations concerned with improving housing and social conditions and the quality of life in neglected neighbourhoods may also be considered as part of the restructuring of the local welfare state described above. In the past, municipalities have used such non-profit organisations to different degrees in different nations, primarily for the delivery of services. But since public funds for community development have dried up everywhere, broader partnerships have been forged involving banks, investors, and voluntary associations — with community development corporations (CDCs) as catalytic actors within them. Now, they are involved in the planning as well as implementation of (social and physical) renewal of urban communities (Selle 1991), their intermediary organisations and renewal agents combine social, environmental and renewal/revitalisation work while also performing lobbying and political functions (Schnepf-Orth and Staubach 1989; Froessler, Selle et al. 1991).

Thus, alongside the private (market) actors and public (state) actors, these community-oriented partnerships importantly involve the so-called voluntary or third sector. A boom of "third sector" literatures reflects the "discovery" of this sector when politicians began to reconsider the division of labour between public and private sectors and to examine ways of reducing state responsibility (Anheier and Seibel 1990, p. 8; Anheier and Salamon 1992). However, while research reports explosive growth rates of the non-market, non-government organisations and activities lumped together under this label, less attention has been paid to the penetration of this sector by the logic of the state and/or market. In fact, simultaneous processes have been under way: while traditional third sector organisations (previously dominated by the Fordist welfare state) tend increasingly to be run for profit as capitalist enterprises, newer ones may function as elements in an alternative economy, which in turn is tied increasingly to municipal programmes (Mayer 1993). In both cases, while serving to make the welfare state more flexible through less rigid bureaucratic forms and more competition, they enlarge and restructure the sphere of local political action. In this expanded system of local politics the public sector reduces its functions, yet plays a more activist role in its interaction with the non-state sectors. No longer the centre of decision-making, as bargaining and decision-making processes are taking place outside of traditional local government structures, the local government takes on the role of a moderator, managing the intersecting areas of interest, and — in successful cases[9] — exerting more leadership and control as it provides its resources on a conditional basis.

While in the more traditional collaboration between the public and the private sector cities would seek to attract investors with cheap land, low taxes, and capital subsidies (without thereby expecting to influence the firms' future behaviour and decisions), the recent urban economic development programmes focus public resources on firms and industries that promise growth, and they hold the private partner responsible for meeting contractual and other obligations (Eisinger 1988, p. 23). While in traditional urban development the redevelopment process was subject to approval by federal bureaucrats, now things are "entirely up to the locality, where communities are mobilised or have gained access to City Hall, they have the potential to influence programmes" (Fainstein and Fainstein 1992, p. 76).

Thus, the role of the municipality has changed from being the (more or less) redistributive local "arm" of the welfare state to acting as catalyst of processes of innovation and cooperation, which it seeks to steer in the direction of improving the community's economic and social situation. These cooperation processes are increasingly replacing state-provided functions to ensure reproduction. In order to win the resources and competences of the various private actors, the local authority has to respect to some degree the peculiar character and particular functional conditions of these non-state organisations.

Regulationist analysis: identifying the constraints and options for local politics

A regulationist analysis may be useful to relate the identified changes in urban governance towards competition-oriented, innovation-oriented policies and new bargaining systems to the larger transition of which they seem to be a part: the crisis of Fordism and the emergence of a new regime of accumulation. Reading the changes in the forms and institutions of urban governance in this framework also brings out some of their implications for progressive political action.

However, the categories of the regulationist framework, originally developed by French political economists during the 1970s,[10] have been adopted and redefined by many other writers. This has led not only to different versions of the approach (cf. Jessop 1990b), but also to a lot of confusion. The British debate, in particular, has been strongly influenced by a version put forth by the journal *Marxism Today*, which sees the breakdown of the monolithic methods of production as leading inevitably to the success of post-Fordist political and social aims. The goal of this tendency is to replace the old debate between the Left and Right by a new opposition between past and future (hence "New Times"[11]); the reorganisation of production around new methods of flexible specialisation is supposed to bring greater individual freedom and the end of centralised bureaucracies; post-Fordism, in this version, is seen as a pre-ordained future[12] (cf. Murray 1988).

Quite contrary to such a "mistranslation" (Barbrook 1990) of the regulationist approach, which has shaped much of the British debate about local state restructuring (cf. Stoker 1990; Lovering 1991b and Chapter 5; Peck and Tickell 1992a; Cochrane 1993b, pp. 81ff), this chapter draws on the French and German analysis of post-Fordism, which offers a framework for assessing the possibilities of *different* compromises under the conditions thrown up by a new regime and new social modes of regulation (cf. Boyer 1990; Lipietz 1992a, b; Hirsch and Roth 1986; Hirsch 1988, 1991; Jessop 1991c, 1992c).

While there are different theoretical explanations within the regulation approach, it is generally assumed that the Fordist regime of accumulation has been in crisis since the mid-1970s and that — without major restructuring and new modes of regulation — this crisis cannot be transformed into a new prosperity constellation. By focusing on the correspondence between the accumulation system and modes of social regulation,[13] and by seeing the latter playing a crucial role in securing (temporary) stability and coherence in the highly dynamic and principally unstable capitalist system, the regulation approach provides the opportunity to explore whether emerging elements of regulation resolve crisis tendencies and address limits of the Fordist models[14] and whether they contribute to securing the conditions for a post-Fordist "virtuous circle" to operate. By, thus, identifying the compatibility requirements of a new mode of regulation, it further allows us to explore the variety of options and scenarios theoretically possible within this model and to recognise the conditions under which more progressive/democratic or more conservative/exclusionary models would emerge.

Compatibility

Can the new entrepreneurial local state as described in the last section be described as post-Fordist? If it can be shown that both the new forms of state intervention (as described under "Shifts in emphasis between different policy fields") and the new institutional relations of the local level (described as "new bargaining systems and public–private partnerships") address the limits and solve the crises of the traditional model and contribute to securing the conditions for a new growth model, then they may indeed prefigure forms of urban governance capable of delivering coherent urban management rather than being mere transitional forms of crisis management.

As we have seen, the new *forms of economic intervention* focusing on competitiveness seek to promote primarily innovation, new sectors, or new processes in established/restructured sectors and thereby do address the problem of insufficient productivity; they move away from the traditional (Keynesian, central government-led) interventionism designed to maintain levels of aggregate demand compatible with full employment (seeking, even, to maintain employment in declining sectors), which contributed to the stagflation of the 1970s and to disrupting the Fordist growth dynamic. Furthermore, as its restructuring of social welfare seeks to subordinate welfare policy to the demands of flexible labour markets and structural competitiveness and to promote more flexible and innovative provision of collective consumption, the entrepreneurial local state not only reduces social consumption expenditures (which had triggered the fiscal crisis of the Keynesian welfare state), but also reorients social policy away from generalising the norms of mass consumption and the forms of collective consumption that were supporting the Fordist growth dynamic. Instead, a fragmented and potentially highly uneven provision of social consumption — tied to economic performance — is established, depending on the skills, political priorities and mobilisation of local political actors.

The new *institutional relations* also contribute to resolving crisis tendencies of the traditional local state by replacing the overbearing, hierarchical state with a more pluralistic and in some ways more egalitarian version. This reorganisation of the local political system reflects the new requirement to make connections between different policy areas, in particular, between economic and technology policies and education, manpower training, infrastructure provision, etc. The sphere of local political action has been expanded: local unions, chambers of commerce, investors, education bodies and research centres have entered into partnership arrangements of different kinds with the local state to regenerate the local economy, and new bargaining systems based on negotiation have evolved. These local networks and bargaining systems address the limits of the centralised, hierarchical, bureaucratic–corporative structures that have been characteristic of the Fordist state and ended up producing huge costs, inefficiency and waste, as well as rebellion. Further, the distribution of territorial management activities among a *range* of private and semi-public agencies as well as local government would seem to prove more capable of contributing to stable reproduction under the new conditions of sharpened interregional and intercity competition.

Identifying these features of compatibility in the local mode of regulation implies that we can describe the requirements for "local economic integrity" or for "success" more specifically than with mere institutional capacity (i.e. the presence of many institutions of different kinds, with high levels of interaction and an awareness of a common enterprise), as Amin and Thrift do in this volume. Not "institutional thickness" would be a condition for success, but the presence of specific institutions compatible with and oriented towards supporting the emerging regime of accumulation. The examples of the North of England or the Ruhr Valley illustrate that the presence of strong alliances based on a "production mission" and of regeneration-oriented institutions and programmes do not necessarily bring about successful regional restructuring (cf. Lehner 1993). Here, "old-fashioned" unions, strong Keynesian welfare institutions, and long-entrenched SPD-labour coalitions have been blocking rather than aiding the generation of a local institutional framework conducive to successful restructuring.

The "new mechanisms for attaining some form of local economic integrity" may be described more specifically than in terms of institutional thickness by focusing on, as regulation theory does, the necessary correspondence between the mode of social regulation and the structures of an emerging post-Fordist accumulation regime.

However, even though this new pattern of entrepreneurial urban policies and partnership style of urban decision-making and implementation are on the agenda of all post-Fordist scenarios (liberal, progressive, conservative), it is quite open whether social and political conflict will permit the actual establishment of these new arrangements as elements of a *dominant* mode of social regulation. Many entrenched habits of those in power, routinised forms of party political competition, occasional powerful political representation of declining sectors (where these were strong, the need for new products and processes did not get articulated), and institutional inertia are known everywhere as stumbling blocks to the *de facto* implementation of strategies that are meanwhile widely applauded in political discourse. But institutions and interventions which *do not* take into account the constraints of the emerging accumulation regime and the elements of the new mode of regulation face the likelihood of failure and the huge costs associated with that.

Possible versions of post-Fordist modes of regulation

As just indicated, a variety of different political platforms pursue this post-Fordist scenario: no matter whether dominated by more left-wing or more right-wing parties, city governments give priority to economic development policies (via the entrepreneurial mobilisation of indigenous potential), thereby pushing one of the formerly central functions of local state politics, the provision of collective consumption goods and welfare services, into the background. This devolution/privatisation of the local (welfare) state and its increased engagement for economic development tend to occur via new forms of negotiation and implementation privileging non-governmental (intermediary) organisations.

We find this basic model applied everywhere, long-held political traditions notwithstanding: subnational state intervention to encourage growth and employment is propagated even in the most liberal environments,[15] and the post-Fordist welfare/workfare state is present on the most diverse political agendas: the right finds it attractive because it involves voluntarism and workfare, allowing state shrinkage; the left, because it is "enabling" people to exercise power for themselves; and the liberals, because it emphasises local community action. Also, as we have seen, new bargaining structures are a reality in many different cities but contrast starkly in terms of their inclusiveness and responsiveness with regard to non-CBD, non-real-estate, non-large investor interests. What is more, cleavages have become apparent not just between neighbourhoods and large developers/large firms, but also between newly included community interests on the one side and groups peripheral to the new arrangements on the other. In any case, city governments *can* and do play a more initiating and more active role than in the past, and this local state activity will obviously reflect the power struggles and political conflicts carried out in a locale.

In other words, more and less democratic versions of this basic model are possible without seriously restraining the transition to post-Fordism. Neither is it a requirement that the new institutions, in order to contribute to "success", must constitute political empowerment within localities (as Amin and Thrift indicate (1992), p. 18), nor are the new bargaining structures *per se* more biased towards private business than the old form of urban governance which emphasised the separation between public benefit and private profit. Their concrete shape, their degree of responsiveness and openness, will depend on how actors on the local level will seize and struggle over the opportunities and forms provided within this basic model.

So what should the (environmental and democratic) movements be arguing for as key elements and practices of urban management? Different proposals have been on the table. Some have argued for "the creation of a new sector dedicated to socially useful tasks of the kind which are provided expensively by the welfare state, by unpaid female work, or not at all (environmental improvement in poor neighbourhoods, etc.)" (Lipietz 1992a, p. 325). Others argue for strengthening national redistributive policies and for challenging the political ideology "that eschews state ownership of housing and industry" (Fainstein and Fainstein 1992, p. 76).

Our analysis, however, shows that the situation is more complicated. The Keynesian welfare state really is in crisis, so we cannot simply return to a social–democratic conception of social and economic policy. A third sector, which has emerged to address its basic contradictions, is not automatically "a school for self-management, gender equality and democracy" as Lipietz (1992a, p. 326) implies. The "new alternative sector" envisioned by him as the way forward is indeed already a widespread practice in many of the municipal programmes that are tying third-sector groups and their polyvalent work[16] to state employment policies. The task for movements, then, is not to *create* it, but to make it accessible and resourceful for marginalised groups threatened by the powerful polarisation processes of post-Fordism. Social movements need to make use of the new channels and forums provided by the new bargaining systems to challenge the powerful trends towards inequality, which the post-Fordist regime entails, and to attack its social forms of division and its political forms of exclusion in order to strengthen the democratic potential of the new forms of urban governance.

On the other hand, while one may conceive of national strategies that redistribute resources from wealthy to poor areas/groups as prop and support for democratic movements, demands for such national projects are improbable today, given the welfare state's overbearing role as it contributed to the crisis of Fordism and the disappearance of the preconditions for a Fordist "deal" embracing the big social blocks. In any case, such demands have to confront the erosion ("hollowing out") of the nation state form, "especially in its Keynesian welfare state guise" (Hirsch 1991, p. 73; Jessop 1992b, p. 3).[17] If these trends are taken into account, a more adequate strategy would be to make use of the forms and structures now available on the subnational level.

Rather than hanging on to "old-fashioned" large-scale, nationally oriented strategies, rather than demanding unspecific third-sector or community representation, social movements will need to use their own chip within the structure of the new bargaining systems. Since urban governance is becoming based on the representation of functional interests active at the local level, and since the local authority has to respect to some degree the particular functional conditions of the other actors involved in the new "partnerships", and since all the involved participants control resources necessary for the policies to be effective, even social movement groups have a real basis for negotiation.

"Negotiation", however, may be a mild term for the struggle at hand. The emerging post-Fordist regime, with the new social modes of regulation including the new forms of urban governance described in this chapter, may function with some temporary stability, but it poses enormous problems of social disintegration. Market-led polarisation processes, the emphasis on economic innovation and competition, and the subordination or social programmes to these economic priorities will tend to deepen societal divisions and threaten the decay of civil society (which, of course, in the long run will cause difficulty for economic stability). Given the increasingly polarised class relations and the highly fragmented local situations, social movements need to mobilise to create pressure on the local authority (1) to develop strategic plans that make evéry effort to avoid social segregation and marginalisation, and (2) to use the resources of large private investors to address local social and environmental needs. At the same time they will have to internationalise, i.e. become active on the same level where capital's global competition takes place. They will have to look towards forging new links with similar movements in other countries, to which global capital movement has "connected" them, and towards addressing those emerging political bodies which are transcending/supplanting national ones to demand the protection and guarantees which were formerly wrested from the nation state.

Notes

1. Cf. for examples Hirsch and Roth (1986), Hirsch (1991), Jessop (1991a), Bonefeld and Holloway (1991) and Amin (1993).

2. Jessop (1993) lists these general characteristics: (a) flexible production process based on flexible machines and a flexible workforce (as opposed to the mass production of consumer durables based on assembly-line techniques operated with the semi-skilled labour of the mass worker); (b) flexible and permanently innovative pattern of accumulation whose growing productivity is based on economies of scope (as opposed to the relatively closed economies of Fordism whose rising productivity was based on economies of scale); (c) supply-side innovation and flexibility in the social modes of regulation (as opposed to the modes of regulation characteristic of the Fordist mode of growth such as: separation of ownership and control in large corporations, union recognition and collective bargaining, wages indexed to productivity growth, state-sponsored social reproduction oriented to the generalisation of norms of mass consumption etc.); (d) there is no predominant post-Fordist mode of "societalisation" obvious yet, but an unresolved competition between the Japanese, German and American models: "a well-developed and relatively stable post-Fordist social formation remains an as-yet unrealised possibility" (the Fordist pattern of social organisation involved the consumption of standardised, mass commodities in nuclear family households and provision of standardised, collective goods and services by the bureaucratic state). This list also illustrates that regulation theory does not specify Fordism (or post-Fordism) merely on the level of the "industrial-organisation paradigm"; therefore Lovering's critique of the "Fordist/post-Fordist shorthand" as diverting attention from the role of the state etc. (in this volume) merely underlines the unfortunate mistranslation of the theoretical language which influenced the British debate (cf. the later section on regulationist analysis in this chapter).

3. It is possible to say, though, that since post-Fordist growth does not need to generalise core workers' rising incomes to other groups, and since post-Fordist accumulation will be more oriented to worldwide demand, global competition could further limit the scope for general prosperity and encourage market-led polarisation of incomes (Jessop 1993, p. 8).

4. For example, in terms of the organisation of capital/labour relations, some countries have developed more negotiated involvement while others have adopted more rigid flexibility strategies: Lipietz (1992a) located the US and UK on the "flexible–liberal–productivist" end of the spectrum, Sweden and to some extent other Scandinavian countries, Germany and Japan have developed "negotiated involvement" modes (p. 318).

5.   Fiscal constraints have become particularly exacerbated in German municipalities since unification, leading to intensified efforts at local economic interventionism and devolution as described in this chapter. In the "new" eastern states of Germany, where institutional structures on all levels have been taken down and had to be newly constructed, local government was the only political-administrative institution to remain in place. But the new constitution and the dramatic social and economic situation confront municipalities with extraordinary difficulties; lack of experience and of adequately trained staff compound the problem (cf. Wollmann 1991). Local politicians eagerly absorb the innovations tried out in the west.

6.   The controversial and painful process of institutionalisation of alternative local politics, which turned movement participation into interest group politics and coproduction of services, has been variously described (Roth 1990; Mayer 1993). Though under pressure, these projects and intermediary organisations are now an integral part of the urban political landscape and the local modes of social regulation. They serve to cushion the labour market and manpower policies which are to flexibilise the labour force, while they are themselves part of a more flexible and innovative provision of collective consumption.

7.   While established welfare associations and churches have long been involved in the provision of social services, community organisations, alternative groups and movement organisations active around health, women, immigrants, youth etc. have been screened by municipal governments since the early 1980s for their usefulness in dealing with long-term unemployment and marginalisation problems; i.e. policy fields where the traditional welfare state mechanisms apparently no longer function effectively. (cf. Offe and Heinze 1992).

8.   Unlike the CBD-oriented partnerships, the community-oriented ones usually suffer, however, from limited staff and financial resources and diversion of staff time to fund-raising rather than project implementation.

9.   Mackintosh (1992) lists some elements joint ventures need to contain for them to be "successful" and for local authorities to establish an active strategic role in them; see pp. 221–222.

10.   Cf. for a summary introduction to the French regulation school, Boyer (1990) and Lipietz (1992b).

11.   Cf. Hall and Jacques (1989): most of the essays reprinted in this volume originally appeared in *Marxism Today*.

12.   Those who disagree with the magazine's celebratory reading of the ongoing transformation processes and its concomitant politics of cross-party coalition often also reject the determinist explanation of its inevitable triumph; e.g. Clarke (1988).

13.   "A mode of social regulation comprises an ensemble of norms, institutions, organizational forms, social networks, and patterns of conduct which sustain and 'guide' an accumulation regime" (Lipietz 1985, p. 121). "Modes of regulation reinforce and underpin these regimes [of accumulation] by institutionalizing class struggle and confining it within certain parameters compatible with continuing accumulation" (Jessop 1990a, p. 309).

14.   "Any feasible reorganization of the welfare state must resolve not only the problems rooted in its own dynamic but also those rooted in its regulatory role in relation to accumulation" (Jessop 1991b, p. 103).

15.   Such as the United States, which is typically described as a "weak state" model where investment/production decisions are left almost entirely to the private sector and government does not pursue a conscious development strategy (cf. Zysman 1983, p. 19).

16. The simultaneous delivery of urban repair, social, lobbying, and political functions.

17. The postwar nation-state "is but one of several distinctive historical forms of the political organization of economic space and as such its development and functions are also shaped and limited by changes in technological paradigms and their modes of social innovation. The crisis in the nation-state form (especially in its KWS guise) is closely tied to the twin crises of nationally constituted economic space and the Fordist technological paradigm. In turn its 'hollowing out' is a political response to these crises which is strongly shaped both by new forms of the internationalisation of capital and by the nature of the emerging post-Fordist technological paradigm" (Jessop 1992, p. 3).

12

Discourses of Integration: Making Frameworks for Democratic Urban Planning

PATSY HEALEY

The early 1990s in Europe have witnessed a renewed interest in strategic spatial planning, and in reviewing the tools available for expressing such concerns. This may be linked to the wider emphasis on a strategic approach to local economic development discussed by Mayer in Chapter 11. The tools of strategic spatial planning have traditionally included development plans and their equivalents which are to be found in the institutional arrangements for spatial, territorial and land-use planning in different countries. A key issue for spatial and land-use planners in the current period is what form, content and preparation processes for such plans should be. This chapter discusses the challenge involved in rethinking the role of the development plan, in the context of land-use planning systems understood as regulatory regimes which act on decisions about property rights, and property development and investment opportunities.

Development plan-making

The determination of how to intervene in and regulate the way land and property is used and developed is a conflictual task for the modern state, as a wide range of interests are affected, cutting across other sectoral policy systems, and levels of government activity, as these affect what happens

Managing Cities: The New Urban Context, edited by P. Healey, S. Cameron, S. Davoudi, S. Graham and A. Madani-Pour. © 1995 The Editors and contributors. Published in 1995 by John Wiley & Sons Ltd.

where and on what terms. This task is made particularly complex at the present time. Land-use planning systems seek to interrelate the various dimensions of the consequences of a land-use decision at a time when socio-spatial relations within localities, as discussed elsewhere in this book, are perceived to be fragmenting. They claim to offer a democratically acceptable machinery for defining the collective interest in environmental issues in places, at a time when social heterogeneity and cross-cutting social cleavages make reaching agreement democratically an increasing problem.

A regulatory regime sets ground rules, "framing" principles and limits on a sphere of activity (Clarke 1992; Francis 1993; Fainstein 1994). In the case of land-use planning, the activity in question is that of public and private landowners, developers, investors, companies and households using and building sites and premises. Within such regimes, provision for development plans is typically found in some form. Plans provide spatially differentiated frameworks for guiding regulatory decisions about land use and development. In theory, they are commonly also intended to provide an explicit framework for public and private investment. The purpose of plans is to provide, in one way or another, a store of decision rules to guide a subsequent stream of regulatory and investment decisions (Faludi 1987).

Given the range of interests involved in land and property development (owners, tenants, developers, infrastructure agencies, all those other households, firms and interest groups concerned about what happens on a particular plot of land), development plan-making involves making choices between a wide range of interest claims. Inevitably, therefore, development plan-making is a potential arena of struggle over strategy, policy and decision rules. Once a plan has been made, struggle then continues over the impact of the plan, over whether the decision rules have leverage over the decisions they are intended to influence, and over the interpretation of the rules.

The preparation and use of development plans involves developing ideas, explicitly and implicitly, about both what places should and could be like, and about appropriate processes for debating such questions. Development plans in land-use planning systems are therefore, potentially, key arenas where the contradictions and challenges of contemporary urban region change are played out. But the attempt to use development plans to frame spatial development decisions raises important questions. If there is increasing diversity in the interests people have in their living and working environment, and less coincidence of interest among those who share the same place, how are the politics of the claims of different interests to be accommodated? If citizens, companies and government agencies operating in places are developing increasingly diverse relationships and networks through which to assert their interests, through what processes and politics will the form and content of development plans be arrived at? And how far are regulatory regimes which embody the notion of a plan framework for subsequent decisions likely to remain a key feature of land use and development regulation? The construction and use of development plans thus present a key challenge to the capacity of contemporary governance processes to mediate among the range of interests in local economic, social and environmental conditions.

This chapter addresses this question, drawing primarily on British experience. This is of particular interest at the present time. Not only does its distinctive administrative form present few barriers to the introduction of new emphases and purposes, if national politicians and civil servants seek to pursue these (Healey 1988; Thornley 1991). Britain has also experienced the energetic adoption of neo-liberal policy ideas in the past decade. This raises possible new directions for the regulatory form of land-use planning which need careful evaluation.

The concept of a development plan in Britain, in relation to land-use regulation, has traditionally had meaning in the context of two regulatory models. In the first, the state is seen as orchestrator and developer, using plans as "blueprints" for its development activities. This model informed new town building and comprehensive redevelopment in the early postwar period. It is an archetypal "command and control" model. In the second, the plan is a store of policy principles and criteria, goals and objectives. It is intended to guide but not determine regulatory decisions. The objective is to provide sufficient flexibility to allow a "reasonable" balance of individual and collective interests in specific decisions. This model, introduced into British planning from public policy theory in the USA, has been the dominant influence on UK plan-making since the 1960s, sitting comfortably with the British tradition of wide-ranging administrative discretion in public policy systems (Thomas et al. 1983). It replaced an earlier zoning model of regulation, still common in Europe and America. This involves precise specification of norms and criteria in a legal zoning ordinance, giving owners rights to develop in line with the plan.

These traditional models assumed a unitary *public interest*. Plan-making could proceed dominated by experts and officials, realising political goals which were assumed to be widely understood and shared. By the 1970s, this assumption was widely criticised, to be replaced by notions of pluralist debate, and by models of structural class conflict (Ravetz 1980; Kirk 1980). As a result, a third regulatory model emerged, focused on the planning system as a process of *conflict mediation* (Healey et al. 1988; Brindley et al. 1989). This term expressed a political model of some form of elite pluralism (Drucker et al. 1986). However, the range of interests finding the opportunity for *voice* within the system challenged the capacity of the political–administrative nexus to keep control of both processes and agendas during the 1980s. The response, informed by neo-liberal political ideology, was to back away from plan-making exercises, and to focus instead on the regulation of projects (Thornley 1991). Behind this was a deliberate concern to prioritise commercial interests, and particularly those of the property sector.

However, by 1990, this position had become politically untenable in the face of widespread and diverse concerns about environmental quality. These concerns were combined with the realisation that property markets benefited from planning frameworks and that effective economic development demanded a flow of available sites and properties, and the safeguarding of key environmental qualities (Healey 1992a; DoE 1992). The development plan was refurbished as a policy tool, and even given further legislative strength (DoE 1992; Young 1992). The development plan is now being presented as an efficient mechanism for "managing" the land-use dimensions of environmental conflicts. Good strategic planning, it is hoped, will reduce political and economic "transactions costs". Implicit in this enterprise is the intention that economic development and environmental issues can be combined, or integrated, in some stable balance. But this raises critical issues about form, content and preparation processes.

How far is it possible, conceptually and practically, to *integrate* the spatial dimensions of the different concerns of diverse interests into a plan which commands the support of the relevant political community? How far is this desirable, given contemporary emphases on individual entrepreneurial initiative and the empowerment of civil society, rather than state management and control?

This chapter explores the nature of development plan-making as an exercise in integrating diverse issues and diverse interests in relation to environmental change in urban regions. Its concern is partly analytical, to explore the role of plans and the interests they serve in the context of emerging forms for the regulatory regimes of land-use planning. It is also normative, to assess the potential and constraints on lodging principles of *discursive democracy* (Drysek 1990), through plans, into the regulatory regimes of land-use planning.

Integration in development plan-making as a political project

Inherent in the concept of a development plan is the notion of a *framework*, a set of relationships which prioritise certain criteria and actions over others, and which provide a point of reference for those making subsequent decisions. Embodied in any framework are views about the world, about human nature, about the issues identified and how to address them. A plan's integrating potential lies in part in these ideas, and in part in the power of the plan over subsequent decisions, the integrating of action within a framework. A plan in effect offers a *framing device*, which serves to shape, or *structure*, the decisions of those who acknowledge its importance. It is thus potentially a powerful tool both in coordinating diverse sets of decisions and actions, and in translating policy into action. Its conceptions offer *structuring ideas* and its policy criteria offer *decision rules* through which influence is exerted on the deployment of *resources*. It thus "carries structure" to agency, and, in use, its reinterpretation remoulds the structuring forces embedded within it.[1] For this reason, the preparation and use of a plan is much more than a technical bureaucratic exercise. It is inherently an arena of political struggle. Struggles focus on both the framework, the ordering or integrating concepts of the plan, and the extent to which the plan is given value, or power, in subsequent decisions. The first lies in the arena of ideology and discourse construction; the second in the arena of the power relations of executive action.

Ideology

Development plan-making involves conceptions of policy content (what kind of place and what kinds of relationships do the plan-makers have in mind), and of the processes through which a plan is formulated and used (who is involved, in what forms of discourse). This has long been recognised in planning theory in the distinction between *substantive* and *procedural* dimensions of planning thought. With respect to substantive issues, development plan-making work expresses assumptions about the interrelations of activities and "sectors" (for example, the Geddesian place–folk–work relation, or the economic base model of location theory), about socio-spatial relations, about the relations between scales of activity, about the relations between present and future, and about space–time relations. These are generally implicit when deployed in a plan, transmuted through the cultures of those dominating the plan-making agenda. There is now a considerable literature aimed at identifying the conceptions and ordering principles historically embedded in plans (Boyer 1983; Hall 1988; Tait and Wolfe 1991; Healey and Shaw 1993). There is also a rich normative literature, upon which the critical literature feeds, offering conceptions of the form of the "ideal city" or settlement, and of the critical relations which produce this form. This literature was sidelined from the late 1960s, under attack for its environmental determinism and for the arrogant utilitarian functionalism of the dominant modernist tendency. Planning theory turned to a preoccupation with conceptions of process. Ideas of form have recently returned, partly in postmodernist conceptions of the re-constitution of space, and most particularly with the increasing political leverage of environmentalist values (see the EC's *Green Book on the Urban Environment* (CEC 1990) and Breheny (1992)). But these new conceptions, while providing a renewed emphasis on urban morphology, reflect very different epistemological and ontological assumptions.

This reinforces the point that different views of the "ideal city" are not just conceptions of form, or even of social order. They embody distinctive *systems of meaning*, within which prioritising certain relations makes sense, and particular attributes of form have value. They vary in the way social and socio-spatial relations are conceptualised, and consequently in the way issues are problematised and interventions designed, valued and implemented. Systems of meaning vary not merely in their priorities and values but in the metaphors and images used to express them, the meaning these metaphors have and the language used to describe them. It is this linguistic differentiation which is encapsulated in the notion of a distinct *discourse*.[2] The preparation and use of a development plan involves not merely establishing meanings for the agendas and priorities in a plan, but a dialogue *between* systems of meaning.

The project for democratic plan-making in a plural democracy is to find ways of exploring the potential substantive agenda of a plan which brings forward such different conceptions or systems of meaning and which thus explicitly engages in such dialogue (Forester 1993; Friedmann 1992; Healey 1992b). If a democratic community searches for agreement, or consensus, the task is further to select a conception around which to agree, embodying both substantive content and principles by which that content is to be arrived at. Such an agreement would then have the potential to act as a powerful integrating force in the social relations of the local management of environmental change. But it is this which is critically difficult in contemporary societies. One result is plans which contain multiple conceptions, uneasily coexisting, or which are merely a collection of disparate claims for status as decision criteria. Such "pluralist" plans are typical products of regulatory systems dominated by interest bargaining (Mazza 1986; Healey 1993). Their contents become merely a collection of claims for attention as policy criteria. How these claims are to be "balanced" in the case of a specific project is not addressed. This diversity tends to undermine the authority of the plan, as conflicts between claims and conceptions can be readily exploited, allowing multiple interpretations when the plan is called upon in subsequent decisions.

The diversity of discourses is not merely about content, but about the *processes* through which people seek to debate their concerns about the environment, and to arrive at some agreement on collective action. Much of planning theory debate is about alternative models for planning processes (Friedmann 1987). The critical literature on planning practice also records the ways in which autocratic or technocratic processes have been used to control the processes and terms of debate even where forms of "public participation" in the formulation of planning policies have been formally encouraged (McAuslan 1980; Tait and Wolfe 1991; Hillier 1994). Yet the planners too have had difficulty establishing their preferred discursive principles, as the frustrated experiences of those seeking to establish the rational process model as the dominant mode of public policy-making illustrate (e.g. Meyerson and Banfield 1955).

The literature on policy processes is rich with accounts of these struggles, and attempts to define the resultant process forms which arise (Healey 1990). Offe (1977) captures the context of this discussion of process forms in his account of the "restless search" by state agencies for appropriate process forms through which to pursue inherently contradictory policy objectives. Fischer (1990) collapses the diversity of forms into a dual opposition between technocratic/technocorporatist forms and discursive process forms. This recognises not merely the dialectical tension between efficient economic organisation and broadly based democratic participation. Fischer's distinction reflects an epistemological and ontological difference between conceptions of social organisation based on the consciousness of individual subjects pursuing instrumental rationality, and those based on conceptions of intersubjective consciousness pursuing intercommunicative rationalities (Friedmann 1992; Forester 1993).

A particular characteristic of contemporary public policy in Britain has been the increasing penetration of the vocabulary of economic evaluation into public policy formulation and implementation. It has become the technical methodology of neo-liberal political ideology. It draws upon US models of regulation through standards, targets and pricing strategies. It aims to construct regulatory regimes which operate through "market signals" and is intended to make those benefiting from a project internalise the full social cost of the impacts they create (Clarke 1992; Dunleavy 1991). The approach appears to offer the dual advantage of efficiency and responsiveness to preferences, by forcing bureaucracies to focus on input–output relations and responsiveness to "customer" requirements. It is thus seen by some as a more progressive alternative than the discursive forms of the political–administrative nexus (Dunleavy 1991). In theory, no integrating or coordinating frameworks or plans are required. However, following the influence of the economics from which it derives, this approach assumes particular forms of behaviour (instrumental rationality), and eschews consideration of the relation between the various regimes or the criteria used within them. Its implicit assumptions lie within the agendas of specific standards, criteria and targets. Local spatial variation is assumed to be of minor significance; hence local spatial frameworks such as development plans are considered unimportant. Environmental protection systems in Europe tend to take this form, with standards, criteria and targets set at supranational, national as well as local levels. This approach is classically technicist, in that it relies on the technical tools of experts to resolve problems of political values. It is particularly narrow in that it converts all issues about environmental change into the language of economic calculation. It rejects communicative processes in policy formulation in favour of calculative ones (Sage 1992). The critical view of the "economisation" of public policy represents it as an attempt to establish a dominant hegemony which crowds out the voices of other systems of meaning, while privileging capital and particularly big capital (Fischer 1990; Friedmann 1992; Mingione 1991).

The alternative put forward by some of those who claim a "postmodern" position is to abandon the possibility of collective action, and encourage anarchic and individualistic expression. In this position, the very idea of *frameworks* for regulatory action is problematised, as an integrating effort which will inherently limit diversity and suppress difference. Yet this position too has been widely criticised, on ontological and moral grounds, as denying the relations we have with each other, and on political grounds, allowing powerful interests to capture control over a range of administrative actions implicitly, rather than through the more transparent forms of plan-making and use (Habermas 1987; Harvey 1989a; Moore Milroy 1991; Healey 1992b).

The third response has been to explore ways of developing *interdiscursive* policy formulation. This challenge is reflected in recent planning theory work. It builds from a concern with *empowerment* in multicultural societies with many dimensions of cleavage and differentiation (gender, ethnicity, race, etc.), and with *forms of communication* — the creation of arenas of debate, of languages and rules of debate, and ways of listening and hearing for difference, out of which richer forms of democratic agreement can be arrived at. The developing regulatory model is of an argumentative form of policy formulation and regulatory decision making, and draws in particular on Habermasian inspiration (see Fischer and Forester 1993; Friedmann 1992; Throgmorton 1992; Bryson and Crosby 1992; Healey 1992b).

The power relations of executive action

The tension in the above efforts at accommodating multiple discourses, whether around substance or process, is that however "democratically" agendas and forms of action are arrived at, they are then used to impose an order or an approach on those who were not involved, or whose views have changed, or who in later times have different conceptions. It is this tension, fuelled by Foucaultian analysis, which underlies the leverage of the postmodernist antagonism to plans and frameworks (Boyer 1983; Moore Milroy 1991). The preparation and use of a plan is an inherently ideological project. The stronger the attempt at consensus formation and at *consistency* and *integration* in the elements of a plan, the more the plan acts as a dominatory influence on the social relations in its sphere of influence and the greater the role of the plan in guiding subsequent review. The arena of plan use, the relation of plan to action, is thus a second critical arena through which to explore the integrating potential of a plan. The literature on policy implementation emphasises the extent to which policy principles are renegotiated in use, shifting the balance of plan frameworks, and often undermining them altogether (Barrett and Fudge 1981). The most obvious form of such challenge in Britain, as McAuslan (1980) perceived in the arena of planning regulation, is the power of the central political administrative nexus. In the USA, local alliances of business and local government have performed a similar role (Logan and Molotch 1987; Plotkin 1987; Feagin 1988). In Italy, the party machines have been revealed, through recent scandals, as corrupting the theory of the administrative–legal process. Through control of the process of "plan-acknowledging", certain groups are able to reinterpret and reprioritise the principles articulated in plan frameworks in order to impose their agendas.

The analytical challenge with respect to development plans is to explore how they are being used to express and to take control of the agendas with respect to the management of environmental change in localities by different groups. This involves not merely assessing who wins and loses with respect to particular issues, but whose terms dominate the discussion and who is included and excluded by this. The normative challenge is to invent forms of interdiscursive communication, which provide space for both multiple systems of meaning and which also have the power to resist or at least limit the discursive domination of powerful groups in plan-making and subsequent use. The power of the plan therefore needs to be explored through its ideology and discursive forms, and its interpretation in use. How far is it possible to imagine that a development plan can be anything other than either a project of the powerful or an ineffective dream of the idealistic?

Integrating traditions in development plan-making in Britain

History gives little encouragement. Boyer (1983) has described the traditions of American planning thought and practice as a search to impose a rationalising order on the dynamic heterogeneity of the city, drawing on Foucaultian inspiration in her analysis. The same kind of critique has been made of British planning. The argument developed here, however, suggests that the issue is not the existence or otherwise of an ordering impetus but what ordering principles have been used, to which cultures and discourses they belong and how widely they are shared among the communities, or interests, affected by the plan.

Each country has its own history of plan-making (e.g. Faludi and Van der Valk 1994). The postwar history of development plan-making in Britain illustrates both the power of dominant conceptions in structuring the content of plans and the continual attempts to challenge such conceptions (Ravetz 1980; Healey and Shaw 1993). Plan-making in the 1940s and 1950s was a key area of planning work, and was strongly influenced by the ideas of a few planners and planning teams. The emphasis was on physical form and spatial arrangement, reorganising the city, and the arrangement between town and country, to produce environments functional to the needs of industry, providing for the material welfare, moral improvement and aesthetic enjoyment of citizens. The key spatial conception was of compact settlements, with planned decentralisation to improve the quality of life in the large conurbations. The emphasis was on the utility of locations within the overall pattern of a settlement and on rebuilding parts of the city to recover functional utility and amenity for modern life.

A moral utilitarian aesthetic pervades the plans of this period, washed over by a paternalist welfarism. The planner as expert was assumed to be the guardian of the idea of the good city, articulating for society what its needs and values were. The planning enterprise was *for* the citizenry, conceptualised as a unified public with a common interest. Surveys of citizens' views and discussions with citizens are sometimes mentioned, but the "planning conception" was allowed to dominate unchallenged as an expression of the "public interest". Politicians were expected to accept the views of the future, as expressed by the experts. The power of the plan was unquestioned. A classic "command and control" model was assumed, with development investment and regulation following strictly the land allocations and development principles articulated in the plan. The state was expected to be the primary developer. Here is Boyer's totalising order in full flourish.

By the 1960s, the moral and aesthetic dimensions of the dominant expert conceptions gave way to an economic functionalism, driven by the national project of facilitating economic growth. Within the arena of urban development, the emphasis was on modernising the city, and particularly town centres, and providing the land-use and development framework for a massive housing programme. Amenity and environmental quality were still important, but primarily as assets to be safeguarded. The principles of spatial form and compact settlements were continued, with an emphasis on functional organisation and use values. There was more attention to strategic infrastructure frameworks as well as the provision of a flow of serviced space in suitable locations to allow development to proceed. The emphasis was on accommodating growth. Planning in this period came to be characterised as *trend planning*, adjusting to the spatial imperatives of where people and firms were locating, thus facilitating metropolitan decentralisation. This functionalism was legitimated once again by a unitary conception of the public interest. Planners, less confident than in the 1960s, saw themselves as realising political objectives. The *rational process* model helped them to conceptualise this role (McLoughlin 1969; Wannop 1985). Citizens were to be "consulted", with legislative encouragement for public participation. But plan-making effort was primarily dominated by economic imperatives. This is reflected in the shift away from "command and control" models of policy implementation to the idea of flexible frameworks, governed by policy goals. This regulatory model, more flexible than the zoning regimes preferred on the continent, has been interpreted by many as functional to a dynamic Fordist economy (Harvey 1989b; Clarke 1992). But just as the welfarist utilitarian aesthetic of 1940s planning faded when challenged by the project of economic growth, so the functional rationalism of the dominant planning paradigm became less influential in the 1970s as recession set in. British society was changing politically towards more populist forms. Meanwhile, the economic "trends" emphasised in the 1960s turned out not to be trends at all, but a particular set of relations which, during the 1970s, were increasingly undermined by the processes of international and technological restructuring. Thus the discursive dominance of the ideology of economic growth and instrumental rationality came into question.

In the 1970s, the plan-making effort initiated by the enthusiasm for strategic "growth accommodation" encountered a very different and more pluralist political climate. The requirements for public consultation during plan-making confronted planners and local politicians with potentially massive challenges to their conceptions, priorities and procedures. The issues which arose were still filtered through professional conceptions, carefully supervised by central government officials. Major disputes arose between local professionals, responding to both local economic and environmental concerns, and central government officials seeking to constrain the range of issues arising locally (Healey 1983). These conflicts were linked not just to policy objectives, but to public expenditure reductions.

The primary concerns of the plans of this period continued to be growth management, but on a reduced scale and accompanied by a rising agenda of economic and social problems generated by recession and restructuring. The thrust of substantive policy was on restricting peripheral expansion in order to promote development in the newly discovered "inner city", hardest hit by economic decline. The dominating conception of most plans was *urban regeneration through peripheral restraint*, supported by a comfortable consensus between countryside protectionists and urban policy in the inner cities (Healey et al. 1988).

But the attempt to sustain a strategic conception of any kind in a plan was difficult to maintain in the face of the "politics of voice" arising in the pressure group arena, the ideological conflicts between central and local government, and the increasingly evident conflicts between different interests over sites and projects. Surrounded by discursive babble at the level of strategy and firmly reined in by central government's administrative discourse, the planning community turned away from plan-making, to an arena where useful expertise could be demonstrated. This focused on putting projects together and deploying regulatory power. Professional concerns for consistency and coherence in strategy evaporated, allowing plans to become in some instances little more than a record of sectoral programmes of action, and sets of often unrelated claims for attention as decision rules in the bargaining process over obtaining planning permission. The encounter with a more pluralist politics thus served to *disintegrate* substantive planning conceptions, while generating the idea of a new role for the planner as an *intermediator* or broker among diverse interests, a role developed initially in the arena of project development and implementation. What remained in place, however, was the strategic conception of settlement structure (the compact settlement, surrounded by countryside) and a regulatory regime dominated by the interpretive opportunities of administrative discretion within which individual rights of challenge were limited and primarily confined to the protection of property interests.

During the 1980s, central government used its interpretive power within the discretionary structure of the planning system to experiment with ways of recasting the regulatory regime. These experiments were largely incoherent and often contradictory (Thornley 1991; Brindley et al. 1989). Two possibilities were explored. One involved a simple balancing of development and conservation, with protected and development areas, in zoning regimes giving property owners rights to develop. Within the latter, land and property markets could be deregulated (Adam Smith Institute 1983; Healey 1989). This radical change to a zoning regime, giving rights linked to simple sets of regulatory decision rules, did not survive the political realisation that the balancing was by no means simple, as citizens were concerned with the fine grain of what happened in their neighbourhoods, as well as with the conservation of national natural and historic assets. The alternative was to implant commercial criteria within the established system. "Market conditions" were emphasised in land allocation policies and plans were to be prepared in consultation with relevant development interests. Certain areas (Enterprise Zones and Simplified Planning Zones) were allocated liberal planning regimes with rights to develop, a proto-zoning system. In parallel, opportunities for public representation in plan-making were marginally reduced, pressure was put on to speed up decision times and existing development plans were progressively sidelined as "out-of-date". Substantive issues in planning were narrowed down in government advice to providing a flow of sites for development. Integration, therefore, was not to be provided via plans. Rather, it took place within the arena of the conception of the regulatory regime itself. Yet the substantive notion of the compact city lived on, notably in the continuing policy leverage of the concept of the greenbelt.

This period came to an abrupt end around 1990. One reason was the enthusiastic adoption of the new environmental agenda. This was partly a response to the well-entrenched policies of safeguarding traditional land-scapes, as reflected in the image of the compact city and the greenbelt. But it was also allied to a concern for global warning, pollution reduction and energy conservation (DoE 1992). The new substantive agenda is now focused in theory around the relation between environmental quality, (understood in biospheric as well as aesthetic and utilitarian terms) and economic development, expressed in the rhetoric of *sustainable develop-ment*. Economic development is understood not merely as the promotion of growth, nor narrowly as property development, but as the promotion of the assets of area. But a second reason for the retreat from a project-based approach to land-use regulation was the financial and political cost of conflict resolution in this form. It is in this context that the develop-ment plan has been refurbished as a device for a strategic resolution of the tension between environmental conservation and economic development, in the search for conflict-stabilising strategies to provide decision criteria for the regulation of land and property development (DoE 1992).

In many ways, this represents a return to tradition, specifically a particular discourse of urban structure, within a discretionary regulatory regime. But how relevant and to whom is this return to tradition, if the socio-spatial relations of urban regions, as discussed elsewhere in this book, are now understood as diverse networks of relations, each with their own spatial and temporal referents overlapping in urban region space, but with no necessary functional or cultural relations with each other? What kinds of arenas are there for articulating mutual concerns? Who has access to these arenas? What discursive practices, in terms of both substance and process, are being promoted? Is there any need for local leverage over the content of plans and the interpretation of the regulatory regime?

There are many levels to these issues, from the ideological debate over the meaning of environmental sustainability in public policy (Jacobs 1991; Hajer 1993) to the struggle to retain control of the debate by central government, and the growth of powerful local spatial alliances which seek to "integrate" local policy agendas across the fragmented field of local governance (Harding 1992; Lovering, this volume). In the mid-1990s, therefore, development plan-making has once again become a significant political arena within which struggles over how to manage local environmental change and for what purposes are being played out.

Managing spatial coexistence in urban regions

The scenario outlined above is of a confused recognition of the significance of what happens where and on what terms in urban regions. In Britain, the current fragmentation of governance institutions means a fragmentation of the arenas for coordination, collaboration and debate. The relative weakness of local government presents difficulties in developing the new enabling and mediating roles for city government suggested by Mayer in Chapter 11. The consequence of this fragmentation is likely to be greater inequality of access to urban region resources, failure to achieve agreed environmental objectives and further crises of democratic legitimacy for any state action on local land use and environmental issues. Through what processes could such fragmentation be overcome?

Policy processes are ways of articulating structuring ideas and policy principles to guide the ongoing stream of governance decisions. Through policy processes, decision criteria and rules are specified, and, more subtly, policy cultures and discourses articulated. What processes are available for addressing socio-spatially differentiated possibilities and impacts of development in urban regions? How can they be made to reflect diversity? How can they work in a situation of institutional fragmentation? And how far and how can interests grounded in concern for the qualities of places get leverage over the diverse extra-local processes which are reconstituting places?

Three possibilities are competing for attention in contemporary debate in Britain on policy processes in the urban region context:

- management by performance criteria and output targets
- management by partnership
- management by argumentation.

Each implies a different form of regulatory regime, and different loci and practices for the articulation of integrating conceptions. Within each, there are potentials for addressing the complex relations identified above. Each also has both progressive and regressive possibilities.

Management by criteria and target

This approach derives from the neo-liberal agenda already described. It is now evolving rapidly in the environmental policy arena and in urban policy, but has not yet been developed in the land-use planning field. It derives its intellectual support from a theoretical approach to public policy which seeks to avoid corporatist and bureaucratic mechanisms in favour of legally specified performance criteria and targets, supported by financial incentives and penalties. This allows individuals, households, firms and agencies to work out for themselves how to adjust their behaviour, how to "cope". It appeals because it accepts and deals in fragments. It appears attractive both to market theorists and to those who consider that attempts at locally integrated development management frameworks are undesirable, unnecessary or impossible to achieve effectively in the conditions of the contemporary city (Dunleavy 1991; Sorenson 1983).

In the land-use planning field, it would involve the specification of norms and standards for development, coupled with incentives to promote certain kinds of development (such as industrial land and buildings, or refurbishment) that the market could not provide. This could be combined with impact assessment requirements linked to standards and targets, addressing economic, property market and social impacts as well as environmental ones, combined with requirements that these impacts be ameliorated in some way. Such an approach could be developed through European Union (EU) or national legislation and/or local legislation. Different aspects of environmental change could be addressed through different regulatory systems, for example land use and development decisions could be subject to one regulatory system, industrial process decisions to another, utility agencies to yet more. This would reflect the British preference in other regulatory spheres for a clear separation of the regulatory function (Francis 1993). The attraction of this approach for land use and development is that, with the exception of perhaps a few special conservation zones, there would be no *a priori* constraint on what happened where. Regulatory constraints would all be worked out on a project-by-project basis in relation to general norms and standards, a fragmented approach to fragmented conditions, through fragmented regulatory systems. Development Plans as spatial frameworks could be replaced by statements of EU, national, regional and/or local norms and criteria, a framework of development rules (as widely used in continental European planning systems — see Davies et al. 1989).

Despite the fragmentation, nevertheless, such an approach represents a strong and consistent regulatory *regime*. The language of criteria and the calculation of impacts and their amelioration would act as a critical framing discourse. The key arenas within which the terms and priorities of the discourse would be set are those where targets and criteria are defined and those where they are interpreted in use. National governments and the EU dominate the first arena. Politicians, civil servants and well-organised business interests have access to such arenas, shadowed by a few well-organised supra-local pressure groups, which often succeed by adopting the discourse forms of the dominant interest. Such a regime thus has, despite the theory, strongly corporatist tendencies. It would require a very strong conception of environmental and social considerations to get leverage on this nexus. Pressure groups would have to fight for the inclusion of specific criteria in legislation. The politics of criteria becomes therefore the key arena within which to constrain the corporatist nexus.

The local arena under such a regime is likely to be dominated by the methodologies used to interpret criteria and targets, and the measures to arrive at these. The increasing tendency in British government to look for standardised performance measures is a way to avoid local influence, and retain control over the substantive agenda (for example, in the case of water charges and impact fees). Such an approach also has the advantage, for those seeking to avoid change, that cumulative impacts are rarely considered. However, it is not easy to arrive at standardised ways of identifying impacts and ways of ameliorating them, given the diversity of development projects and the configuration of locales. It is not likely to reduce conflict over development projects. Nor does this approach deliver the frameworks for strategic investment that business and property interests call for, still less the re-invention of substantive "framing" ideas which would help demolish traditional models of urban structure and invent new ones.

This regulatory model has a powerful attraction to the British government at the present time. It is strongly technicist, structured by the methodology and politics of criteria and targets. It treats urban region qualities and citizens in the language of individual rational interest, commodities and impacts. It would allow access to debate to the powerful and knowledgeable, governed only by the construction of citizens' rights. Development plans would not be needed. The framing principles are instead contained in the criteria. Only if linked to the strong specification of substantive targets and criteria related to environmental and social considerations, and the existence of powerful rights for citizens to challenge government decisions, would it be possible to limit the power of business and big government. It is more likely that such an approach would tend to be undemocratic and ineffective in achieving spatial coordination. So far, however, this approach has not been systematically elaborated with respect to land-use regulation.

Management by partnership

This approach responds to the demands within urban regions for more spatial coordination. It also offers the opportunity of capturing control over policy agendas from EU and national government arenas. It allows development principles to be articulated locally, and EC and national norms and standards to be interpreted to accommodate local consider-ations. It assumes that local business, political and community alliances of interest will take control of the policy process within urban regions. Such alliances are typically reasserting or seeking to establish narrow corporatist frameworks, as Lovering discusses in Chapter 5 and essentially reflect elite pluralist models of political organisation (Drucker et al. 1986). However, the very fragmentation which encourages the search for coordinative mechanisms also creates opportunities for a wider range of interests to enter the arena of alliance formation, creating progressive opportunities, as Mayer argues in Chapter 11.

In Britain, such alliance formation was greatly encouraged in the urban policy arena in the 1980s with increasing emphasis on a government–business partnership. But, as Mackintosh (1992) and Harding (1992) and Mayer argue, partnerships can take many forms. They vary in terms of the arena or forum around which partnerships form (to advise, to disburse resources, to devise programmes, to implement them); the terms of access to the arena (by right, by invitation, by informed contact); and the terms of discussion and decision (the discourse forms). In the British context, the agency forms arising are typically voluntarist (promotional agencies, development trusts etc.) or merely informal networks (business clubs). Business-dominated arenas show a preference for private decision arenas, within which issues are managed rather than debated. Strategies and policies may be precisely identified, often in terms of political influence. But they will not necessarily be declared. Any "plan" thus has existence primarily in the minds of alliance makers and, carefully packaged, in marketing material (e.g. Wilkinson 1992). Policy making thus tends to focus on the construction of agreed "storylines", marketable to an external audience of inward investors and EU and national government subsidy programmes, rather than a broadly based, locally sustainable, long-term urban region strategy. This is often avoided as too complex, or not appropriate for the partnership, even though the need for a wider strategic framework may be recognised.

The framing device in such "management by spatial alliance" typically exists as an informal articulation of ideas, structured by the concerns of the dominant partners in any alliance. The significant recent shift in Britain in urban governance alliances has been from a politico-administrative nexus, dominated by the discussion of central–local relations, to a business–administrative nexus, with government represented primarily by officials (see, for example, the Urban Development Corporations and the Training and Enterprise Councils). Curiously, however, such alliances have not been strongly encouraged in the management of the land-use planning system. One reason for this is the recognition that planning involves authoritative mediation *among* conflicting interests. To privilege one interest group explicitly in this situation would antagonise others.[3] This recognises implicitly the limitations of spatial alliances for managing local spatial–environmental conflicts. In essence, while they may embody the power relations to deliver their strategies, their policy discourses are likely to be narrowly based, excluding the interests of many within localities, and subject to challenge by groups left out of the arenas.

Management by argumentation

The challenge for the democratic management of spatial change in urban regions is to find ways of including a wider range of interests, to represent the fragments, with respect to access to the arenas of policy formation and the discursive forms through which policy is developed within them. Traditional forms of representative democracy and administrative–professional delivery on which the planning system has long rested for its legitimacy are now widely rejected as narrowly based and conservative. During the 1980s, as discussed above, the system in Britain developed into an interest-bargaining arena. As a result, the "framing" role of the system was allowed to decay, with plans becoming a collection of claims, which could not deliver coordination, nor transform established policies nor provide strategic stability over the long term. Accepting the democratic requirement for approaches to strategy formation and implementation which are open and inclusionary while capable of reaching agreement, new ideas are developing in the field of policy analysis and planning theory around the conception of policy development through democratic argumentation. These ideas focus on the construction of arenas for debate, on the forms of policy discussion, and on the mediation of conflicts. By focusing normatively on the processes of argumentation in this way, the concepts also provide a vocabulary with which to critique the previous two approaches.

In land-use planning systems, there are typically two arenas for debate, those where strategy is formed, and the processes upon which strategy is supposed to have leverage. Land-use planning systems typically include careful specification of rights and/or consultation requirements with respect to both arenas. The problem with such rights and requirements is firstly that they tend to be skewed towards property interests and are often bureaucratically and legally difficult and expensive to use. Secondly, the professional–administrative perception of the processes taking place tends to construct them as necessary procedures to check the content of policy frameworks, rather than as the critical arena within which frameworks are actively developed. Recent work has in contrast highlighted the way planners actively manage argumentation processes, without explicitly formulating the task they are engaged in (Bryson and Crosby 1989, 1992; Forester 1989). As Forester (1992) has argued, there is a critical difference between an interest bargaining approach to conflict mediation, and an approach which seeks to invent new ideas around which more agreement can cluster. In the former, the key arena is the arbitration mechanism (in Britain the public inquiry into a plan or project). In the latter, it is the processes of argumentation which shape the plan's form and content.

Critical to this approach are the discursive forms which develop within debating arenas. That interactive forms of policy articulation are important arenas of mutual learning, developing understanding and ownership of problems and solutions, has long been understood (Friedmann 1987; Bryson and Crosby 1992; Forester 1993). It is one of the key strengths of effective spatial alliances that the participants to the alliance learn about each other's concerns and are prepared to "empathise" with the situation of the "other". In doing so, as Hajer (1993) argues, discourses are changed. The challenge is to move this approach into a wider strategic arena, and to develop it to allow different discursive forms; that is, systems of meaning, to be articulated, expressed and heard. This means recognition that neither the discursive forms of administrative procedure, nor political ideology, nor business boardrooms, nor technical analysis nor pressure group politics are privileged discourses. Argumentation processes require instead that the diversity of discursive forms is recognised and that agreement is arrived at on the rules of debating procedure as substantive debate proceeds.

Agreements reached, on discursive forms as well as substantive content, are always likely to be incomplete and unstable. Mechanisms are therefore needed to provide a process for arbitration over disputes, and to force leverage of agreed policies over subsequent events. As in the construction of arenas, this requires the specification of requirements and rights: requirements to attend to an agreed strategy in subsequent action and rights to challenge decisions which appear to evade the requirement. Typically in a planning system, such requirements and rights exist in some form. Where they are active, they create pressure on the processes of strategy formulation, encouraging active debate and agreement on strategy (Healey 1986). This arises because those developing plans need reasons when challenged. The problem in many planning systems is that the opportunities for challenge are firmly limited.

The plan, in such argumentation processes, then becomes a record of arguments, about structuring ideas, about why a particular strategy or approach has been undertaken, about reasons why specific policies and policy criteria have been selected and about impacts and who bears them. It acts as a *store of reasoning* for use in subsequent debates, about specific projects, or about the strategy itself. It becomes in effect a key tool in a cultural project for reaching interdiscursive consensus. It thus privileges *reasoning* in democratic discussion, but accepts the diversity of forms which such reasoning can take. As with any policy process, it is open to "capture" by powerful groups. It is in this context that the specification of rights and requirements is as important as the explicit focus on the methods of interdiscursive argumentation. But it holds out an approach which both encourages spatial alliances to expand to incorporate a broader interest base, and forces the politico-administrative nexus into a transparent and answerable relation with the rest of us.

Management by argumentation thus accepts the contemporary fragmentation of activities and interests in urban region space and recognises that this diversity extends beyond interests to systems of meaning. But it is premised on the belief that, through forms of interdiscursive reasoning, democratic debate is both possible and desirable in contemporary pluralist societies. In the long run, such processes are also probably more efficient in achieving multiple objectives in the management of spatially differentiated change in urban regions, because they will be more informed and more capable of discovering lasting bases, if any, for consensus on strategy.[4]

Conclusions

This chapter has been premised on the assumption that the institutional forms of land-use planning regimes matter. This premise holds in spite of, and in part because of, the fragmentation of the socio-spatial relations within regions. The arguments to support this assumption are both technical and moral. The technical arguments focus on the contribution to economic competitiveness and efficiency of the effective management of spatial development in regions. The moral arguments centre on the acceptance of collective responsibility for managing our environmental inheritance sustainably and on a socio-political responsibility to accommo-date lifestyle diversity fairly. However strong the pressures for the disintegration of the connections between firms and households and the territories they occupy, there are nevertheless many reasons why collective mechanisms are needed to provide frameworks for "cohabitation" within shared spaces. There are also many reasons why these mechanisms should allow local interests, those actually experiencing the cohabitation, to influence the form, contents and practices surrounding the articulation and use of frameworks.

How far and which interests are able to obtain such influence depends critically on the institutional forms of planning systems. These reflect the way national politico-institutional cultures relate to professional debate on planning machinery and to local circumstances. This chapter has mapped out the general evolution of regulatory regimes within the planning field in Britain, providing a more nuanced account of the modernist/post-modernist tendencies in planning discussed by Dear in Chapter 1.

At a rather crude level, it is possible to link this evolution to debates about the relation between economic organisation and forms of governance, as encapsulated by Harvey (1989b), and discussed by Mayer in this volume. It is more revealing to use Offe's notion of the "restless search" by political communities for appropriate governance forms for the management of relations which are both dynamic and contradictory (Offe 1977). Perhaps the critical difference between the early postwar period and the end of the century is in the scale of the "restlessness", a product of a general uncertainty and experimentation about appropriate governance forms for contemporary western late capitalist societies.

Following Fischer (1990) and Forester (1993), however, underlying this "restlessness" is not merely a search for appropriate tools from a "repertoire" of instrumental management techniques. There are more fundamental epistemological and political issues at stake. The choices focusing the contemporary search for appropriate regulatory models for land-use planning regimes centre on longstanding alternatives. The state could be left to operate as some kind of self-interested bureaucratic or clientelistic machine. In this case, planning systems merely provide a stock of assets (land-use rights) to be captured and distributed by bureaucracy for material or political gain to the political–institutional nexus. Without policy principles, plans or decision rules, any planning system can decay into this form and there are many pressures encouraging this regress at the present time. Or systems can be based on principles and criteria which work well for dominant interests, primarily economic ones. Two forms for this are currently being explored, as discussed above: a criteria-based approach leading to general codes for development types, or a framework of policy principles which express an accommodation among the key interests which constitute a local spatial alliance. The first approach is being developed strongly in Britain in other governance fields, but its failure to address spatial relations explicitly makes its application in the land-use planning arena problematic. It is therefore unsurprising to find government in Britain currently apparently preferring the second and more traditional model. But both of these technocorporate forms are only marginally concerned with the wide range of interests in places in the changing local environment and their emphasis is primarily to limit the "noise" created by these other claims.

The model of plan-based argumentation offers an alternative which challenges the technocorporatist argument. This latter tends to dismiss democratic debate as time-wasting and unlikely ever to lead to agreement. Yet there are a number of examples of argumentative practices developed within the context of planning systems (e.g. Innes 1992; Alty and Darke 1986; Hillier 1995). One task for the planning community is to develop and evaluate more such practices, so that a vocabulary and methodology develop out of which a more pervasive regulatory regime of this kind can emerge (see Friedmann 1992).

But argumentative forms within the existing arenas of policy debate in planning systems are not by themselves sufficient. In Britain in particular, the discretionary flexibility of the planning system provides an easy opportunity for the agendas defined by community debate to be subverted by the political–administrative nexus. In this context, the criteria-based approach provides valuable resources for the project of democratising British public policy. Precise specification of both procedural *and* substantive performance criteria for the planning system, combined with specification of rights of access to representation in debates and to challenge decisions, would serve to reinforce the democratic potential of argumentative forms of land-use regulation. In such a context, development plans would become a store of democratically debated arguments and ideas about possible futures and about ways of managing the collective dimensions of cohabitation within urban regions. They would have value within a regulatory regime which encouraged checks and challenges designed to support both inclusionary forms of debate and the use of the arguments in subsequent executive action.

This leads to a further conclusion. The struggle over the form, content and influence of land-use planning systems is engaged at many levels. The fine grain of detailed practice is as important for the potential invention and subversion of regulatory regimes as is the enactment of legislation. This means that as researchers, we need to analyse the ethnography of institutional practices to identify the way regulatory regimes are shaping and being shaped by the political, economic and social processes in which they are embedded. Normatively, it is necessary to engage both at the level of theory and system form, and at the level of method and practice, to be able to identify what is a movement towards, and what is a movement away from, more democratic forms of land-use planning.

Notes

1. This reflects a Giddensian view of the structure–agency relation, in which structuration is achieved through authoritative and allocative relations (Giddens 1984). For a development of this idea in relation to land policy, incorporating the domain of ideas, see Healey and Barrett (1990).
2. This conception of discourses has been developed from Geertz (1983); see Healey (1993).
3. Property interests already have privileged rights in the British planning system but this is not widely understood. However, government efforts to privilege the housebuilding industry in plan-making discussion in the 1980s brought considerable opposition from interest groups and their political supporters, on environmental grounds.
4. These ideas have been influenced by the epistemology and normative proposals of Habermas (1987) and Forester (1989, 1993). Bryson and Crosby (1992) provide an interesting parallel, focusing on the methods of strategic plan-making.

13

Challenges for Urban Management

THE EDITORS

A world of structural change

This book is infused with references to instability; to disruption and rupture; conflict and break up; and to the complex and intertwined adverse effects of contemporary processes of change. This instability is not confined to particular arenas, sectors of the economy or of policy; to the public or the private; to particular classes, genders, races or cultural communities. One of the key general messages of the book is that the forces of change are pervasive across all dimensions of our societies, reconstituting previous relations between the economic, political and socio-cultural worlds in which we live such that changes in one part reverberate across all dimensions of our lives. The world of contemporary western society is presented as one of systemwide change in structures, rather than of change within structures. The contributions in this book also record efforts at coping, adapting, inventing and making sense of these changes. Typically, these seem to appear at the margins of the "old" structures — the vertically integrated industrial firm, the hierarchically organised political adminis-tration, the nuclear family of the industrial age, the clearly divided urban and rural landscape.

Some of the authors stress the importance of these new sites of dynamic intervention. Liberated from the confines of the rationalist, hierarchical world of modernist conceptions, these new sites of social diversity, new forms of economic organisation and political mobilisation suggest the

Managing Cities: The New Urban Context, edited by P. Healey, S. Cameron, S. Davoudi, S. Graham and A. Madani-Pour. © 1995 The Editors and contributors. Published in 1995 by John Wiley & Sons Ltd.

potential of a new world, within which it could be possible, through a broadly based reflexive politics (see Mayer in Chapter 11, and Beck 1992), to work in new ways towards the original enlightenment promise of a humane democracy grounded in respect for individuals and an appreciation of their diversity (Drysek 1990). Other contributors stress the constraints on such possibilities. Behind these changes, they argue, still lie the forces of capitalist economic organisation, more powerful it seems than ever now that they are increasingly freed from national bonds.

While all the contributors carefully steer clear of reducing the political and the social to the determinacy of the economic, nevertheless the power of major actors — transnational companies and financial institutions — to structure the opportunities for the rest of us is recognised as fundamental. Similarly, while formal political structures of the old orders are increasingly challenged by new alliances and movements, political elites continue to manage to hold on to the strings of political power. But the organisational forms through which such power is exercised are not the formal hierarchical political structures of the past. Instead, as in the sphere of economic organisation, they are being replaced by horizontal alliances and networks, cutting across divides between the political and the economic, the public and the private. The negotiation of adaptation and transformation in the face of change takes place not at the apex of system hierarchies, but across all the intersecting relations of economic and social life. It is within such adaptation and transformation that new structures are imagined and created; both unconsciously and explicitly. Efforts which are judged by participants as "successful" are typically those where institutional structures have been put in place which have the capacity to stabilise the conflicting dynamics; to "pin down" the forces of global economic change; and to achieve some degree of "coherence" (Harvey 1985a) between economic, social and political relations, for however brief a period. "Unsuccessful" efforts either fold back into the rough seas of conflicting initiatives and adaptations or are colonised by successful structuring efforts elsewhere.

If the interpretation presented in these chapters has merit, then it follows that the critical challenge for efforts in managing change at the level of the urban region is whether and how to act in relation to these unfolding dynamics. Can governance efforts achieve anything by acting strategically, to engage not merely in adapting to change but in actively building structures and systems to stabilise the changing dynamics and capture some degree of control over economic and social life? How and where can any kind of beneficial coexistence between economic development and environmental sustainability be achieved? What are the prospects that this can be done in humane and democratic ways? And specifically where does governance at the level of the urban region fit into such an enterprise? Is it a victim of the sloughing-off of past orders, part of the "relict apparatus" of the removal of modernist constraint, or does it have a newly significant role in a world where the power of hierarchical nation states has been "hollowed out", by globalisation, deregulation and individualisation, as discussed by Amin and Thrift, Lovering and Mingione in this book?

In this final chapter, we briefly restate the tendencies identified and the arguments for building up urban governance capacity. We then examine the nature of the relation between urban governance forms and economic relations. This leads on to more specific comments on the institutional capacities for urban governance. Throughout, our particular concern is not merely to explore the general challenge of *managing cities*. We also have a normative concern. Our commitment is to open out the opportunities for, and threats to, forms of governance which encourage the project of humane and pluralist democratic practices in contemporary western urbanised societies. This commitment arises out of both our moral attitude as researchers at the service of our societies and our analytical observations of the changes unfolding in front of us. The sustainability of our societies, their capacity to reproduce the conditions for survival across generations, requires the evolution of democratic forms of policy process through which we can discuss, imagine and consolidate ways of thinking and acting through which we can invent creative and relevant re-integrations of the fragmented and polarising worlds in which we currently seem to live.

Tendencies

Mingione captures the reiterated theme of these chapters. Cities are "in the frontline" of the multifaceted destructuring and recomposing of contemporary western societies. Within them are concentrated the opportunities and the seeds of innovation, along with the costs and debris resulting from the realignment and renegotiation of multiple relationships. The dangerous and the developmental exist side by side in our cities, just as they did in the burgeoning industrialising cities of the nineteenth century. But then we saw cities as the way to the future. Now we wonder if they are a relict of our past.

What then must those seeking to govern the city attend to? Within the economic sphere, these contributions stress that the critical phenomenon for cities is the visible incorporation of every economic relation within a globalised economy which sets places and workforces in competition with each other on a transnational scale. As a consequence, the attachment of companies to particular places is increasingly tenuous, while people at work are forced to live with the constant threat of change. Yet people are "tied down" to places by links of kinship and association, by culture and sentiment, and by opportunities and the lack of them. It is the continuing rootedness of activity in particular places which generates the place-based interests which people have — as citizens, as producers of goods and services, as investors, through cultural and sentimental associations, which provides the basis for claims for a strategic political response to the qualities of places. This is a major factor behind the continuing pressure for an urban governance capacity. Helping workforces adjust to change, continuously producing new sites and locations to attract companies while coping with the consequences of abandoned sites, reorganising infrastructures to suit new spatial patterns, becomes the pressing agenda for city governments. This matches with the interests of national and transnational companies, who seek out local governance cultures which will make them comfortable during their sojourn in a place.

A major concern of several of the contributors is how urban governance can move beyond surviving and adapting in this global economic flux, to set the terms of engagement with it. Fainstein suggests this could be done by the development of coherent strategies. Lovering focuses on structuring the bargains with the economic sphere. Mayer proposes mobilising across disparate groups to create both consciousness and capacity to "localise" the global.

The scale of the task is daunting, given the power of global capital, as the contributions emphasise. The capacity to grasp these changes and take strategic initiatives is itself further undermined by changes in social organisation. As Wheelock shows, the spatial instability of company investment strategies penetrates the daily lives of people in households as workforces are forced to adjust to job insecurity or long-term unemployment. This comes at a time when the other supports of social life — family relations, welfare support, church and other associations — are themselves in a flux, as Mingione argues. As the nation state withdraws from models of universalist welfare provision, individuals are increasingly thrown on to their own resources, to renegotiate life support relations (Beck 1992). The consequence for some is liberation and innovation. For others, and particularly many women, it means added burdens, and the threat of poverty. Behind the beneficial perception of the diversity of lifestyles and cultures lies the tension of urban street life, tendencies to polarisation, and the active marginalisation of those who are too poor to conform. The recognition of diversity and difference, so much celebrated by the postmodernists, has had positive emancipatory effects, as in the increasing visibility of women, of issues concerning race, culture and physical ability. But it may also lead to the entrenchment of political majorities in defence of governance measures which appear to safeguard their way of life, but which make conditions worse for others and which do not help in the adjustment to new economic conditions. In Britain, this political response is encapsulated in the concept of "Essex man",[1] but it is echoed elsewhere in Europe in the support for neo-fascist parties.

Yet in such unstable conditions, what constitutes "conformity" is itself challenged. By noticing difference, people become reflective about themselves. This has the effect of encouraging social mobilisation around the defence of specific interests. One of the most dynamic developments in the political canvas of western societies in recent years has been the springing up of a multiplicity of campaigning groups, arguing for the right to be heard and for an active voice in policy making by a whole spectrum of interest groups — women's groups, groups of the disabled, support groups for those with particular social or medical problems, those affected by adverse environmental impacts, those concerned with children and the elderly. These not only protest against their previous invisibility and demand fair consideration. They demand to be heard *as themselves*, not filtered through the politics of representative democracy or the concepts and vocabulary of professional advocacy. As a result, as Mayer argues, city politics in many places combines both defensive maintenance of the status quo and pressure to accommodate to a babel of often conflicting demands. This may give the appearance of a vigorous democratic polity. In some cities and urban regions, a richly democratic political life supports urban governance. But elsewhere, the consequences are more conflictual, with groups capturing control for short periods, to be displaced by others, pursing sequences of ideological and/or special-interest politics.[2] Meanwhile, at an individual level, many who are able to select where to live – within and beyond the city — choose places where they feel physically safe and socially comfortable. The urban penumbra, the once-rural areas of the urban region, attracts many by nostalgic illusions of a past rural community while at the same time it reinforces socio-spatial segregation, as Lowe, Murdoch and Cox show. The dynamic political life of Mumford's urban crucible is thus progressively undermined as the city-as-container spreads out across the urban region, becoming a collection of niche habitats rather than a world of spatially and socially intersecting relations, as celebrated in traditional concepts of *urbanity*. The political bases for articulating urban governance strategies and practices thus evaporate.

Is the city in space then to be replaced with a *virtual* urbanity, a city of the mind, enabled by telematics? The hope of this new technological revolution is that it will provide channels through which knowledge and information can be democratised, dispersed around the diversity of relational webs in urban regions. Could this clever technology provide the basis for dispersing power out from current nodes, and empowering and articulating diverse democratic voices? Could it provide a route through which marginalisation could be reduced? If so, the constraint of space could finally be annihilated, allowing people to network globally with similar communities of interest, thereby mobilising the power to contest specific developments. The need for place-based political mobilisation would thus disappear (Toffler 1980). The chapters in Part 3 suggest a different story. The new technology may instead be used to increase the power of the main actors, and their ability to control the rest of us (Robins and Hepworth 1988). The democratising potential of telematics thus has to be fought for. Without conscious action, both social groups and territories may be left out of these new electronic highways.

Faced with such tendencies to social fragmentation and technological exclusion, the project of urban governance comes into focus as a deliberate effort to assist the expression of the diverse voices of the various interest communities which cohabit in a place and to help to spread benefits across territories. The justification for an urban governance can also be made more prosaically. Whatever the emerging spatiality of evolving economic and social relations, the future is being constructed from an urban past. In western societies, most people have for some time lived in towns and cities. Most still spend much of their life in such places, often the same place. Where people are moving, and if city cores are losing people, it is not back to a subsistence economy or an agricultural lifestyle. Firms and households are dispersing across urban regions, incorporating rural relations and cultures into the array of possibilities which have evolved in complex interaction with urban contexts and cultures, as Lowe, Murdoch and Cox show. Villages become neighbourhoods within the urban region. Any strategic action thus requires a capacity to integrate across "urban" and "rural" space. The urban region then becomes the focus of attention of strategic political action generated by both the need to sort out the problems of those living in an area and to capture opportunities and resist damage generated by global forces.

But this conclusion highlights the question of the capacity of urban regions to articulate not just a political voice but an institutional equipment to take such strategic action. Several of the contributions emphasise the dislocation of established institutional mechanisms for mobilisation. Local governance units are frequently too small to encompass the labour market, land market and infrastructure relations of urban regions. Regional levels of government which could provide a locus of mobilisation have atrophied in several cases (e.g. Italy) or been abolished (e.g. England). New organisations have been created on an *ad hoc* basis to cope with what are seen as new functions and approaches. Whatever the distinctive form of these tendencies, the result seems to be a fragmentation of urban governance efforts and a consequent loss of capacity to mobilise for strategic action. Those places with institutional arrangements which provide arenas for strategic articulation have a considerable asset in this situation. Yet everywhere, capturing opportunity and resisting damage requires an effort in political mobilisation across the disrupted relations of the economic, social and political worlds by those with interests in urban regions. Through such mobilisation, institutional capacity for integration at the urban region level is generated with which to undertake the political project of strategic repositioning of urban regions within new transnational economic and political relations. Without such institutional integration, the institutional capacity which exists will be merely the product of multiple and conflicting adaptations. As the discussion in the March 1993 Seminar on Amin and Thrift's concept of *institutional thickness* highlighted, it is not just the density of institutional relations and the extent to which they tap into access to economic, social and political resources that matters. The coherence, process forms and agendas of urban governance agencies themselves are also critical to an urban region's institutional capacity. Thus a key message of this book is that institutional capacity matters. It matters to the future trajectory of an urban region; to whether the intersecting relational webs within a region flourish, whether they are merely locked into a cycle of constant reactive adaptation, or whether they decay, with damaging social and environmental consequences.

Rupture and coherence

The hope expressed in the contributions to this book is that, through intelligent mobilisation, urban region interests can create the capacity to stabilise and even shape the flux of forces around them in such a way as to provide opportunities for the diversity of innovative efforts to flourish and produce locally beneficial effects. This raises three areas of discussion. Firstly, what kind of future is emerging? Is it just wishful thinking to imagine that action at the urban region level can make a difference, as Lovering tends to argue, or is there a real theoretical and empirical case to support such a hope? The second area of discussion centres on the theoretical and practical question of the relation between economic and political forces. The third considers the role of actions initiated at the urban level in these relations.

All the contributions present a conception of a trajectory of change, from a Fordist, or industrial, or modernist, Keynesian welfarist or managerial past, to something else. Where the authors differ is in their conceptions of the path of this trajectory. For Dear and Mayer, we are already in a new world. For Amin and Thrift, Lovering and Robins, we still carry much of the old with us. Clearly it would be very helpful for urban policy makers if the academic community could not only explain what has happened, but give an idea of what will happen next — to predict. Is the contemporary world of fragmenting, differentiating and differing relations, with its polarising and marginalising tendencies and economic instability and vulnerability, now a constant phenomenon, the "new times" referred to by Mayer, drawing on Hall and Jacques (1989)? Or is it in a stage of reconstruction on the way to some new order? The literature is full of metaphors for a new order: Harvey's *entrepreneurial* state (Harvey 1989a); Jessop's *Schumpeterian workfare state* (Jessop 1992c); Beck's *risk society* (Beck

1992). Most of our authors are more cautious. They either resist the impetus for a new *order* as such, celebrating a world beyond unifying orders (for example, Dear). Or they argue that whether a new order will emerge and what its lineaments will be is a matter of conjecture (for example, Amin and Thrift, Robins). Several (Mayer, Healey, Fainstein) go on to argue that what will emerge is not only contingent on the particularities of time and place. It also has to be actively constituted. Consequently policymakers face significant choices, and those in urban regions have a real political agenda.

These three ways of thinking about the future — a continual fragmentation and differentiation; an emerging new order in the making unfolding before us; or a historically and geographically shaped potentiality and constraint, awaiting our capacity to grasp the opportunities — suggest different responses from urban region policy communities. Following the first, policymakers would feel legitimated in avoiding any attempt at integrated strategic actions. Their stance would be facilitative and responsive to diverse, individualised claims for policy attention. A postmodern urban governance would thus continue the project-led approach described by Healey in Chapter 12. Following the second, the policy response would be to develop an acute research and intelligence role, to help in reading the contextual future as it emerges, and in working out how to position an urban region within it. The focus of such a research function would be more than the study of individual economics sectors, workforce skills etc. Instead, it would concentrate on the structuring dynamics of the relational context for economic activity and social life. Following the third, urban region policymakers would recognise that they are involved in active and risky experimentation in building up the structure of the future. All the research and intelligence of the second approach would remain important, but urban region policy communities could believe that their role is not merely to respond intelligently to external pressure but actively to seek to construct futures for their places.

A second area of concern is what kinds of relations are emerging between economic activity and the political sphere. As Mayer argues, recent theorisation within the regulationist school of urban and regional analysis has sought to escape from the reductionism of standard Marxist analysis of the 1970s. There is now much agreement within political economy analysis that economic forces do not simplistically determine political responses. Some argue that economic and political forces are interrelated but subject to their own dynamics. What happens in urban regions is thus the outcome of the complex negotiation of codetermining forces. Others who maintain the primacy of the economic at a general level (e.g. Harvey 1985a), recognise that the dynamics of the relations between the economic and the political are unlikely to be coterminous in particular places. Both strands of argument emphasise the conclusion that possibilities and outcomes are likely to vary significantly from place to place. Further, economic and political relations are not homogeneous forces but are broad groupings with often conflicting strands. This all serves to emphasise that the way the links between the economic and the political work out cannot be simply "read off" from an analysis of economic dynamics. They must be actively thought through by urban region policymakers in the specificity of local conditions.

As several of the contributions in this book point out, empirical research on the political and economic relations of urban governance shows that such relations are typically matters of constant negotiation and reinterpretation (e.g. Logan and Molotch 1987). Further, this negotiation takes place in urban region contexts structured not just by economics and politics but also by local culture and history, local *pathways* (North 1990). Further, broader *cultural* forces have significant effects on urban region values and attitudes, as the cultural power of the contemporary environmental movement shows (Beck 1992). The interlocking of economic, social and political relations to be found in one place, Harvey's *structured coherence* (Harvey 1985a), must be understood not just as a one-way flow of influence *from* the economic to the social and political. It is a product of active negotiation at a multiplicity of nodes and levels, structuring the economic relations themselves. That many places seemed to have had in the 1960s, and seem now to have, rather similar relational patterns is thus the result of negotiated codeterminacy at the urban region level rather than economic determinacy. The implication for urban region policymakers is that, firstly, strategic repositioning of places in the context of wider changes involves not just thinking about the economy, but about socio-cultural changes too. Secondly, in any strategic management project, it is necessary to identify sensitively, and with an eye to local particulars, what specific *coherences* are sought between economic, socio-cultural and political relations, and how the negotiation of these relationships can be affected by urban governance interventions.

The perspective of these chapters also argues for a significant conceptual shift in the understanding of social relations and what "managing" them involves. This challenges neo-liberal conceptions which focus on individual preferences. Instead it argues for more attention to people in relationship to each other and in the context of relational webs structured by economic, political and cultural forces. But these structuring forces are understood not in the terms of the mechanical, hierarchical systems envisaged by urban systems theorists of the 1960s, or the impersonal "forces of history" driving social change, as envisaged by the structuralist marxists. They are to be understood as intersecting and actively negotiated relational webs, within which the tensions of conflicting demands are actively worked out.

If this is so, then the preoccupation of the contemporary economic development literature with building up alliances and creating networks, both within and between urban regions, is not a sideshow. It is and should be a central concern of urban management. But networking activity, the effort of creating relationships and re-assembling new alliances from the fragments and disruption of recent years, can take many forms. An urban management which makes a difference needs to develop an appreciation of what are the critical relations, the key links, which need to be fostered in an area. What are the networks aimed to get access to and which existing relational nodes are the best route to this? What practices and ways of behaving, and what manipulation of rules and resources, will help achieve such relation-building work? This moves the debate about urban networking (Cooke and Morgan 1993) beyond a narrow preoccupation with public–private partnerships, of *Eurocities* networking,[3] or creating business–community links to a strategic consideration of the evolving relations within an urban arena and their consequences for democratic process, for material welfare, social cohesion and environmental quality. It shifts the locus of discussion from merely the analysis of the formation and mobilisation of bias inherent in spatial alliance formation, as discussed by Lovering, towards the active social process of consensus forming, and to dialogical and argumentative conceptions of policy processes, as Healey emphasises (see Forester 1989; Bryson and Crosby 1992; Fischer and Forester 1993; Sager 1994). In such conceptions, the task of urban governance moves beyond that of provider of welfare and support services for economic activity, to that of a strategically shaping enabler of the lively coexistence of multiple relations.

Building up key urban region relations has tended in the past to be a *consequence* of urban governance, as the relationships of governance activity link into the different areas of economic, social and political life in an urban region. The implication of the above discussion is that it should become a *direct object* of policy attention. Effectively done, such relation-building work has the potential to release substantial local institutional capacity; to mobilise the fragments of coexisting networks in urban regions. But such relational capacity building involves moving beyond consideration of who controls resource flows and how to influence them, and how to set ground rules for interactions. It requires careful attention to the *processes* through which relations are built up and maintained, to the discursive forms through which interests and objectives are identified, conflicts delineated and consensus developed. It involves building up commitment and belief in what could be done, as well as breaking down old conventions. It in effect needs the reverse of the ideological neo-liberal strategies designed to *break up* institutional capacity pursued so vigorously in Britain in the 1980s. It is not so difficult to break down traditions, as the neo-liberal experiment in Britain has shown. By changing rules, shifting resource flows and continual ideological bombardment, established practices and attitudes disintegrate. Building up sustainable institutional capacity and cultures is, in contrast, a slow process. Generating hope and commitment to future possibilities is one element of such work. But these need to be grounded in more than exhortation and the "talking up" of possibilities, as was so actively used in British urban policy in the Thatcher years. *Active debate* about imagining possibilities is as important as strategic research and intelligence work.

As several of the contributors have argued, strategic policy rhetoric makes a difference. The construction and dissemination of storylines of the future has substantial mobilisation potential, so long as these are honed to the multiple realities of urban region dynamics. Thus the preoccupation with "vision" of urban regeneration policies in British and American cities in the 1980s was not misguided as such. The critique which can be made is rather of the narrowness of the vision and the failure to attach conceptions of possibilities to rich analysis of the changing conditions of urban regions. As a result, policy "visions" typically became mere ephemeral marketing labels in a political competition for voter and investor attention (Wilkinson 1992) rather than strategic conceptions around which urban interests could cluster and focus their thinking over the long term. Yet as Fainstein shows in Battery Park, New York, in appropriate institutional contexts, some visions are realised. There are many other examples across western cities — for example, the way Barcelona and Manchester City used the opportunity to bid for (and in Barcelona's case to run) the Olympic Games, or the interlocking of strategic infrastructure investment at national level with urban development projects, as in Lyons or Lille in France. What makes the difference in the approach to "vision" and "urban marketing" is the degree of richness and social breadth in the storylines and metaphors, and the relation between dreaming about the future and the reality of the present.

Thus a relational perspective on urban region governance emphasises the importance of local institutional capacity and its role in mobilising interconnections between the relational webs which coexist within an urban region through encouraging network building and through discourse. A critical strategic asset for urban regions then becomes the people, groups and forums within a region which have the ability to develop ideas about key relations and key policy ideas. A critical *moral* issue accompanying such work is whose interests and values this mobilisation effort supports. The project of humane democratic urban region governance would judge such efforts by their inclusionary potential and their capacity to accommodate multiple life histories within an overall strategic storyline.

To conclude, urban management in this perspective is not about ways of delivering local government services fairly, efficiently and effectively, as it was in the 1960s. It is instead about how people in firms, agencies and households with shared interests in the relational webs and environmental qualities of urban areas can come together to identify common concerns, develop strategic ideas and generate the momentum to bring forward investment in building links and constructing discourses. Through these, the possibility of new forms of institutional coherence could be realised.

Forms of urban governance

The argument which this book develops is that the tasks of urban management in the contemporary period centre on an active effort in building up local relational structures which have the capacity to sustain those kinds of economic activity which can coexist comfortably with local social and environmental agendas. A critical task is to draw down from these activities, through fostering the fine grain of links between economic and social relations, as broad a spread of benefits locally as can be achieved. In parallel, and encouraging those points of constructive inter-section with key economic relations (i.e. encouraging *coherence-building*), urban management efforts need to develop a relational infrastructure for diverse social lives and cultural worlds. This requires access to research and intelligence capacity, with respect to the critical relations of the economic, social and cultural spheres to be found in an urban region. It also requires skills in "making links", setting contexts to foster relation-building work; and "strategic vision", mobilising ideas about the future. But how is this to be done? And how can it be done in ways which extend and include rather than reduce, exclude and polarise?

The chapters offer many suggestions. They also point to the potential in the practices emerging in many cities: the shift to enabling government agencies rather than service providing ones; the pervasive interest in "partnership"; the creation of special quasi-governmental bodies; the efforts in building networks between city governments across Europe: the proliferation of interest-group politics. Yet such new practices are not of themselves carriers of possibilities for an effective broadly based institutional capacity-building. Much critical analysis of the working out of such initiatives points in quite the opposite direction (consider, for example, the British case; Imrie and Thomas 1993; Healey et al. 1992). They may merely increase the contemporary tendency to governance fragmen-tation. Or they may be used to re-establish control by a narrow range of traditionally dominant interests. To build up an urban institutional capacity capable of "pinning down" the global, spreading out the benefits of this, and sustaining diversity, it is necessary to move beyond individual organisational initiatives as such, in order to consider their informing ideas, their working practices and the underpinning structure of rules which are drawn upon to guide the development of ideas and practices. The structuring of institutional capacity thus centres, following Giddens, on building "coherence" through ideas and through rules, which have the capacity to act on the acquisition and flow of resources. This focuses attention on arenas, arguments and rights; the forums and arenas where strategies and principles are articulated, the management of argument within such forums and arenas, and the formal structure of rules which can be activated to call any urban region actor to account in relation to the others. It is these ingredients which have the potential to *make a difference* in urban governance capacity-building, generating the possibility of strategic action, rather than continual responsive adaptation.

Building up relational links requires more than networking activity. It requires the identification of key nodes in the networks, accepted as places where what constitute shared problems and objectives can be identified and discussed. In the fragmented agency structure of contemporary urban management, it is clear that governance activity is no longer coterminous with the formal structures of local and regional governance. This makes identifying a locus for discussing common problems particularly difficult. As Bryson and Crosby argue (1992), developing strategic organising ideas to guide the actions of diverse agencies involves a discursive effort in raising issues and identifying a need for some consensus-building. Some *forum* is needed for such debate, but this can be relatively fluid, perhaps generated by the media, or by an *ad hoc* temporary alliance. Such problem-defining work then needs to move on to the articulation of strategies and policies. Bryson and Crosby suggest this requires a more defined organisational *arena*, with some legitimacy and leverage over key urban region actors. They then argue that some form of *court* is needed for arbitration of disputes which remain unresolved. The problem for contemporary fragmented urban governance is that the traditional arenas have lost much of their legitimacy, and forums are lacking in which to recreate new agendas and principles which could breathe legitimacy back into them. As a result, too much of the agenda of urban region management ends up in actual courts, or other and sometimes more violent forms of dispute and confrontation. A key effort in institutional capacity-building for urban region governance is therefore the construction of appropriate forums within which strategic debate can take place. Interesting examples of such strategic forums can be found in the field of growth management in the USA, where many interests seek to control growth, but getting agreement to act above the level of the individual local government or the utility company or the major landowning interests requires building up consensus which will legitimise rewriting the rules in state legislatures (Innes 1992).

In many European countries, the traditional institutions of hierarchical governance may contain arrangements which have the potential to provide such strategic arenas. Those concerned about urban region management look enviously at the regional machinery available elsewhere, such as the German Länder, since these appear to provide ready-made forums and arenas. Some countries have political cultures which strive towards consensus-building. In the Netherlands, for example, government structures created on the basis of a hierarchical model have been remoulded to become a vehicle for "co-sociational" consensus-building strategies. It is such consensus-building, Faludi and Van der Valk (1994) argue, which has underpinned the stability in Dutch spatial policy over the years. In France, many city mayors have vigorously responded to the 1983 decentralisation of power in the government system to become the focal point of strategic urban region action. In Britain, many local governments, which are relatively large by comparison with their US and continental counterparts, are seeking to restructure themselves from service providers to "strategic enablers" (Stoker and Young 1993). But such a reformulation of existing institutional forums and arenas is not an easy task. It involves a *cultural transformation* away from a past in which typically local government was pitted against central government and the public sector was seen as the guardian of the public interest, in opposition to the private sector and its private interests. The new urban management is not about capturing power understood as *control* back from economic and political forces which have taken it away. It is about reconstituting the bases for power, understood as *opportunity*, in a world of open, dynamic and diverse relational webs. It is in this sense that Fainstein in Chapter 6 supports the entrepreneurial turn in contemporary urban governance. But the creation of entrepreneurial urban development agencies of themselves does not build up relational capacity. It is the broader effort of consensus-building which can help to provide the coordination and integration with other initiatives which maximises the effectiveness of urban development agencies, as Fainstein shows.

The core of strategic urban region management thus seems to lie in careful consensus-building work across the contemporary fragments. But this involves more than constituting the forums and arenas. How effective forums are in identifying possibilities and building up support for new ways forward depends on how discussion proceeds on the mechanisms of consensus-building and cultural change. It is in this context that the ideas about policy argumentation referred to by Healey in Chapter 12 come into play. The expanding literature in policy analysis and planning on communicative and dialogical forms of argumentation provides an increasingly rich array of possibilities (Fischer and Forester 1993; Bryson and Crosby 1992; Sager 1994). This body of work seeks to break out of concepts of instrumental rationality which have dominated policy analysis since the 1940s, to embrace a richer conception of reasoning which includes moral and expressive forms of understanding. Drawing on Habermas in particular, it explores how public discussion can take place in ways which generate ideas and possibilities, rather than merely following the zero-sum game of interest-mediation. This conception assumes, as Habermas does, that arguments carry power and that the process of argumentation can shift the balance of power in any situation. It further assumes that ideas about the future are not specialist creative objects to be produced by experts through design or analysis, or by visionary politicians. They arise out of argumentation, through which participants learn about their interests, about their shared concerns and the conflicts which may arise between them, about possibilities, and about strategic ideas which could help express and organise what many are thinking. In this effort, strategic policy experts are no longer skilled in the production of strategies. They are rather, as Forester (1989, 1993) argues, sensitive managers of policy attention and strategic argumentation, raising questions as to who might be involved in debate and how, and about the structure and interrelations of arguments.

Such a scenario, of strategic debate among urban region actors drawn from alliances built up across the webs of relations which coexist within an urban region, raises complex questions of accountability and legitimacy. What is the status of debates conducted outside the elected council chambers of local government bodies? Does this not presage yet a further limitation of local democracy? Comments of this kind implicitly reify the model of representative democracy. Such a model may work in a world where consensus exists, or where simple majorities need their interests protected against the power of "big capital". The contemporary problem is that the representative model does not easily provide voice for the multiple interests generated by the relational webs within urban areas. Further, the political structures which have evolved to manage the representation process often entrench the power of old elites, whether representing landowners, industrial capital, or labour. The model also focuses primarily on the citizen's role as voter, electing representatives and leaving them to it, whereas the struggle by many interests these days is to have a say in the detail of policy development and delivery. The neo-liberal arguments tap a real demand in their emphasis on giving consumers a voice in evaluating the delivery of public services, through customer charters and the like.[4] But the neo-liberal case focuses on the individual service consumer, whereas many interests seek a say in the *production* of ideas about services and strategies (i.e. a form of democracy with a participatory element (Drysek 1990)) and recognise the difference between their personal interest and a collective interest in an issue.

What is needed is a form of accountability which allows for the active involvement of various parties in policy development and delivery, as expressed, for example, in the partnership idea, while at the same time setting the parameters of *attention to interests* to which any governance activity, whether strategic or specific, is required to refer. It is here that the traditional liberal idea of citizen's rights can be brought into play. The notion of rights, which used to be linked to rights to the enjoyment of private property and to vote, is now being extended to other spheres, as in the right to information. Perhaps the critical right for the citizens of urban regions is the right, in strategic policy debate and in policy actions, for their interests to be considered. The equal opportunities movement and its legislative gains provides a precursor of how such rights might be used. The existence of rights of this kind, especially if actively used, would have a double benefit. It could lead to much more active involvement in governance activity. More likely, it would encourage those who are involved to bear in mind the potential for challenge from the diverse interests in an urban region and the need to be able to show how they have done this. Where citizens are willing to activate such rules, this could lead to a form of potentially direct accountability, rather than the mediation of citizens' interests through the processes of political representation. Accountability lies not in *who* makes decisions, but in what decision-makers take account of when making decisions.

Key areas for urban management capacity-building would therefore appear to centre on constructing forums and arenas for broadly based policy debate, managing argumentation and drawing up ground rules for the relation between governance activity and urban region interests. If this can lock into and sustain existing tendencies for both entrepreneurial opportunity-taking and for the mobilisation of the diversity of political movements and groupings seeking a voice and an involvement in aspects of the management of their places, then it may be possible to build up a reasonable coherent local view about how to reposition an urban region in the dynamic world of transnational economies and supranational politics.

But any conclusion about future forms of governance is difficult to make because we still know so little about how urban life and urban economies are evolving, and how this relates to governance activity. This book had its origins in an attempt to promote more research on urban region management. The various contributions have indicated both conceptual and empirical lines of enquiry. Most of the chapters draw from attempts to synthesise a scattered empirical research effort combined with intelligent interpretation of contemporary events and ideas. We have suggested in this chapter ways in which urban governance may be evolving, and the kinds of management capacity which may be of value in these new worlds. But without much more research, governance efforts will be ill-prepared for the tasks ahead. Research agendas, in effect, need to be reconstituted, along with our understanding of the nature of the urban in the contemporary period. This book has emphasised the significance of the institutional capacity of urban regions in influencing the future quality of life and economic possibility for people in households, firms and agencies. It has also emphasised that, to grasp the dimensions of such capacity, the conceptual and methodological tools of the institutionalist approach expressed in the various chapters have much to offer. These tools now need to be harnessed to the task of building up the research capacity for reflective evaluation of the urban region relations unfolding before us.

Notes

1.   The term "Essex man" came into currency in Britain in the early 1980s to describe the newly affluent Thatcherite voter.
2.   A good example is the fraught local "politics of turf" in racially mixed areas such as Tower Hamlets and Brent in London, or Toxteth in Liverpool.
3.   The *Eurocities* network was established under the EC's auspices, to encourage exchange of technology and policy.
4.   The customer charter movement has been used in Britain in an attempt to demonstrate that public sector agencies and newly privatised utilities meet quality standards deemed to be of relevance by customers.

References

Abercrombie, P. (1930). The English countryside, in Robson, W. (ed), *The Political Quarterly in the Thirties*. London, Allen and Unwin.

Abercrombie, P. (1933). *Town and Country Planning*. London, Butterworth.

Adam Smith Institute (1983). *Omega Report: Local Government Policy*. London, Adam Smith Institute.

Aglietta, M. (1979). *A Theory of Capitalist Regulation: The US Experience*. London, Verso.

Ahmed, Y., Gilchrist, A. and Miller, C. (1993). Economic restructuring in the city and the contradictions of community action, in Smith, R, and Blanke, B. (eds), *The Future of the Medium-Sized City*. Anglo-German Foundation.

Aigrin, P. and Salge, F. (1992). Vers L'Europe de l'Information Géographique. Acts of the Second International Forum on Geographical Instrumentation and Information, Strasbourg (France), 25–27 May.

Alger, C.A. (1990). Local responses to global intrusions. Mimeograph, Department of Political Science, Ohio State University.

Allen, J. (1988). The geography of services, in Massey, D. and Allen J. (eds), *Uneven Redevelopment*. Hodder and Stoughton, London.

Altshuler, A.A. (1965). *The City Planning Process*. Ithaca, NY, Cornell University Press.

Alty, R. and Darke, R. (1986). A city centre for people, *Planning Practice and Research*, (3), 7–12.

Ambrose, P. (1986). *Whatever Happened to Planning?* London, Methuen.

Ambroso, G. and Mingione, E. (1992). Diversità etnico-culturale e progetti migratori, in Mottura, G. (ed), *L'Archipelago Immigrazione*. Rome, Ediesse, pp. 71–92.

Amin, A. (ed) (1994). *The Geography of Post-Fordism*. Cambridge, Basil Blackwell.

Amin, A. and Malmberg, A. (1992). Competing structural and institutional influences on the geography of production in Europe, *Environment and Planning A*, **22**, 401–416.

Amin, A. and Robins, K. (1991). These are not Marshallian times, in R. Camagni (ed), *Innovation Networks*. London, Belhaven.

Amin, A. and Taylor, P. (1994). Forum for heterodox international political economy, *Radical International Political Economy*, **1**(1), 1–12.

Amin, A. and Thrift, N. (1992). Neo-Marshallian nodes in global networks, *International Journal of Urban and Regional Research*, **16**, 571–587.

Amin, A. and Thrift, N. (1994). Holding down the global, in Amin, A. and Thrift, N.

(eds), *Globalisation and the Regions: Examples from Europe*. Oxford University Press, Oxford.

Amin, A. and Tomaney, J. (1993). Turning the tide: the impact of urban and regional regeneration initiatives in North East England, in Fasenfest, D. (ed), *Community Economic Development*. London, Macmillan.

Anheier, H.K. and Salamon, L.M. (1992). Genese und Schwerpunkte internationaler Forschung zum Nonprofit-Sektor, *Forschungsjournal Neue Soziale Bewegungen*, 5(4), 40–48.

Anheier, H.K. and Seibel, W. (eds) (1990). *The Third Sector: Comparative Studies of Nonprofit Organizations*. Berlin, de Gruyter.

Anzieu, D. (1984). *The Group and the Unconscious*. London, Routledge & Kegan Paul.

Appadurai, A. (1990). Disjuncture and difference in the global cultural economy, *Theory, Culture and Society*, 7, 295–310.

Ascherson, N. (1993). A diverse England we can shape to our taste, *Independent on Sunday*, 3 October.

Ashworth, C.J. and Voogd, H.J. (1990), *Selling the City*. London, Belhaven Press.

Association of London Authorities (ALA), and Docklands Consultative Committee (DCC) (1991). *10 Years of Docklands: How the Cake was Cut*. London, ALA and DCC, June.

Bagnasco, A. (1990). The informal economy, in Martinelli, A. and Smelser, N.J. (eds), *Economy and Society: Overviews in Economic Sociology*. London, Sage.

Bakis, H., Abler, R. and Roche, E. (1993). *Corporate Networks, International Telecommunications and Interdependence*. London, Belhaven.

Baldwin, S. (1926). *On England*. London.

Balibar, E. and Wallerstein, I. (1990). *Race, Nation, Classe: Les Identités Ambigües*. Paris, La Découverte.

Banham, R. (1973). *Los Angeles: Architecture of the Four Ecologies*. Harmondsworth, Penguin.

Barbrook, R. (1990). Mistranslations, Lipietz in London and Paris, *Science as Culture*, 8, 80–117.

Barr, A. and York, P. (1982). *The Official Sloane Ranger Handbook: The First Guide to What Really Happens in Life*. London, Ebury Press.

Barrett, S. and Fudge, C. (ed) (1981). *Policy and Action*. London, Methuen.

Batley, R. and Stoker, G. (eds) (1991). *Local Government in Europe*, London, Macmillan.

Bauman, Z. (1990). Modernity and ambivalence, *Theory, Culture and Society*, 7(2–3), 143–169.

Bauman, Z. (1992). *Intimations of Postmodernity*. London, Routledge.

Beauregard, R. (1993). *Voices of Urban Decline*. Oxford, Blackwell.

Beck, U. (1992). *The Risk Society*. Sage, London.

Becker, G. (1965). A theory of the allocation of time, reprinted in Amsden, A.M. (ed), *The Economics of Women and Work*. Harmondsworth, Penguin.

Begg, I. and Moore, B. (1992). Industrial regeneration and economic redistribution, in Miliband, D. (ed), *A More Perfect Union? Britain and the New Europe*. London, Institute of Public Policy Research.

Benevolo, L. (1980). *The History of the City*. London, Scolar Press.

Bennett, R., Krebs, G. and Zimmermann, H. (eds) (1990). *Local Economic Development in Britain and Germany*. London, Anglo-German Foundation.

Ben-Porath, Y. (1980). The F-connection: families, friends, and firms and the organisation of change, *Population and Development Review*, 6, 1–30.

Bensoussan, A. (1991). *Les SIG et le Droit*. Paris, Hermes.

Berger, P. and Luckman, T. (1971). *The Social Construction of Reality*. Harmondsworth, Penguin.

Berman, M. (1982). *All That is Solid Melts into Air: the Experience of Modernity*. New York, Penguin.

Berrie, T. and Berrie, T. (1993). Utility management, ownership and accountability in the 1990s, *Utilities Policy*, January, 81–85.

Best, S. and Kellner, D. (1991). *Postmodern Theory: Critical interrogations*. New York, Guilford Press.

Bianchini, F. and Parkinson, M. (eds) (1993). *Cultural Policy and Urban Regeneration: The West European Experience*. Manchester, Manchester University Press.

Bianchini, F. and Schwengel, H. (1991). Re-imaging the city, in J. Corner and S. Harvey (eds), *Enterprise and Heritage: Crosscurrents in National Culture*. London, Routledge.

Biehl, D. (1986). *The Contribution of Infrastructure to Regional Development*. Final Report. Infrastructure Study Group, CEC, Brussels.

Bimbi, F. (1991). Doppia presenza, in Balbo, L. (ed), *Tempi de Vita*. Milano, Feltrinelli.

Blackhurst, C. and Cope, N. (1993), The new barons, *Independent on Sunday*, 3 January.

Blanke, B. et al. (eds) (1987). *Großstadt und Arbeitslosigkeit, ein Problemsyndrom im Netz lokaler Sozialpolitik*. Opladen, Westdeutscher Verlag.

Boddy, M. (1993). The restructuring of training provision: training and enterprise councils and market-led training in the skills decade, in Campbell, N. and Duffy, K. (eds), *Local Labour Markets: Problems and Policies*. London, Longman.

Boden, D. (1993). *The Business of Talk*. Cambridge, Polity Press.

Bonefeld, W. and Holloway, J. (eds) (1991). *Post-Fordism and Social Form: A Marxist Debate on the Post-Fordist State*. London, Macmillan.

Bottles, S.L. (1987). *Los Angeles and the Automobile*. Berkeley, University of California Press.

Boyer, C. (1986). *Dreaming the Rational City*. Cambridge, Mass, MIT Press.

Boyer, R. (1990). *The Regulation School: A Critical Introduction*. New York, Columbia University Press.

Brabher, G. (1990). On the weakness of strong ties: the ambivalent role of inter-firm relations in the decline and reorganization of the Ruhr. Discussion paper FS 1, 90–4 Wissenschaftszentrum, Berlin.

Bradshaw, J. and Holmes, H. (1989). *Living on the Edge: A Study of Living Standards of Families on Benefit in Tyne and Wear*. London, Child Poverty Action Group.

Breheny, M. (ed) (1992). *Sustainable Development and Urban Form*, London, Pion.

Brenner, R. and Glick, M. (1991). The regulation approach: theory and history, *New Left Review*, (188), 45–120.

Brewer, H. (1989). Diversification attempts by electric utilities: a comparison of potential vs. achieved diversification, *Energy Policy*, June, 228–234.

Brindley, T., Rydin, Y. and Stoker, G. (1989). *Remaking Planning*. London, Unwin Hyman.

Brodsly, D. (1981). *L.A. Freeway: An Appreciative Essay*. Berkeley, University of California Press.

Bruce, A. (1993). Prospects for local economic development: a practitioner's view, *Local Government Studies*, **19**(3), 319–340.

Bryden, J. and Houston, G. (1978). *Agrarian Change in the Scottish Highlands*. London, Martin Robertson.

Bryson, J. and Crosby, B. (1989). The design and use of strategic planning arenas, *Planning Outlook*, **32**(1), 5–13.

Bryson, J. and Crosby, B. (1992). *Leadership for the Common Good: Tackling Public Problems in a Shared Power World*. San Francisco, Jossey Bass.

Buck, N. (1991). Social polarisation in the inner city: an analysis of the impact of labour market and household change, in Cross, M. and Payne, G. (eds), *Social Inequality and the Enterprise Culture*. London, Falmer Press.

Buck, N. and Fainstein, N. (1992). A comparative history, 1880–1973, in Fainstein, S., Gordon, I. and Harloe, M. (eds), *Divided Cities*. Oxford, Basil Blackwell.

Buck, N., Gordon, I.R. and Young, K. (1986). *The London Employment Problem*. Oxford, Oxford University Press.

Bullman, U. (1991). *Kommunale Strategein gegen Massenarbeitslosigkeit*. Opladen, Leske & Budrich.

Bullman U. (ed) (1993). *Die Politik der dritten Ebene: Regionen im EG Integrationsprozess*. Baden-Baden, Nomos.

Burrow, J.W. (1966). *Evolution and Society*. Cambridge, Cambridge University Press.

Button, K. and Rothengather, W. (1993). Global environmental degradation: the role of transport, in Banister, D. and Button, K. (eds), *Transport, Environment and Sustainable Development*. London, E & FN Spon.

Cain, P.J. and Hopkins, A.G. (1993). *British Imperialism*. London, Longman.

Campbell, B. (1993). *Goliath: Britain's Dangerous Places*. London, Methuen.

Campbell, M. (ed) (1990). *Local Economic Policy*. Cassell, London.

Cannadine, D. (1990). *The Decline and Fall of the British Aristocracy*. London, Yale University Press.

Capello, R. and Gillespie, A. (1993). Transport, communication and spatial organisation: future trends and conceptual frameworks, in Giannopoulos, G. and Gillespie, A. (1993). *Transport and Communications in the New Europe*. London, Belhaven.

Carroll, D. (ed) (1990). *The States of Theory*. New York, Columbia University Press.

Cashmore, E. (1991). Flying business class: Britain's new ethnecelite, *New Community*, **17**, 547–58.

Castells, M. (1977). *The Urban Question*. London, Edward Arnold.

Castells, M. (1989). *The Informational City*. Oxford, Blackwell.

Caton, C.L.M. (ed) (1990). *Homeless in America*. New York, Oxford University Press.

Chambers, I. (1990). *Border Dialogues: Journeys in Postmodernity*. London, Routledge.

Champion, A.G. and Green, A.E. (1992). Local economic performance in Britain during the late 1980s: the results of the third Booming Towns study, *Environment and Planning A*, **24**, 243–272.

Champion, T. and Townsend, A. (1990). *Contemporary Britain: A Geographical Perspective*. London, Edward Arnold.

Chapin, F.S. (1965). *Urban Land Use Planning*. Urbana, University of Illinois Press.

Cheshire, P. and Hay, D. (1989). *Urban Problems in Western Europe: an Economic Analysis*. London, Unwin Hyman.

Chesnaux, J. (1992). *Brave Modern World: The Prospects for Survival*. London, Thames and Hudson.

Church, A. (1988). Urban regeneration in London Docklands: a five-year policy review, *Environment and Planning C*, **6**, 187–208.

Clarke, G. (1992). "Real" regulation: the administrative state, *Environment and Planning A*, **24**, 615–627.

Clarke, S. (1984). The local state and alternative economic development strategies: gaining public benefits from private investment. Boulder: Centre for Public Policy Research, discussion paper 16.

Clarke, S. (1988). Overaccumulation, class struggle and the regulation approach, *Capital and Class*, **36**, 59–92.

Clarke, S. and Gaile, G.L. (1992). The next wave: postfederal local economic development strategies, *Economic Development Quarterly*, 6 (2), 187–198.

Clifford, J. (1988). *The Predicament of Culture*. Cambridge, Mass, Harvard University Press.

Cloke, P. and Little, J. (1990). *The Rural State: Limits to Planning in Rural Society*. Oxford, Clarendon Press.

Cochrane, A. (1993a). Das veränderte Gesicht der Städtischen Politik in Sheffield: vom "municipal labourism" zu "public–private partnership" in Heinelt, H. and Mayer, M. (eds), *Politik in europäischen Städten: Fallstudien zur Bedeutung lokaler Politik*. Basel, Birkhäuser, pp. 119–136.

Cochrane, A. (1993b). *Whatever Happened to Local Government?* Buckingham, Open University Press.

Cockburn, C. (1977). *The Local State*. London, Pluto Press.

Colenutt, B. and Ellis G. (1993). The next quangos in London, *New Statesman and Society*, 26 March.

Commission of the European Community (CEC) (1990). *Green Book on the Urban Environment*. Luxembourg, CEC.

Commission of the European Community (CEC) (1992a). *Europe 2000: Outlook for the Development of the Community's Territory*. Luxembourg, CEC.

Commission of the European Community (CEC) (1992b). *Community Activities in Urban Matters: the Development of the Urban System and the Urban Dimension in Community Policies*. Luxembourg, CEC.

Commission of the European Community (CEC) (1993). *Growth, Competitiveness, Employment: the Challenges and Way Forward into the 21st Century*. Luxembourg, CEC, Com (93) 700.

Connolly, W.E. (1991). *Identity/Difference: Democratic Negotiations of Political Paradox*. Ithaca, Cornell University Press.

Cooke, P. (1988). Flexible integration, scope economies and strategic alliances: social and spatial mediations, *Environment and Planning D: Society & Space*, **6**, 281–300.

Cooke, P. (ed) (1989). *Localities*. London, Unwin.

Cooke, P. (1990a). *Back to the Future: Modernity, Postmodernity and Locality*. London, Unwin Hyman.

Cooke, P. (1990b). Manufacturing miracles: the changing nature of the local economy, in Campbell, M. (ed), *Local Economic Policy*. London, Cassell.

Cooke, P. and Imrie, R. (1989). Little victories: local economic development in European regions, *Entrepreneurship and Regional Development*, **1**, 313–327.

Cooke, P. and Morgan, K. (1993). The network paradigm: new departures in corporate and regional development, *Environment and Planning D: Society & Space*, **11**, 543–564.

Cooke, P., Moulaert, F., Swyngedouw, E., Weinstein, O., and Wells, P. (1992). *Towards Global Localisation*. London, UCL Press.

Coopers & Lybrand Deloitte (1991). *London, World City*. Consultants' Stage II Report, London, LPAC.

Corbridge, S. (1992). Discipline and punish: the new right and the policing of the international debt crisis, *Geoforum*, **23**, 285–301.

Cornford, J. and Gillespie, A. (1992). The coming of the wired city: the recent development of cable in Britain, *Town Planning Review*, **63**(3), 243–264.

Coster, G. (1991). Another country, *Guardian*, 1 June.

Costonis, J.J. (1990). Tinker to evens to chance: community groups as the third player in the development game, in Lasser, T.J., (ed), *City Deal Making*. Washington, Urban Land Institute.

Cox, G. (1988). Reading nature: reflections on ideological persistence and the politics of the countryside, *Landscape Research*, **13**(3), 24–34.

Cox, G. (1993). Shooting a Line? Field sports and access struggles in Britain, *Journal of Rural Studies*, **9**(3), 267–276.

Cox, K. (1993). The local and the global in the new urban politics: a critical view, *Environment and Planning D: Society & Space*, **11**, 433–448.

Cox, K. and Mair, A. (1988). Locality and community in the politics of local economic development, *Annals of the Association of American Geographers*, **78**(2), 307–325.

Cox, R.W. (1992). Global perestroika, *Socialist Register*. London, Merlin.

Cox, R.H. (1993). Creating welfare states in Czechoslovakia and Hungary: why policy makers borrow ideas from the west, *Environment and Planning C: Government & Policy*, **11**, 349–364.

Cross, M. and Keith, M. (eds) (1993). *Racism, the City and the State*. London, Routledge.

Crouch, D.P., Carr, D.J. and Mundingo, A.I. (1982). *Spanish City Planning in North America*. Cambridge, Mass, MIT Press.

Crozier, M. (1964). *The Bureaucratic Phenomenon*. Chicago, University of Chicago Press.

Crudington, I.M. and Baker, D.J. (1979). *The British Shotgun. Vol 1: 1850–1870*. London, Barrie and Jenkins.

Curr, T. and King, D. (1987). *The State and the City*. London, Macmillan.

Curry, N. and Comley, A. (1986). Who enjoys the countryside?. *Strathclyde Papers in Planning 9*, University of Strathclyde, Department of Urban and Regional Planning, Glasgow.

Daly, M. (1990). The 1980s — a decade of growth in enterprise: data on VAT registrations and deregistrations, *Employment Gazette*, November, 553–565.

Daly, M. (1991). The 1980s — a decade of growth in enterprise: self-employment data from the Labour Force Survey, *Employment Gazette*, March, 109–134.

Davies, H.W.E., Edwards, D., Hooper, A. and Punter, J. (1989). *Planning Control in Western Europe*. London, HMSO.

Davis, M. (1987). *Prisoners of the American Dream*, New York, Verso.

Davis, M. (1990). *City of Quartz: Excavating the Future in Los Angeles*. New York, Verso.

Davis, M. (1992). Fortress Los Angeles: the militarization of urban space, in Sorkin, M. (ed), *Variations on a Theme Park*. New York, Hill and Wang.

Davis, M. (1993). Who killed Los Angeles? A political autopsy, *New Left Review*, (197), 3–28.

Davoudi, S. and Healey, P. (1994). City challenge, sustainable development or temporary gesture? *Environment and Planning C: Government & Policy*, **12**.

Dear, M. (1986). Postmodernism and planning, *Environment and Planning D: Society & Space*, **4**, 367–384.

Dear, M. (1988). The postmodern challenge: reconstructing human geography, *Transactions of the Institute of British Geographers*, **45**, 262–274.

Dear, M. (1989). Privatization and the rhetoric of planning practice, *Environment and Planning D: Society & Space*, **7**, 449–462.

Dear, M. (1991). The premature demise of postmodern urbanism, *Cultural Anthropology*, **6**(4), 538–552.

de Certeau, M. (1984). *The Practice of Everyday Life*. Berkeley, University of California Press.

de Gournay, C. (1988). Telephone networks in France and Great Britain, in Tarr, J.A.

and Dupuy, G. (eds), *Technology and the Rise of the Networked City in Europe and America*. Philadelphia, Temple University Press.

Dekker, A.M. (1992). Cross-national comparison of large scale entrepreneurial city renewal: building a theoretical framework, Manuscript, University of Amsterdam.

Dematteis, G. (1985). L'ambiente come contingenza e il mondo comorete, *Urbanistica*, 85(11), 113–117.

Department of the Environment (DoE) (1992). *Planning Policy Guidance 12: Development Plans and Regional Guidance*. London, HMSO.

Derrida, J. (1987). In *Deconstruction and philosophy: the texts of Jacques Derrida*, Sallis, J. (ed). Chicago, University of Chicago Press.

Deutsche, R. (1990). Men in space, *Strategies*, 3, 130–137.

Dicken, P. and Tickell, A. (1992). Competitors or collaborators? Inward investment promotion in Northern England, *Regional Studies*, 26, 99–106.

Di Maggio, P. (1993). On metropolitan dominance: New York in the urban network, in Shefter, M. (ed), *Capital of the American Century: The National and International Influence of New York City*. New York, Russell Sage Foundation.

Docherty, T. (1993). Postmodernism, an introduction, in T. Docherty (ed), *Postmodernism: A Reader*. Hemel Hempstead, Harvester Wheatsheaf.

Docklands Consultative Committee (DCC) (1988). *Urban Development Corporations: Six Years in London's Docklands*. London, Docklands Consultative Committee, February.

Donald, J. (1993). How English is it? Popular literature and national culture, in Carter, E., Donald, J. and Squires, J. (eds), *Space and Place: Theories of Identity and Location*. London, Lawrence and Wishart.

Dosi, G., Pavitt, K. and Soete, L. (1990). *The Economics of Technical Change and International Trade*. New York, New York University.

Douglas, M. (1987). *How Institutions Think*. London, Routledge and Kegan Paul.

Drucker, H., Dunleavy, P., Gamble, A. and Peele, G. (eds) (1986). *Developments in British Politics Vol. 2*. London, Macmillan.

Drysek, J. (1990). *Discursive Democracy*. Cambridge, Cambridge University Press.

Ducatel, K. (1990). Rethinking retail capital, in *International Journal of Urban and Regional Research*, 14(2), 207–221.

Duckworth, R.P., Simmons, J.M. and McNulty, R.H. (1985), *The Entrepreneurial City*. Washington, Partners of Livable Places.

Dunford, M. (1990). Theories of regulation, *Environment and Planning D: Society & Space*, 8, 297–322.

Dunford, M. and Kafkalas, G. (1992). The global–local interplay, corporate geographies and spatial development strategies in Europe, in Dunford, M. and Kafkalas, G. (eds), *Cities and Regions in the New Europe*. London, Belhaven Press.

Dunford, M. and Perrons, D. (1983). *The Arena of Capital*. London, Macmillan.

Dunford, M. and Perrons, D. (1992). Strategies of modernisation: the market and the state, *Environment and Planning C: Government & Policy*, 10, 367–405.

Dunleavy, P. (1991). *Democracy, Bureaucracy and Public Choice*. Hemel Hempstead, Harvester Wheatsheaf.

Dupuy, G. (1991). *L'Urbanisme des Réseaux: Théories et Méthodes*. Paris, Armand Colin.

Dupuy, G. (1992a). *L'Informatisation des Villes*. Paris, Presses Universitaires de France.

Dupuy, G. (1992b). New information technologies and utility management, in *Cities and New Technologies*. Paris, OECD, pp. 51–76.

Dyson, K. (1988). *Local Authorities and New Technologies: the European Dimension*. New York, Croom Helm.

Eagleton, T. (1991). *Ideology: an Introduction*. London, Verso.

Eden, R. (1979). *Going to the Moors*. London, John Murray.

Ehrenreich, B. (1987). Foreword, in Theweleit, K. (ed), *Male Fantasies*, Vol 1. Cambridge, Polity Press, pp. ix–xvii.

Eisinger, P.K. (1988). *The Rise of the Entrepreneurial State: State and Local Economic Development Policy in the United States*. Madison, University of Wisconsin Press.

Ekins, P. and Max-Neef, M. (eds) (1992). *Real-life Economics: Understanding Wealth Creation*. London, Routledge.

Ellul, J. (1970). *The Meaning of the City*. Grand Rapids, Mich, William B. Eerdmans Publishing.

Emery, F. and Trist, E. (1965). The casual texture of organizations, in Emery, F. (ed), *Systems Thinking*. Harmondsworth, Penguin.

Emery, F. and Trist, E. (1972). *Towards a Social Ecology: Contextual Appreciation of the Future in the Present*. New York, Plenum Press.

Erie, S.P. (1992). How the urban west was won: the local state and economic growth in Los Angeles, 1880–1932, *Urban Affairs Quarterly*, **27**, 519–554.

Esping-Andersen, G. (1990). *The Three Worlds of Welfare Capitalism*. Cambridge, Polity Press.

Esping-Andersen, G. (1993). Post-industrial class structures: an analytical framework, in Esping-Andersen, G. (ed), *Changing Classes: Stratification and Mobility in Post-industrial Societies*. London, Sage.

European Foundation (1992). *Out of the Shadows: Local Action Towards Social and Economic Problems*. European Foundation for the Improvement of Living and Working Conditions, EF/92/12/EN, Dublin.

Evers, A. (1991). Pluralismus, Fragmentierung und Vermittlungsfähigkeit. Zur Aktualität intermediärer Aufgaben und Instanzen im Bereich der Sozial- und Gesundheitspolitik, in Heinelt, H. and Wollmann, H. (eds), *Brennpunkt Stadt*. Basel, Birkhäuser.

Fainstein, N., Fainstein, S.S. and Schwartz, A. (1989). Economic shifts and land-use in the global city, New York, 1940–87, in Beauregard, R. (ed), *Atop the Urban Hierarchy*. Totowa, NJ, Rowan and Littlefield.

Fainstein, S. (1990). The changing world economy and urban restructuring, in Judd, D. and Parkinson, M. (eds), *Leadership and Urban Regeneration*. London, Sage.

Fainstein, S. (1994). *The City Builders*. Oxford, Blackwell.

Fainstein, S. and Fainstein, N. (1991). Public–private partnerships for economic development in the United States, Working Paper No. 35A, Center for Urban Policy Research, Rutgers University, New Brunswick, New Jersey.

Fainstein, S., Gordon, I. and Harloe, M. (eds) (1992). *Divided Cities*. Oxford, Basil Blackwell.

Fainstein, S. and Young, K. (1992). Politics in economic restructuring, in Fainstein, S., Gordon, I. and Harloe, M. (eds), *Divided Cities: New York and London in the Contemporary World*. Oxford, Blackwell.

Faludi, A. (1987). *A Decision-Centred View of Environmental Planning*. London, Pion.

Faludi, A. and Van der Valk, A. (1994). *Rule and Order: Dutch Planning Doctrine in the Twentieth Century*. Lancaster, Kluwer Academic Publishers.

Feagin, J. (1988). *Free Enterprise City*. New Brunswick, Rutgers.

Featherstone, M. (1988). In pursuit of the postmodern: an introduction, *Theory, Culture & Society*, **5**, 195–215.

Featherstone, M. (1993). Global and local cultures, in Bird, J. et al. (eds), *Mapping the Futures: Local Cultures, Global Change*. London, Routledge.

Fischer, F. (1990). *Technology and the Politics of Expertise*. London, Sage.

Fischer, F. and Forester, J. (eds) (1993). *The Argumentative Turn in Planning Theory*. Durham, North Carolina, Duke University Press.

Fisher, M. and Owen, U. (eds) (1991). *Whose Cities?* Harmondsworth, Penguin.

Fishman, R. (1990). Metropolis unbound: the new city of the twentieth century, *Flux*, **1**, 43–56.

Flyvberg, B. (1993). Aristotle, Foucault and progressive phronesis: outline of an applied ethics: a reader, in Winkler, E.R. and Coombes, J.R. (eds), *Applied Ethics: A Reader*. Oxford, Blackwell.

Fogelson, R.M. (1967). *The Fragmented Metropolis: Los Angeles 1850–1930*. Cambridge, Mass, Harvard University Press.

Fogelson, R.E. (1986). *Planning the Capitalist City*. Princeton, Princeton University Press.

Foucault, M. (1979). *Discipline and Punish*. Harmondsworth, Penguin.

Forester, J. (1989). *Planning in the Face of Power*. Berkeley, University of California Press.

Forester, J. (1992). Envisioning the politics of public sector dispute resolution, in Sibley, S. and Sarat, A. (eds), *Studies in Law and Society*, Vol 12. Greenwich, Conn, JAI Press.

Forester, J. (1993). *Critical Theory, Public Policy and Planning Practice*. Albany, NY, State University of New York Press.

Forrest, R. and Gordon, D. (1993). *People and Places*. School for Advanced Urban Studies, University of Bristol.

Fothergill, S. and Gudgin, G. (1982). *Unequal Growth*. Heinemann, London.

Francis, J. (1993). *The Politics of Regulation*. Oxford, Blackwell.

Frieden, B.J. and Sagalyn, L.B. (1989). *Downtown Inc.: How America Rebuilds Cities*. Cambridge, Mass, MIT Press.

Friedmann, J. (1986). The world city hypothesis, *Development and Change*, (17), 69–83.

Friedmann, J. (1987). *Planning in the Public Domain*. New Jersey, Princeton University Press.

Friedmann, J. (1992). *Empowerment: The Politics of Alternative Development*. Oxford, Blackwell.

Friedmann, J. and McMichael, H. (1989). Agriculture and the state system: the rise and decline of national agricultures, 1870 to the present, *Sociologia Ruralis*, **29**, 93–117.

Friend, J., Power, J. and Yewlett, C. (1974). *Public Planning: the Intercorporate Dimension*. London, Tavistock.

Froessler, R., Selle, K. et al. (1991). *Auf dem Weg zur sozial und ökologisch orientierten Erneuerung? Der Beitrag intermediärer Organisationen zur Entwicklung städtischer Quartiere in der BRD*. Dortmund, Dortmunder Vertrieb f. Bau- und Planungsliteratur.

Gans, H. (1968). *People and Plans*. New York, Basic Books.

Garreau, J. (1991). *Edge City: Life on the New Frontier*. New York, Doubleday.

Gaze, J. (1988). *Figures in a Landscape*. London, Barrie and Jenkins.

Geertz, C. (1983). *Local Knowledge: Further Essays in Interpretive Anthropology*. New York, Basic Books.

Geertz, C. (1988). *Works and Lives: the Anthropologist as Author*. Stanford, Calif, Stanford University Press.

Geltmaker, T. (1992). The Queer Nation ACTS UP, *Environment and Planning D: Society & Space*, **10**, 609–650.

George, L. (1992). *No Crystal Stair: African-Americans in the City of Angels*. New York, Verso.

Gertler, M. (1992). Flexibility Revisited: districts, nation states and the forces of production, *Transactions of the Institute of British Geographers*, **17**(3), 259–278.

Getimis, P. (1992). Dezentralisierungspolitik und Handlungsmöglichkeiten des lokalen Staates in Griechenland — am Beispiel der örtlichen Arbeitsmarktpolitik in Athen, in Heinelt, H. and Mayer, M. (eds), *Politik in europäischen Städten. Fallstudien zur Bedeutung lokaler Politik*. Basel, Birkhäuser.

Giannopoulos, G. and Gillespie, A. (1993). *Transport and Communications in the New Europe*. London, Belhaven.

Giddens, A. (1984). *The Constitution of Society*. Cambridge, Polity Press.

Giddens, A. (1990). *The Consequences of Modernity*. Cambridge, Polity Press.

Giddens, A. (1991). *Modernity and Self-Identity*. Cambridge, Polity Press.

Gill, S. (1992). The emerging world order and European change, *Socialist Register*. Merlin, London.

Gilroy, P. (1987). *There Ain't No black in the Union Jack*. London, Hutchinson.

Gilpin, R. (1987). *The Political Economy of International Relations*. Princeton, Princeton University Press.

Girouard, M. (1981). *Return to Camelot: Chivalry and the English Gentleman*. London, Yale University Press.

Glasmeier, A. (1994). Flexible districts, flexible regions? The institutional and cultural limits to districts in an era of globalisation and technological paradigm shifts, in Amin, A. and Thrift, N. (eds), *Globalisation and the Regions: Examples from Europe*. Oxford, Oxford University Press.

Glyn, A. (1992). Paying for the 1980s, *New Left Review*, 195.

Glyn, A. and Sutcliffe, R. (1992). Global but leaderless: the new capitalist order, *Socialist Review 1992*. Merlin, London.

Gökalp, I. (1988). Global networks: space and time, in Muskens, G. and Gruppelaar, J. (eds), *Global Telecommunications: Strategic Considerations*. Dordrecht, Kluwer.

Gökalp, I. (1992). On the analysis of large technical systems, *Science, Technology and Human Values*, **17**(1), 587–588.

Goodhart, D. (1993). Industrialist predicts mass joblessness and underclass, *Financial Times*, 8 November.

Goodwin, M., Duncan, S. and Halford, S. (1993). Regulation theory, the local state, and the transition of urban politics, *Environment and Planning D: Society & Space*, **11**, 67–88.

Gordon, D. (1988). New edifice or crumbling foundations?, *New Left Review*, March/April, 112–140.

Graham, S. (1994). Networking cities: telematics in urban policy — a critical review, *International Journal of Urban and Regional Research*, **18**(3), 416–432.

Graham, S. and Marvin, S. (1994a). Cherry picking and social dumping: utilities in the 1990s. *Utilities Policy*, **4**(2), 113–119.

Graham, S. and Marvin, S. (1994b). Telematics and the convergence of urban infrastructure: implications for contemporary cities, *Town Planning Review*, **65**(3), 227–242.

Granovetter, M.N. (1985). Economic action and social structure: the problem of embeddedness, *American Journal of Sociology*, **91**, 481–510.

Granovetter, N. and Swedberg, M. (1992). *The Sociology of Economic Life*. Boulder, Westview Press.

Green, F. (ed) (1989). *The Restructuring of the UK Economy*. Hemel Hempstead, Harvester Wheatsheaf.

Greenstein, P., Lennon, N. and Rolfe, L. (1992). *Bread & Hyacinths: The Rise and Fall of Utopian Los Angeles*. Los Angeles, California Classic Books.

Gudeman, S. and Rivera, A. (1990). *Conversations in Colombia: the Domestic Economy in Life and Text*. Cambridge, Cambridge University Press.

Gurr, T. and King, D. (1987). *The State and the City*. London, Macmillan.

Gyford, J. (1985). *The Politics of Local Socialism*. London, Allen and Unwin.

Haas, P.M. (1992). Introduction: epistemic communities and international policy coordination, *International Organisation*, **46**, 1–35.

Habermas, J. (1984). *The Theory of Communicative Action. Vol 1: Reason and the Rationalization of Society*. Cambridge, Mass, MIT Press.

Habermas, J. (1987). *The Philosophical Discourse of Modernity*. Cambridge, Polity Press.

Habermas, J. (1993). Modernity — an incomplete project, in Docherty, T. (ed), *Postmodernism: a reader*. Hemel Hempstead, Harvester Wheatsheaf.

Hajer, M. (1993). The politics of environmental discourse: a study of the acid rain controversy in Great Britain and the Netherlands. Unpublished PhD thesis, University of Oxford.

Hall, P. (1988). *Cities of Tomorrow*. Oxford, Blackwell.

Hall P. and Preston, P. (1988). *The Carrier Wave: New Information Technology and the Geography of Innovation, 1846–2003*. London, Unwin.

Hall, P., Thomas, R., Gracey, H. and Drewett, R. (1973). *The Containment of Urban England*. London, Allen & Unwin.

Hall, S. and Jacques, M. (1989). *New Times: The Changing Face of Politics in the 1990s*. London, Lawrence and Wishart.

Hambleton, R. (1990). Urban government in the 1990s: lessons from the USA. School for Advanced Urban Studies, occasional paper 35, University of Bristol.

Hambleton, R. (1991). The regeneration of US and British cities. Public lecture to the Centre for Regional, Economic and Social Research, Sheffield City Polytechnic, 20 March.

Handy, C. (1979). *Understanding Organizations*. Harmondsworth, Penguin.

Hannerz, U. (1992). *Cultural Complexity*. New York, Columbia University Press.

Harding, A. (1991). The rise of urban growth coalitions, UK-Style?, *Environment and Planning C: Government & Policy*, **9**, 295–317.

Harding, A. (1992). Property interests and urban growth coalitions in the UK: a brief encounter, in Healey, P. et al. (eds), *Rebuilding the City: Property-led Urban Regeneration*. London, E & FN Spon.

Harrison, B. (1992). New wine in old bottles?, *Regional Studies*, **26**, 469–484.

Harrison, C. (1991). *Countryside Recreation in a Changing Society*. TMS Partnership.

Hart, D. (1983). Urban economic development measures in West Germany and the United States, in Young, K. and Mason, C. (eds), *Urban Economic Development: New Roles and Relations*. London, Macmillan.

Harvey, D. (1978). Planning the ideology of planning, in Burchell, R. and Sternlieb, G. (eds), *Planning Theory in the 1980s*. New Brunswick, NJ, Rutgers/University Center for Urban Policy Research.

Harvey, D. (1985a). *The Urbanisation of Capital*. Oxford, Blackwell.

Harvey, D. (1985b). *Consciousness and the Urban Experience*. Oxford, Blackwell.

Harvey, D. (1989a). *The Condition of Postmodernity*. Oxford, Blackwell.

Harvey, D. (1989b). From managerialism to entrepreneurialism: formation of urban governance in late capitalism, *Geografisker Annaler*, **71B**, 3–17.

Harvey, D. (1993). From space to place and back again, in Bird, J., Curtis, B., Putnam, T., Robertson, G. and Tickner, L., (eds), *Mapping the Futures*. London, Routledge.

Hassard, J. (1993). Postmodernism and organizational analysis: an overview, in Hassard, J. and Parker, M. (eds), *Postmodernism and Organizations*. London, Sage.

van Hauff, M. (1989). *Neue Selbsthilfebewegung und staatliche Sozialpolitik*. Wiesbaden, Deutscher Universitätsverlag.

Haughton, G. and Lawless, P. (1992). *Policies for Potential: Recasting British Urban and Regional Policies*. London, Regional Studies Association.

Hayois, F. (1993). Utilisation des systèmes d'information géographique dans des problématiques de réseau. DEA thesis, University of Paris/Val de Marne.

Healey, P. (1983). *Local Plans in British Land Use Planning*. Oxford, Pergamon.

Healey, P. (1986). The role of development plans in the British planning system, *Urban Law and Policy*, **8**, 1–32.

Healey, P. (1988). The British planning system and managing the urban environment, *Town Planning Review*, **59**, 397–417.

Healey, P. (1989). Directions for change in the British planning system, *Town Planning Review*, **60**, 125–149.

Healey, P. (1990). Policy processes in planning, *Policy and Politics*, **18**, 91–103.

Healey, P. (1992a). Development plans and markets, *Planning Practice and Research*, 7(2), pp. 12–20.

Healey, P. (1992b). Planning through debate, *Town Planning Review*, **63**, 143.

Healey, P. (1992c). Urban regeneration and the development industry, *Regional Studies*, **25**, 97–110.

Healey, P. (1993). The communicative work of development plans, *Environment and Planning B*, **20**, 83–194.

Healey, P. and Barrett, S. (1990). Structure and agency in land and property development processes, *Urban Studies*, **27**, 89–100.

Healey, P., Davoudi, S., O'Toole, M., Tavsanoglu, S. and Usher, D. (eds) (1992). *Rebuilding the City: Property-Led Urban Regeneration*. London, E & FN Spon.

Healey, P., McNamara, P., Elson, M. and Doak, J. (1988). *Land Use Planning and the Mediation of Urban Change*. Cambridge, Cambridge University Press.

Healey, P. and Shaw, T. (1993). The treatment of "environment" by planners: evolving concepts and policies in development plans. Working paper 31, Department of Town and Country Planning, University of Newcastle.

Heinelt, H. and Mayer, M. (eds) (1993). *Politik in europäischen Städten: Fallstudien zur Bedeutung lokaler Politik*. Basel, Birkhäuser.

Heinz, W. (1993). *Public–Private Partnership — Stadtentwicklung durch partnerschaften*. Stuttgart, Kohlhammer.

Held, D. (1991). Democracy, the nation-state and the global system, *Economy and Society*, **20**, 138–172.

Hepworth, M.E. and Ducatel, K. (1992). *Transportation in the Information Age: Wheels and Wires*. London, Belhaven Press.

Hesse, J.J. (1987). Aufgaben einer Staatslehre heute, in Ellwein, Th. et al. (eds), *Jahrbuch zur Staats- und Verwaltungswissenschaft*, Vol. 1. Baden-Baden, Nomos.

Hewett, E.A. (1992). *Open for Business: Russia's Return to the Global Economy*. Washington, Brookings Institution.

Hill, O. (1899). The open spaces of the future, *The Nineteenth Century*, **46**, 26–35.

Hillier, J. (1995). Deconstructing the discourse of planning, in Mandelbaum, S. and Mazza, L. (eds), *Planning Theory in the 1990s*. New Brunswick, New Jersey, CUPR Press.

Hirsch, J. (1988). The crisis of Fordism, transformations of the "Keynesian" security state, and new social movements, *Research in Social Movements, Conflicts and Change*, **10**, 43–55.

Hirsch, J. (1991). From the Fordist to the post-Fordist state, in Jessop, B. et al. (eds), *The Politics of Flexibility*. Aldershot, Edward Elgar.

Hirsch, J. and Roth, R. (1986). *Das neue Gesicht des Kapitalismus: Vom Fordismus zum Post-Fordismus*. Hamburg, VSA.

Hirst, P. and Thompson, G. (1992). The problem of globalisation, international economic relations, national economic management and the formation of trading blocs, *Economy and Society*, **21**, 357–396.

Hirst, P. and Zeitlin, J. (1991). Flexible specialisation vs. post-fordism: theory, evidence and policy implications, *Economy and Society*, **20**, 1–56.

Hobsbawn, E. (1983). Mass producing traditions: Europe, 1870–1914, in Hobsbawn, E. and Ranger, T. (eds), *The Invention of Tradition*. Cambridge, Cambridge University Press.

Hodge, I. and Monk, S. (1987). Manufacturing employment change within rural areas, *Journal of Rural Studies*, **3**, 65–69.

Hodgson, G.M. (1988). *Economics and Institutions*. Oxford, Polity Press.

Hodgson, G.M. (1993). *Economics and Evolution: Bringing Life Back into Economics*. Cambridge, Polity Press.

Hoggett, P. (1987). Farewell to mass production? Decentralisation as an emergent private and public sector paradigm, in Hambleton, R. and Hoggett, P. (eds), *Decentralisation and Democracy*. School for Advanced Urban Studies, University of Bristol.

Hoggett, P. (1992a). A place for experience: a psychoanalytic perspective on boundary, identity and culture, *Environment and Planning D: Society & Space*, **10**, 345–356.

Hoggett, P. (1992b). *Partisans in an Uncertain World: The Psychoanalysis of Engagement*. London, Free Association Books.

Holston, J. (1989). *The Modernist City: An Anthropological Critique of Brasilia*. Chicago, University of Chicago Press.

Hudson, R. (1992). Institutional change, cultural transformation and economic regeneration: myths and realities from Europe's old industrial areas, in Amin, A. and Thrift, N. (eds), *Globalization, Institutions and Regional Development in Europe*. Oxford, Oxford University Press, pp. 196–216.

Hughes, T. (1983). *Networks of Power: Electrification in Western Society, 1880–1930*. Baltimore, Johns Hopkins.

IBRD (1991). *Urban Policy and Economic Development: An Agenda for the 1990s*. Washington, IBRD/World Bank.

Ikenberry, J. (1992). A world economy restores: expert consensus and Anglo-American postwar settlement, *International Organisation*, **46**, 289–321.

Imrie, R. and Thomas, H. (1993). *British Urban Policy and the Urban Development Corporation*. London, Paul Chapman.

Ingham, G. (1984). *Capitalism Divided? The City and Industry in British Social Development*. London, Macmillan.

Innes, J. (1992). Group process and the social construction of growth management: Florida, Vermont, New Jersey, *Journal of the American Planning Association*, **58**, 440–453.

Institute for Alternative Journalism (1992). *Inside the L.A. Riots*. New York, Institute for Alternative Journalism.

IRES (1992). *Caratteristiche e Tipologia della Disoccupazione in Italia: Sperimentazione di Strumenti di Analisi e Valutazione*. Rome, IRES.

Itzkowitz, D.C. (1977). *Peculiar Privilege: a Social History of English Foxhunting 1753–1885*. London, Harvester Press.

Jacobs, J. (1985). *Cities and the Wealth of Nations*. Harmondsworth, Penguin.

Jacobs, M. (1991). *The Green Economy*. London, Pluto Press.

Jahoda, M. (1982). *Employment and Unemployment: a Social–Psychological Analysis.* Cambridge, Cambridge University Press.

Jameson, F. (1991). *Postmodernism or the Cultural Logic of Late Capitalism.* London, Verso.

Jeffers, S. (1993). Is race really the sign of the times or is postmodernism only skin deep?, in Cross, N. and Keith, M. (eds), *Racism, the City and the State.* London, Routledge.

Jessop, B. (1990a). *State Theory: Putting Capitalist States in their Place.* Cambridge, Polity Press.

Jessop, B. (1990b). Regulation theory in retrospect and prospect, *Economy and Society*, **19**(2), 153–216.

Jessop, B. (1991a). Thatcherism: the British road to post-Fordism, in Jessop, B., Kastendiek, H., Nielson, K. and Pedersen, O.K. (eds), *The Politics of Flexibility.* Aldershot, Edward Elgar.

Jessop, B. (1991b). The welfare state in the transition from Fordism to post-Fordism, in Jessop, B. et al. (eds), *The Politics of Flexibility.* Aldershot, Edward Elgar.

Jessop, B. (1992a), Fordism and post-Fordism, a critical reformulation, in Storper, M. and Scott, A.J. (eds), *Pathways to Industrialisation and Regional Development.* London, Routledge.

Jessop, B. (1992b). From the Keynesian welfare to the Schumpeterian workfare state. Lancaster Regionalism Group working paper 45, Lancaster University.

Jessop, B. (1992c). Towards a Schumpeterian workfare state? Preliminary remarks on post-Fordist political economy, *Studies in Political Economy*, **40**, 7–37.

Jessop, B. (1994). Post-Fordism and the state, in Amin, A. (ed), *The Geography of Post-Fordism.* Cambridge, Blackwell.

Johnston, R. (1993). The rise and decline of the corporate welfare state, in Taylor, P. (ed), *Political Geography of the Twentieth Century.* London, Belhaven Press.

Jones, E. (1990). *Metropolis: The World's Great Cities?* Oxford, Oxford University Press.

Jordan, B., James, S., Kay, H. and Redley, M. (1991). *Trapped in Poverty? Labour Market Decisions in Low-Income Households.* London, Routledge.

Judd, D. and Parkinson, M. (eds) (1990a). *Leadership and Urban Regeneration.* London, Sage.

Judd, D. and Parkinson, M. (1990b). Urban leadership and regeneration, in Judd, D. and Parkinson, M. (eds), *Leadership and Urban Regeneration: Cities in North America and Europe.* London, Sage.

Judd, D.R. and Ready, R.L. (1986). Entrepreneurial cities and the new politics of urban development, in Peterson, G.W. and Lewis, C.W. (eds), *Reagan and the Cities.* Washington, DC Urban Institute.

Keeble, D., Owens, P. and Thompson, P. (1983). The urban–rural manufacturing shift in the European Community, *Urban Studies*, **20**, 405–418.

Keith, M. (1993). From punishment to discipline? Racism, racialisation and the policing of social control, in Cross, M. and Keith, M. (eds), *Racism, the City and the State.* London, Routledge.

King, A.D. (1990). *Global Cities.* London, Routledge.

King, A.D. (ed) (1991). *Culture, Globalisation and the World System.* London, Macmillan.

Kirk, G. (1980). *Urban Planning in a Capitalist Society.* London, Croom Helm.

Kirlin, J.J. and Kirlin, A.M. (1983). Public/private bargaining in local development, in B.H. Moore (ed), *The Entrepreneur in Local Government.* Washington, International City Management Association.

Knox, P. (ed) (1993). *The Restless Urban Landscape*. Englewood Cliffs, NJ, Prentice Hall.

Kristeva, J. (1991). *Strangers To Ourselves*. New York, Harvester Wheatsheaf.

Kristeva, J. (1992). Strangers to ourselves: the hope of the singular, in Kearney, R. (ed), *Visions of Europe*. Dublin, Wolfhound Press.

Krueckeberg, D.A. (ed) (1983). *Introduction to Planning History in the United States*. New Brunswick, Center for Urban Policy Research.

Lash, S. and Urry, J. (1993). *Economics of Signs and Space: After Organized Capitalism*. London, Sage.

Lassar, T.J. (ed) (1990). *City Deal Making*. Washington, DC, Urban Land Institute.

Laterasse, J. (1991). Intelligent city: utopia or reality of tomorrow. Paper presented at "Communications and the future of European cities", Seminar, Glasgow, September.

Laterasse, J. and Deutsch, J.C. (1991). Gestion des reseaux techniques urbains et nouvelles technologies de l'information. Paper presented at "La citta interrativa", Seminar, Milan, June, pp. 175–186.

Lawless, P. (1987). Urban development, in Parkinson, M. (ed), *Reshaping Local Government*, New Brunswick, NJ, Transaction Books.

Lawless, P. (1989). *Britain's Inner Cities*, 2nd edn., London, Paul Chapman.

Lawless, P. and Haughton, G. (1992). Urban policy initiatives: trends and prospects, in Townroe, P. and Martin, R. (eds), *Regional Development in the 1990s*. London, Regional Studies Association, Jessica Kingsley Publishers.

Le Corbusier (1947) [1924]. *The City of Tomorrow*. London, Architectural Press.

Le Gales, P. (1992). New directions in decentralisation and urban policy in France: the search for a postdecentralisation state, *Environment and Planning C: Government & Policy*, **10**, 19–36.

Lehner, F. (1993). "Die Politik kann verflucht wenig tun" — Interview with F. Lehner on the steel crisis and restructuring in the Ruhr Valley, *Die Tageszeitung*, 5 March.

Lesthaeghe, R. (1991). The second demographic transition in western countries: an interpretation. IPD working paper 2, Bruxelles, Vrjie Universiteit.

Leyshon, A. (1992). The transformation of regulatory order; regulating the global economy and environment, *Geoforum*, **23**, 249–267.

Leyshon, A. and Thrift, N. (1990). The chartered surveying industry, in Healey, P. and Nabarro, R. (eds), *Land and Property Development in a Changing Context*. Aldershot, Gower.

Lin, P. (1991). The super-agency, *City Limits*, 16 November, 8–10.

Linton, R. (1936). *The Study of Man: an Introduction*. New York, Appleton Century.

Lipietz, A. (1985). Akkumulation, Krisen und Auswege aus der Krise: Einige methodische Überlegungen zum Begriff "Regulation", *Prokla*, **15**(1), 109–137.

Lipietz, A. (1992a). The regulation approach and capitalist crisis: an alternative compromise for the 1990s, in Dunford, M. and Kafkalas, G. (eds), *Cities and Regions in the New Europe*. London, Belhaven Press.

Lipietz, A. (1992b). *Towards a New Economic Order: Postfordism, Ecology and Democracy*. New York, Oxford University Press.

Little, J. (1987). Rural gentrification and the influence of local-level planning, in Cloke, P. (ed), *Rural Planning: Policy into Action?*. London, Harper and Row.

Lloyd, G. (1992). Property-led partnership arrangements in Scotland: the private sector domain, in Healey, P. et al. (eds), *Rebuilding the City*. London, E & FN Spon.

Logan, J. and Molotch, H. (1987). *Urban Fortunes: The Political Economy of Place*. Berkeley, University of California Press.

Logan, J. and Swanstrom, T. (1990a). Urban restructuring: a critical view, in Logan, J. and Swanstrom, T. (eds), *Beyond the City Limits: Urban Policy and Economic Restructuring in Comparative Perspective*. Philadelphia, Temple.

Logan, J. and Swanstrom, T. (eds) (1990b). *Beyond the City Limits: Urban Policy and Economic Restructuring in Comparative Perspective*. Philadelphia, Temple University Press.

Logan, J., Taylor-Gooby, P. and Reuter, M. (1992). Poverty and income inequality, in Fainstein, S., Gordon, I. and Harloe, M. (eds), *Divided Cities*. Oxford, Basil Blackwell.

Los Angeles 2000 Committee (1988). *LA 2000: A City for the Future*. Los Angeles, LA 2000 Committee.

Los Angeles Department of City Planning (1964). *City Planning in Los Angeles*. Los Angeles, Department of City Planning.

Lovering, J. (1988). The local economy and local economic strategies, *Policy and Politics*, **16**, 145–157.

Lovering, J. (1989). The restructuring debate, in Peet, R. and Thrift, N. (eds), *New Models in Geography*, Vol 2. London, Unwin Hyman.

Lovering, J. (1990a). A perfunctory post-Fordism, *Work, Employment and Society*, special issue, May, 9–28.

Lovering, J. (1990b). Fordism's unknown successor: a comment on Scott's theory of flexible accumulation, *International Journal of Urban and Regional Research*, **14**, 159–174.

Lovering, J. (1991a). *Bridging the Gap: Skills Training and Barriers to Employment in Bristol*. Bristol Inner City Task Force, Bristol City Council, Avon County Council.

Lovering, J. (1991b). Theorising post-Fordism: why contingency matters, *International Journal of Urban and Regional Research*, **15**, 298–301.

Lovering, J. (1993). After the Cold War: the defence industry and the new Europe, in Brown, P. and Crompton, B. (eds), *A New Europe? Economic Restructuring and Social Exclusion*, University of London Press.

Lovering, J. and Thrift, N. (1993). Bristol at the end of the old road, in *The Future of the Medium Sized City*. London, Anglo-German Foundation.

Lowe, A. (1988). Small hotel survival — an inductive approach, *International Journal of Hospitality Management*, **7**(3), 197–223.

Lowe, P. (1977). Amenity and equity: a review of local environmental groups in Britain, *Environment and Planning A*, **9**, 35–58.

Lowe, P. and Bodiguel, M. (eds) (1990). *Rural Studies in Britain and France*. London, Belhaven.

Lowe, P., Murdoch, J., Marsden, T., Munton, R. and Flynn, A. (1993). Regulating the new rural spaces, *Journal of Rural Studies*, **9**, 205–222.

Lustiger-Thaler, H.J. and Salée, D. (eds) (1994). *Artful Practices: the Political Economy of Everyday Life*. Montreal, Black Rose.

Lyotard, J.F. (1979). *The Postmodern Condition*. Minneapolis, University of Minnesota Press.

Lyotard, J.F. (1992a). *The Postmodern Explained: Correspondence 1982–1985*. Minnesota, University of Minnesota Press.

Lyotard, J.F. (1992b). Answering the question: what is postmodernism?, in Jencks, C. (ed), *The Post-Modern Reader*. London, Academy Editions, pp. 138–150.

Mabbott, J. (1993). City challenge — faith, hope and charities, *Town and Country Planning*, **6**, 137–138.

Mackintosh, M. (1992). Partnership: issues of policy and negotiation, *Local Economy*, **7**(3), 210–224.

Mackintosh, M. and Wainwright, H. (1987). *A Taste of Power: The Politics of Local Economies*. London, Verso.

Madden, D. (1992). Light at the end of the tunnel, *Financial Times*, 30 Jan.

Magatti, M. and Mingione, E. (1994). Family strategies and economic development: the two Italian cases, *Ethnographia*, 90(1).

Maier, H.E. and Wollmann, H. (eds) (1986). *Lokale Beschäftigungspolitik*. Basel, Birkhäuser.

Marcuse, P. (1989). Gentrification, homelessness, and the work process: housing markets and labour markets in the quartered city, *Housing Studies*, 3, 211–220.

Marcuse, P. (1993) What's so new about divided cities? *International Journal of Urban and Regional Research*, 17, 355–365.

Marsh, J. (1982). *Back to the Land*. London, Quartet Books.

Marshall, J.N. (1989). New industrial horizons and local responses, *Local Government Studies*, Nov/Dec, 17–22.

Marshall, M. (1987). *Long Waves of Regional Development*. London, Macmillan.

Martinand, C. (1986). *Le Génie Urbain*. Report to the Ministry of Public Works and the Research Ministry, Paris, La Documentation Française.

Martinez, R. (1993). *The Other Side: Notes from LA, Mexico and Beyond*. New York, Vintage.

Martinotti, G. (1993). *Metropoli*. Bologna, Il Mulino.

Marvin, S. (1992). Urban policy and infrastructure networks, *Local Economy*, 7, 225–247.

Marvin, S. and Cornford, J. (1993). Regional policy implications of utility regionalization, *Regional Policy*, 27, 159–165.

Marvin, S. and Graham, S. (1993). Utility networks and urban planning: an issue agenda, *Planning Practice and Research*, 8(4), 6–14.

Marx, K. and Engels, F. (1926). *The Essentials of Marx*. London, Vanguard Press.

Massey, D. (1984). *Spatial Divisions of Labour: Social Structure and the Geography of Production*. London, Macmillan.

Massey, D. (1991a). A global sense of place, *Marxism Today*, June, 24–29.

Massey, D. (1991b). A global sense of place, in *The Making of the Regions*. Open University Press, Milton Keynes, pp. 12–51.

Massey, D. (1992). A place called home?, *New Formations*, 17, 3–15.

Massey, D. (1993). Power-geometry and a progressive sense of place, in Bird, J., Curtis, B., Putnam, T., Robertson, G. and Tickner, L. (eds), *Mapping the Futures*. London, Routledge.

Massey, D. and Meegan, R. (1982). *The Anatomy of Job Loss*. London, Macmillan.

Mayer, M. (1990). Lokale Politik in der unternehmerischen Stadt, in Borst, R. et al. (eds), *Das neue Gesicht der Städte*. Basel, Birkhäuser.

Mayer, M. (1992). The shifting local political system in European cities, in Dunford, M. and Kafkalas, G. (eds), *Cities and Regions in the New Europe*. London, Belhaven Press.

Mayer, M. (1993). The role of urban social movement organizations in innovative urban policies and institutions, *Topos Review of Urban and Regional Studies*, special issue, 209–226.

Mazmanian, D. and Sabatier, P. (1990). *Implementation and Public Policy: With a New Postscript*. Lanham, MD, University Press of America.

Mazza, L. (1986). Giustificazione e autonomia degli elementi di piani, *Urbanistica*, 82, 56–63.

Mazzoleni, D. (1993). The city and the imaginary, in Carter, E., Donald, J. and Squires, J. (eds), *Space and Place: Theories of Identity and Location*. London, Lawrence and Wishart.

308 References

McAuslan, P. (1980). *The Ideologies of Planning Law*. Oxford, Pergamon.

McGowan, F. (1993). Transeuropean networks: utilities as infrastructures, in *Utilities Policy*, July, 179–186.

McLoughlin, B. (1969). *Urban and Regional Planning: a Systems Approach*. London, Faber.

McPhee, J. (1989). *The Control of Nature*. London, Hutchinson Radius.

McWilliams, D. (1993). *London's Contribution to the UK Economy*. Centre for Economics and Business Research Ltd, available from Corporation of London, Guildhall, London, EC2P 2EJ.

Meager, N. (1991). "TECS" — A revolution in training and enterprise, or old wine in new bottles?, *Local Economy*, **6**, 4–21.

Metcalfe, J.S. (1988). Evolution and economic change, in Silberston, A. (ed), *Technology and Economic Progress*. Basingstoke, Macmillan.

Meyerson, M. and Banfield, E. (1955). *Planning, Politics and the Public Interest*. New York, Free Press.

Micheli, G.A. (1992). La riproduzione sociale tramite la famiglia, in Mauri et al., *Vita di famiglia. Social Survey in Veneto*. Milano, Angeli, pp. 35–78.

Michie, J. (ed) (1992). *The Economic Legacy 1979–1992*. Academic Press Ltd for the Cambridge Political Economy Society, pp. 33–37.

Middleton, A. (1985). Marking boundaries: men's space and women's space in a Yorkshire village, in Lowe, P., Bradley, T. and Wright, S. (eds), *Deprivation and Welfare in Rural Areas*. Norwich, Geo Books.

Miles, I., Rush, H., Turner, K. and Bessant, J. (1988). *Information Horizon: The Long Term Social Implications of New Information Technology*. Aldershot, Elgar.

Miller, D. (1990). The future of local economic policy: a public and private sector function, in Campbell, M. (ed), *Local Economic Policy*. London, Cassell.

Mingione, E. (1991). *Fragmented Societies: A Sociology of Economic Life beyond the Market Paradigm*. Oxford, Blackwell.

Mingione, E. (1993a). Italy: the resurgence of regionalism, *International Affairs*, **69**(3), 305–318.

Mingione, E. (1993b). The new urban poverty and the underclass, *International Journal of Urban and Regional Research*, **17**, 324–325.

Mingione, E. (1994a). New aspects of marginality in Europe, in Hadjimichalis, C. and Sadler, D. (eds), *Europe at the Margins: New Mosaics of Inequality*. Wiley, Chichester, forthcoming.

Mingione, E. (1994b). Family strategies and social development in Northern and Southern Italy, in Lustiger-Thaler, H. and Salée, D. (eds), *Artful Practices: the Political Economy of Everyday Life*. Montreal, Black Rose.

Mollenkopf, J.H. and Castells, M. (1991). *Dual City: Restructuring New York*. New York, Russell/Sage Foundation.

Molotch, H. (1990). Urban deals in comparative perspective, in Logan, J. and Swanstrom, T. (eds), *Beyond the City Limits: Urban Policy and Economic Restructuring in Comparative Perspective*. Philadelphia, Temple UP.

Montgomery, J. (1990). Cities and the art of cultural planning, *Planning Practice and Research*, **5**(3), 17–22.

Moore, B.H. (1983). *The Entrepreneur in Local Government*. Washington: International City Management Association.

Moore, C. (1991). Reflections on the new political economy, *Policy and Politics*, **19**, 73–85.

Moore Milroy, B. (1991). Into postmodern weightlessness, *Journal of Planning Education and Research*, **10**, 181–187.

Morris, A.E.J. (1979). *History of Urban Form*. London, George Godwin.

Morris, L. (1990). *The Workings of the Household*. Oxford, Polity Press.

Morris, L. (1993). Is there a British underclass?, *International Journal of Urban and Regional Research*, **17**, 404–412.

Motte, A. (1994). Innovation in development plan-making in France: 1967–1993, in Healy, P. (ed), *Trends in Development Plan-Making in European Planning Systems*, Working Paper No. 32. Department of Town and Country Planning, University of Newcastle upon Tyne.

Mottura, G. (ed) (1992). *L'Arcipelago Immigrazione*. Rome, Ediesse.

Moulaert, F., Swyngedouw, E. and Wilson, P. (1988). Spatial responses to Fordist and post-Fordist accumulation and regulation, *Papers of the Regional Science Association*, **64**, 11–23.

Mumford, L. (1961). *The City in History*. London, Secker and Warburg.

Murdoch, J. and Marsden, T. (1994). *Reconstituting Rurality*. London, UCL Press.

Murray, R. (1988). Life after Henry Ford, in *Marxism Today*, October, 8–13.

Murray, R. (1991). *Local Space: Europe and the New Regionalism*. Manchester, Centre for Local Economic Strategies.

Nairn, T. (1988). *The Enchanted Glass: Britain and its Monarchy*. London, Radius.

National Congress for Community Economic Development (1989). *Against All Odds: Achievements of Community-based Organizations*. Washington, DC, NCCED.

Newby, H. (1980). *Green and Pleasant Land*. London, Hutchinson.

Newman, P.W.G., Kenworthy, J.R. and Lyons, T.J. (1988). Does free-flowing traffic save energy and lower emissions in cities?, *Search*, **19**, 267–272.

Nijkamp, P. (1991). Evaluation of environmental quality in the city, *International Journal of Development Planning Literature*, 9(3/4), 119–134.

Nijkamp, P. (1993). Towards a network of regions: the United States of Europe, *European Planning Studies*, 1(2), 149–167.

Norris, C. (1982). *Deconstruction: Theory and Practice*. London, Methuen.

North, D.C. (1990). *Institutions, Institutional Change and Economic Performance*. Cambridge, Cambridge University Press.

Offe, C. (1977). The theory of the capitalist state and the problems of policy formation, in Linberg, L.N. and Alford, A. (eds), *Stress and Contradiction in Modern Capitalism*. Lexington, Mass, D.C. Heath.

Offe, C. (1984). *Contradictions of the Welfare State*. London, Hutchinson.

Offe, C. and Heinze, R.G. (1992). *Beyond Employment*. Cambridge, Polity Press.

Ohmae, J. (1989). Planting for a global harvest, *Harvard Business Review*, 67(4), 136–145.

Ohmae, K. (1990). *The Borderless World*. New York, Harper.

Page, E.C. (1993). The future of local government in Britain, in Bullmann, U. (ed), *Die Politik der dritten Ebene*. Baden-Baden, Nomos.

Pahl, R. (1965). Class and community in English commuter villages, *Sociologia Ruralis*, **5**, 5–23.

Pahl, R. (1966). *Urbs in Rure*. London, Weidenfeld and Nicolson.

Pahl, R. (1970). *Readings in Urban Sociology*. Oxford, Pergamon.

Pahl, R.E. (1988). Some remarks on informal work, social polarisation and the social structure, *International Journal of Urban and Regional Research*, **12**, 247–267.

Pahl, R.E. and Wallace, C. (1985). Household work strategies in economic recession, in Redclift, N. and Mingione, E. (eds), *Beyond Employment: Gender, Household and Subsistence*. Oxford, Blackwell.

Painter, J. (1991). Regulation theory and local government, *Local Government Studies*, Nov/Dec, 23–44.

Park, R.W. (1969) [1928]. Human migration and the marginal man, in Sennett, R. (ed), *Classic Essays on the Culture of Cities*. New York, Appleton–Century–Croft.

Parkinson, M. (1990). Leadership and regeneration in Liverpool: confusion, confrontation or coalition? in Judd, D. and Parkinson, M. (eds), *Leadership and Urban Regeneration*. London, Sage.

Parkinson, M., Foley, B. and Judd, D. (eds) (1988). *Regenerating the Cities: The UK Crisis and the US Experience*. Manchester, Manchester University Press.

Peck, J. (1992). TECs and the local politics of training, *Political Geography*, **11**, 335–354.

Peck, J. and Emmerich, M. (1993). Tyneside TEC: rather less than a "skills revolution", *Northern Economic Review*, **20**, 23–41.

Peck, J. and Tickell, A. (1992a). Accumulation, regulation and the geographies of post-Fordism: missing links in regulationist research, *Progress in Human Geography*, **16**(2), 190–218.

Peck, J. and Tickell, A. (1992b), Local modes of social regulation? Regulation theory, Thatcherism and uneven development, *Geoforum*, **23**, 347–363.

Perry, R., Dean, K. and Brown, B. (1986). *Counterurbanisation*. Norwich, Geo Books.

Peterson, P. (1985). Introduction: Technology, race and urban policy, in Peterson, P. (ed), *The New Urban Reality*, Washington, Brookings Institution.

Petrosino, D. (1991). *Stati, Nazioni, Etnie, Il Pluralismo Etnico e Nazionale nella Teoria Sociologica Contemporanea*. Milan, Angeli.

Philips, M. and Kettle, M. (1993). The murder of innocence, *Guardian*, 16 Feb.

Piccinato, G. (1993). *Urban landscapes and spatial planning in industrial districts: the case of Veneto, European Planning Studies*, **1**(2), 181–198.

Picciotto, S. (1991). The Internationalisation of the state, *Capital and Class*, **43**, 43–64.

Pickvance, C. and Preteceille, E. (1991). *State Restructuring and Local Power: A Comparative Perspective*. London, Pinter.

van der Pijl, K. (1989). The formation of an international capitalist class, in Bottomore, T., (ed), *The Capitalist Class*, London, Macmillan.

Pinch, S. (1986). *Cities and Services: The Geography of Collective Consumption*. London, Routledge & Kegan Paul.

Pinch, S. (1993). Social polarization: a comparison of evidence from Britain and the United States, *Environment and Planning A*, **25**, 779–795.

Piore, M.J. and Sabel, C.F. (1984). *The Second Industrial Divide: Possibilities for Prosperity*. New York, Basic Books.

Plotkin, S. (1987). *Keep Out! The Struggle for Land Use Control*. Berkeley, University of California Press.

Polanyi, K. (1946). *Origins of Our Time: The Great Transformation*. London, Victor Gollancz.

Port Authority of New York and New Jersey (PANYNJ) (1993). *The Arts as an Industry: Their Economic Importance to the New York–New Jersey Metropolitan Region*. New York, PANYNJ.

Porter, M. (1990). *The Competitive Advantage of Nations*. London, Macmillan.

Porter, R. (1992). Introduction, in Porter, R. (ed), *Myths of the English*. Cambridge, Polity Press.

Powell, W.W. and Di Maggio, P.J. (ed) (1991). *The New Institutionalism in Organisational Analysis*. Chicago, University of Chicago Press.

Pratt, A. (1992). Review of Laura Ashley: A Life by Design, *Journal of Rural Studies*, **8**, 126–127.

Pred, A. (1989). The locally spoken word and local struggles, *Environment and Planning D: Society & Space*, **7**, 211–233.

Preteceille, E. (1990). Political paradoxes of urban restructuring: globalization of the economy and localisation of politics, in Logan, J. and Swanstrom, T. (eds), *Beyond the City Limits*. Philadelphia, Temple University Press.

Przeworski, J. Fox (1986). National government responses to structural changes in urban economies, in H.J. Ewers, et al. (eds), *The Future of the Metropolis*. Berlin, de Gruyter.

Pugh, M. (1994). *State and Society: British politics and Social History 1870–1992*. London, Edward Arnold.

Pudup, M.B. (1992). Industrialisation after (de)industrialisation: a review essay, *Urban Geography*, **13**, 187–200.

Pugliese, E. (1993a). *Sociologia della Disoccupazione*. Bologna, Il Mulino.

Pugliese, E. (ed) (1993b). *Razzitsi e Solidali: L'Immigrazione e le Radici Sociali dell'Intolleranza*. Rome, Ediesse.

Rainbird, H. (1991). The self-employed: small entrepreneurs or disguised wage labourers?, in A. Pollert (ed), *Farewell to Flexibility*. Oxford, Blackwell.

Ravetz, A. (1980). *Remaking Cities*. London, Croom Helm.

Redfield, R. and Singer, M.B. (1954). The cultural role of cities, *Economic Development and Cultural Change*, **3**, 53–73.

Rees, G. and Lambert, J. (1985). *Cities in Crisis: the Political Economy of Urban Development in Post-War Britain*. London, Edward Arnold.

Reich, R.B. (1991). *The Work of Nations*. Hemel Hempstead, Harvester Wheatsheaf.

Reid, D. (ed) (1992). *Sex, Death and God in LA*. New York, Pantheon.

Reynolds, D.R. (1992). Political geography, thinking globally and locally, *Progress in Human Geography*, **16**, 393–405.

Rhind, D. (1991). Les systèmes d'information géographique et les problèmes environnementaux, *Revue Internationale des Sciences Sociales*, (130), 693–714.

Rhodes, R. (1981). *Control and Power in Central–Local Relations*, Aldershot, Gower.

Roberts, I. and Holroyd, G. (1992). Small firms and family firms, in Gilbert, N., Burrows, R. and Pollert, A. (eds), *Fordism and Flexibility: Divisions and Change*. London, Macmillan.

Robertson, R. (1990). Mapping the global condition: globalisation as the central concept, *Theory, Culture and Society*, **7**, 15–30.

Robins, K. (1991). Tradition and translation: national culture in its global context, in Corner, J. and Harvey, S. (eds), *Enterprise and Heritage*. London, Routledge.

Robins, K. (1993). Prisoners of the city: whatever could a postmodern city be?, in Carter, E., Donald, J. and Squires, J. (eds), *Space and Place: Theories of Identity and Location*. London, Lawrence and Wishart.

Robins, K. and Hepworth, M. (1988). Electronic spaces: new technologies and the future of cities, *Futures*, April, 155–176.

Robinson, C.J. (1989). Municipal approaches to economic development: growth and distribution policy, *American Planning Association Journal*, **55**(3), 283–295.

Robinson, F. and Shaw, K. (1991). Urban regeneration and community involvement, *Local Economy*, **6**, 61–71.

Rose, G. (1993). *Feminism and Geography*. Oxford, Polity Press.

Roth, R. (1990). Stadtentwicklung und soziale Bewegungen in der Bundesrepublik, in Borst R. et al. (eds), *Das Neue Gesicht der Stadt*. Basel, Birkhäuser.

Rubinstein, W.D. (1993). *Capitalism, Culture and Decline in Britain 1750–1990*. London, Routledge.

Rueschemeyer, D. and Evans, P.B. (1985). The state and economic transformation: toward an analysis of the conditions underlying effective intervention, in Evans, P.B., Rueschemeyer, D. and Skocpol, T. (eds), *Bringing the State Back In*. Cambridge, Cambridge University Press.

Ruffer, J.G. (1977). *The Big Shots*. London, Debretts.

Rustin, M. (1989). The shape of "New Times", *New Left Review*, (175), 54–78.

Rydin, Y., (1986). *Housing Land Policy*. Aldershot, Gower.

Sabel, C.F. (1992). *Studied Trust*, Discussion Paper, Berlin, Science Centre.

Sabel, C.F., Herrigel, G.B., Deeg, R. and Kazis, R. (1988). Regional prosperities compared: Massachusetts and Baden-Württemburg in the 1980s, *Economy and Society*, **18**, 374–404.

Sage, T. (1992). *Communicate or Calculate: Planning Theory and Social Science Concepts in a Contingency Perspective*. Stockholm, Nordplan.

Sager, T. (1994). *Communicative Planning Theory*. Aldershot, Avebury.

Salais, R. and Storper, M. (1992). The four "worlds" of contemporary industry, *Cambridge Journal of Economics*, **16**, 169–193.

Sassen, S. (1988). *The Mobility of Labour and Capital*. New York, Cambridge University Press.

Sassen, S. (1991). *The Global City: New York, London, Tokyo*. Princeton, NJ, Princeton University Press.

Saunders, P. (1981). *Social Theory and the Urban Question*. London, Hutchinson.

Savage, M., Barlow, J., Dickens, P. and Fielding, T. (1992). *Property, Bureaucracy and Culture*. London, Routledge.

Savage, M. and Warde, A. (1993). *Urban Sociology, Capitalism and Modernity*. London, Macmillan/British Sociological Association.

Savitch, H.V. (1988). *Post-Industrial Cities: Politics and Planning in New York, Paris and London*. Princeton, NJ, Princeton University Press.

Saxenian, A. (1991). *Regional networks: industrial adaption in Silicon Valley and Route 128*. Department of City and Regional Planning, University of California, Berkeley.

Sayer, A. (1989). Postfordism in question, in *International Journal of Urban and Regional Research*, **13**, 666–695.

Sayer, A. and Walker, R. (1992). *The New Social Economy*. Oxford, Blackwell.

Schaffer, D. (ed) (1988). *Two Centuries of American Planning*. Baltimore, Johns Hopkins University Press.

Scharpf, F. (1991). Die Handlungsfähigkeit des Staates em Ende des 20. Jahrhunderts, *Politische Vierteljahresschrift*, **32**, 621–634.

Schnepf-Orth, M. and Staubach, R. (1989). *Bewohnerorientierte Stadterneuerung. Erfahrungen aus Beispielfällen ortsnaher Beratungs-und Kommunikationsstellen*, Dortmund, ILS.

Schutz, A. (1944). The stranger: an essay in social psychology, *American Journal of Sociology*, **49**, 499–507.

Scott, A.J. (1988). *Metropolis: From Division of Labor to Urban Form*. Berkeley, University of California Press.

Scott, A.J. and Cooke, P. (1988). The new geography and regional development; the rise of new industrial spaces in North America and Western Europe, *International Journal of Urban and Regional Research*, **12**, 171–185.

Scott, J. (1982). *The Upper Classes: Property and Privilege in Britain*. London, Macmillan.

Sebba, A. (1990). *Laura Ashley: A Life by Design*. London, Weidenfeld and Nicolson.

Security Trust and Savings Bank (1929). *La Reina: Los Angeles in Three Centuries*. Los Angeles, Security Trust and Savings Bank.

Selbourne, D. (1993). *The Spirit of the Age*. London, Sinclair-Stevenson.

Selle, K. (1991). *Mit den Bewohnern die Stadt erneuern. Der Beitrag intermediärer Organisationen zur Entwicklung städtischer Quartiere. Beobachtungen aus sechs Ländern*. Dortmund, Dortmunder Vertrieb f. Bau- und Planungsliteratur.

Sennett, R. (1973). *The Uses of Disorder*. Harmondsworth, Penguin.

Sennett, R. (1990). *The Conscience of the Eye: The Design and Social Life of Cities*. New York, Alfred A. Knopf.

Sennett, R. (1992). The body and the city, *Times Literary Supplement*, 18 Sept, 3–4.

Sert, J.L. (1944). *Can Our Cities Survive? An ABC of Urban Problems, Their Analysis, Their Solution*. Cambridge, Mass, Harvard University Press.

Sharp, T. (1932). *Town and Countryside*. Oxford, Oxford University Press.

Sharp, T. (1944). *Town Planning*. London, Pelican.

Sheets, R.G., Nord, S. and Phelps, J.J. (1987). *The Impact of Service Industries on Underemployment in Metropolitan Economies*. Lexington, Mass, D.C. Heath.

Shefter, M. (ed) (1993). *Capital of the American Century: The National and International Influence of New York City*. New York, Russell Sage Foundation.

Short, J.R. (1991). *Imagined Country: Society, Culture, Environment*. London, Routledge.

Silver, H. (1993). National conceptions of the new urban poverty: social structural change in Britain, France and the United States, *International Journal of Urban and Regional Research*, **17**, 336–354.

Simmel, G. (1971) [1908]. The stranger, in Levine, D.N. (ed), *Simmel On Individuality and Social Forms*. Chicago, University of Chicago Press.

Simmons, J.M.D., Kelleher, W. and Duckworth, R.P. (1985). *Business and the Entrepreneurial American City*. Washington, US Chamber of Commerce.

Simon, J. (1993). The origins of US public utilities regulation: elements for a social history of networks, *Flux*, **11**, 33–41.

Singh, A. (1992). The political economy of growth, in Michie, J. (ed), *The Economic Legacy 1979–1992*. Academic Press Ltd, for the Cambridge Political Economy Society.

Smart, B. (1993). *Postmodernity*. London, Routledge.

Smith, A.D. (1990). Towards a global culture?, *Theory, Culture and Society*, **7**, 171–191.

Smith, G. (1994). Towards a framework for comparative ethnography of "informal economies" in Western Europe, in Lustiger-Thaler, H. and Salée, D. (eds), *Artful Practices of Everyday Life*. Montreal, Black Rose.

Smith, M.P. (1988). The uses of linked-development policies in US cities, in Parkinson, M., Foley, B. and Judd, D. (eds), *Regenerating the Cities*. Manchester, Manchester University Press.

Smith, R. (1992). On the margins: uneven development and rural restructuring in the Highlands of Scotland, in Marsden, T., Lowe, P. and Whatmore, S. (eds), *Labour and Locality*. London, Fulton.

Soja, E. (1989). *Postmodern Geographies*. New York, Verso.

Soja, E. and Hooper, B. (1993). The spaces that difference makes: some notes on the geographical margins of the new cultural politics, in Keith, M. and Pile, S. (eds), *Politics of Identity*. London, Routledge.

Solesbury, W. (1990). Property development and urban regeneration in Britain, in Healey, P. and Nabarro, R. (eds), *Land and Property Development in a Changing Context*. Aldershot, Gower.

Solesbury, W. (1993). Reframing urban policy, *Policy and Politics*, **21**, 31–38.

Sonenshein, R.J. (1993). *Politics in Black and White: Race and Power in Los Angeles*. Princeton, Princeton University Press.

Sorenson, A. (1983), Towards a market theory of planning, *The Planner*, **69**(3), 78–80.

Sorkin, M. (1992). *Variations on a Theme Park*. New York, Hill and Wang.

Springhill, J. (1977). *Youth, Empire and Society*. London, Croom Helm.

Squires, G.D. (ed) (1989). *Unequal Partnerships: The Political Economy of Urban Redevelopment in Postwar America*. New Brunswick, Rutgers University Press.

Stafford, D. (1994), Who buys this stuff?, *Guardian*, 8 Feb.

Stallybrass, P. and White, A. (1986). *The Politics and Poetics of Transgression*. London, Methuen.

Stanfield, J.R. (1982). Towards a new value standard in economics, *Economic Forum*, **13**, 67–85.

Stöhr, W.B. (ed) (1990). *Global Challenge and Local Response: Initiatives for Economic Regeneration in Contemporary Europe*. London, Mansell.

Stoker, G. (1988/1991). *The Politics of Local Government*, London, Macmillan.

Stoker, G. (1989). Creating a local government for a post-Fordist society: the Thatcherite project, in Steward, J. and Stoker, G. (eds), *The Future of Local Government*. Basingstoke, Macmillan.

Stoker, G. (1990). Regulation theory, local government and the transition from Fordism, in King, D.S. and Pierre, J. (eds), *Challenges to Local Government*. Newbury Park, Sage.

Stoker, G. and Mossberger, K. (1992). *The Post-Fordist Local State: The Dynamics of its Development*. Middlesbrough, The University of Teesside.

Stoker, G. and Young, S. (1993). *Cities in the 1990s*. London, Longman.

Stone, I. (1993). Re-making it on Wearside — de-industrialisation and re-industrialisation, *Northern Economic Review*, Spring, 6–22.

Stone, I. and Stevens, J. (1986). Employment on Wearside: trends and prospects, *Northern Economic Review*, **12**, 39–56.

Storper, M. (1989). The transition to flexible specialisation in the US film industry, *Cambridge Journal of Economics*, **13**, 273–305.

Storper, M. (1991). Technology districts and international trade: the limits to globalisation in an age of flexible production. Mimeograph, School of Planning, University of California, Los Angeles.

Storper, M. (1993). Regional worlds of production: learning and innovation in the technology districts of France, Italy and the USA, *Regional Studies*, **27**, 433–455.

Storper, M. and Walker, R. (1989). *The Territorial Imperative*. Oxford, Basil Blackwell.

Strange, S. (1988). *States and Markets*. London, Frances Pinter.

Strange, S. (1991). An eclectic approach, in Murphy, C.N. and Tooze, R. (eds), *The New International Political Economy*. Boulder, Lynne Rienner.

Suisman, D.R. (1989). *Los Angeles Boulevard*. Los Angeles, Los Angeles Forum for Architecture and Urban Design.

Svedinger, B. (1991). *The Technical Infrastructure of Urban Communities*. Stockholm, Swedish Council for Building Research.

Swedberg, R. (1991). Major traditions of economic sociology, *Annual Review of Sociology*, **17**, 251–276.

Swyngedouw, E. (1989). The heart of the place: the resurrection of locality in the age of hyperspace, *Geografiska Annaler*, **71**(b), 31–42.

Swyngedouw, E. (1992a). The Mammon quest. "Globalisation", interspatial competition and the monetary order: the construction of new scales, in Dunford, M. and Kafkalas, G. (eds), *Cities and Regions in the New Europe*. London, Belhaven.

Swyngedouw, E. (1992b). Territorial organization and the space/technology nexus, *Transactions of the Institute of British Geographers*, **17**, 417–433.

Tagliaventi, G. and O'Connor, L. (eds) (1992) *A Vision of Europe: Architecture and Urbanism for the European City*. Florence, ALINEA Editrice.

Tait, A. and Wolfe, J. (1991). Discourse analysis and city plans, *Journal of Planning Education and Research*, **10**(3), 193–200.

Tapper, D. (1992). *Game Heritage*. Fordingbridge, Game Conservancy.

Tarr, J.A. (1984). The evolution of urban infrastructure in the nineteenth and twentieth centuries, in Hanson, R. (ed), *Perspectives of Urban Infrastructure*. Washington, DC. National Academy Press, pp. 4–66.

Tarr, J.A. and Dupuy, G. (eds) (1988). *Technology and the Rise of the Networked City in Europe and America.* Philadelphia, Temple University Press.

The Economist (1993). Hell is an American city, 6 Nov, 13–14.

Thomas, D., Minett, J., Hopkins, S., Hamnet, S., Faludi, A. and Barrell, D. (1983). *Flexibility and Commitment in Planning.* The Hague, Martinus Nijhoff.

Thornley, A. (1991). *Urban Planning under Thatcher.* London, Routledge.

Thrift, N. (1983). On the determination of social action in space and time, *Environment and Planning D: Society & Space,* 1, 23–57.

Thrift, N. (1988). New times and spaces? The perils of transition models, *Environment and Planning D: Society & Space,* 7, 127–130.

Thrift, N. (1989). Images of social change, in Hamnet, C., McDowell, L. and Sarre, P. (eds), *The Changing Social Structure.* London, Sage.

Throgmorton, J. (1992). Planning as persuasive story-telling about the future: the case of electric power rate settlement in Illinois, *Journal of Planning Education and Research,* 12(1), 17–31.

Tobias, G. and Boettner, J. (1992). *Von den Hand in den Mund: Armut und Armutsbewältigung in einer westdeutschen Großstadt.* Essen, Klartext.

Toffler, A. (1980). *Third Wave.* London, Pan.

Tomer, J.F. (1987). *Organisational Capital: the Path to Higher Productivity and Well Being.* New York, Praeger.

Toulmin, S. (1990). *Cosmopolis: The Hidden Agenda of Modernity.* New York, Free Press.

Townroe, P. and Martin, R. (eds) (1992). *Regional Development in the 1990s: The British Isles in Transition.* Regional Studies Association/Jessica Kingsley Publishers.

Tuan, Y. (1979). *Landscapes of Fear.* New York, Pantheon.

Turok, I. (1991). Developing skills, securing jobs? Evaluating an integrated local employment initiative, *Regional Studies,* 19, 207–226.

Turok, I. (1992). Property-led urban regeneration: panacea or placebo? *Environment and Planning A,* 24, 361–379.

Urry, J. (1990). *The Tourist Gaze.* London, Sage.

Vance, J.E. (1977). *This Scene of Man.* New York, Harper & Row.

Veblen, T. (1919). *The Place of Science in Modern Civilization and Other Essays.* New York, Huebsch.

Wacquant, L. (1993). Urban outcasts: stigma and division in the black American ghetto and the French Urban Periphery, *International Journal of Urban and Regional Research,* 17, 366–383.

Waller, W. and Jennings, A. (1991). A feminist institutionalist reconsideration of Karl Polanyi, *Journal of Economic Issues,* 25, 485–497.

Walton, J. (1990). Theoretical methods in comparative urban politics, in Logan, J. and Swanstrom, T. (eds), *Beyond the City Limits: Urban Policy and Economic Restructuring in Comparative Perspective.* Philadelphia, Temple.

Wannop, U. (1985). The practice of rationality: the case of the Coventry–Solihull–Warwickshire Subregional Planning study, in Breheny, M. and Hooper, A. (eds), *Rationality in Planning.* London, Pion.

Ward, S. (1990). Local industrial promotion and development policies 1899–1940, *Local Economy,* 2 Aug, 100–118.

Watson, J. (1978). *Victorian and Edwardian Field Sports from old Photographs.* London, Batsford.

Watts, M.J. (1991). Mapping meaning, denoting difference, imagining identity: dialectical images and postmodern geographies, *Geografiska Annaler,* 73(b), 7–17.

Weir, M. (1993). From equal opportunity to the "new social contract": race and the politics of the American "underclass", in Cross, M. and Keith, M. (eds), *Racism, the City and the State*. London, Routledge

Whatmore, S. (1991). *Farming Women: Gender, Work and Family Enterprise*. London, Macmillan.

Wheelock, J. (1990a). *Husbands at Home: The Domestic Economy in a Post-industrial Society*. London, Routledge.

Wheelock, J. (1990b). Self-respect and the irrelevance of "rational economic man" in a post-industrialist society", *Journal of Behavioural Economics*, 19, 221–236.

Wheelock, J. (1992a). The household in the total economy, in Ekins, P. and Max-Neef, M. (eds), *Real-Life Economics: Understanding Wealth Creation*. London, Routledge.

Wheelock, J. (1992b). The flexibility of small business family work strategies, in Caley, K., Chittenden, F., Chell, E. and Mason, C. (eds), *Small Enterprise Development: Policy and Practice in Action*. London, Paul Chapman Publishing.

Wiesel, E. (1991). Welcome, stranger, *Guardian*, 14 June.

Wievel, W. and Weintraub, J. (1990). Community develoment corporations as a tool for economic development finance, in Bingham, R., Hill, E. and White, S. (eds), *Financing Economic Development: An Institutional Response*. Newbury Park, Sage.

Wilkinson, S. (1992). Towards a new city? A case study of image-improvement initiatives in Newcastle upon Tyne, in Healey, P. et al. (eds), *Rebuilding the City*. London, E & FN Spon.

Williams, R. (1975). *The Country and the City*. London, Paladin.

Williams, R. (1990). Between country and city, in Pugh, S. (ed), *Reading Landscape*. Manchester, Manchester University Press.

Williams, V. (1993). The village people, *Guardian*, 13 Nov.

Williamson, O.E. (1975). *Markets and Hierarchies*. New York, Free Press.

Williamson, O.E. (1985). *The Economic Institutions of Capitalism*. New York, Free Press.

Wilson, E. (1991). *The Sphinx in the City*. London, Virago.

Wilson, E. (1992). The invisible flâneur, *New Left Review*, (191), 90–110.

Wilson, R. (1992). Communications and power struggle, *Financial Times*, 30 Jan.

Wolch, J.R. (1990). *The Shadow State: Government and Voluntary Sector in Transition*, New York, Foundation Center.

Wolch, J.R. and Dear, M. (1993). *Malign Neglect: Homelessness in an American City*. San Francisco, Jossey-Bass.

Wollmann, H. (1991). Kommunalpolitik und Verwaltung in Ostdeutschland, in Blanke, B. (ed), *Stadt und Staat, PVS-Sonderband*. Opladen, Westdeutscher Verlag.

Wood, M.M. (1934). *The Stranger: A Study in Social Relationships*. New York, Columbia University Press.

Wolf, E. (1982). *Europe and the People without History*. Berkeley, University of California Press.

Worpole, K. (1992). *Towns for People: Transforming Urban Life*. Buckingham, Open University Press.

Wright, E.O. and Martin, B. (1987). The transformation of the American class structure, 1960–1980, *American Journal of Sociology*, (93), 1–29.

Wright, G. (1991). *The Politics of Design in French Colonial Urbanism*. Chicago, University of Chicago Press.

Wright, P. (1985). *On Living in an Old Country*. London, Verso.

Yeandle, S. (1984). *Women's Working Lives*. London, Tavistock.

Young, G. (1992). Keynote address, in Hart, G. (ed), *Development Plan: Master or Servant*. Journal of Planning and Environmental Law occasional paper 10, Sweet and Maxwell, London.

Young, I.M. (1990a). *Justice and the Politics of Difference*. Princeton, Princeton University Press.

Young, I.M. (1990b). The ideal of community and the politics of difference, in Nicholson, L.J. (ed), *Feminism/Postmodernism*. London, Routledge.

Zeitlin, J. (1989). Local industrial strategies, *Economy and Society*, **18**, 367–373.

Zukin, S. (1991). *Landscapes of Power*. Berkeley, University of California Press.

Zysman, J. (1983). *Governments, Markets and Growth*, Ithaca, NY, Cornell University Press.

Index